APPLIED GRAMMATOLOGY

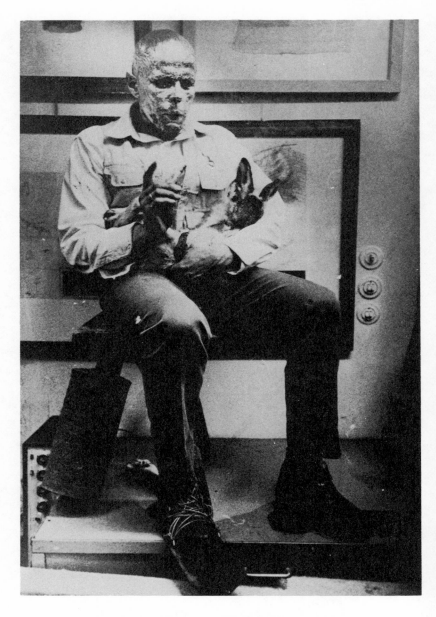

Joseph Beuys, "How to explain pictures to a dead hare."
1965. (Photograph by Ute Klophaus.)

Applied Grammatology

Post(e)-Pedagogy from Jacques Derrida to Joseph Beuys

GREGORY L. ULMER

The Johns Hopkins University Press
Baltimore and London

©1985 by The Johns Hopkins University Press
All rights reserved
Printed in the United States of America

The Johns Hopkins University Press, Baltimore, Maryland 21218
The Johns Hopkins Press Ltd., London

Library of Congress Cataloging in Publication Data
Ulmer, Gregory L., 1944–
Applied grammatology.

Includes index.
1. Languages–Philosophy. 2. Humanities–Study and
teaching. 3. Derrida, Jacques. 4. Philosophy, Modern–
20th century. I. Title.
P106.U46 1984   401'.41   84–47941
ISBN 0–8018–3256–X
ISBN 0–8018–3257–8 (pbk.)

for Kathy

Contents

Preface

I will not work very hard to compose the thing, it is a rough draft of confused tracks which I will leave in their hands. Certain ones will put it into their mouths, to identify the taste, sometimes to spit it out with a grimace, or to gnaw at it, or to swallow it in order to conceive, even, I mean, a child." So says Jacques Derrida in "Envois," the dramatic narrative prefacing *La carte postale* (191). His description applies, retroactively, to the generation of my book, in that I am one of those who swallowed. As a graduate student, writing a dissertation on Rousseau and several modernist authors, I unsuspectingly purchased a copy of *De la grammatologie*, thinking I would find out something about Rousseau. The book was just lying there in a pile of other books, waiting, looking as harmless, as attractive, as a puppy in a pet store window (as Georges Poulet once put it). The effect of reading it, however, was more like Baudelaire's *flacon*, except that I was overwhelmed by a sense of the future rather than of the past. Soon I was more interested in Derrida than in Rousseau.

My interest in grammatology as a pedagogy emerged out of my experience teaching courses in literary criticism, or rather, out of the relation of this course to my other courses, a juxtaposition that made me aware of the disparity between the contemporary understanding of reading, writing, and epistemology and the institutional framework in which this understanding is communicated (pedagogy, curriculum, evaluation). I resolved to try to reduce this gap between theory and practice, but not before I had figured out what might take the place of conventional pedagogy. This book is an installment on that initial proposal (a partial and inadequate re-port), undertaken to inform myself first of all of what steps to take, of how to achieve a postmodernized pedagogy. As such, it might be read as an outline for a possible course of action, although one might also prefer to ignore the general argument, the attempt at application, and read it as a comparative study of Derrida, Lacan, Beuys, and Eisenstein.

Let me try to state very briefly what I myself learned from the project. The bias of the research lies in my selection of Derrida as the tutor figure. I believe that his texts constitute a vanguard of academic writing in the humanities, bringing together the most vital aspects of philosophy, literary criticism, and experimental (creative) writing. I also decided not to review the deconstructionist movement, not only because several excellent books already do this, but also because I wanted to discover an alternative to deconstruction—another, perhaps more comprehensive, program that might be available in Derrida's texts. The pleasure in this project was precisely *not* knowing what a close study of the entire *oeuvre* would reveal, espe-cially one that focused on the more recent texts not yet assimilated by deconstructionism.

My intention, in replacing "deconstruction" with "grammatology" as the principal name for Derrida's program, is not to impose a binary opposi-tion on Derrida's thinking, but to reread his *oeuvre* from a perspective that turns attention away from an exclusive concern with deconstruction ("I use this word [deconstruction]," Derrida says in "The Time of a Thesis" (Alan Montefiore, ed., *Philosophy in France Today* [Cambridge, 1983]), "for the sake of rapid convenience, though it is a word I have never liked and one whose fortune has disagreeably surprised me"—44). Grammatology (I have no illusions about the status of this term, either) is a more inclusive notion, embracing both deconstruction and "writing" (understood not only in the special sense of textualist *écriture,* but also in the sense of a compositional practice). Deconstruction and Writing are complementary operations, the relationship of which is suggested in this statement at the beginning of "Plato's Pharmacy": "Since we have already said everything, the reader must bear with us if we continue on awhile. If we extend our-selves by force of play. If we then *write* a bit." Writing is privileged in my study, then, in order to explore the relatively neglected "affirmative" (Derrida's term) dimension of grammatology, the practical extension of deconstruction into decomposition.

The difference between Writing and deconstruction may be seen most clearly in the different ways Derrida treats philosophical works (which he deconstructs) and literary or artistic texts (which he mimes). The metho-dologies in the two instances bear little resemblance to each other: the philosophical work is treated as an object of study, which is analytically articulated by locating and describing the gap or discontinuity separating what the work "says" (its conclusions and propositions) from what it "shows" or "dis-plays" (its examples, data, the materials with which it, in turn, is working). Literary or plastic texts (a "new new novel" by Sollers, or drawings by Adami, for example) are not analyzed but are adopted as models or tutors to be imitated, as generative forms for the production of another text. Jonathan Culler, in *On Deconstruction* (Ithaca, 1982), makes a similar point: "Derrida's own discussions of literary works draw attention to important problems, but they are not *deconstructions* as we have been using the term, and a deconstructive literary criticism will be primarily influenced by his readings of philosophical works" (212). Because Derrida's readings of art texts are not deconstructions, Culler ignores them in his book, whereas my study foregrounds them. Derrida's experimental texts are just now becoming available in English translation. The intervention of texts such as *Glas, La carte postale,* and *La vérité en peinture* in the current debate surrounding deconstruction should substantially reorient the entire problematic. *Applied Grammatology* is an introduction to this second Derridean influence.

I should add that while Derrida has always seen the difference between literary and philosophical styles as representing alternative theories of language—ever since his first book, in which he opposed Husserl to Joyce and declared his preference for the latter—his decision to Write in a fully experimental style himself came after 1968. In "The Time of a Thesis," delivered on the occasion of his much-delayed thesis defense in June 1980, Derrida, recounting his development for the academic jury, divided his career into three periods, based on his shifting attitude toward the thesis. The important point for me is that he submitted to the jury only his "philosophical" works, none of his experimental texts, thus acknowledging this division in his *oeuvre.*

Part I is devoted to reporting the results of a close reading of Derrida's corpus. I learned that Writing, as Derrida practices it, is something other than deconstruction, the latter being a mode of analysis, while the former is a mode of composition. The interest of what I report lies not so much in the inventory of elements, which are apparent to anyone who reads something by Derrida, and which Derrida himself identifies as a "picto-ideo-phonographic" (or sometimes -phonogrammic) style. He utilizes, that is, three levels of communication—images, puns, and discourse. But what I have come to understand (and attempt to describe in what follows) is the extent to which Derrida systematically explores the nondiscursive levels—images and puns, or models and homophones—as an alternative mode of composition and thought applicable to academic work, or rather, play. His detractors accuse him of superficial wordplay, and sometimes even the deconstructors consider the images and puns as nonfunctional subversion of academic conventions. What I had not expected, what in fact astonished me, is the fully developed homonymic program at work in Derrida's style, a program as different from traditional academic discourse and assumptions as it is productive in its own terms of knowledge and insight. I say I was astonished because it is one thing to engage in wordplay, but another thing to sustain it and extend it into an epistemology, into a procedure that is not just a tour de force but that is functional, replicable. This Writing, however, is not a method of analysis or criticism but of invention (and here Writing departs from deconstruction). Writing is the *inventio* of a new rhetoric, with "invention"—or even "creativity"—being the "mana" word of the new pedagogy associated with Writing.

The other major innovation of Writing is its reliance on images. Again, Derrida's contribution is not simply the use of images, but his sustained expansion of images into models. Thus he gives considerable attention in his texts (much to the frustration of normal readers trained to look for arguments, concepts, evidence, and theses—all of which are included, but seemingly obscured by ornament) to the description of quotidian objects—an umbrella, a matchbox, an unlaced shoe, a post card—whose functioning he interrogates as modeling the most complex or abstract levels of thought. In the process he reveals a simplicity, an economy, underlying the so-called esotericism of intellectual discourse which, if properly tapped, could eliminate the gap separating the general public from specialists in cultural studies.

The two elements—homophones and models—supplement one another in that the vocabulary associated with the model is scrutinized, as well as its operation as an object, for double inscriptions joining the sensible with the intelligible realm. The world of Western thought is investigated at the levels of both words and things, giving fresh insight into the ancient problem of motivation in language. The resultant achievement could be described as non-Euclidean—the humanities equivalent of non-Euclidean geometry—in that it builds, in defiance of the axioms of dialectics, a coherent, productive procedure out of the elements of writing considered traditionally to be mere ornament, not suitable for fostering true knowledge. The ultimate deconstruction of the logocentric suppression of writing is not to analyze the inconsistency of the offending theories, but to construct a fully operational mode of thought on the basis of the excluded elements (in the way that the non-Euclideans built consistent geometries that defied and contradicted the accepted axioms).

The new compositional attitude, however, exceeds what we have come to identify as deconstruction and reflects a larger program that might be derived from Derrida's texts, a program I label "grammatology." Grammatology as composition (Writing) is not confined to books and articles, but is addressed more comprehensively to the needs of multichanneled performance—in the classroom and in video and film as well. In this respect,

Writing as Derrida practices it could be called Scripting, since a recent text such as *La carte postale,* although published as a book, has the status of a script. It is to the program of grammatology what a screenplay is to a film —a set of descriptions and directions which for its full effect must be "enacted." It is research undertaken in a dramatic rather than in a conceptual form. The title itself, manifesting Derrida's paragrammatic style, indicates that the essay format of the printed book is just a transitional or STOP-GAP measure. *Carte,* as Derrida notes, is an anagram of *écart,* or "gap." And *postale,* in a series with *post,* as a member of the semantic family related through the S-T phonex (according to Mallarmé's *English Words*), is a relative of "style," but more importantly here, of "stop." *La carte postale (The Post Card)* is a "stop-gap" production, a holding action, an antibook awaiting relief by a Writing beyond the book. Or, to put it another way, it is a work of theoretical grammatology which contains the script for an *applied* grammatology. The applied phase of grammatology, which I introduce here, is meant to be the pedagogical equivalent of this scripting beyond the book, adequate to an era of interdisciplines, intermedia, electronic apparatus.

Part II summarizes Derrida's explicit statements about pedagogy and also describes the pedagogical implications of his full *oeuvre.* To indicate the feasibility of the Writing strategy, I offer three examples of teachers who have used similar techniques—Jacques Lacan, exemplifying a homophonic lecture style; Joseph Beuys, exemplifying the demonstration of models; and Sergei Eisenstein, exemplifying filmic writing—with the understanding that the application of grammatology to the present classroom will be a translation, an approximation or adaptation of these exemplary procedures. Grammatology, in any case, requires the introduction of the subject into the scene of teaching—the inscription of one's own signature on the curriculum (each one is read by what he/she writes "on"), leading to the decentering of disciplinary identities. The relevant motto here is: "We must begin *wherever we are* and the thought of the trace which cannot take the scent into account, has already taught us that it was impossible to justify a point of departure absolutely. *Wherever we are:* in a text where we already believe ourselves to be" (*Of Grammatology,* 162).

I should emphasize the preliminary nature of my book—which has some of the tone of Saussure's suggestion that there ought to be something like "semiology." I argue that there ought to be something like "applied grammatology." Given that the task of theoretical grammatology (the closure of Western metaphysics) is infinite, there can be no thought of sequence or order in the three phases. For that matter, historical grammatology—the scientific exposition of the history of writing—is not yet completed, and applied grammatology, as I show in the examples of Lacan, Beuys, and

Eisenstein, is already under way (had Saussure looked around he would have noted, possibly, that semiology already existed).

I offer here an outline for an alternative to the current aporia stalling literary criticism. But to choose applied grammatology over deconstruction is to shift paradigms, a move that, as Thomas Kuhn pointed out, does not solve the old problems but exchanges them for an entirely new set of problems. These new problems offer, however, an extremely interesting and challenging future for teaching scholars in the humanities, making this a particularly happy time to be a pedagogue. Nor would it have been possible for me to glimpse this threshold without the work of the Yale School critics and other explorers of and commentators on deconstructionism. My "beyond" (deconstruction) is really an "elsewhere" or "other than," since I cannot pretend to surpass the work of my predecessors.

The debts I have accumulated along the way are extensive, and in spite of Derrida's suggestion that it is sometimes better to default on one's creditors (and auditors), I would like to include a few acknowledgments. I thank the University of Florida for its generous support of my research, including in addition to a sabbatical in 1980–81 (when I started the actual composition of this manuscript) a semester of release time, spring 1982 (the Division of Sponsored Research), and funding for a research trip (spring 1980) enabling me to consult with Jacques Derrida in Paris and Joseph Beuys in Düsseldorf, both of whom provided me with valuable advice and documentation. A summer grant from the National Endowment for the Humanities (1979) enabled me to initiate my research on Beuys, a considerable detour from the domains of discourse with which I was familiar.

I thank the students and colleagues with whom I have had an opportunity to discuss these ideas, among whom I must single out Alistair Duckworth, Robert B. Ray, Hayden White, and J. Hillis Miller. Thanks also to Ronald Feldman and to John P. Leavey, Jr.

Chapter 5 includes a revised version of a piece that appeared in *Diacritics;* parts of chapters 2 and 4 appear in Mark Krupnick, ed., *Displacement,* Indiana University Press. My thanks for permission to reprint.

PART I

Beyond Deconstruction:

Derrida

*C'est la logique inimaginable, impensable même
de ce pas au-delà qui m'intéresse.*

—Jacques Derrida

1

Grammatology

W

BEYOND DECONSTRUCTION

hat is the importance of Jacques Derrida's theories for the disciplines of the humanities? Thus far, as indicated by such book titles as *Deconstruction and Criticism, Deconstructive Criticism, On Deconstruction*, and *Marxism and Deconstruction*, the application of Derrida's ideas has focused on the principle (or method) of deconstruction. The one point of agreement in the controversy surrounding this topic is that the initial phase of the importation of Derrida into American higher education is now over. This initial phase, as several critics have noted, took place in language and literature departments (rather than in philosophy or human sciences departments) and was concerned almost exclusively with the practice of literary criticism. Whatever the interest of the Yale School critics (Paul de Man, J. Hillis Miller, Geoffrey Hartman) who sponsored this introduction, there is now a general feeling of dissatisfaction, a sense of a discrepancy between the first application of Derrida's texts and the fuller program outlined in his theories. From the point of view of literary criticism, Rodolphe Gasché notes,

> Derrida's philosophical work can be turned into a theory to be applied to the regional science of literary criticism as well as to the literature it deals with, without the categories of literature and criticism (and the institutions supporting them) being put into question. This naive and intuitive reception of Derrida's debate with philosophy, its reduction to a few sturdy devices for the critic's use, represents

nothing less than an extraordinary blurring and toning-down of the
critical implications of this philosopher's work.[1]

The tendency among those discussing these "critical implications" is to
consider the political potential of deconstruction. The point that the
institution of literary studies may be radically altered, that the very disciplines promoting such study may disappear or be transformed beyond
recognition, is frequently mentioned but is subordinated as an issue to the
more directly political question. Michael Ryan, for example, believes that
even in its attenuated form, New French Theory is politically subversive:
"If bourgeois ideology is general and consistent, that is, if it rests on certain values and principles which turn up predictably in each one of its
domains—from law and science to culture and politics—then the fact that
domestic NFT, without being self-consciously political, manages to set the
teeth of bourgeois literary critical ideologists on edge should give leftists
pause before rejecting it out of hand."[2]

Edward Said, however, characterizes the apparent radicalization of
thought in New French Theory as an illusion or as a pose without effect,
because its professors accept all the assumptions and conventions of present
academic practice. The result, Said says, is an ever greater isolation of
critics from the major intellectual, moral, and political issues of the day.
Against de Man's embracement of the aporia at the heart of discourse which
inhibits communication and knowledge, Said recalls F. O. Matthiessen's
"Responsibility of the Critic"—to keep open a life-giving communication
between art and society.[3] Interestingly enough, Gerald Graff, who has become the spokesman for conservative humanists, professes an ideal similar
to Said's of an interaction between literary culture and general society. A
useful function for the humanities now, Graff argues, is to shore up our
sense of reality by means of a referential theory of analysis which resists the
vanguardist tendency to turn lying into a universal principle.[4] That critics
of such radically different political persuasions could be in agreement
about the general area of the limitations of deconstructionism is itself a
signal of the direction to be taken in further research.

I propose, in the present book, to approach the question of the application of Derrida's theories, not in terms of deconstruction (although that
topic remains an important aspect of Derrida's work), but in terms of
grammatology. To enter the question at this level opens up the disciplinary implications of New French Theory in a way that illuminates the full
extent of the challenge Derrida poses to current academic practice. I will
argue that grammatology, a name designating a new organization of cultural
studies, is first of all a new mode of writing whose practice could bring the
language and literature disciplines into a more responsive relationship with
the era of communications technology in which we are living.

At the very least, a grammatological perspective has the advantage of offering an alternative to the present impasse in critical theory brought about by the emphasis on deconstruction. As a result of this emphasis or selection within Derrida's program, some of the best younger critics, even while promoting deconstruction, are beginning to settle for an artificial limitation on the application of the theory. Jonathan Culler, for example, has stated persuasively the view with which I wish to take issue:

> Undertaking a rigorous investigation of signs and signification, semi-otics produces a discipline which, ultimately, reveals the fundamental contradictions of the signifying process as we understand it. Semiotics leads, necessarily, to a critique of semiotics, to a perspective which shows the error of its ways. But that perspective is never a viable al-ternative. It is not a position from which one could undertake an alternative analysis of signs and systems of signs, for the notions of analysis, of explanation, of production of models are all part of the semiotic perspective, and to undertake any of them is immediately to revert to that perspective. The alternative, then, is not a discipline, not another mode of analysis, but acts of writing, acts of displace-ment, play which violates language and rationality. The tense interplay between the opposed yet inseparable activities of semiotics and de-construction is already a major source of energy in literary studies, and it would be rash indeed to predict when or how its dominance will end. [5]

Culler's assumption is that "escape from logocentrism is impossible because the language we use to criticize or to formulate alternatives works accord-ing to the principles being contested" (41). A review of Derrida's program at the level of grammatology will reveal a mode of writing, and ultimately of pedagogical practice, that is designed to overcome the logocentric limitations of discourse.

MANIFESTO

Part I of *Of Grammatology* ("Writing before the Letter"), which relates writing as idea and as phenomenon to the mainstream of Western philos-ophy and to modern linguistics, constitutes the manifesto of grammatol-ogy. Derrida does not claim grammatology as his invention; rather, he intervenes in a tradition of scholarship at a crucial moment in its history. His intervention consists of providing a theory for a mode of research that up until now has produced almost exclusively (at least among its modern representatives) histories of writing. The historians of writing, such as I. J. Gelb (who actually entitled his book *Grammatology* in one edition) or André Leroi-Gourhan (whom Derrida cites several times), to mention only two examples, have made available a considerable knowledge of the evolution of writing.[6] But since the historians, according to Derrida, tend to confuse the question, What is writing?—asking after the essence of writing —with the problem of the *origin* of writing (a question that finally paralyzed the research of facts), the theoretical questions were never attempted. The phase of grammatology in which Derrida participates has as its task the formation of a theory which will organize and conceptualize these facts.

Like most modern fields of study, which were at one time part of philosophy, grammatology is now beginning to distinguish itself from its parent discipline. Indeed, from a disciplinary perspective, the import of Derrida's attack on logocentrism concerns just this work of emergence of a new knowledge practice. In addition to his critique of the impingement of philosophy on the history of writing (including discussions of such figures as Plato, Aristotle, Warburton, Condillac, Rousseau, Kant, Hegel, Husserl, Freud, and Heidegger), Derrida has offered suggestions for another stage of grammatology altogether, one that would go beyond the current episteme to develop an *applied* grammatology. Thus, three phases are included in the field: a history of writing (still under way), a theory of writing (one version now formulated by Derrida), and a grammatological practice (the application of the history and theory to the development of a new writing). My book is an introduction to the third phase—applied grammatology.

Derrida identifies two major breakthroughs leading to the current status of grammatology. The first occurred in the eighteenth century, a period in which the search for a universal language was accompanied by the beginnings of grammatology as a positive science. During this period there were two obstacles to a science of writing. One had to do with a theological prejudice —the myth of an original, primitive language given to man by God. The other obstacle (another form of "blindness") concerned the period's "hallucinatory" misunderstanding of hieroglyphics. Far from being rejected owing to ethnocentric scorn of things non-Western, the hieroglyph was excessively admired as a form of sublime, mystical writing. Derrida credits the work of Frerét and Warburton (one working with Chinese and the other with Egyptian writing) with creating an "epistemological break" that overcame these obstacles, thus "liberating a theoretical field in which the scientific techniques of deciphering were perfected by the Abbé Barthélemy and then by Champollion. Then a systematic reflection upon the correspondence between writing and speech could be born. The greatest difficulty was already to conceive, in a manner at once historical and systematic, the organized cohabitation, within the same graphic code, of figurative, symbolic, abstract, and phonetic elements."[7]

Following this historical leap in the eighteenth century, the next breakthrough needed to realize a science of writing occurred in literature during the modernist period. Derrida credits here the graphic poetics of Mallarmé and Ezra Pound's advocacy of Ernst Fenollosa's "The Chinese Written Character as a Medium for Poetry." The graphological concerns of Mallarmé (one of the founders of "concrete poetry") and Pound-Fenollosa showed the limits of the logico-grammatical structure of the Western model, offering instead a writing that balanced the ideographic with the phonetic elements of writing. The hieroglyph, it is worth noting, provides a common denominator relating these two moments in the development of grammatology.

The present theoretical phase of grammatology, Derrida says, requires more than an intrascientific and epistemological liberation analogous to the one brought about by Freret and Warburton. "Now a reflection must clearly be undertaken, within which the 'positive' discovery and the 'deconstruction' of the history of metaphysics, in all its concepts, are controlled reciprocally, minutely, laboriously" (*Grammatology*, 83). In short, the metaphysical tradition itself is the primary obstacle to a grammatology, an obstacle whose undoing has absorbed nearly all of Derrida's attention. The conceptual structure imposed by Western metaphysics on our thinking (which opposes soul to body and valorizes the spiritual or the ideal over the material throughout a long list of polar oppositions) entailed an instrumentalist and technicist view of writing. The obstacle Derrida wishes to remove is this conception (even this habit of thought) of the exteriority of writing to speech and of speech to thought—the view that language is an instrument of thought, and writing only "the extension of an instrument." The applied stage of grammatology will come about through the transformation of this dualistic and subordinating attitude toward writing.

At the same time that he has undertaken a critique of the themes of logocentrism, then, Derrida has begun to practice a mode of writing which is no longer subordinated to speech or thought—a writing no longer functioning as a representation of speech, in which the hierarchy of thought, speech, and writing is collapsed. Derrida's books and essays, it must be remembered, are not yet an applied grammatology. Working at the level of theory, they provide a model from which may be projected an understanding of how to apply grammatology. To facilitate this understanding, Derrida has addressed himself to several problems, foremost among these being the contemporary condition of composing books. One of Derrida's assumptions, essential to a sympathy for the grammatological project, is that written language, every bit as much as spoken language, evolves and changes, and that the evolution of writing is not necessarily dependent upon the evolution of speech.

The first fact to be confronted in this evolution of writing is the development and perfection of the alphabet by the Greeks. The problem that circulates through every field of reflection, Derrida maintains, constituting the fundamental condition that the grammatologist must address, is *the phoneticization of writing:* "On this subject, what does the most massive, most recent, and least contestable information teach us? First, that for structural or essential reasons, a purely phonetic writing is impossible and has never finished reducing the nonphonetic. The distinction between phonetic and non-phonetic writing, although completely indispensable and legitimate, remains very derivative with regard to what may be called a synergy and a fundamental synesthesia" (*Grammatology,* 88–89).

In its early stages of development, writing was associated with drawing and the visual arts in general, never having more than a loose association with speaking until phoneticization transformed it into a representation of the spoken word. But, as Gelb notes, there can never be an exact correspondence between the spoken and the written, his examples including certain visual morphemes such as spellings, which convey meaning only in writing, silently (homophony) (18). Derrida makes this point by noting that phonetic and nonphonetic are never pure qualities of writing systems, but are characteristics of elements more or less dominant within all systems of signification in general. "The cuneiform, for example, is at the same time ideogrammatic and phonetic . . . the cuneiform code playing alternately on two registers. In fact, each graphic form may have a *double value*—ideographic and phonetic" (*Grammatology,* 89). Moreover, Derrida adds, "this is true of all systems of writing." Applied grammatology is the search for a writing that recognizes and brings into balance this double value.

Another name for phoneticization, according to Leroi-Gourhan, is "linearization." Grammatology confronts nothing less than the sediment of four thousand years of the history of language, during which time everything that resisted linearization was suppressed. Briefly stated, this suppression amounts to the denial of the pluridimensional character of symbolic thought originally evident in the "mythogram" (Leroi-Gourhan's term), or nonlinear writing (pictographic and rebus writing). In the mythogram, meaning is not subjected to successivity, to the order of logical time, or to the irreversible temporality of sound. The linear schema of unfolding presence, where the line relates the final presence to the originary presence according to the straight line or the circle, became a *model,* Derrida says, and as such became inaccessible and invisible. Given Heidegger's demonstration that this mundane concept of temporality (homogeneous, dominated by the form of the now and the ideal of continuous movement, straight or circular) is the determining concept of all ontology from Aristotle to Hegel, and the assumption that the linearity of language entails just this concept of time, Derrida concludes that "the meditation upon writing and the deconstruction of the history of philosophy become inseparable" (*Grammatology,* 86). Part of my concern will be to disentangle these two questions, to set aside the philosophical investigations (which have already received considerable attention anyway) while highlighting instead the meditation on writing as the clue to an applied grammatology.

WRITING

The subordination of writing to speech, which began with phoneticization in hieroglyphic writing and approached completion in the phonetic alphabet is incapable of imposing itself absolutely, its limits being discreteness, spacing, differance: "But however important it might be, and were it in fact universal or called upon to become so, that particular model which is phonetic writing *does not exist;* no practice is ever totally faithful to its principle. Even before speaking, as I shall do further on, of a radical and a priori necessary infidelity, one can already remark its massive phenomena in mathematical script or in punctuation, in *spacing* in general, which it is difficult to consider as simple accessories of writing" (*Grammatology,* 39). From these margins or pockets within phoneticization, grammatology will begin to counter the effects of linearization. Indeed, Derrida notes that all the revolutions in philosophy, science, and literature during this century can be interpreted as shocks that are gradually destroying the linear model.

The association of the new writing with mathematical script indicates what is at stake in this counterattack. George Steiner, for example, noting like Derrida the primacy given to the word, to the verbal, in Western civilization, the effort (in the humanities) to enclose reality within language, finds in mathematics the insuperable symptom of the "two cultures" split, which is forcing the humanities into increasing irrelevance. Humanists today who do not know that mathematics has cut them off from the greater part of modern reality, Steiner says, are like those who persisted in believing the world was flat after it had been circumnavigated.[8] Steiner's belief that the problem of silence, representing the retreat from the word in the sciences and the arts alike, is the central question of our time is shared by many observers.

Derrida, however, does not share Steiner's pessimism. The modernist aesthetics of silence and the mathematicization of science are for Derrida signs that the culture is shifting away from a paradigm based on language toward one based on writing. The humanities need not become mute, are not helpless in the face of modern science, but may find support precisely in the nonphonetic features of mathematical operations for exploring the resources of spacing in writing. The resurgence of the graphic element, escaping from the domination of the spoken word, is a symptom of the end of the metaphysical era.

It is clear by now that "writing" is being redefined in grammatology:
For some time now, as a matter of fact, here and there, by a gesture

and for motives that are profoundly necessary, whose degradation
is easier to denounce than it is to disclose their origin, one says "language" for action, movement, thought, reflection, consciousness,
unconsciousness, experience, affectivity, etc. Now we tend to say
"writing" for all that and more: to designate not only the physical
gestures of literal pictographic or ideographic inscription, but also
the totality of what makes it possible; and also, beyond the signifying
face, the signified face itself. And thus we say "writing" for all that
gives rise to an inscription in general, whether it is literal or not and
even if what it distributes in space is alien to the order of the voice:
cinematography, choreography, of course, but also pictorial, musical,
sculptural "writing." One might also speak of athletic writing, and
with even greater certainty of military or political writing in view of
the techniques that govern those domains today. All this to describe
not only the system of notation secondarily connected with these
activities but the essence and the content of these activities themselves.
It is also in this sense that the contemporary biologist speaks of
writing and *pro-gram* in relation to the most elementary processes of
information within the living cell. And, finally, whether it has essential limits or not, the entire field covered by the cybernetic *program*
will be the field of writing. (*Grammatology*, 9)

All these manifestations of writing, so visibly different, share an irreducible
and invisible element—the *gramme,* or the *grapheme,* the trace: hence,
grammatology. A grammatologist may be able to bring this range of materials together within a field of study, but my concern in this book is with
grammatology's own compositional practice.

SCIENCE

Grammatology participates in the current trend, marking the close of
an epoch of specialization, toward the formation of disciplinary syntheses,
including in the area of information studies such composites as semiology
and cybernetics. Grammatology cuts across the old divisions of knowledge,
being concerned with all manner of inscription, with the question of how
any form of knowledge or mode of knowing relates to writing. "The science
of writing should therefore look for its object at the roots of scientificity.
The history of writing should turn back toward the origin of historicity. A
science of the possibility of science? A science of science which would no
longer have the form of *logic* but that of *grammatics*?" (*Grammatology*,
28). Far from simply opposing science, as opponents of New French Theory
sometimes claim, "grammatology must pursue and consolidate whatever,
in scientific practice, has always already begun to exceed the logocentric
closure," Derrida notes. "This is why there is no simple answer to the ques-

tion of whether grammatology is a 'science.' In a word, I would say that it *inscribes* and *delimits* science; it must freely and rigorously make the norms of science function in its own writing; once again, it *marks* and at the same time *loosens* the limit which closes classical scientificity." [9]

Derrida contributed to this vigilance with his first book, an introduction to Husserl's *Origin of Geometry,* concerned with the problem of how knowledge establishes itself as truth—the passage from prescience to science —and with how such truth transmits itself through tradition, changing or evolving as a field of knowledge, yet remaining true. This interest in geometry—the mathematics that is at once closest to writing as drawing, yet the most logocentric, being the very figure of linearization—involves the problematic relation of spacing to spatialization in language, the whole history of the metaphor of structure, which includes everything having to do with "the order of forms and sites," "the internal unity of an assemblage, a *construction,*" and extending, by transfer of topography to rhetoric, "the theory of commonplaces in language and the manipulation of motifs or arguments." [10] Here we have one of the principal concerns of grammatology as a field of study: "This geometry is only metaphorical, it will be said. Certainly. But metaphor is never innocent. It orients research and fixes results. When the spatial model is hit upon, when it functions, critical reflection rests within it" (*Writing,* 17). Grammatology, as we shall see, interrogates the relation of knowledge to metaphor.

In order to loosen and displace spatialization from the logocentric model, Derrida, reflecting his status as a *post*structuralist and *de*constructionist, raised the question of energetics, force, duration, motion, topics that led him to investigate a contemporary example of how a domain of knowledge emerges and establishes itself as a science—psychoanalysis. Psychoanalysis offers an especially interesting example for a science of writing, being a mode of knowledge constructed out of an idiomatic memory technique of one individual—it is the "science of Freud's name." The question Derrida poses is "how an autobiographical writing, in the abyss of an unterminated auto-analysis, could give *its* birth to a world-wide institution." [11]

Part of Derrida's interest in the foundation of geometry and psychoanalysis as sciences, of course, has to do with the establishment of grammatology itself as a science. In a sense, Derrida explores the possibility that the best way to study the foundations of knowledge is to instigate oneself the establishment of a discipline, one whose aim is to provide a model that will expose the operations of the existing disciplinary structure. At the theoretical stage of its development, then, grammatology is borrowing extensively from psychoanalysis: "Outside of linguistics, it is in psychoanalytic research that this breakthrough [the "deconstitution of the founding concept-words of ontology"] seems at present to have the greatest likelihood of being expanded" (*Grammatology,* 21). His intention, Derrida explains, is to attempt the "theoretical articulation of the new general question of the gram . . . with the question of psychoanalysis" (*Positions,* 83), not only to "fracture the closure that shelters the question of writing (in general, and notably philosophical and literary writing) from psychoanalysis, but equally the closure that so frequently blinds psychoanalytic discourse to a certain structure of the textual scene" (84).

The articulation of writing and psychoanalysis permits a "radicalization of the thought of the trace," which, Derrida suggests, opens up numerous fields of study, including, in addition to the history of writing, "a psychopathology of everyday life," extending Freud's interpretation of slips of the pen and tongue to the full domain of writing; "a becoming-literary of the literal," being a "psychoanalysis of literature respectful of the *originality of the literary signifier*"; and finally, "a new *psychoanalytic graphology,*" following Melanie Klein's lead in "The Role of the School in the Libidinal Development of the Child," concerned with "all the investitures to which a *graphie,* in form and substance, is submitted" (*Grammatology,* 87); "As concerns the forms of signs, even within phonetic writing, the cathexes of gestures, and of movements, of letters, lines, points, the elements of writing apparatus (instrument, surface, substance, etc.)" (*Writing,* 230–31).

Grammatology, then, is a science that functions as the deconstruction of the concept of science. The current norm of science is used temporarily to interrogate the conditions in which a grammatology might be possible, since the undoing of logocentrism—the model of the line and of forms—which is the fundamental condition for the emergence of grammatology, would destroy the present concept of science as well, making a science as such of writing impossible. Thus, "graphematics or grammatography ought no longer to be presented as sciences; their goal should be exorbitant when compared to grammato*logical knowledge*" (*Grammatology,* 74). Grammatology, if it comes into being, will not be an abstract discipline, nor a determined science: "The necessary decentering cannot be a philosophic or scientific act as such, since it is a question of dislocating, through access to another system linking speech and writing, the founding categories of language and the grammar of the *episteme.* The natural tendency of *theory* — of what unites philosophy and science in the episteme—will push rather toward filling in the breach than toward forcing the closure" (92). The challenge of an applied grammatology is to define how this other writing can function as knowledge *without being theoretical.*

The movement of difference itself, of course, strategically nicknamed *trace, reserve,* or *differance,* is called writing only within the limits of science and philosophy. But, Derrida adds, there is a *thought* ("*thought* is here for me a perfectly neutral name, the blank part of the text, the necessarily indeterminate index of a future epoch of differance"—*Grammatol-*

ogy, 93), of the trace which must also point beyond the field of the episteme: "The future can only be anticipated in the form of an absolute danger. It is that which breaks absolutely with constituted normality and can only be proclaimed, *presented,* as a sort of monstrosity" (5).

BEYOND THE BOOK

"The end of linear writing," Derrida declares in his manifesto, "is indeed the end of the book," even if, he continues, "it is within the form of a book that the new writings—literary or theoretical—allow themselves to be, for better or for worse, encased" (*Grammatology,* 86). Asked in an interview to clarify what he meant by "the end of the book," Derrida explained that while *Of Grammatology* inquires into the "current upheavals in the forms of communication, the new structures emerging in all the formal practices, and also in the domains of the archive and the treatment of information, that massively and systematically reduce the role of speech, of phonetic writing, and of the book," one would be mistaken to conclude that grammatology implies the "death of the book": in the first place because grammatology itself, as a "theory," is caught in the limits of science; second, because the end of the book and the beginning of writing involve the notion of closure, not of end. The book thus may continue indefinitely—it has no "end," any more than writing has an "origin" (writing is always already at work) (*Positions,* 13). He could have added a third reason, revealed in his projection for a psychoanalytic graphology: any attempt to move beyond the book must contend with the libidinal investment in the form of the book. The book is perhaps the most charged, cathected object in Western civilization, representing, according to Freud's analysis of his own dream of the botanical monograph, the Mother. Derrida's frequent allusions to the need for mourning (a process associated with the child's defenses for dealing with the loss of or separation from the mother, an essential element of the entry into language), signaled by the funeral knell in *Glas,* suggest that grammatological writing exemplifies the struggle to break with the investiture of the book.

The empirical basis for this question, of course, is the development of the electronic media. Every theorist who has addressed the question of the role of communications technology in the evolution of cognition, representing every shade of thought from the Catholic Walter Ong to the Marxist Hans Enzensberger, agrees that the new media are bringing about a radical cultural transformation whose imperatives may no longer be ignored by intellectuals.

Derrida's participation in the meeting of "the Estates General of Philosophy," which took place at the Sorbonne for two days in June 1979, indicates his interest in the problem of the new media. The purpose of the meeting was to call attention to, and find remedies for, the diminishing role of philosophy in French education. Derrida, one of the five-member preparation committee for the meeting, delivered the principal address, an essential point of which was an appeal for the humanities disciplines to enter into the media revolution. He reminded the professors present that many of the changes taking place that seem so threatening to philosophy may not simply be condemned and rejected. "We would be making a grave error to ignore that if we are often shocked or made indignant by certain of these effects, it is because, even in our bodies, we live our relation to philosophy behind protective selecting filters, in laboratories whose social, political and philosophical conditioning especially merits interrogation."[12] He called upon the group to concern itself with what passes for philosophy not only in other disciplines but especially outside the scholarly and university circle.

Derrida's purpose was to focus the attention of the educators on a new object (and mode) of study and communication—the very object that most held responsible for the atrophying of the humanities: "I am thinking here in particular," Derrida stated, "of what conveniently may be gathered under the generic name 'media' and the 'power of the media'" (*Etats,* 32). Given a cultural situation in which the media have replaced the educational institutions as the purveyors of whatever philosophy or humanities the public is exposed to, and given the complete absence of any critical element in this new education ("There is there a complementarity often scarcely readable, but solid, between the most immobilized, contracted academicism and all that, outside the school and the university, in the mode of representation and spectacle, taps almost immediately into the channels or chains of the greatest receivability"—43), the primary task for the Estates General was to concern itself with "the functioning of the market-place, the techno-politics of the 'media' and with what the government administers under the name of 'Culture' and 'Communication.' It is desirable that this work on the techno-politics of the media becomes from now on a regular part, let me repeat, of the 'philosophical education' to come" (40).

Derrida's interest in the media is an aspect of his general concern for writing as a "technology," an evolving technology, constrained for three millennia in the service of language. This adventure—of "a narrow and historically determined concept of writing"

> now seems to be approaching what is really its own *exhaustion;* under
> the circumstances—and this is no more than one example among
> others—of this death of the civilization of the book, of which so much
> is said and which manifests itself particularly through a convulsive

proliferation of libraries. All appearances to the contrary, this death
of the book undoubtedly announces nothing but a death of speech
and a new mutation in the history of writing, in history as writing. Announces it at a distance of a few centuries. . . . "Death of speech" is
of course a metaphor here: before we speak of disappearance, we must
think of a new situation for speech, of its subordination within a
structure of which it will no longer be the archon. (*Grammatology*, 8)

The facilitator of Derrida's exploration of this shift, then, will not be
Marshall McLuhan, who projected the return of an oral civilization (or
rather, Derrida will psychoanalyze that orality), but Martin Heidegger.
Working philologically, Heidegger located the essence of modern technology
in the family of terms related to *Gestell* (enframing), including thus all the
stellen words, translated as "to order, to represent, to secure, to entrap, to
disguise, to produce, to present, to supply."[13] Derrida took up the question of enframing, as indicated in his exploration of all marginal and parergonal phenomena, in order to prepare the way for the shift away from,
or the deemphasis of, speech in favor of writing. From Heidegger's point
of view, the danger of technology is that its rigid cause-and-effect enframing order might blind humanity to alternative orders. It is not technology itself, but this blindness to its enframing, that must be confronted:
"Because the essence of technology is nothing technological, essential reflection upon technology and decisive confrontation with it must happen
in a realm that is, on the one hand, akin to the essence of technology, and,
on the other, fundamentally different from it. Such a realm is art" (*Technology*, 35). Enframing, in short, concerns not any given form of technology, but the production and relaying of information by whatever means,
which is to say that the *techne* itself cannot "end" or "arrive at its completion," since it is what allows anything at all to become present. *Techne*,
thus, overlaps as a question differance (*Carte*, 206-7). Grammatology,
then, studies enframing, not "literature" or "science," which is to say that
ultimately it is a pedagogy rather than a system of knowledge.[14]

In his address to the Estates General, Derrida urged the academic worker
not only to study the effects of the media but to engage in media practice:
"It is within the media that the battle ought to be established" (*Etats*,
169). But before grammatology can attain its applied status by working in
the video medium, whose audiovisual capacity seems to fulfill the require-
ments of a *double-valued* writing (phonetic and ideographic—to be discussed in chapter 9), certain theoretical problems must be resolved (to be
discussed in chapter 3). Meanwhile, theoretical grammatology accepts the
limits of the book, just as it does those of science, as the point of departure
for its deconstruction of the current paradigm. "And yet did we not know
that the closure of the book was not a simple limit among others? And

that only in the book, coming back to it unceasingly, drawing all our resources from it, could we indefinitely designate the writing beyond the
book?" (*Writing*, 294).

The idea of a unified totality upon which the concept of the book depends is the notion that a totality of the signified preexists the totality of
the signifier, "supervises its inscription and its signs, and is independent of
it in its ideality" (*Grammatology*, 18). In the metaphysical tradition, in
spite of the fact that it served as a metaphor for the soul and the divine,
the book as a written space had no intrinsic value. Rather, the "Platonic"
book records a discourse that has already taken place (the voice of thought
in dialogue with itself—self-presence) and therefore is testable in terms of
truth—the resemblance to what is "engraved on the psychic surface"—
intention.[15] The concept of the book in logocentrism, thus, is essentially
representation, mimetic; but the destiny of the book, as Heidegger said
about the future of technology, is not determined, is still open, free. The
book may become "text," lend itself to writing, as in the example of Edmond Jabes, for whom a return to the book is an escape from it. "The
book has lived on this lure: to have given us to believe that passion, having
originally been impassioned by *something,* could in the end be appeased
by the return of that something. Lure of the origin, the end, the line, the
ring, the volume, the center" (*Writing,* 295). To pass through the book,
repeating the lure at every point along the way, changes everything without anything having budged—such is the enigmatic power of repetition to
expose the derived status of origins. This repetition refers to the fact that
the closure of the book occurs *when the book lets itself be thought as such*
(296), a moment emblematized in Mallarmé's project for The Book. This
strategy of (parodic) repetition will play an important role in Derrida's
texts.

HIEROGLYPHS

Theoretical grammatology, thus far, has used the book format, although
its genre, to the extent that the term applies in this case, is the essay. These
essays are rather the simulacra of books ("This [therefore] will not have
been a book"—*Dissemination,* 3) because the principle directing their production is no longer logocentric, no longer a Platonic metaphysics in which
writing is secondary. The new essays are written in and for an age of electronic media, written both against the old model of the book and as a supplement to the new media, to assist and stimulate the transition to the new
epoch.

The generating principle guiding the production of Derrida's texts is a literal transformation, or rather *a point-by-point repetition, of the history of writing into a theory of writing.* Grammatology, that is, was founded in the eighteenth century as a science of decipherment of nonalphabetic scripts—most specifically, the decipherment of Egyptian hieroglyphics. Theoretical grammatology (the second stage of the science of writing) could be characterized as a "new Egyptology," being a writing modeled upon the works of the two principal decipherers of the modern world—Champollion and Freud (himself, of course, a collector of Egyptian artifacts). The importance of this background to Derrida's theories is shown in his description of his single most influential proposal—the definition of differance:

> Now, in point of fact, it happens that this graphic difference (the *a* instead of the *e*), this marked difference between two apparently vocalic notations, between vowels, remains purely graphic: it is written or read, but it is not heard. It cannot be heard, and we shall see in what respects it is also beyond the order of understanding. It is put forward by a silent mark, by a tacit monument, or, one might even say, by a pyramid—keeping in mind not only the capital form of the printed letter but also that passage from Hegel's *Encyclopaedia* where he compares the body of the sign to an Egyptian pyramid. The *a* of differance, therefore, is not heard; it remains silent, secret, and discreet, like a tomb.[16]

In the history of decipherment, Warburton is credited with discovering, or realizing, that the hieroglyphic scripts were not occult or secret codes, but were meant for public monuments and popular use, and as such were readable, in principle.[17] The next step leading to decipherment was the discovery that the obelisk cartouches contained the proper names of kings or gods. The decipherment effort thereafter always began with the location of the proper names in the text. The names in the cartouches were discovered in a number of cases to contain foreign names written phonetically, with ideographs assigned phonetic value, leading to the conclusion that it was the need to record the proper name that stimulated the development of phoneticization.

Another essential aspect of decipherment was the trilingual interaction of translation made possible by the Rosetta stone, a surviving example of the basalt stele placed in every temple in ancient Egypt, bearing an inscription in hieroglyphic, demotic, and Greek characters in praise of Ptolemy, king of Egypt from 205 B.C. to 182 B.C. The importance of this stele as a theoretical emblem is related to Heidegger's discussion of enframing, the essence of technology, which "sets upon man and challenges him forth" (*Technology,* 15). As such, according to Heidegger, it is related to *poiesis,* a type of unconcealment of the real, etymologically linked with setting up or erecting statues in a temple. The elements of the story of the Rosetta stone—the cartouches with their phoneticized hieroglyphic recordings of proper names, the funerary setting of this writing (the common presence of the cartouches in tombs and on monuments to the dead), the multi-lingual, macaronic interaction of the languages along with the act of decipherment itself, carried out finally in the era of the French Revolution, and even the theme of praise signified in the inscription—all serve as a pre-text or model to guide Derrida's theoretical discourse, giving it thus an allegorical status.[18] This story (taking theory to be the stories we tell about certain facts), associating writing with the themes of identity (the name), death, praise, and the fortuitous play of sense, is the point of departure for Derrida's theoretical research.

Derrida finds, that is (and here is the clue to his methodology and strategy), that *the proper name is as much the key to the theory of writing as it was to the history of writing.* Thus, in his manifesto he turns to the proper name precisely as it was treated in ideographic script to illustrate the all-important lesson of the double-valued stratification of writing: "The problem of the picture-puzzle (*rébus à transfert*) brings together all the difficulties. As pictogram, a representation of the thing may find itself endowed with a phonetic value. This does not efface the 'pictographic' reference which, moreover, has never been simply 'realistic.' The signifier is broken or constellated into a system: it refers at once, and at least, to a thing and to a sound" (*Grammatology,* 90).

He provides an example from the writing of the Aztecs which covers all these possibilities: "Thus the proper name *Teocaltitlan* is broken into several syllables, rendered by the following images: lips (*tentli*), road (*otlim*), house (*calli*), and finally tooth (*tlanti*). The procedure is closely bound up with that . . . of suggesting the name of a person by images of the beings or things that go into the making of his name. The Aztecs achieved a greater degree of phoneticism. By having recourse to a truly phonetic analysis, they succeeded in rendering separate sounds through images" (*Grammatology,* 90).

The nonphonetic moment in writing threatens and subverts the metaphysics of the proper ("self-possession, property, propriety, cleanliness") first of all by decomposing the substantive: "Nonphonetic writing breaks the noun apart. It describes relations and not appellations. The noun and the word, those unities of breath and concept, are effaced within pure writing" (*Grammatology,* 26). "It is to speech," Derrida notes of nonphonetic writing, "what China is to Europe (25)—the outer margin of logocentrism. Theoretical grammatology adopts hieroglyphic writing as a model, translating it into a discourse, producing thus in philosophy distortions similar to those achieved in those movements, labeled "cubist" and "primitivist," which drew on the visual arts of non-Western cultures in order to deconstruct the look of logocentrism.

SIGNING

Derrida's application of Egyptology, or the hieroglyphic principle, to critical writing, because it focuses on the proper name—the signature, or autograph—could be called "signing," a label that calls attention to his critique of semiotics and Saussure's theory of the sign. Continuing his practice of allegorizing in theory the historical origin of writing, Derrida adopts as an operational device the exploitation of the pun, alluding to the wealth of homophones in the Egyptian language, which originally contributed to its phoneticization. Homophony and homonymy, history reveals, played a crucial role in extending the resources of language: "The otherwise motivated sign has acquired arbitrary uses, which are derived, by homonymy, from its continuing motivated occurrences. At the same time, the sign's ties with the specific spoken language are greatly strengthened." [19] Countering Saussure, Derrida offers a theory of signing, then; and the extent of his reliance on such puns for the generation of his strategies can never be overestimated, although he does not always pursue their consequences as systematically as he does in the case of signing. Derrida's "sign," then, is not a noun but a verb. It is not constituted by the signifier-signified but by the signature.

Derrida's essay on Francis Ponge, part of which was delivered at the Cerisy-la-Salle colloquium devoted to that poet, exemplifies his use of the hieroglyphic signature as a generative device. "Let us inscribe without saying a word," Derrida states at the conclusion of his paper, "the legend, in large monumental characters . . . the event of language [*langue*] on the *stele* (without punctuation, therefore), let us inscribe the luck (chance) of a trait, on a stone, on a table, that is on a blackboard [*tableau*] offered (exposed) to the sponge, this." [20] There follows in the published proceedings a paragraph in capital letters containing the puns on Ponge's name, the anagrams or homophones that were elaborated in the paper. The erasable blackboard in the modern classroom is, thus, the heir of the ancient basalt stele upon which was eternalized the names of royal and divine beings. Part of Derrida's strategy is to exploit the polysemy of the terms generated by his procedures. Stele is not only an upright stone slab, bearing an inscription or design, serving as a monument or marker, but also the central cylinder or cylinders of vascular and related tissue in the stem, root, leaf, and so on of higher plants. The botanical meaning is foregrounded in *Glas,* although the connection with Egyptology is always available as well, as it is in all of Derrida's writings on the proper name.

The spongeable, erasable blackboard literally puts the Egyptian stele under erasure (the device of crossing out while using terms being deconstructed), a gesture emphasizing the method of the paper which amounts to *a reversal of the phoneticization process* originally employed by the scribes in order to be able to write non-Egyptian names in the hieroglyphic script —the procedure, as described above with the Aztec name, being to match the sounds of the foreign name with those of Egyptian words, whose hieroglyphs were then used to write the name. Thus "Ptolemy" (the subject of the Rosetta stone) is inscribed with the signs of a door, a cake, a knotted rope, a lion, two reeds, and a chairback, with each character being used only for the sound of the first letter of the object's name.[21] Whereas the scribes started with pictures or images to build the sound of the name, Derrida uses the name to return to the images, miming in an alphabetized language while reversing the direction of the hieroglyphic operation. His paper on Ponge has nothing to do with Ponge as person or as poet, but only with "Ponge" as name—the name "Ponge" serves as the generative rule of the piece: "a discourse on his signature, its praise rather" ("Signéponge," 117). His approach, resembling Saussure's anagrammatic and hypogrammatic studies seeking the names of gods or heroes that provide the rule for Latin poems, is to reveal the dissemination of Ponge's name in the images of his texts, reducing his reading to a "cartouche" principle. "Ponge," thus, becomes (among other things) *"éponge"* (sponge and turkish towel), *"éponger"* (to clean with a sponge), and *"ponce"* (pumice). In the course of his paper, however, Derrida demonstrates that these items or actions do appear in the poetry, turning chance into necessity and manifesting the dissemination of the name in the images of the text.

At issue is the ancient problem of designation—the relation between a word and a thing, between a name and its referent—in which the status of the proper name serves as a limit-case. The sponge in "Ponge" may be used for erasing blackboards and for washing and cleaning in general; that is, to make proper (*propre*) in the sense of clean, emblematizing the poet's effort (the subject) to establish the propriety of his identity. Derrida's purpose, however, is to question the very notion of the proper, of "belonging together" in the relation between subject and a predicate, an object and its attributes as property and propriety, a question that he entitles "economimesis."[22] To move from the proper to common nouns (the rhetorical figure of antonomasia) reverses the idealization of nomination, desublimàtes the name. This impropriety is happily dramatized in the insignificance, the commonness and banality of the things constituting Ponge's signature, providing the *blason* of his name. Having discovered in Ponge's texts the image of a piece of blotting paper (*"tissu-éponge"*), for example, Derrida poses the question of the consequences of such events for our understanding of writing: "The *rebus* signature, the metonymic or anagrammatic signature is the condition of possibility and impossibility, the *double bind* of the signature event. As if the thing (or the common name of a thing) should absorb the proper, drink it and retain it in order to keep it. But at the same time, holding it, drinking it, absorbing it, it is as if it (or its name) lost or sullied the proper name" ("Signéponge," 138). What constitutes the "event"—the double bind or contra-band or double band—is the following homophonic sequence: *"l'e* [the e], *l'est* [the is], *lait* [milk], legs [legacy]." The "thing *and* (*et*) its name" thus easily becomes the "thing *is* (*est*) its name." The legacy involves the falling due (*la chance et l'échéance*) of the debt each one owes to the father for the gift of the name (an aspect of the problem which I will consider in the next chapter).[23]

Ponge provides not only the example of his ambivalent process (the *Aufhebung,* the lifting up that cancels and preserves, like sponging—free-loading on the name—which cleans the common and dirties the proper), Derrida says, but its science. His work demonstrates systematically the unilateral contract that the writer may sign with things. Observing the "regional science," Derrida notices and generalizes into his own procedures the particular "happiness" of the sponge—the way the aleatory material becomes necessary, the way the qualities of the sponge, taken as a model, can be extended, theorized—a model for the interaction between metaphor and concept. In this case, it is the sponge's status as a zoophyte that turns out, on reflection, to support concretely the theoretical principle of the undecidability, the fundamental ambiguity, of the proper so basic to Derrida's position. The sponge is neither proper nor improper; that is, it is an entity neither animal nor vegetable. Moreover, upon examination (in its status as a model), the sponge possesses a number of equivocal *properties*—it may be filled alternatively with water or air; it can ignobly "make water" everywhere, or wipe things clean (dirtying itself). As zoophyte, and given its other equivocal properties, the sponge serves as an analogue of writing and of metaphoricity itself ("Signéponge," 142).

Briefly stated, the cartouche principle is used as a mode of analysis (a literalization of analysis, after all, which term means the breakup or dissolution of something) for studying the author-text relation, first by locating in the text the images whose terms pun in some manner on the author's name, and then by scrutinizing these concrete elements to the fullest extent, unlimited by notions of context or intention, for their theoretical potential. Such interrogation invariably reveals (and here lies much of the importance of the technique) that the name and the text *do* stand in a *motivated* relationship one to the other. It is astonishing, once one notices this technique, how systematically Derrida applies it. At one level he uses it to provide a point of entry, an organizing device, a mode of invention (*inventio*) for his essays. Thus, he discusses Kant from the point of view of the "parergon" because "Kante" means border, or edge.[24] Blanchot opens up to the play of *"pas"* (the motion of a step, but also the negation of *"ne pas"*) because of the "o"—zero, or naught—in his name. To appreciate this procedure fully, one more example should be discussed—perhaps the most important one, outside of Derrida's own signature—before turning to a consideration of the implication of the cartouche principle for an applied grammatology.

SEMINAR

Jean Genet's signature is shown in *Glas* to be inscribed on the other side of the stele, that part of the term having to do with flowers. Genet embraces the original arbitrariness of language that gave the sponge to Ponge. His name, taken from his mother rather than his father, imitates a type of flower called the *genêt* (or *genets*)—broom flower, gorse, or greenweed, a luck that he doubles as author by naming many of his characters after flowers.

Part of the interest of Genet's example—a signature of flowers—is that the flower is, conventionally, the very trope of rhetoric itself ("the flowers of rhetoric"). Hence Derrida asks, "What is rhetoric such that flowers can be its figure?" Flowers, he decides, do not constitute a language, but take the place of zero signification (the place of the proper name). So the problem is to determine how the flowers, as things, take hold in "the jungle of natural language: question of *physis* as *mimesis.*" [25]

To help the reader follow his study of de*sign*ation in *Glas,* Derrida recommends that his essay "White Mythology" be consulted (even "grafted" onto *Glas*). Modern theory, best represented by Nietzsche, mounted a critique of philosophy, Derrida explains in "White Mythology," based on the view that the concept has its origin in metaphor, that every abstract figure hides a sensible figure that has been effaced in the course of the speculative *Aufhebung* (sublation) that raises words from the physical to the metaphysical. Derrida's purpose is to deconstruct this metaphysical and rhetorical schema at work in the Nietzschean critique—not to reject it, of course (his own project is to undo sublation), but to reinscribe it with an obliqueness that avoids the traps of the dialectic.

In a section entitled "Flowers of Rhetoric: Meliotrope," Derrida notes that metaphor, and mimesis in general, is held by tradition to be proper to man, aiming at an effect of knowledge. Such knowledge is acquired from metaphor in terms of resemblance—one of the terms in the substitution must be known in its proper sense as the basis for the comparison. The problem with this traditional understanding of metaphor or analogy, Derrida argues, is that the *aistheton*—the sensible or concrete referent whose term serves as the basis for the comparison—can always *not* present itself, and can not be perfectly known or mastered. The sun, for example, is the sensible object par excellence, and also *the* metaphor of philosophy (as in Plato's famous analogy of the sun to the good). The whole language of appearing and disappearing, the lexicon of *aletheia* (truth as unconcealment), would not be possible without the sun's determination of human perception. The dilemma for philosophy is that in spite of Aristotle's arguments to the contrary, the metaphor as such (resting its case on this key example) must necessarily be "bad" (there can never be a properly "good" metaphor) because metaphors can never furnish anything but improper knowledge. In other words, Aristotle's comparison of philosophy to the sun, for example, and the philosophic metaphor of the heliotrope (the flower that turns as it follows the path of the sun) may be empty (semantically) because no one actually has an exact knowledge of the sun or the heliotrope, the vehicles of the comparison. In short, Derrida here is challenging the description theory of naming, in which theoretically, in order to designate an object, a speaker must know something about it and so be able to identify it without relying on substitute names. This requirement of knowledge is evaded temporarily by the circular argument that the speaker may borrow a name from a community of users, the weakness of this move being that some "lender" in the "economy" must finally be able to make the reference on his own—must have real knowledge. The description theory, that is, relies finally on a group of experts to pay its semantic debts.[26]

Derrida, against description theories, and also against phenomenological epistemologies dependent on perception, intuition, or experience, is developing a theory of naming that does not depend on intelligibility or prior knowledge.[27] His procedure in *Glas,* with regard to the relation of flowers to rhetoric (representing the analogical process in general), exemplifies his alternative. *The principle underlying Derrida's method for researching the relation of metaphors to concepts is exactly the same one that governs the signature*—a systematic exploitation of the chance-necessity effects produced by the event of homophony or homonymy. In order to discover how flowers take root in language, according to Derrida's theory of concept formation, *the place to look is in the discourses that describe flowers* —literature and botany. The initial step of the operation is "mechanical" or "objective"—a cross-referencing of an artistic and a scientific terminology. What this research reveals is that a number of botanical terms relate homophonically, and even etymologically, to certain rhetorical terms. At stake is a theory of creativity, classically stated in terms of an analogy between sexual and spiritual creation and conception, as well as a pedagogy, also classically posed in terms of husbandry (as in Rousseau's famous image in *Emile* of the seedling in the roadway).

Rather than assuming that he (or we) will know what these analogies mean, Derrida systematically explores them by citing long passages from encyclopedic dictionaries containing definitions of the sex of flowers— information concerning the reproductive, or fertilization, process. The result of these collages is that certain lexical overdeterminations appear, producing the effect of the double band, a double-entry bookkeeping. Thus, pollen in certain orchids is said to "agglutinate," recalling the linguistic process of word formation in which morphemes are fused (*"l'est"* = *"lait,"* and so forth). Similarly, "cryptogam," an old division of plants (comprising those without true seeds or flowers, such as ferns or mosses), opens up the domain of cryptography, with all its strategies of decipherment. Since the proper-common shift in Genet's text always involves the names of flowers, Derrida states that in *Glas* he will replace "antonomasia" with "anthonymy," a portmanteau word combining anthography—the study of flowers—and anthology—itself extended to identify a collection of verse from the original reference to a collection of flowers.

Although Sartre, in *Saint Genet,* was certain that Genet's career was determined when he was named thief (*voleur*), Derrida shows that the meaning of the term in the other band—the flight (*vol*) of seeds in dissemination (the most important of the botanical-rhetorical transactions)—deserves equal recognition: "It is in terms of what concerns the seed, fertilized ovule, that one believes oneself to be speaking properly of dissemination (with respect to angiosperms or gymnosperms). The seeds are sometimes projected in every direction [*sens*] by the explosion of the fruit. More often, they escape by slits or holes opened in its wall, to be dispersed by wind or animals" (*Glas,* 279). Botanists call the wind-borne seed the *"genêt ailé"* (282), making Genet not only a thief but a flying seed. The description also exposes another term linking the two domains of botany and rhetoric —*"sens,"* meaning direction (the scattered seeds), and sense (meaning).

Having educated his reader in the terminology of plant fecundation, Derrida declares, "One is not going to produce here the theory of pollen and of seed scattering [*dissemence*]" (*Glas,* 283). The botanical information, rather, as the "vehicle" of the analogy between flowers and rhetoric, constitutes a didactic model in a textual "seminar": "Good or bad, the cries of the thief [*voleur*] . . . tried incessantly to withdraw, to initial the semen (seeds) [*semence*], to sign [*ensigner*] the dissemination, to paralyze the signature's sperm, to reappropriate the genealogy, to reconstitute the gilded monument of his own [*propre*] (seminar), to direct, to lock without a trace his clean [*propre*] and white sign manual [*seing*], to be the son, not the daughter, please note, of himself" (280). The passage displays not only the contraband relationship between seme and semen, which is one of the motivating, legitimating "events" of differance, but also the connotations of *seminar,* recalling Plato's analogy in *Phaedrus* characterizing the proper end of teaching: "The dialectician selects a soul of the right type, and in it he plants and sows his words founded on knowledge, words which can defend both themselves and him who planted them, words which instead of remaining barren contain a seed whence new words grow up in new characters, whereby the seed is vouchsafed immortality, and its possessor the fullest measure of blessedness that man can attain unto."[28]

The homophonic resemblance between "to sign" (*ensigner*) and "to teach" (*enseigner*) reveals the import of the entire demonstration, for in grammatology *the theory of signing is also a theory of teaching*. The research into dissemination, revealing the variations in human and plant sexuality, reopens the analogy between spiritual and sexual procreation, the idea being, based on the sexual operations described in the literature, to formulate a new approach to writing and teaching. The new approach, obviously, will not be platonic.

Glas teaches dissemination, a theory of writing, by means of its namesake in botany—a seminar technique in which, as we shall see, signing becomes a model for pedagogy. The method involved is crucial to applied grammatology, which is why I shall reiterate its principle. The whole process by which certain plants conceive—an immaculate conception (whose overtones on the spiritual band are picked up in the other column, in Hegel's discussion of Christianity)—emblematized in the explosion of the pod and the scattering of seed, is offered as an analogy for an intellectual conception generated in the process of writing—the flowers of rhetoric: "Everything leads to the importance of change. It can never subvert and corrode necessity except at the matchless moment when the proper name breaks language [*langue*], destroys itself in an explosion—dynamite—leaving there a hole. Very soon recovered: a vegetation parasitic and without memory" (*Glas*, 264).

The feature of language highlighted here is the very structure (a structural unconsciousness) of iteration—the same inherent quality that prevents phoneticization from ever totally reducing writing to voice also assures that the "intention animating the utterance *will never be through and through present to itself and to its content*": "I have underlined *dehiscence*. As in the realm of botany, from which it draws its metaphorical value, this word marks emphatically that the divided opening, in the growth of a plant, is also what, in a *positive* sense, makes production, reproduction, development possible. Dehiscence (like iterability) limits what it makes possible, while rendering its rigor and purity impossible. What is at work here is something like a law of undecidable contamination, which has interested me for some time."[29] Thus is the oval enclosure of the cartouche, separating the name from the text, broken, producing not "denotation" but "detonation." Keeping in mind the relation of grammatology to science, Derrida's use of the botanical definitions may be recognized as a deconstruction of description theories of designation which rely on expert knowledge. Derrida's strategy, displacing science within the constraints of its own rigor, is to use the expert definitions, not to close or reduce ambiguity, but to open it; not as guarantee of the univocal, but as generative model: documentation as allegory.[30]

HOMONYMY

The premise of applied grammatology is that the cartouche principle of the signature, directing the relation of the proper name to common nouns (the images generated by "anthonomasic" dissemination), may be generalized to include the process of concept formation—the relation of an abstract term to the metaphors from which the term is "derived." The method of the signature here demonstrates its affirmative nature, in that it not only calls attention to the weakness of the Nietzschean critique of conceptual language—which retained the myth of an original language (deconstructed by the homophonic event, which parodies the science of etymology)—but provides in its place an alternative to the metaphor-concept opposition. Against the traditional process of abstraction dependent on a systematic exclusion of properties, gathering "properties" into sets of terms based on synonymy or resemblance of meaning (identity, identification), Derrida proposes a homonymic procedure that blows a hole in the cartouche-like boundaries of conceptual categories, thus allowing terms to circulate and interbreed in a festival of equivocality.

In "White Mythology," Derrida allies his operation with Bachelard's "psychoanalysis of objective knowledge." Bachelard's most influential insight, dating back to the early thirties, was that the new physics rendered conventional thinking in philosophy obsolete. In order to overcome the obstacles to a new epistemology relevant to the new science, Bachelard argued that a pedagogy would have to be devised capable of reeducating human sensibility at its very root. One of his favorite examples dealt with the microphysics of Heisenberg and Bohr—the uncertainty principle and the complementarity principle—having to do with the nature of light, which behaves sometimes as a wave and sometimes as a particle. Keeping in mind that light is *the* philosophic metaphor, any change in our understanding of its nature should affect its analogical extensions in such concepts as form and theory. Thinking, in Einstein's universe, Bachelard stated, requires a new logic that breaks with all absolutes, whether Newtonian or Hegelian, but especially a logic that frees itself from the identity principle (the principle of noncontradiction and the excluded middle) of Aristotelian logic. The basic feature of this non-Aristotelian logic (to accomplish for the concept what non-Euclidean geometry and non-Newtonian physics accomplished for the object) would be a three-valued operation, including, in addition to the usual "true" and "false" values, a value labeled "absurd." Derrida's borrowing, by way of analogy (as he stresses), of Gödel's notion of undecidability to characterize his own "quasi-concepts," not to mention the Einsteinian or fourth-dimensional (space-time synthesis) tone of differance itself, which at once "differs" (spatial) and "defers" (temporal), indicates his sympathy for Bachelard's project.

The pedagogy implicit in grammatology, as we shall see, resembles the new pedagogy that Bachelard feels is required to reorganize conceptual thinking in a world of quantum physics (although, for Derrida, the life sciences rather than physics provide the motivation for research). Dubbed "dialectical surrationalism," defined as the realm in which the scientific mind dreams,[31] Bachelard's method does not abandon, but reorients, the theory of representation away from empirical or experiential reality. The consequences for the traditional use of analogy are radical, for against the traditional reliance on the familiar or the known as the vehicle of the comparison, Bachelard's pedagogy locates itself fully in the realm of the unknown: here even the doctrine of the "as if" of conventional heuristics gives way to a practice of the "why not," whose purpose is to submit "reality" to the extremes of human imagination. Thus, "realization" (invention) replaces "reality" in such theoretical fictions as "negative mass," the virtue of such fictions being that they allow theoretically precise questions to be posed with regard to totally unknown phenomena. In short, *the traditional order of realist or empirical experimentation is inverted,* so that the noumenon now explains the phenomenon (*No,* 53). Derrida's conceptual experiments function in a similar way, involving the movements of thought and language in a formal space entirely free of phenomenal, perceptual, or commonsensical reality. Indeed, the lesson of the new science, as in the case of Mendeleev's periodic table (arranging chemical elements into rows and columns, exemplifying the importance of writing's listing capacities to science), which permitted scientists to predict the existence of natural elements before they were discovered in nature (another one of Bachelard's favorite examples), suggests that theoretical fictions organized into a pedagogy that would collapse the distinctions separating teaching, research, and art might have also the power to guide transformations of the lived, social world.

With Bachelard's surrationalism in mind, and remembering that the French "non" and "nom" (name) are homophones, Derrida's textuality may be understood as non-Aristotelian—his philosophy of the name as a philosophy of the "non"—a context that is made explicit in "White Mythology." In Aristotle's system, of course, there is no place for differance:

> For human language is not uniformly human in all its parts to the same degree. It is still the criterion of the noun which is decisive: its literal elements—vocal sounds without meaning—include more than letters alone. The syllable too belongs to *lexis,* but of course has no sense in itself. Above all there are whole "words" which, though they have an indispensable role in the organization of discourse, remain nonetheless quite devoid of sense, in the eyes of Aristotle. Conjunction (*sundesmos*) is a *phone asemos.* The same goes for the article, and in general for every joint (*arthron,* everything which operates *be-*

tween significant members, between nouns, substantives, or verbs.
A joint has no sense because it does not refer to an independent unit,
a substance or a being, by means of a categorematic unit. It is for
this reason that it is excluded from the field of metaphor as an ono-
mastic field. From this point on, the anagrammatic, using parts of
nouns, nouns cut into pieces, is outside the field of metaphor in general, as too is the syntactic play of "joints."[32]

Against Aristotle's influential doctrine that "in non-sense, language is not
yet born," Derrida builds an alternative onomastics based precisely on
what Aristotle excludes from metaphor.

The extent of Derrida's non-Aristotelian inspiration may be seen in
Aristotle's condemnation of homonymy as the figure that doubled and
thus threatened philosophy. One of the first "places" to check for the
obscurity that characterizes bad metaphors, according to Aristotle, is to
determine whether the term used is the homonym of any other term
("White Mythology," 53, 74). Derrida, with his interest in discerning and
then transgressing the limits of philosophical discourse, takes his cue from
Aristotle and builds an entire philosophical system on the basis of the
homonym (and homophone). In this respect he resembles the nineteenth-
century mathematicians who, challenged by the axiomatic absoluteness of
Euclid's principles, were able to prove that it was possible to devise a
geometry that Euclid's system held to be impossible. Considered at first to
be playful monstrosities or abstract exercises, these non-Euclidean geometries provided eventually the mathematics of relativity.

The philosopher, and especially the teacher of applied grammatology,
must learn like poets and revolutionary scientists to explore the frivolities
of chance. The dehiscence of iteration, an economimesis that redistributes
the property or attributes of names, is exemplified in its generalized mode
in "Dissemination," an essay that, as Derrida explains, is a systematic and
playful exploration of the interval of the gap itself, leading from *"écart"*
(gap) to *"carré, carrure, carte, charte, quatre, trace."* He calls this play of
the interval, set to work within the history of philosophy,

> undecidables, that is, unities of simulacrum, "false" verbal properties
> (nominal or semantic) that can no longer be included within philo-
> sophical (binary) opposition, but which, however, inhabit philosophical
> opposition, resisting and disorganizing it, *without ever* constituting
> a third term, without ever leaving room for a solution in the form of
> speculative dialectics (the *pharmakon* is neither remedy nor poison,
> neither good nor evil, neither the inside nor the outside, neither speech
> nor writing; the *supplement* is neither a plus nor a minus, neither an
> outside nor the complement of an inside, neither accident nor essence,
> etc. (*Positions,* 43)

These double negations "severely crack the surface of philosophy," contest the logic of noncontradiction while forcing the dehiscence that permits invention by dissemination—a strategy of "objective creation": "Its proper route is not that of an 'either this . . . or that,' but of a 'neither this . . . nor that.' The poetic force of metaphor is often the trace of this rejected alternative, this wounding of language. Through it, in its opening, experience itself is silently revealed" (*Writing,* 90).

In the next chapter I shall submit the name of "theory" itself to this "anthonomasic" detonation.

2

Theoria

LIMITS

The concept of limit is one of the fundamental issues, not only for Derrida, but for that group of writers currently identified as "poststructuralist." As Foucault notes in a 1963 article on Bataille, limit and transgression are interdependent: "Perhaps one day [transgression] will seem as decisive for our culture, as much a part of its soil, as the experience of contradiction was at an earlier time for dialectical thought. But in spite of so many scattered signs, the language in which transgression will find its space and the illumination of its being lies almost entirely in the future."[1]

The problem facing philosophy (conceptual discourse) is that "no form of reflection yet developed, no established discourse, can supply the model, its foundation, or even the riches of its vocabulary" (Foucault, 40). In short, to attempt to treat the concept of limit places the writer at the limits of concept and at the limits of language. The cause of this difficulty, revealing by its very existence the limitations of philosophical discourse, "is that philosophical language is linked beyond all memory (or nearly so) to dialectics" (40).

Derrida could agree completely with Foucault's assessment of the problem. Indeed, Derrida's texts provide the most elaborate effort yet to discover the nondialectical language and mode of thought which can be the model for a new methodology. The concept of limit poses special problems for the writer who attempts transgression because, as Derrida remarks in "Tympan" (the preface to *Marges de la philosophie*), philosophy admits of no "outside": philosophy is precisely that discourse which has taken as its object its own limit. It appropriates the concept of limit and believes that it can dominate its own margin and think its other. Derrida noted this quality in his first book (an introduction to Husserl's *Origin of Geometry*) in terms of the teleological nature of tradition. Geometry (or, by extension, any science), according to Husserl, is a unity—"However far its building up progresses, however generous the proliferation of its forms and metamorphoses may be, they do not call again into question the unified sense of what, in this development, is to be thought of as *the* geometrical science."[2] Truth, then, can have a history, and science can appropriate all its own revolutions because of the transcendental, idealizing function of dialectical thinking.

The machinery of this power of appropriation is the Hegelian *Aufhebung,* the dialectical sublation that permits philosophy to talk about itself and its other in the same language, essentializing the accidental and sensible into the substantial and intelligible. Against this appropriation Derrida states his resolve: "One must simultaneously, by means of rigorous conceptual analyses, philosophically *intractable, and* by the inscription of marks [*marques*—"this is the same word as *marche* as limit, and as margin"] which no longer belong to philosophic space, not even to the neighborhood of its other, displace the framing, by philosophy, of its own types. Write in another way."[3]

Marges does not itself attempt this new writing, but rather it works a certain question: "What form could the play of limit/passage have, the logos which itself poses itself and denies itself in allowing its own voice to arise?" (ix). How pass a limit that is not one, or proceed without taking a step? The problem must be approached otherwise, avoiding all dialectic, all confrontation or oppositional thinking. Instead, in the essays included in *Marges,* Derrida exposes the "inner border" of philosophy (thus implying the outer border), which is constituted by the "philosophemes," or founding ideas of philosophy. His strategy is to interrogate the relationship between sense and sense: "This divergence between sense (signified) and the senses (sensible signifier) is declared through the same root (*sensus, Sinn*). One might, like Hegel, admire the generosity of this stock and interpret its hidden sublation speculatively and dialectically; but before using a dialectical concept of metaphor, it is necessary to investigate the double twist which opened up metaphor and dialectic by allowing the term *sense* to be applied to that which should be foreign to the senses" ("White Mythology," 28-29).

With this homonymic relationship (in the word *sens*) between the sensible and the intelligible in mind, we may understand the phrase placed at the opening of "Tympan" which, Derrida says, is capable of generating all the sentences of the book: *"l'être à la limite."* The generating power of this phrase arises out of the punning, agglutinative relationship between

"L'être" (being) and *"lettre"* (letter). The sonorous vibration linking these senses, their inaudible difference, is assigned "a quasi-organizing role" in *Marges* (and in all of Derrida's texts). Nietzsche's Zarathustra suggested that philosophers should have their eardrums broken, Derrida remarks, in order to teach them to hear with their eyes. But Derrida wishes to extend this philosophizing with a hammer by analyzing "the metaphysical exchange, the circular complicity of the metaphors of the eye and hearing" (*Marges*, iv).

THEORY

In the statement "science is the theory of the real," Heidegger asks, What does the word "theory" mean? He explains that "theory" stems from the Greek *Theorein,* which grew out of the coalescing of *thea* and *horao.* "*Thea* (cf. Theatre) is the outward look, the aspect, in which something shows itself. Plato names this aspect in which what presences shows what it is, *eidos.* To have seen this aspect, *eidenai,* is to know." And the second root, *horao,* means "to look at something attentively, to look it over, to view it closely." When translated into Latin and German, *theoria* became *contemplatio,* which emphasizes, besides passivity, the sense of "to partition something off into a separate sector and enclose it therein. *Templum* means originally a sector carved out in the heavens and on the earth (the region of the heavens marked out by the path of the sun)"—in short, an entirely different experience from that conveyed by the Greek, stressing now *temenos: "Temnein* means: to cut, to divide" (Heidegger, *Technology,* 164-65).

Moreover, Heidegger complains, the translation into *contemplatio* loses the other possibility of meaning available in the Greek when the root terms are stressed differently in pronunciation (pun). For *thea* is goddess, relating to *Aletheia* (translated as *veritas*), "the unconcealment from out of which and in which that which presences, presences." And *ora* (the other root) "signifies the respect, honor and esteem we bestow." Theory in this sense means, "the beholding that watches over truth" (164-65). But not only have the meanings of fundamental terms such as "theory" undergone several metamorphoses during their history, they were deliberately invented in the first place:

> We, late born, are no longer in a position to appreciate the significance of Plato's daring to use the word *eidos* for that which in everything and in each particular thing endures as present. For *eidos,* in the common speech, meant the outward aspect [*Ansicht*] that a visible thing offers to the physical eye. Plato exacts of this word, however, something utterly extraordinary: that it name what precisely is not

and never will be perceivable with physical eyes. But even this is by no means the full extent of what is extraordinary here. For *idea* names not only the nonsensuous aspect of what is physically visible. Aspect (*idea*) names and is, also, that which constitutes the essence in the audible, the tasteable, the tactile, in everything that is in any way accessible. (Heidegger, 20)

Derrida shares Heidegger's interest in this philological evidence and draws several important conclusions: theory—the term and the activity—is not fixed, is still evolving or is capable of change; the direction of that change, using Plato's audacity against Platonism, must be to emancipate the other senses from the tyranny of *eidos.*

Everything in talk about metaphor which comes through the sign *eidos,* with the whole system attached to this word, is articulated on the analogy between *our* looking and sensible looking, between the intelligible and the visible sun. The truth of the being that is present is fixed by passing through a detour of tropes in this system. The presence of *ousia* as *eidos* (being set before the metaphorical eye) or as *upokeimenon* (being that underlies visible phenomena or accidents) faces the theoretic organ, which, as Hegel's *Philosophy of Fine Art* reminds us, has the power not to consume what it perceives, and to let be the object of desire. Philosophy, as a theory of metaphor, will first have been a metaphor of theory. ("White Mythology" 55–56)

Derrida questions whether such defining tropes, productive of philosophemes, even should be called "metaphors." Metaphor assumes that one of the terms in the comparison has a "proper" meaning, but the philosophemes are produced by catachresis, "the imposition of a sign on a sense not yet having a proper sign in the language. And so there is no substitution here, no transfer of proper signs, but an irruptive extension of a sign proper to one idea to a sense without a signifier" ("White Mythology," 57). Catachresis, Derrida suggests, should be removed from its traditional placement as a "phenomenon of abuse" and recognized as an irreducibly original production of meaning. "Catachresis does not go outside the language, does not create new signs, does not enrich the code; yet it transforms its functioning: it produces, with the same material, new rules of exchange, new meanings." Deconstruction, in other words, is a form of catachresis, but one that must be distinguished from the traditional use of this device, since philosophy always interpreted its catachresis as "a torque turning back to a sense already present, a production (of signs, rather than of meanings), but this as revelation, unveiling, bringing to light, truth" (59–60). Against philosophy's tendency to present "forced metaphors" as "natural and correct," deconstruction uses catachresis openly, to carry thought not forward to the origins (teleology), but "elsewhere." Hence, the first term defined in *Glas* is "catachresis," signaling the operation that is to be explored in that text.

The metaphorization apparent in the philosophemes consists of two processes: *idealization* and *appropriation* ("White Mythology," 55). Against these processes, in search of a different writing, Derrida proposes two processes of his own: *articulation* and *decomposition.*

    1. *Articulation.* The first process is non-Aristotelian in that Aristotle allows no place in "metaphor" for differance, the joint of spacing, the interval (as explained in chapter 1) that joins and separates homophones.

    2. *Decomposition.* The second process in Derrida's new "metaphorology" (a term used in "White Mythology") could be described as non-Hegelian. The issue is that the founding ideas of the Western tradition are structured by a family of metaphors related to sight and hearing—the two distancing and idealizing senses—which thus excludes from the metaphor of concept the properties of the other senses (although the hand provides the literal sense of the term).

> Hearing holds a certain privilege among the five senses. The classification of *Anthropologies* places it among the objective senses (touch, sight and hearing) which give a mediated perception of the object (sight and hearing). The objective senses put one in relation with an outside, which taste and smell do not. The sensible mixes itself in with these, for example with saliva and penetrates the organ without keeping its objective subsistence. Mediated objective perception is reserved to sight and hearing which require the mediation of light and air. Touch is objective and immediate. (*Mimesis,* 84)

Derrida's project to displace the dialectic includes an attempt to isolate the specific features of those senses that have not been conceptualized—taste in particular, and smell—and to pose them as an alternative, as models of thinking and writing, to the distancing, idealizing notions based on sight and hearing. The theorization or thematization of the non-objective senses provides the new concept of the methodological procedures derived from the principle of articulation.

As we saw in the case of the botanical analogy leading to the theory of creativity as dissemination, Derrida's method is first to analyze the literal (the letter) level of the metaphor, then to extend the comparison to include any material available in the semantic domain of the vehicle, but which has been excluded from the received sense of the analogy. In the present instance, the analogy, fundamental to philosophy, is between the sensible and the intelligible domains, with thought conceptualized in terms of sight and hearing. Derrida's move is simply to hypothesize a thinking, an intelligibility, that would function in terms of that part of the sensible excluded from consideration—the chemical senses ("why not?").

This procedure also represents a discovery process by which Derrida investigates (rather like a chemist using Mendeleev's chart to predict the possible existence of as yet unknown elements) the new balance in the sensorium emerging because of the shift in communications technology. Derrida's engagement of this issue indicates another aspect of the participation of his thought in a larger field of study which could be called "grammatology," for, as Walter Ong notes, the interest in the sensorium has become widespread, with Whitehead's *Modes of Thought* (1938) being "one of the earliest to call rather specific attention to the need for study of the effects of changes in the communications media on the organization of the sensorium."[4] The modern age, "as a child of typography," is now over, Ong adds; although, like Marshall McLuhan, Ong believes that we are returning to the auditory (telephone, radio, television) after an epoch dominated by visualization. Even though Ong notes how "Freudians have long pointed out that for abstract thinking the proximity senses—smell, taste, and in a special way touch (although touch concerns space as well as contact and is thus simultaneously concrete and abstract)—must be minimized in favor of the more abstract hearing and sight" (6), he fails to connect this understanding with the new physics and thus misses the crucial contribution to this question achieved by Derrida. Derrida realizes that at the level of technology the reorganization of our sensorium is being carried out, not so much in terms of the audiovisual properties of the television message (television is not simply an addition of the two previous stages of communications culture—oral and typographic), but in response to the electronic nature of the medium (McLuhan also stressed this point, but focused on the viewer as screen being bombarded with light impulses). Derrida, interested in the *techne* as enframing (the essence of technology, which is not itself technological but artistic), examines the science of electronics, which reveals that a major difference between Newtonian and Einsteinian physics is that the former is a theory of *action at a distance,* while the latter is a theory of *action by contact,* based on the experiments of Faraday and Maxwell in electromagnetism. "The old 'action at a distance' theory postulated that the electrostatic field was merely a geometrical structure without physical significance, while this new experiment ["that the mutual action between two electrically charged bodies depends upon the character of the intervening medium"] showed that the field had physical significance. Every charge acts first upon its immediate surroundings."[5]

Derrida's conceptualization of the chemical or contact senses, then, correlates with Einstein's physics just as Kant's and Hegel's idealizations based on the objective senses correlate with Newton's. In this respect,

Derrida has found a way to apply Nietzsche's admonition that we "overcome the spirit of gravity," understood now as the principle of action at a distance, which governs not only the motions of the planets but the conception of truth as well. The mode of science culminating in Newton's law, that is, corresponds with the notion of truth whose image is "women and their effect from a distance"—seduction. The history of the "idea," Derrida suggests, may be divided into three periods. In the first period the philosopher himself is the truth—"I, Plato, am the truth" (science in the first period is Platonic). In the second period, history begins, the idea becomes woman, Christian, castrating: "Now the stories start. Distance—woman—averts truth—the philosopher. She bestows the idea. And the idea withdraws, becomes transcendent, inaccessible, seductive. It beckons from afar. Its veils float in the distance. The dream of death begins. It is woman."[6] It is the history of truth as an error, as that from which the sage is exiled, whose recovery becomes the goal of all his research, desiring to unveil the hidden thing. Nietzsche's supposed antifeminism, then, as an attack on this paradigm of truth, is the philosophical equivalent of the discoveries in geometry and electricity which were transforming science, challenging the empirical model while preparing for the third age, the one now emerging, the one Derrida himself is formulating, a truth that will direct the pedagogy of grammatology.

This point is of central importance, since applied grammatology is meant precisely to provide the mode of writing appropriate to the present age of electronic communications. As Ong reminds us, the Greek word *idea,* meaning the look of a thing, comes from the same root as the Latin *video* (I see)—"ideas thus were in a covert sense like abstract pictures" (Ong, 35). The way an era formulates its notion of the idea—and hence how it proposes to educate its population (pedagogy as the transmission of ideas)—will be directly affected by the balance in the sensorium. Thus, Derrida's theorization of the chemical senses (described below in the section on decomposition), in the context of action by contact informing the new physics, permits a significant advance in our thinking about how to use the video medium in relation to thought. Writing with video (or in any medium in the video age) will be directed (in applied grammatology, at least) by a new epistemology and a new set of philosophemes whose metaphors are derived from the chemical senses.

I turn now to an examination of each of the components—articulation and decomposition—of Derrida's metaphorology.

ARTICULATION

Moiré. Let us say, then, that Derrida's goal is to shift the ratio in the sensorium away from the domination of *eidos* to a new balance in which taste and smell bring sight and hearing under their control, thus requiring a new term to replace "idea" as the name for thought. Derrida himself suggests that the other of *eidos* is *force* (which, as movement, duration, quality, energetics in general, lends itself to electronic formulations), but he rejects any temptation to reduce the problem to a simple dialectical opposition. The situation, rather, is that "force is the other of language without which language would not be what it is" (*Writing*, 27). Thus, Derrida's concern for what lies outside of and shapes language is what locates his work within the concerns of poststructuralism: "In order to respect this strange movement within language, in order not to reduce it in turn, we would have to attempt a return to the metaphor of darkness and light (of self-revelation and self-concealment), the founding metaphor of Western philosophy as metaphysics. The founding metaphor not only because it is a photological one—and in this respect the entire history of our philosophy is a photology, the name given to a history of, or treatise on, light—but because it is a metaphor" (27).

Metaphor in general, that is, all analogical displacement of Being, "is the essential weight which anchors discourse in metaphysics." And yet, "this is a fate which it would be foolish to term a regrettable and provisional accident," as do those who would "cure" language of its "fallen" condition. "Fate," it is important to note, as a determinant of the relationship between force and *eidos*, alludes to Heidegger's essay on *Moira* in Parmenides and Heraclitus. *Moira*, according to Heidegger's analysis of several pre-Socratic fragments, is a force that binds the duality of presencing and that which is present—it is the unfolding of the twofold (in Derrida's terms, the articulation of the twofold). With respect to the question before us, only what is present attains appearance, excluding thus from knowledge all the rest: "Destiny altogether conceals both the duality as such and its unfolding. The essence of *aletheia* remains veiled. The visibility it bestows allows the presencing of what is present to arise as outer appearance (*eidos*) and aspect (*idea*). Consequently the perceptual relation to the presencing of what is present is defined as 'seeing.' Stamped with this character of *visio*, knowledge and the evidence of knowledge cannot renounce their essential derivation from luminous disclosure."[7]

The "fateful yielding" of what is present to ordinary perception by means of "name-words," Heidegger states, occurs "already only insofar as the twofold as such, and therefore its unfolding, remain hidden. But then does self-concealment reign at the heart of disclosure? A bold thought. Heraclitus thought it" (*"Moira,"* 100). This bold thought, relevant to the entire question of enframing, is extremely important to Derrida's project. It comes into view here in terms of his notion that "light is menaced from within by that which also metaphysically menaces every structuralism: the possibility of concealing meaning through the very act of uncovering it. *To comprehend* the structure of a becoming, the form of a force, is to lose meaning by finding it. The meaning of becoming and of force, by virtue of their pure, intrinsic characteristics, is the repose of the beginning of the end" (*Writing,* 26). Or, as Heidegger poses it, "What is the significance of the fact that destiny releases the presencing of what is present into the duality, and so binds it to wholeness and rest?" (*"Moira,"* 98).

Derrida's strategy at the level of articulation, then, is to treat the binding destiny that limits what it makes possible by asking, "How can force or weakness be understood in terms of light and dark?" (*Writing,* 27). The purpose of this question (and here is the justification for the parentheses on *Moira*) is to "solicit" this founding philosopheme: "Structure then can be *methodically* threatened in order to be comprehended more clearly and to reveal not only its supports but also that secret place in which it is neither construction nor ruin but lability. This operation is called (from the Latin) *soliciting.* In other words, *shaking* in a way related to the *whole* (from *sollus,* in archaic Latin 'the whole,' and from *citare,* 'to put in motion')" (6). In terms of the homonymic event (dehiscence of iteration or articulation), the destiny of language, its relation to *Moira* and the *Moirae,* may be solicited in the same way that structural engineers, using computer analyses of moiré patterns, examine buildings (or any structure) for defects. The cracks and flaws in the surface of philosophy may thus be located. Of course, an interrogation of this vibration or trembling, the analogy of thought to the wave motion of light and sound, as Derrida notes, is the key to Hegel's *Aesthetics* (100), which is to say that it remains within the limits of philosophical language. Nor is Derrida certain, at the time of writing the essays under discussion here (the middle sixties), that any movement other than that of light and sound is possible (92).

To understand how Derrida carries out his solicitation of the eye's contribution (as metaphor) to thought, it is helpful to consider the analogy between grammar and geometry, both of which superimpose figures, one on the lexical and the other on the pictorial world.[8] Geometry, in other words, is the helping science for articulation, just as psychoanalysis is the helping science for decomposition. The analogy between grammar and geometry marks the abstracting power of both systems—especially their respective capacities for defining *relations* among objects or words without regard for their specific embodiments or meanings. Geometry and grammar, that is, *function at the level of the concept,* which in modern thinking is understood as a set of relations rather than as a common substance inhering in a group of phenomena.[9] It is not surprising, considering that one of the principal goals of grammatology is to break with the logocentric model of representation, in which writing has been conceived as a representation of speech, that Derrida should look to the nonobjective movements in the arts for models of how to proceed. Of course, "nonobjective"

ultimately refers, in grammatology, to a writing based on the conceptualization of the nonobjective senses (in the method of decomposition), but
for now it alludes to the practice of constructivist art, including not only
cubism but especially the "Group for Research in the Visual Arts" (GRAV
—founded in France in 1960 by Julio le Parc), which serves as a model and
resource for grammatological experimentation.

The artists of GRAV, inspired by the work of Victor Vasarely (active in
Paris during the fifties and after), developed the style dubbed "op art"—
the creation of optical effects through the manipulation of geometric
forms, color dissonance, and kinetic elements, all exploiting the extreme
limits of the psychology of optical effects or visual illusions, thus continuing the constructivist interest (manifested as early as Cézanne) in the interdependence of conception and perception. The experimental production
of optical illusion directly in abstract forms (rather than indirectly, as in
the mimetic tradition, in forms subordinated to representational demands),
is relevant to an understanding of Derrida's attempt to identify the illusory
effects of grammar in a similarly pure way. Researching Nietzsche's insight
that grammar is the last refuge of metaphysics ("I am afraid we are not rid
of God because we still have faith in grammar,"[10] Nietzsche said, alluding
to the "crude fetishism" of the belief, produced in language, in a cause and
an effect, a doer and a doing, and so forth), Derrida inventories some of
the irreducible deceptions that grammar plays on our conceptual system,
demonstrating these effects in exercises that are the grammatical equivalent
of the geometrical experiments of the constructivists working at the limits
of optical perception, and which deserve the label of "op writing."

Op art, then, provides a guide for an appreciation of the "trembling" or
"shaking" effect that Derrida wishes to achieve in his solicitation of the
idea as form. One of Vasarely's chief techniques, for example, was the
development of a "surface kinetics," which set off a two-dimensional surface into an apparently three-dimensional pulsation: "In black-and-white
patterns—parallel bands, concentric circles or squares, chessboard patterns
and the like—pulsating effects are the commonest. A disturbing element,
for instance a diagonal or curved line crossing a pattern of stripes, may be
added to produce the 'moiré effect.'"[11] Disturbing effects are also produced by irradiation, the spread of a color beyond its actual surface area.
The "Mach strip," or edge contrast, on either side of a line dividing two
adjacent color areas produces a flutter or vibration along the line depend-
ing on the relationship of the two colors. Two structures that are superimposed but separate, two different line systems or a line system and a color
surface will also generate the kinetic moiré effect (Rotzler, 150).

The optical effects mentioned are only a few of those taken over by the
artists from color theory and cognitive psychology as well as those de-

veloped in their own research (for their program was to practice art as a
kind of scientific research, with their ultimate goal being, as Vasarely declares in one of his manifestoes, to reintegrate art into society). My purpose
is not to undertake even a brief comparative study of the relation of
Derrida to *GRAV* (although such a study is needed), but only to note the
analogy of their interests—translated between geometry and grammar—in
such issues as framing, grids, networks, movement, and double bands. The
moiré effect alone serves not only as a didactic model for "solicitation,"
but constitutes—by virtue of its peculiar feature of being a static form that
produces the effect of motion—an emblem of *Moira*, destiny, whose nature
is to be at once the motion of Becoming and the rest of Being. This homophone opens the way into a major aspect of Derrida's methodology.

Ornament. A comparison of E. H. Gombrich's study of decorative art [12]
with Derrida's op writing reveals that many of the effects Derrida seeks are
those inherent in the history of ornament—decorative or parergonal art—of
which constructivism and other abstract art movements, as Gombrich explains, are the modern heirs. Derrida's research into these decorative devices, of course, is a deliberate aspect of his metaphorology, challenging
the logocentric prejudice against rhetoric as ornament and showing that
ornamentation itself can provide the methodology of a science (grammatology).

Derrida's interest in the features and history of ornament is evident in
his concern for everything marginal, supplementary, everything having to
do with borders rather than centers. Gombrich mentions that he thought
of calling his book "the unregarded art," since decoration, as parergon or
by-work, is not noticed, its effects being assimilated inattentively with
peripheral vision. Against the logocentrism of Western metaphysics, which
thought of style as something added on to thought as decoration, and
which valorized the center of structure—the notion of presence which is
both inside the structure yet outside, controlling it, out of play—Derrida
proposes that our era is beginning to think of the structurality of structure,
realizing that the center is not a natural or fixed locus but a function, "a
sort of non-locus in which an infinite number of sign substitutions come
into play." Replacing the old notion of center is the notion of supplementarity, described as a movement of freeplay: "A field of infinite substitutions
in the closure of a finite ensemble . . . instead of being an inexhaustible
field, as in the classical hypothesis, instead of being too large, there is
something missing from it: a center which arrests and founds the freeplay
of substitutions. . . . One cannot determine the center, the sign which supplements it, because this sign adds itself, occurs in addition, over and
above, comes as a supplement." [13]

The entities used as models for supplementarity (the effect of enframing) include, for example, the device known as the passe-partout (matting —a frame for the display of prints or engravings, open in the center for the infinitely substitutable image; but also a master key) and the cartouche (in one sense, the decorative border, whose convolutions may be extended infinitely within the closure) surrounding or framing a blank space ready to receive an inscription (not to mention its meaning in hieroglyphics). Both these examples are discussed in Derrida's *La vérité en peinture,* his collection of essays dealing with the visual arts, which I will discuss in more detail later.

I would like now to itemize some of the topics elaborated in Gombrich's study of ornament which are relevant to Derrida's op writing (a deconstruction of the optical effects in conceptual discourse).

1. Reading Gombrich, who notes that pattern is a form of rhythm, made me realize that when Derrida talks about rhythm as replacing dialectic in a new theory of change ("Inseparable from the phenomena of *liaison* . . . the said unities of time could not help but be also metrical and rhythmic values. Beyond opposition, the difference and the rhythm"—*Carte,* 435), he is referring to spatial relationships as well as temporal ones. The laws of repetition (repetition as the surrogate that is not a copy of anything, being the principle of decentering—the structurality of structure, as in Edmond Jabes's repetition of the Book—in Derrida's program) governing pattern formation, Gombrich explains, include *translation* (rhythmic rows extended along an axis), *rotation,* and *reflection.* By each of these principles, grids or lattice forms may be generated and extended infinitely.

The mathematical employment of these concepts, as James Ogilvy demonstrated, serves to map one set of axes onto another (remember that Jakobson defines poetry as the projection or mapping of one axis of language—paradigmatic and syntagmatic—onto the other), making them useful operations for understanding (or even bringing about) relationships among the various dimensions of discourse—for the circulation of philosophemes through all the divisions of knowledge:

> The usefulness of the concept of transformation [read translation, rotation, reflection] consists in the fact that, unlike the more familiar notion of analogy, transformation permits the more radical move toward taking the basic parameters themselves—the political, psychological and religious dimensions—as transforms of one another. Unlike symbolism and analogy, which tend to assume a basic or literal foundation on which an analogy is built or a symbol drawn, the concept of transformation assumes no fundamental dimension.[14]

The purely relational and mathematical operations of ornament, applied to

the conceptual dimension, make irrelevant the notions of proper and figurative meanings.

2. The *interlacing* pattern—the structure of chiasmi and of "double invagination" which, in Derrida's texts, constitutes the structurality of
structure, the form of force (to be discussed later)—is a major feature of
ornament throughout history. The seventeen symmetries producible by
the three principles of rhythm (rotation, reflection, translation) can be
multiplied to eighty possible arrangements by the simple device of interlacing the lines above and below one another, a procedure that, as Gombrich notes, introduces the fiction of a mirroring plane. The illusion of
depth thus introduced, *giving the effect of weaving, plaiting, knotting,*
places the interlacing device undecidably between abstract form and representational meaning—between geometry and a perceptual thing, thus providing an analogy, which Derrida exploits in "Spéculer—sur 'Freud,'" for
the ambiguous status of *speculation.* A universal device, one of the ones
most frequently encountered in designs all over the world, the interlace is
also one of the favorite patterns of op art (and also of op writing, in which
it serves as an image of syntax). One of the effects of interlacing, of course,
is the moiré effect—the flicker produced when two grids are superimposed
or made to overlap in a dissymmetrical or off-centered way.

3. Gombrich explains that op art achieves many of its effects by means
of a *systematic overload of the perceptual apparatus,* as in the "Fraser
Spiral," "which is not a spiral at all, but a series of concentric circles superimposed on vortex lines. These lines, it turns out, tend to deflect our
searching gaze so that we always lose our place and settle for the most
plausible 'templet,' the continuous spiral" (134). Lightening the load of
information by covering half the page or tracing the lines with a pencil
reveals the trick. Op art pushed such basic decorative figures to an extreme
of "restlessness," a feature also of op writing, as exemplifed by the unstable
character of the term *restance.* When he originally introduced *restance* in
the article "Signature Event Context," Derrida equipped it with several
warning signals. It is, to begin with, a neologism, translated into English as
remainder, explicitly avoiding the word *permanence,* with *restance* being
retained in brackets. The graphics utilized—the italic print and the bracketed
term—serve as a warning light, Derrida explains. In its context, the term is
also associated with *"non-present,"* which "adds a spectacular *blinking-
effect* to the warning light. . . . Blinking is a rhythm essential to the mark
whose functioning I would like to analyze" ("Limited Inc" 188–89). The
graphics of *remainder* signal that this term marks a "quasi-concept" whose
structure, implying alteration as well as identity, deconstructs the logic of
permanence associated with its traditional meaning, a point that John
Searle, in his critique of "Signature Event Context" (to which "Limited
Inc" is a response) completely missed. *Restance,* or remainder, then, is not

only unstable itself but marks the instability and restlessness of all of Derrida's quasi-concepts: "To remain, in this sense, is not to rest on one's laurels or to take it easy" (190).

Op writing exploits for its effects the tendency to receive concepts in terms of presuppositions and the encoded habits of expectation, in the same way that op art exploits the fact that the eye "is good in recognizing continuities and redundancies, but bad in 'locking in' on a particular feature of repeated elements." Thus, an art—or a philosophy of writing—*based on repetition* will cause problems for the habits of seeing or thinking: "By strictly repeating this *circle* in its own historical possibility, we allow the production of some *elliptical* change of site, within the difference involved in repetition. . . . Neither matter nor form, it is nothing that any philosopheme, that is, any dialectic, however determinate, can capture" (*Speech*, 128).

As with Vasarely, who took as the basic element of composition (his plastic unit) two contrasting color shapes, many op art effects play with the contrasting relation of figure and ground and with the oscillation and interferences set up in the play between "two bands" (recalling Derrida's contra-band strategy). Much of this effect is due to an "extrapolator" device in visual perception which goes beyond mere registration to the production of continuous shapes, a performance of habit and anticipation which the artist uses to create the illusion. Derrida similarly plays with our conceptual habits favoring the continuities of common sense, and he overloads our conceptual apprehension with a paradoxical syntax that displaces the normal line of logic, resulting in a conceptual vertigo akin to the Fraser Spiral.

4. Gombrich's study of ornament also helps account for Derrida's manner of interrogating framing effects. One of the basic features of visual perception, framing delimits or borders the field of vision, determining what is excluded and included. Gombrich defines the frame as a continuous break setting off the design from the environment. The crucial point, however, is that there can be no center without a frame: "The frame, or the border, delimits the field of force, with its gradients of meaning increasing towards the center. So strong is this feeling of an organizing pull that we take it for granted that the elements of the pattern are all oriented towards their common center" (Gombrich, 157). Patterning, like ordering of any kind, is the ordering of elements of identity and difference. In ornamentation, its two steps are framing and filling. The geometrical tendency in design starts at the outside or frame of the surface and works in to the center, while representational (naturalistic) designs tend to begin at the center and work out toward the frame.

5. A principal aspect of the history of ornament, whose features Gombrich explains by a kind of "etymology" or "paleonymy" of motifs (similar

to Derrida's science of "old names," with which he extends conventional terms into new settings), is the balance of, or relation between, decoration and symbolism (design and meaning). He mentions the Egyptian hieroglyphics as a writing that fuses these two purposes (the very fusion sought by grammatology). Gombrich studies in this regard the flourish that people sometimes attach to their signature. Such flourishes, carried to extremes, may make the letter illegible. The monogram, a variation on the flourish, involves an interlacing of letters which is finally only recognized rather than read (such is the effect of the PS monogram—Plato-Socrates—which Derrida studies in "Envois"—*Carte*). The functional aspect of the flourish, in addition to its manifestation of self-display and playfulness, is that its personal rhythms make the signature extremely difficult to imitate or counterfeit. "The flourish is easily understood as a playful product, a paradigm of the relation between sign and design. Even where it enters into a symbiosis with the sign, serving as a means of emphasis or enhancement, it never quite surrenders its freedom from the constraints of signification" (Gombrich, 241). Stressing throughout *The Sense of Order* "the degree of autonomy we must grant to ornament," Gombrich offers a resource for comprehending Derrida's study of parerga as the structurality of structure. Op writing has available in the history of ornament an index of devices all potentially translatable from geometry to the graphics of grammatology.

6. If the flourish tends to tip the balance of decoration and symbol in the direction of decoration, the *cartouche,* defined as a transformed and reified flourish, tends in the opposite direction of representation. "In its origins it [the cartouche] transforms the abstract heraldic field or shield into a real or fictitious object. Such a transformation is natural in the medium of sculpture, in which the coat of arms is held or displayed as a real tablet or shield. In Renaissance painting this play with a fictitious support also led to a simulated piece of paper or parchment being affixed to the panel for the signature or some other inscription" (Gombrich, 241). Beginning with the Renaissance, the cartouche—the shield-shaped writing support with its curling framework—was in demand wherever inscriptions or symbols were to be inserted into a decorative ensemble. The great advantage of the animated flourish around the cartouche, Gombrich explains, is that it so effortlessly absorbs additional symbols or emblems within its swirling shapes.

Moiré-Moirae.   Derrida gets his ideas from the systematic exploitation of puns, used as an *inventio* to suggest nondialectical points of entry for the deconstruction of the philosophemes. His best-known version of this strategy involves the deflation of proper names into common nouns (antonomasia), as in *Glas,* in which Genet's texts are discussed in terms of flowers (the flowers of rhetoric), beginning with *genêt* (a broomflower). Blanchot, Hegel, Kant, and Ponge have all received similar treatment, described as research into the signature effect. Discussing this methodology in his essay on Ponge, Derrida exposes his mood: "It is necessary to scandalize resolutely the analphabet scientisms, . . . before what one can do with a dictionary. . . . One must scandalize them, make them cry even louder, because that gives pleasure, and why deprive oneself of it, in risking a final etymological simulacrum" (*Digraphe,* 33).

The technique works as well for concepts, both for subverting old ones and for building new (pseudo-) concepts. Part of my discussion of the critique of theory as metaphor is to discern the homophone that (in retrospect, as an aftereffect at least) could be said to be the organizing articulation of Derrida's approach to this project. This search may result in the formulation of an aspect of deconstructive writing which as yet has found few, if any, imitators. The *idea* (*i–d*) accounting for the specific terms used to deconstruct *theoria* has its source in the "constellation" O–I–R, originally discerned in Mallarmé. (It is worth noting that *oir* is the Spanish equivalent of *entendre,* meaning to hear and to understand, a propos both of Derrida's Joycean macaronics and of his suggestion that the idea itself could not be seen but only heard.) The principle at work here involves "a hymen between chance and rule. That which presents itself as contingent and haphazard in the *present* of language . . . finds itself struck out anew, retempered with the seal of necessity in the uniqueness of a textual configuration. For example, consider the duels among the *moire* [watered silk] and the *memoire* [memory], the *grimoire* [cryptic spell book] and the *armoire* [wardrobe]" (*Dissemination,* 277).

What especially interests Derrida is precisely the *articulation:* "Rhyme—which is the general law of textual effects—is the folding-together of an identity and a difference. The raw material for this operation is no longer merely the sound of the end of a word: all 'substances' (phonic and graphic) and all 'forms' can be linked together at any distance and under any rule in order to produce new versions of 'that which in discourse does not speak'" (*Dissemination,* 277). Derrida is interested in the way in which the arbitrarily rhyming terms have some motivated relationship. To perceive the motivation of the series of O–I–R words for the deconstruction of *theoria* requires that I add one more term to the sequence which Derrida himself neglects (but thus imitating his own addition of *pharmakos* to the series set going in Plato's dialogues: "Certain forces of association unite—at diverse distances, with different strengths and according to disparate paths—the words 'actually present' in a discourse with all the other words in the lexical system"—129–30). The term, of course, is *Moira*

(*Destiny* in Greek). Let us say that the antonomasia, the exchange between proper and common, governing this project involves *Moirae*—the
fates—and *moiré* (not "watered silk," but the visual illusion known as the
moiré effect). *Grimoire* is drawn in with respect to the thirteenth-century
fortune-telling book featured in *La carte postale* (whose wheel of fortune
might be associated with Destiny); *memoire* with respect to the artificial
memory (hypomnemics) associated with the mechanics of the *inventio*.
This *inventio* (an aspect of Derrida's "new rhetoric") functions on the
assumption that language itself is "intelligent," hence that homophones
"know" something. Derrida's deconstruction of *theoria* reveals what
Moirae-moiré knows.

In "Envois" Derrida states, "no matter what I say, I seek above all to
produce effects" (*Carte,* 124). The specific effect he seeks, in fact, is the
textual equivalent of the moiré effect, whose pattern is woven into language
on the loom of fate (*Moira*). As already noted in terms of his interest in the
ideographic or nonphonetic features of writing, Derrida wants to restore to
writing the balance between design and symbol it had in hieroglyphics. His
pursuit of the moiré effect, as an attempt to write the structurality of
structure, contributes to this project by assigning to ornamentation a
generative role in text production.

The moiré effect manifests itself in the special functioning of Derrida's
terminology, best illustrated by the term "differance." The verb "to differ"
(*differer*) differs from itself in that it conveys two meanings: "On the one
hand it indicates the difference as distinction, inequality, or discernibility;
on the other, it expresses the interposition of delay, the interval of a *spacing* and temporalizing." Derrida concludes that "there must be a common,
although entirely differant [*differante*] root within the sphere that relates
the two movements of differing to one another. We provisionally give the
name *difference* to this sameness which is not *identical*" (*Speech,* 129).

We see here why Derrida calls Hegel the first philosopher of writing as
well as the last philosopher of the book, since the articulation of the undecidability in differance is a generalization of Hegel's speculative procedure (a generalization with anti- or non-Hegelian consequences):

> Without naively using the category of chance, of happy predestina-
> tion or of the chance encounter, one would have to do for each
> concept what Hegel does for the German notion of *Aufhebung,* whose
> equivocality and presence in the German language he calls *delightful:*
> "*Aufheben* has in the German language a double sense: that of pre-
> serving, *maintaining,* and that of leaving off, *bringing to an end.* . . . It
> is remarkable that a language comes to use one and the same word
> to express two opposed meanings. Speculative thought is delighted to
> find in language words which by themselves have a speculative sense."
> (*Writing,* 113–14)

Derrida, believing that "since this equivocality [in ordinary language] is original and irreducible, perhaps philosophy must adopt it, think it and be thought in it," proposes not to follow Hegel's laborious analysis of each concept but to adopt a homonymic principle that, in a sense, automatically locates all possible equivocality.

As opposed to the clarity and distinctness that is part of philosophy's founding opposition between the sensible and the intelligible (themselves qualities of "literality" suggested by the clarity and distinctness of the alphabetic letter), differance marks a *movement between two letters—e* and *a,* a "marginal" difference—and between two "differences," a movement that articulates a strange space "*between* speech and writing and beyond the tranquil familiarity that binds us to one and to the other, reassuring us sometimes in the illusion that they are two separate things" (*Speech,* 133-34). The strategy of paleonymy (the science of old names) extends this beat, or rhythm, set in motion by the proximity of two meanings, two spellings, that are the same and different, offset, *like the two overlapping but not quite matching grids that generate the flicker of the moiré effect.* Deconstruction, as a double science, is structured by the "double mark," by means of which a term retains its old name while displacing the term (only slightly or marginally at first) toward a new family of terms: "The rule according to which every concept necessarily receives two similar marks—a repetition without identity—one mark inside and the other outside the deconstructed system, should give rise to a double reading and a double writing. And, as will appear in due course: a *double science"* (*Dissemination,* 4).

Elsewhere Derrida not only characterizes differance as a movement, he actually describes the nature of this movement, understood to be "virtual," like the moiré effect, while referring to the "path" followed by thought, traced by a step (*pas*) which is not one (because the *pas* is also the negative in *ne pas*), which does not advance.[15] The moiré effect in op writing, the movement between the disparate semantic domains of a homophonic series of terms, is the effect of *marginal* spelling differences: "Each cited word gives an index card or a grid [*grille*] which enables you to survey the text. It is accompanied by a diagram which you ought to be able to verify at each occurrence" (*Glas,* 223). The term Derrida chooses to name this movement in *Glas* is *"la navette"* (shuttle, referrring to the "to and fro" motion which bears this name in weaving, sewing, and transportation). In French, moreover, the term also names a type of seed, a plant in the family of crucifers. "It is [the term] I sought earlier in order to describe, when a gondola has crossed the gallery, the grammatical to and fro between *langue* [language, tongue] and *lagune* [lagoon] (*lacuna*)" (232).

In short, the grids involved are the two spellings, the paragram, with only one letter out of order between them. The shuttle motion between these two words is the binding necessity of their chance occupation of the same letters. The motion is set up within the shuttle itself, joining its meanings or semantic domains, which in French (*"la navette"*) include, besides those already mentioned, a liturgical sense (it is a small vessel for incense). "To and fro woven in a warp [*chaîne*]. The woof [*trame*—also *plot*] is in the shuttle. You can see all that I could do with that. Elaboration, isn't it a weaver's movement?" (*Glas,* 233). But Derrida states that he distrusts this textile metaphor, however, because finally it retains a "virtue" of the natural, the originary, of propriety. He decides instead to think of the motion of *Glas* as the interlacing stitching of *sewing.* In either case, the vibration or to and fro motion of articulation carries or displaces the sensorium only to the vicinity of handicrafts, evoking the hand (writing as a hand-eye relation rather than a voice-ear relation) and, in the textile metaphor, the sense of touch. But the hand has been the philosopheme of "concept" from the beginning (to grasp and to hold), so that "textuality," with its associations with textile and the sense of touch, only initiates the transition to the new notion of idea as *action by contact* (in place of the action as a distance which characterizes the idealizing senses), touch being the intermediate sense, which is both abstract and concrete.

Derrida is particularly interested in the way the shuttle motion (the soliciting vibration, whose homophonically overlapping terms offer an alternative metaphorics that challenges the logocentric structure of concept formation), is manifested in other systems of thought, especially in psychoanalysis (the science, along with geometry, that Derrida uses to think his way toward grammatology). It is not surprising, then, that Freud's famous anecdote of the game his grandson played with a bobbin on a string (the bobbin itself being part of the apparatus of weaving and sewing, symbolizing in this moment of language acquisition the mother, whose loss is repaired with the *fort-da* stitch), should serve Derrida as the pretext or emblem guiding his reading of Freud's *Beyond the Pleasure Principle.*

For now it is important to note that the conceptual equivalent of the back and forth motion of sewing in the composition of the text is the undecidability of the fetish, the very topic being treated in the Hegel column of *Glas* next to the discussion of the shuttle in the Genet column: "Here, he [Freud] comes to recognize the 'fetishist's attitude of splitting' and the oscillation of the subject between two possibilities" (*Glas,* 235). The oscillation or shuttle motion of the fetish enters the Genet column later: "He oscillates like the beating of a truth which rings. Like the clapper in the throat, that is to say in the abyss of a bell" (254). *Glas,* having found in the homophonic shuttle a different intonation of one of the philosophemes of logocentrism, sounds the death knell of dialectics.

Grotesquery. The question of fetishism, "an economy of the undecid-able," in the context of the sensorium shift, concerns membranes—their tension and capacity for vibration or permeability (the tympanum or the hymen)—which is also the problem of inside-outside, companion to the philosopheme of light and dark. When the fetishist looks at woman un-veiled, he sees and denies the absence of the phallus, sees the mother's phallus, model of all simulacra. Working free of the paradigm of the idea become woman, Derrida looks for evidence of this oscillation in the vicin-ity of the "vagina" as term. He considers, to begin with, the undecidable nature of the hymen occupying the space *between* (*entre*) the inside and the outside. He discovers the shuttle at work here (the ersatz phallus imaged as braided pubic hair) in the very name of this space—the between— *entre,* since the word *antre* (a cavern or grotto) also alludes to the vagina and finally, in its etymology, to *entre* itself. The hymen, in Derrida's rhetoric, is the structurality (the vibration of a membrane) of these two words together. The homophones *entre-antre* enact a repetition of signifiers which is the device constitutive of grammatological "space."

> Without reducing all these to the same, quite the contrary, it is pos-sible to recognize a certain serial law in these points of indefinite pivoting: they mark the spots of what can never be mediated, mas-tered, sublated, or dialecticized through any *Erinnerung* or *Auf-hebung.* . . . Insofar as the text depends upon them, *bends* to them, it thus plays a *double scene* upon a double stage. It operates in two absolutely different places at once, even if these are only separ-ated by a veil, which is both traversed and not traversed, *inter-*sected. Because of this indecision and instability, Plato would have conferred upon the double science arising from these two theaters the name *doxa* rather than *episteme.* (*Dissemination,* 221)

Such is the nature of the liaison of the two semantic domains articulated by the joining of the shuttle—what is only a marginal displacement at the level of the letter, setting up the grammatical equivalent of a blur, reaches catastrophic proportions at the conceptual level, prohibiting the unifying effects, the clarity and distinctness, of dialectics.

That the between is also a grotto (*entre-antre*) is important for under-standing the place of grammatology in the history of ornament, since it suggests that op writing is a form of grotesquery. An example on a small scale of Derrida's participation in the genre of the grotesque is "Tympan," the preface to *Marges de la philosophie.* Its topic, relevant to the title of the collection, is the margins and limits of philosophy. The double-column format is used (anticipating *Glas*), the right side being a citation from Michel Leiris, and the left side being Derrida's discussion "touching" on Leiris, marginal writing. The citation concerns what can only be described as a cartouche, a version of the flourish in ornament; that is, it is an inventory of network, grid, woven, or winding patterns found in nature and society, all of which Leiris gathers under the name "Persephone":

> "The acanthus leaf which one copies at school when one learns to
> handle charcoal more or less well, the stems of a concolvulus or other
> climbing plants, the spiral inscribed on a snail shell, the meanders
> of an intestine, the curl of childhood hair enshrined in a medallion,
> the modern style ironwork of metro entrances, the interlacings of
> embroidered monograms on sheets and pillow cases, the windings of
> a path, everything that is festoon, volute, scroll, garland, arabesque.
> It is a question therefore, essentially, of a name in *spirals.*" (*Marges,*
> ii–v)

Persephone as signature, in other words, is inscribed in the framing flourish, whose shapes recall the name. And, just as Gombrich notes in a chapter of *The Sense of Order* entitled "The Edge of Chaos," the margin with its overgrowth of tendrils, in baroque artists like Albrecht Dürer, may spawn monsters, grotesques, resulting from the playful invention permitted in this "zone of license": "Much learning and ingenuity has been expanded in assigning symbolic meanings to the marginal flourishes, monsters and other motifs created by Dürer and his medieval predecessors, and there is no reason to doubt that once in awhile the text offered a starting point to the artist for his playful invention. But even where we are prepared to strain our credulity, the majority of inventions must still be seen as creations in their own right" (Gombrich, 251). Dürer, the example of this tradition of virtuosity and free invention in marginal decoration, mixed every known tradition in a search for ideas. The resulting enigmatic images are classified as grotesques or drolleries. Dürer's own term was "dreamwork" (Whoever wants to dream must mix all things together"), creating an effect of "bewildering confusion."

It is helpful to consider op writing within this tradition of the grotesque. Leiris, in the passage cited in "Tympan," provides an example of how the grotesque, in its original or technical sense (which refers to a kind of ornament, similar to the arabesque, consisting of medallions, sphinxes, foliage), can be extended in writing to the fantastic sense of the term, thus combining like Dürer the decorative and the monstrous. The spiraling foliage (decorative grotesque) reminds Leiris of the name Persephone, but the name itself sounds to him like *perce-oreille*—earwig, a boring insect—which is the appearance of the monster. Derrida's own homophonic or punning strategy results in a similar "fantasy etymology," which has much the same distorting effect in a philosophical discourse as had Dürer's drawings of thistles, cranelike birds, and gargoyles on the margins of the prayer book the emperor Maximilian had commissioned for his newly founded Order of St. George.

As suggested by *antre*—the grotto, recalling the Italian grottoes in which the ancient decorations were discovered, hence their dubbing as grotesquery —the "betweenness" of grammatological space is a zone of license. Part of the lesson of the grotesque genre for understanding Derrida, keeping in mind Gombrich's stress on the independence of grotesqueries—and all ornamentation, for that matter—from what it decorates, is that Derrida's writing deals only *marginally* with what it is "about" (with what it surrounds or enframes, like a passe-partout). Nonetheless, the moiré effect of op writing, giving rise to grotesque etymologies, constitutes a new theory of mimesis (Derrida is opposed, he says, not to mimesis, but to a determined interpretation of mimesis, to "mimetologism"—*Positions,* 70): "Here we are *playing* on the fortuituous *resemblance,* the purely simulated common parentage of *seme* and *semen.* There is no communication of meaning between them. And yet, by means of this floating, purely exterior collusion, accident produces a kind of *semantic mirage:* the deviance of meaning, its reflection-effect in writing, sets something off" (45). The new mimesis, in short, is based on homophonic resemblance.

The metaphorics of non-Aristotelian articulation, I have argued, generate a discourse between the pulsating moiré effect (emblem of solicitation as vibration) and *Moira,* or destiny. The hinge jointing these two domains may be found within the tympanum itself, whose meanings, as Derrida notes in "Tympan," include of course the vibrating ear drum (sound and light being susceptible to the same effects, the beat of dissonance being the acoustic equivalent of the moiré blur—both effects of proximity), a part of the apparatus of printing presses, and a type of water wheel—suggesting an image of the wheel of fortune. Derrida is redefining idea, working on its root metaphor of sight and light, analyzing it no longer in terms of its effect (the light bulb that lights up when we have an idea in cartoons and advertisements) but in terms of its physics, energy waves (the vibrations mediated by air, the level at which light and sound are equivalents, identified in relation to the body in terms of the "objective senses" of sight and hearing). What electricity is to light, *Moira* is to language. To think grammatologically is not to have an idea, but to have a "moira" (so to speak).

DECOMPOSITION

Voice. The second step in Derrida's solicitation of the founding metaphors of Western thought (the philosophemes upon which are based our notion of theory, idea, concept, and of metaphor itself)—decomposition—extends articulation to the chemical senses by finding an analogy for thought that does not depend on touch, sight, or hearing. Challenging the idealizing and appropriating operations of metaphysics, which lifted metaphors into con-

cepts and which exalted the *episteme* over *aisthesis* as the only genuine
source of truth, Derrida reverses the direction (*sens*) of sublation, returning the concepts to their bodily metaphors, just as he used the rebus or
cartouche principle to transfer proper names into common nouns. His experiments with decomposition begin as a reversal of Hegel's hierarchy of
the senses:

> This hierarchic classification combines two criteria: objectivity and
> interiority, which oppose one another only in appearance, idealiza-
> tion having tended (from Plato to Husserl) to confirm them simulta-
> neously one by the other. Ideal objectivity maintains all the better
> its identity to itself, its integrity and its resistance, in not depending
> any longer on an empirical perceptible exteriority. Here, the com-
> bination of two criteria permits the elimination from the theoretical
> domain touch (which has to do only with a material exteriority:
> masterable objectivity), taste (consumption which dissolves objec-
> tivity in interiority), odor (which allows the object to dissociate
> itself in evaporation). Sight is imperfectly theoretical and ideal (it
> permits the objectivity of the object to be but is not able to in-
> teriorize the sensible and spatial opacity). According to a metaphor
> coordinated with the whole system of metaphysics, only hearing,
> which preserves at once objectivity and interiority, could be called
> fully ideal and theoretical. (*Marges,* 108)

In Hegel's system, then, the material of ideality is light and sound.
Light is the milieu of phenomenality, the element of appearing. Voice, in
relation to hearing (the most sublime sense), animates sound, permitting the
passage from more sensible existence to the representational existence of
the concept (*Marges,* 103-7). Derrida analyzed the theorizing effect of the
complicity between voice and hearing at length in *Speech and Phenomena:*

> The ideality of the object, which is only its being-for a nonempirical
> consciousness, can only be expressed in an element whose phenom-
> enality does not have worldly form. *The name of this element is the
> voice. The voice is heard* [*entendus* = "heard" plus "understood"].
> . . . The subject does not have to pass forth beyond himself to be im-
> mediately affected by his expressive activity. My words are "alive"
> because they seem not to leave me: not to fall outside me, outside my
> breath, at a visible distance, not to cease to belong to me, to be at
> my disposition "without further props." (*Speech,* 76)

The special status of the voice-ear circuit (cf. the O-I-R series linking
moira with *theoria*) is that every other form of auto-affection must pass
through what is outside the sphere of "ownness" in order to claim universality—they must risk death in the body of the signifier given over to
the world and the visibility of space—thus sacrificing purity. Derrida asks,
however, "Are there not forms of pure auto-affection in the inwardness of

one's own body which do not require the intervention of any surface displayed in the world and yet are not of the order of the voice?" (*Speech,* 79). He does not answer this question in *Speech and Phenomena,* but it is a clue to the direction his thinking will take elsewhere. Philosophy does not recognize even that "hearing oneself speak" *is* auto-affection, for "as soon as it is admitted that auto-affection is the condition for self-presence, no pure transcendental reduction is possible" (82). Moreover, such an admission would require philosophy to conceive of the *logos* as a form of "excrement," the word falling outside oneself.

The theoretical senses (sight and hearing) are praised in Hegel's *Esthetics* for leaving objects free to exist for themselves, "unconsumed." Indeed, as Derrida points out, "the Hegelian theory of desire is the theory of the contradiction between theory and desire. Theory is the death of desire, death in desire if not the desire of death. The entire introduction to the *Esthetics* shows this contradiction between desire which drives toward consumption, and the 'theoretical interest,' which lets things be in their liberty" (*Marges,* 105). Art, Hegel maintains, occupying the milieu between the sensible and the intelligible, must be addressed by the two theoretical senses. Taste, odor, and touch are excluded from any contribution to the comprehension of art (and from the philosophemes). Against this theoretical bias, Derrida notes Freud's observation, made in the case of the Rat Man, that the progress of civilization has been made at the expense of sexuality— the atrophy of the chemical senses in humans is in sharp contrast to the animal world, where they are closely linked with sexual instinct. Moreover, our relation to the abandoned sexual zones ("the regions of the anus and of the mouth and throat") provides Freud with a metaphor for repression as such: "To put it crudely, the current memory stinks just as an actual object may stink; and just as we turn away our sense organ (the head and nose) in disgust, so do the preconscious and our conscious apprehension turn away from the memory. This is *repression.*" [16]

Taste. Experimenting with a non-Hegelian speculation, Derrida begins to define a conceptual system that would be based on the nontheoretical senses, which would efface the contradiction between theory and desire. This strategy is necessary, given his belief, stated in *Of Grammatology,* that grammatology's project to deconstruct science cannot be theoretical: "The necessary decentering cannot be a philosophic or scientific act as such, since it is a question of dislocating, through access to another system linking speech and writing, the founding categories of language and the grammar of the *episteme.* The natural tendency of *theory*—of what unites philosophy and science in the *episteme*—will push rather toward filling in the breach than toward forcing the closure" (92). Just as "praxis" is used to name the integration of theory and practice, so too is a new term needed to designate the convergence of theory and desire in poststructuralist writing in general, and in Derrida in particular. A Greek or Latin translation of "taste" itself will not do, since part of what is at stake includes a challenge to the traditional (figurative) use of taste to refer to the process of judgment—"The abstraction of a human faculty to a generalized polite attribute," as in Addison: " 'Rules . . . how we may acquire that fine Taste of Writing, which is so much talked of among the Polite World.' "[17] "Epithymia" (desire)[18] is perhaps adequate to at least hold a place for the needed term. "Epithymics," then, is to "taste" (within the operation of decomposition) what "moira" is to "idea" (within the operation of articulation). Epithymics and moira name Derrida's alternative strategy, replacing our traditional understanding of concept formation.

Derrida's epithymics is most fully developed in *Glas* (the Genet column), in which he employs a technique introduced in "Tympan": an analysis of the organs associated with the metaphorics of the philosophemes. In "Tympan," the voice-hearing circuit of self-presence was treated in terms of the physiology, psychology, and etymology of the tympanum. "The copulating correspondence, the question/response opposition is lodged already in a structure, enveloped in the hollow of an ear where we want to go see. To know how it is made, how it is formed, how it functions" (*Marges,* ix). This procedure challenges the metaphysical or dialectical interpretation of metaphor as a transfer from the sensible to the intelligible (the *Aufhebung*). But a mode of thought so habitual to our civilization is not easily changed. The first step is to reverse the direction of the metaphorics. Given that the French *"sens"* also means "direction," this third meaning provides the place from which to question the other two meanings by calling attention to the sublimating movement that joins them.[19] The philosophemes are to be deconstructed by an examination of their metaphors—specifically, the vehicles, the senses or sensible aspect of the organs. The goal is the conceptualization of the chemical senses, excluded thus far from theory.

"You must also work like an organist the word tongue [*langue*]," Derrida advises at the beginning of *Glas,* "tongue" being a classic example of catachresis, extending its name to cover "language." *Glas,* then, proposes to investigate a philosopheme based on the tongue and its "sheath" or hollow envelope, the mouth. Throughout *Glas* there are references to the organs of the subjective senses, olfactory as well as gustatory and textural (the latter—touch—being set aside, finally, as too representational, which would indicate that it might be misleading to call *Glas* a text). What will be identified as the "decompositional" features of the subjective senses elaborated in the Genet column are juxtaposed with the objective senses of the *Aufhebung* in the Hegel column, whose central example is Christ's Last Supper, the transsubstantiation of bread and wine. Against this sublation and subliming, the Genet column insists on the physiology of the organ through which nourishment enters the body. The tongue, of course, plays a major role in two bodily functions—speaking and eating. According to one theory, in fact, language developed from the sounds made during the chewing of food.[20] A logical place to begin the deconstruction of the logocentric privilege of speech is to take note of the other function performed by the same organs that make speech possible—to explore the surplus of operations excluded from the philosopheme.

> The dividing membrane which is called the soft palate, fixed by its upper edge to the border of the roof, *floats* freely, at its lower end, above the base of the tongue. Its two lateral sides (it is a quadrilateral) are called "pillars." In the middle of the floating end, at the entrance of the throat, hangs the fleshy appendage of the uvula, like a small grape. The text is spit out. It is like a discourse in which the unities model themselves after an excrement, a secretion. And because it has to do here with a glottic gesture, the tongue working on itself, *saliva* is the element which sticks the unities together. Association is a sort of glue-like contiguity, never a reasoning or a symbolic appeal; the glue of the aleatory makes sense and the progress punctuates itself by little jerks. (*Glas*, 161)

The olfactory is included as well as the saliva so important to taste, again as a metaphor for the structurality of writing:

> The essence of the rose is its non-essence: its odor as it evaporates. Hence its affinity as effluvium with a fart or a belch: these excrements are not preserved, are not even formed. . . . How could ontology get hold of a fart? One must therefore read the anthropy of a text which makes roses fart. And yet the text, itself, does not entirely disappear, not entirely as fast as the farts which it exhales. . . . This suspension of the text which delays a little—one must not exaggerate—its absolute dissipation, could be called effluvium. Effluvium designates in general decomposing organic substances, or rather their product floating in the air, that sort of *gas* which is preserved awhile above marshes, as well as magnetic fluids. The text is thus a gas. (*Glas*, 69–70)

The motivation for this discussion, of course, is that Hegel explicitly condemns odor (and taste) as useless for artistic pleasure, given that esthetic contemplation requires objectivity, without reference to desire or will, whereas "things present themselves to smell only to the degree in which they are constituted themselves by a process, in which they dissolve into the air with practical effects" (*Marges*, 109). The larger issue, relevant to the entire tradition of Western thought, concerns the consequences of the rigid separation of the intelligible from the sensible. Posed in its most extreme form by Parmenides (who denies the reality of Becoming), the separation of the sensible particular from the intelligible general entails that such things as mud or hair, not to mention effluvium, are not real, do not "provoke thought." Against the Eleatic bias against empty space in favor of substance, Derrida finds a way to localize the gap of difference in the body, metaphorizing the new philosopheme out of the resonating chambers, the hollows of the body—ear and vagina, mouth and rectum. He approaches here the Swiftian insight that proposes as an alternative to the metaphysical voice-ear circuit the equally auto-effective circuit of the anus-nose.

The issue in *Glas* may be appreciated by taking into account another version of the same argument in "Economimesis," in which Kant's esthetics of taste becomes a meditation on the mouth:

> The mouth in any case no longer occupies here one place among others. It is no longer locatable *in* a topology of the body but attempts to organize all the places and localize all the organs. The *mouth* [*os*] of the system, the place of gustation or of consumption but also of the emitive production of the *logos,* is this still a term in an analogy? Could one, figuratively, compare the mouth to this or that, to some other orifice, lower or higher? Is not it itself the analogy, in which everything has its origin as in the *logos* itself? (*Mimesis,* 79)

The split between all opposed values passes through the mouth, whether sensible or ideal, judging the good and the bad, "as between two manners of entering and two manners of leaving the mouth: of which one would be expressive and transmitting (of a poem optimally), the other vomitive or emetic" (*Mimesis,* 80). Against Kant's "exemplorality" (exemplary orality) concerning taste in the ideal sense, having to do with singing and hearing, without consumption, Derrida raises the question of "distaste," or rather, disgust (*dégoût*).

The question has to do with the relation of Kant's "exemplorality" to the structure of the *gustus*—the relations among the palate, lips, tongue, teeth, throat—in short, the *articulators.* The point of Derrida's interrogation is to find out, with regard to exemplorality, "what is excluded from it, and from what exclusion, gives it form, limit and contour? And what of this excess with regard to what is called the mouth?" (*Mimesis,* 87). Derrida's response is an inverted duplication of the question. If taste orders a system of pleasure of assimilation, the excluded will be that which cannot be digested, represented, spoken. What cannot be swallowed is what "makes one vomit": "The *vomi* gives its form to an entire system, that is, the schema of vomit, as experience of disgust." Kant noted that the Beaux-Arts can make ugly things beautiful. The only thing that cannot be assimilated to beauty, Kant maintained, is that which is disgusting. Beauty puts things at a distance, takes up an attitude of "indifference," disinterest, detachment so that the object may be enjoyed "for itself." But an art object or work which presents the disgusting prohibits the experience of the beautiful because " 'the artistic representation of the object is no longer distinguishable, in our sensation, from the nature of that object and therefore it can no longer be considered beautiful' " (90).

The effect of the *vomi* is the destruction of representation and the pleasure associated with it, exposing one instead to the experience of *jouissance* (beyond pleasure). The essential point, Derrida insists, is that the term "disgust" does not designate the repugnant or negative in general —it does not depend on literally disgusting things, but is directed beyond the opposition taste/distaste. The disgusting is dissymmetrical with the system of taste: "What is absolutely foreclosed, is not the *vomi,* but first of all the possibility of the vicariousness of the *vomi,* . . . any other which forces *jouissance* and whose irrepressible violence comes to undo the hierarchizing authority of the logocentric analogy: its power of identification" (*Mimesis,* 92). The *vomi,* in its essence, then, is the effacement of the distinction between the fictional and the real, between art and life. And it is also the "gag" alluding to the tongue-in-cheek bite of this alternative to voice.

Mouth. The *vomi* explicitly engages not the "objective" senses of hearing and sight, nor even touch, which Kant describes as "mechanical," all three of which involve perception of or at surfaces, but the "subjective" or "chemical" senses of taste and smell: "One could say that both of these [senses] are affected by salts (fixed or volatile) of which some may be dissolved by saliva in the mouth, the others by the air" (*Mimesis,* 92). Here we have the principal trait of the chemical, nontheoretical senses—to dissolve, the act of dissolution, hence the transformation of the object. This characteristic provides the metaphor for Derrida's new philosopheme, for his counter to the conceptualizing process of dialectics, which gathers together or collects elements into a set. The dissolving action of the chemical senses, involving the breakdown and transformation of substances, offers a model for a methodology of decomposition by means of which the limits of theoretical philosophy might be transgressed. The organ of this new philosopheme is the mouth, the mouth that bites, chews, tastes: the organs of speech in the mouth and throat are examined now for their metaphoric potential in terms of their other function—not to exclude speaking in the way that the orthodox philosopheme of the voice-ear circuit excludes eating, but to "think" their "surplus."

The first step of decomposition is the bite. To understand the rationale for all the interpolations, citations, definitions used in *Glas,* Derrida says, one must realize that "the object of the present work, its style too, is the *'morceau'* [bit, piece, morsel, fragment; musical composition; snack, mouthful]. Which is always detached, as its name indicates and so you do

not forget it, with the teeth" (*Glas,* 135). The "teeth," as Derrida explained in an interview, refer to quotation marks, brackets, parentheses:
when language is cited (put between quotation marks), the effect is that of
releasing the grasp or hold of a controlling context. With this image of biting out a piece, Derrida counters the metaphor of concept—grasping, holding (*Begriff*).[21]

The image Derrida uses to describe his procedure in *Glas* indicates the
scale of the project attempted in that text: "I see rather (but it is perhaps
still a matrix or a grammar) a kind of dredging machine. From the hidden,
small, enclosed glassed cabin of a crane I manipulate levers from afar. I
saw it at Saint-Maries-de-la-Mer at Easter. I plunge a steel mouth into the
water. And I rake the bottom, and pick up rocks and seaweed which I
carry back to dump on the land while the water rapidly falls back out of
the mouth" (*Glas,* 229).

Decomposition, then, is another version of what Derrida describes as
the most fundamental feature of language—iterability, the principle shared
by both speech and writing. The nuclear traits of a "general writing" consist of three modes of "absence"—examples of the spacing, gap, differance
of articulation that Derrida opposes to Aristotle's onomastics. The written
mark is iterable in the absence of its producer and in the absence of a
referent or signified. The mark may also continue to function *in the absence of its context.* Here we encounter the crucial element of the decompositional mode of writing. The grapheme—the *restance,* or nonpresent
remainder of the differential mark inaccessible to any experience, cut off
from the origins of a receiver or ends of a referent, from a signified or a
context—remains iterable and still functions as sense (because language is
a system).

Husserl gave as an example of meaninglessness, with regard to which no
truth or communication was possible, the agrammatical phrase, "The
green is either" (*le vert est ou*). But Husserl himself admitted that, translated into French (from German) and by means of homophony, the phrase
could be understood to mean, "Where is the glass?" (*vert* as *verre, ou* as *où*)
(*Marges,* 381). With this example in mind, Derrida proposes the fundamental generalization of his writing:

> And this is the possibility on which I want to insist: the possibility
> of disengagement and citational graft which belongs to the struc-
> ture of every mark, spoken or written, and which constitutes every
> mark in writing before and outside of every horizon of semio-
> linguistic communication; in writing, which is to say in the possi-
> bility of its functioning being cut off, at a certain point, from
> its "original" desire-to-say-what-one-means and from its participa-
> tion in a saturable and constraining context. Every sign, linguistic
> or non-linguistic, spoken or written (in the current sense of this

opposition), in a small or large unit, can be *cited*, put between quotation marks; in so doing it can break with every given context, engendering an infinity of new contexts in a manner which is absolutely illimitable. [22]

Derrida in fact takes this possibility of cutting free and regrafting as his (de)compositional principle. Iterability, as a mode of production, may be recognized as *collage*. [23] Indeed, Derrida has referred to his style as "a parody, a collage, a juxtaposition," carried out "as gaily and scientifically as possible" ("Crochets," 112). The parody may be seen in his exploitation of puns, for if the tradition of aesthetics, following Kant and Hegel, advocated the distancing, "detached" attitude of the objective senses, Derrida responds with the bite that "detaches" the piece in order to dissolve it: "That the sign detaches itself, that signifies of course that one cuts it out of its place of emission or from its natural relations; but the separation is never perfect, the difference never consummated. The bleeding detachment is also—repetition—delegation, commission, delay, relay. Adherence. The detached [piece] remains stuck by the glue of differance, by the a. The a of gl agglutinates the detached differents. The scaffold of the A is glutinous" (*Glas*, 188).

The effectiveness of collage is that, like metaphor, the piece, displaced into a new context, retains associations with its former context. The two operations constituting the collage technique—selection and combination—are the operations characteristic of all speaking and writing. Moreover, as in language usage, the operations are carried out on preformed material. Derrida uses his decompositional, dissolving, collage technique to break up the clear and distinct outlines of the concept, with distorting effects similar to those achieved in cubism with regard to the conventions of representation in the visual arts. In fact, given that the collage in general is *the* most characteristic mode of composition in the modernist arts and that Derrida is the first to develop fully a theory (epithymics) that conceptualizes this mode, it is fair to say that Derrida's grammatology is to the collage what Aristotle's poetics was to Greek tragedy. The comparison is also a contrast, since decomposition (deconstruction extended from a mode of criticism to a mode of composition) as a practice relies on the very elements Aristotle excluded from metaphor—articulation and the homonym.

Orality. The project to "deconstitute the founding concept-words of ontology," Derrida states in *Of Grammatology,* "has the greatest likelihood of success, at present, in psychoanalytic research" (21). Nicolas Abraham considered psychoanalysis to have as its "object" of study precisely what is excluded by, or escapes the notice of, phenomenology (or any philosophy of consciousness). Psychoanalysis expands the narrow limits allowed to the sign by philosophy—"the conscious representation of 'words' and 'things' for a self speaking within the 'internal' system of language."[24] The use of collage permits Derrida to escape the traditional "intentionality" in favor of a writing that is productive outside the ideology of communication. Collage, that is, makes possible a rigorous yet creative *unconscious* writing.

> For a writing to be a writing it must continue to "act" and to be
> readable even when what is called the author of the writing no longer
> answers for what he has written, for what he seems to have signed.
> . . . This essential drift bearing on writing as an iterative structure, cut
> off from all absolute responsibility, from *consciousness* as the ulti-
> mate authority, orphaned and separated at birth from the assistance
> of its father, is precisely what Plato condemns in the *Phaedrus*. If
> Plato's gesture is, as I believe, the philosophical movement par excel-
> lence, one can measure what is at stake here. ("Signature," 181)

The model for an unconscious writing—its rationale—is provided by the theories devised to explain the language of the Wolf Man, whose compulsive or unconscious condition separating him from his "name," or "signature," makes him a test case for a new theory of writing. Derrida's strategy for exceeding the limits of philosophical discourse is to learn to write the way the Wolf Man spoke. (Freud, in any case, had already compared the fragmenting effect of the processes he was studying to chemical processes: "Phantasies are constructed by a process of fusion and distortion analogous to the decomposition of a chemical body which is combined with another one"—*Origins*, 204.) In their analysis of the Wolf Man's case, Abraham and Torok developed a special topographical theory (referring to the "locational relationship" of the Unconscious to the Conscious systems) to account for the resistance of the patient's language to decipherment. The topography consists of a kind of vault or crypt built within the Self; nor is this topography simply the usual version of a hidden or buried unconscious. The crypt belongs to the discussion of "taste" and "disgust" (the *vomi*) because it involves the mouth in terms of oral fixation, of the "oral stage" as the first phase of libidinal development: "Sexual pleasure at this period is bound predominantly to that excitation of the oral cavity and lips which accompanies feeding. The activity of nutrition is the source of the particular meanings through which the object-relationship is expressed and organised; the love-relationship to the mother, for example, is marked by the meanings of *eating* and *being eaten*."[25]

Part of the interest of drawing on theories of orality (as the first libidinal experience, it forever marks desire, determining the nature of our satisfaction and dissatisfaction) for the deconstruction of the philosophemes is that against the appropriation of all the other senses by sight in Plato's use of *eidos*, "psychoanalysis reveals that in childhood phantasies this mode is not attached solely to oral activity but that *it may be trans-*

posed on to other functions (e.g. respiration, sight)" (Laplanche, and Pontalis, 288). Moreover, in support of a methodology attempting to theorize (epithymize) repulsion, this stage includes an "oral-sadistic" phase concurrent with teething in which the activity of biting and devouring implies a destruction of the object; "as a corollary of this we find the presence of the phantasy of being eaten or destroyed by the mother" (288).

Psychoanalysis defines the element of phantasy life that is involved in personality formation in terms of the functioning of the erotogenic zones (including especially those sensory organs excluded from the philosophemes). Incorporation—the nourishment process of taking things into the mouth, but also the spitting out of the breast—provides a model for relationships with the external world in general. Thus, the child will assimilate the image of the mother as an ideal self, as part of ego-development, in a process an important aspect of which is termed "mourning." Mourning—the idealization and interiorization of the mother's image—enables the child to accept the separation from (loss of, "death" of) the physical mother.

Abraham and Torok distinguish sharply between introjection and incorporation, with the latter—defined as a pathology inhibiting mourning—being responsible for the formation of the "crypt." The love-object (in phantasy life) is walled up or entombed and thus preserved as a bit of the outside inside the inside, kept apart from the "normal" introjections of the Self. (Collage, of course, is the formal equivalent of incorporation in this sense, and was similarly considered, from the point of view of traditional esthetics with its valuation of unity, to be a pathology of form.) "Faced with the impotence of the process of introjection (gradual, slow, laborious, mediated, effective), incorporation is the alternative choice—fantasmatic, unmediated, instantaneous, magical, sometimes hallucinatory" ("Fors," 72). The refusal to mourn a lost love object causes the object to be preserved like a mummy (mom) in a crypt, the passageway sealed off and marked (in the psyche) with the place, date, and circumstances in commemoration, a monument to an unacceptable desire (hence the *vomi*). "And if the work of mourning consists always in eating the bit [*mors*], the disgusting can only be vomited" (*Mimesis*, 90).

Since Hegel's *Aufhebung* resembles introjection, it is understandable that Derrida would be interested in the functioning of incorporation, which resists introjection. Introjection, it should be remembered, is a process of auto-affection, relevant to the hearing-oneself-speak of logocentrism. The satisfactions associated with the maternal breast are replaced in introjection by filling the mouth with words. The language is a *figure* of the presence of self-presence (an auto-apprehension of the absent object). Against this passage to the figural or representational, incorporation "transforms the oral metaphor presiding over introjection into a *reality*" ("Fors," 102)—a destruction of representational distance, a reversal of the sensible-intelligible *Aufhebung.* "But the fantasy involves eating the object (through the mouth or otherwise) in order *not* to introject it, in order to vomit it, in a way, into the inside. The metaphor is taken *literally* in order to refuse its introjecting effectiveness" (103). Thus, the limit prohibiting introjection is situated in the mouth: "No longer able to articulate certain forbidden words, the mouth takes in—as a fantasy—the unnameable thing" (103). The incorporation, thereafter, passes through a crypt of language, *a crypt which grammatology mimes in order to write otherwise.* Epithymics, that is, challenges the catachreses of the philosophemes by taking the metaphors of the founding ideas literally.

Sealed in the Wolf Man's psychic vault, then, is a word-thing, a word treated as a thing that is unspeakable and yet (because the walls of the crypt, being metaphors for the membranes of the erotogenic organs, are permeable) achieves utterance by means of a complex translation process. *Glas* may be considered a kind of philosophical surrealism in that it uses the principles of this "mad" speech to generate a text. This hieroglyphic system is what the cryptologists (Abraham and Torok) were finally able to decipher, using techniques, like those used by Champollion to decipher the Rosetta stone (their own analogy), that require translations across three languages—in this case Russian, German, and English (but in Derrida's case, French replaces Russian). The word-thing *functions as the Wolf Man's name,* naming the singularity of his desire, dissociated entirely from the names of his fathers, both civil and psychoanalytic: "When in secret he dares, barely aware of it, to *call himself,* when he wishes to call himself and to call his wish by its (his) name, he calls himself by the unspeakable name of the Thing. He, but who? The Thing is part of a symbol. It no longer calls itself. The entire body of a proper name is always shattered by the *topoi.* As for the 'word' which says the Thing in the word-thing, it is not even a noun but a verb, a whole collapsed sentence" ("Fors," 112).

The word—*Tieret* (alluding to the various usages meaning to rub, to scrape)—is the privileged but not exclusive magic word that carries with it the effect of a proper name. The other words—*goulfik* (the fly of his father's trousers) and *vidietz* (a witness, alluding to the glimpse of the primal scene)—are also part of the name. The name is magic because it has only to be uttered for the bearer to obtain "actual or sublimated sexual satisfaction" (the name as symptom).

The cryptonomy of verbal material that the Wolf Man derived from his fetish scene (the maid on her knees scrubbing the floor, invested as a sign of the primal scene) did not operate by the usual procedures of representation—the symbolizing or hiding of one word behind another, or one thing by a word or a word by a thing. Rather, his names were generated by picking out from the extended series of "allosemes"—the catalogue of uses available for a given word—a particular usage, which is then translated into a synonym (creating thus even greater distance from the secret name). The path from crypt to speech may follow either semantic or phonic paths, with the play between homonyms and synonyms being part of the mechanism. Thus, the allosemes of *Tieret,* for example—to rub, to grind, to wound, to polish—provide a range of associations and dissociations among the semantic fields related to rubbing and/or wounding-scrubbing that provide the Wolf Man with his vocabulary. The linkage of the uttered word to the secret name is so tortuous, a relay-labyrinth of "non-semantic associations, purely phonetic combinations," that the translation may not be classified by the available rhetorical figures:

> The *Verbarium* shows how a sign, having become arbitrary, can re-motivate itself. And into what labyrinth, what multiplicity of heterogeneous places, one must enter in order to track down the cryptic motivation, for example in the case of *TR,* when it is marked by a proper-name effect (here, *Tieret*), and when, consequently, it no longer belongs simply to the internal system of language. Such motivation does nevertheless function within the system and no linguistic consciousness can deny it. For example, when *Turok* (Turk, the Turkish flag in the dream of the moon with a star) says (?), means (?), translates (?), points out (?), represents (?), or *in any case* also imitates, induces the word-thing *Tieret.* ("Fors," 114)

The TR of the *Verbarium* accounts for the GL of *Glas*—the Wolf Man, or rather, Abraham and Torok's theory of the Wolf Man's language, teaches Derrida to write "orally," an operation between words and things, with the mouth meta-(mor)phorized as the philosopheme beyond theory.

Signature. The key to the production of the text is the author's proper name: the proper name is the permeable membrane (the tympan, the hymen, allowing contamination between the inside and outside). The method of decomposition as the conceptualization of the chemical senses functions at the level of writing as the break-up of words: "Of what clacks here—and decomposes the word's cadavre (*balc, talc, algue, eclat, glace,* etc.) in every sense this is the first and last time that, as an example, you are here forewarned" (*Glas,* 9). Liberated from the unity of the word, "gl remains open, ready for all concubinations, all collages" (263). Decomposition is part of Derrida's definition of writing in terms of death—the death of the author, and as an artificial mnemonics, not animated by living intentions. The proper name occupies the masterpiece like a body in a tomb, decomposing. "The proper name does not resonate, losing itself immediately, except at the moment of its *debris,* in which it breaks, jumbles itself, skids in contacting the sign manual [*seing*]" (41). The death knell (*glas*) sounds with the decomposition of the name, a decomposition that

passes through at least two stages of decay. The first stage consists of the
desublimation of the proper into the common noun—the common noun is
the remains of the proper name: "The great stake of discourse—I mean to
say discourse—of literature: the patient transformation, crafty, almost animal or vegetal, untirable, monumental, derisive but also turning itself into
ridicule, of its proper name, *rebus,* into things, into names of things" (10–
11). Hegel decomposes into *aigle* (eagle), Genet into *genêt* (a flower)—the
idiom of the name passes into the general circulation of a system with a
small set of signifiers and an unlimited supply of signifieds. The decomposition of the name begins, then, as antonomasia (the rhetorical figure of
this passage from proper to common), reversing the *Aufhebung* that cancels
the literal and lifts it into the figurative.

The second stage of decomposition enacts another usage of "signature,"
meaning the "key" of a musical composition (*morceau*). *Glas,* in this sense,
is written in the key of GL, "as music composed 'in,' a book written in—
such and such letters" (*Glas,* 94). The whole labor is undertaken in a sense,
he adds, to emit GL, decomposed now to a nonrepresentational level where
the discourse is governed no longer by a rebus of the name but by a certain
rhythm, the "time" of the piece. As an example of the formal principle involved, Derrida cites Mallarmé's translation of Poe's "The Bells": "There is
an appearance of a simple nucleus around which all seems to gather: gl, cl,
kl, tl, fl. . . . The two letters recomposing the attraction elsewhere, from a
distance, in the poem, according to numerous and complex games" (178).
The words included in the poem are selected not for their sense but for
their "L"—the "+ L" effect. Mallarmé's favorite combination joins the L
with I. Since Mallarmé, author of *English Words,* must be considered an
English poet as well as French, Derrida explains, the "I" carries the sense
of "je." The "I" is the "subject" of Mallarmé's poetry, then, but as a letter
only, and not finally as a person. Thus, it enters into many compositions—
IL, LIT, LIS—and as a fragment, "enseveLI," "aboLI," and so forth. In
short, this technique escapes semantics, since the poetry is directed not by
metaphor or metonymy but by a rule of repetition of kernel letters. Being
nonrepresentational in its compositional technique, the poetry exemplifies
the possibility of a text free of the rules of "good" rhetoric: the semantic
properties that might be attributed to it—meaning, truth, dialectics—are
simply *effects* generated by the nature of language.[26]

That the strategy is an explicit alternative to theory as *eidos,* the idea
as the sublation of the sensible into the intelligible, may be seen in Derrida's allusion to the key of I-D itself (not an insignificant combination of
letters in this context, "Id" suggesting the relation of Derrida's Mallarméan
method to "unconscious thought"). "The reader is now invited to count
the dots, to follow the fine needlepoint pattern of *i*'s and *iques*'s [*-ic* or
-ical] which are being sprinkled rapidly across the tissue being pushed by

another hand. Perhaps he will be able to discern, according to the rapid, regular movement of the machine, the stitches of Mallarmé's idea, a certain instance of *i*'s and a certain scattering of dice [*d*'s]" (*Dissemination*, 238). As the translator notes, "The word *idée* [idea] is composed of the two syllables in question here: *i* and *de* [de = the letter 'd' and the word 'dice']." The idea put to work hypomnemically (the *idea*, *i-d*, operating according to the mechanical repetition of the signifier—a sophistic technique of artificial memory, rather than the living memory favored by Plato and dialectics) is not the signified concept, then, but the letters/phonemes of the word itself, which are set free to generate conceptual material *mechanically* (without the intention or presence of the subject) by gathering into a discourse terms possessing these letters (often using the pun or homophone).

Glas, at this level of decomposition, becomes a performance of the fricative properties of the guiding consonants, which turn out to be perfect opposites—caesura and flow: "Even while remaining a fragment effect among others, gl remarks also in itself the angular cut of opposition, the differential schize and the continuous flowing of the couple, distinction *and* copulating unity (for example of the arbitrary and of motivation)" (*Glas*, 262). Citing a work on the instinctual drives of phonation, Derrida notes that the L alludes to milk, archetype of all nourishing liquids (hence, the L in "liquid" itself), and the properties of milky colors and flowing sensations in general. These properties of the phonated L, associated with the Milky Way (galaxy), move Derrida to entitle this mode of production "galactics," in opposition to Hegel's dialectics. The "+ L" effect is the procedure appropriate to an aesthetics of the *vomi* for two reasons, then: first, because of its "chemical" associations ("the same gl begins to squirt, trickle, drip . . . sperm, saliva, mucus, clotted slaver, milk tears, vomit, all those heavy, white substances flowing into one another, agglutinating" [158]); second, and more important, because it works not by representational distance but (*nonobjectively*) by rhythm.

Unlike dialectics, which works by confrontation, opposition and assimilation, *galactics* (which alludes in its own way to a segment of the heavens, if not the same one identified by *contemplatio*) functions as a kind of metamorphosis, generating and changing signification not by synthesis but by dissemination at the levels of both the signifier and signified. The unity of a signified (whether of a proper name, or the name of a concept) is *dissolved into its component usages*. *Glas* itself, for example, in the course of the writing, spits out a long sequence of allosemes: "the bearings and peals of all the bells, the sepulchre, funeral ceremony, legacy, testament, contract, signature, proper name, given name, classification and the class struggle, the work of mourning in the relations of production, fetishism, disguise, attire of the dead, the incorporation, the introjection of the cadaver, idealization, sublimation, rejection, remainder, etc." (this list being the one Derrida provided in the blurb he prepared for *Glas*). In decomposition (the mode of writing needed for the epithymics of taste and smell), whose direction (*sens*) is downward (dissolving, breaking apart), a term does not generate its opposite but metamorphoses into its own allosemes, without unity, conclusion, or hierarchy, but only scattering, which is the equivalent at the level of the concept of the translation of the proper name into its rebus.

The Genet column of *Glas* is not a composition, then, but a decomposition, dissolving at two levels (the first and second signature), producing a collage of fragments which interpolates long passages from Genet's texts and dictionary definitions of the "+ L" allosemes with Derrida's own discourse. This column, juxtaposed with the Hegel column, allows for a non-dialectical, chance interaction of the materials presented on either side of the page. The text as a "whole" constitutes a simulacrum of a Renaissance commonplace book, in which the humanist collected the "flowers of rhetoric" ("anthology" being first a botanical term). The effect is one of material encountered in a pre- or post-compositional state (composition as compostition), incorporated rather than introjected (in either case, giving the effect of material ready to be made into a composition, or left over from a completed composition, against the traditional treatment of Taste as Judgment, in which the digestion metaphor suggested that the materials were to be assimilated and transformed into one's *own* thought). The commonplace book—a form of artificial memory (hypomnesis)—was used in the invention stage of composition. We might conclude that *Glas* itself is an image of invention and that its strategies, considered within the context of the "new rhetoric" as "rules for writing," provide a postmodern *inventio*.

The capacity for metamorphosis within words may also be recognized as the chemical rationale of grotesquery. The discursive line of op writing, that is, resembles the sinuosities of ornamental foliage which, amongst its tendrils, blossoms forth with a great variety of gargoyles and curiosities, just as the homophonic or paragrammatic hymen metamorphoses "Ponge" into "sponge" or *"entre"* into *"antre."*

The use of psychoanalysis to investigate decomposition, similar to the way the geometry of ornament and optical illusion was used to research articulation, brings us back full circle to the proper name as the model for a new mode of concept formation (and deformation). The Wolf Man's fetishism and his dissemination of his secret name through his conversations (a name no longer corresponding to his given name, nor to the name of his analyst) extend the association of the moiré pattern with the oscillating undecidability of the fetish, as well as the analysis of the dissemination of the proper name carried out in the first chapter. That the proper name should have a major place in Derrida's new metaphorology is understandable, given Jacques Lacan's demonstration that the name-of-the-father is the first metaphor—the first substitution (of the father's name for the desire of the mother: the father's name as a metaphor of this desire), which constitutes the entry into language or the Symbolic.

The usefulness of psychoanalysis is that it makes available a discourse on identity, with knowledge or certainty of one's own name (identification with the name) providing, in grammatology, a model for the operation of "knowledge" in general (of the relation of the subject to knowledge). Just as an examination of the discourse of botany revealed, in the context of a solicitation of the analogy of creativity as fertilization, an excess of alternative manners of procreating (dissemination, for example), so too does psychoanalysis reveal (in family procreative relationships) a plurality of possible reactions to the family name, among which the *Aufhebung* (Freud's usage now) is but one possibility (the one defining normality). An inventory of other possibilities is available, however, such as *Verwerfung*— foreclosure or repudiation—the schizophrenic refusal of the name, which is *the psychological equivalent of dehiscence,* since in place of the name-of-the-father, a *hole* opens in the unconscious—the symbol, the symbolic significance of the phallus (symbolic castration), is excluded from the unconscious, to reappear in the real in hallucinations, as exemplified in the case of the Wolf Man, who "sees" that acne has eaten away his nose (Waelhens, 128). Thus, the Wolf Man's fantasies are thrown into the real; the inside is disseminated in the outside.

The linguistic symptom of foreclosure, in other words, is the loss of a metaphoric understanding of language—words lose their symbolic dimension and are retained as non-symbolic signifiers in the real (Waelhens, 11). The loss of subject and of identity in schizophrenia (and its linguistic symptoms) provide a further model—foreclosure as dehiscence—which an applied grammatology can exploit in its search for a new writing. The literalization of the symbolic which takes place in foreclosure, an alternative to the *Aufhebung* (the internalization of the name and the acceptance of symbolic castration), as described in psychoanalytic discourse, gives access at the level of knowledge to a refusal of the proper, which Derrida translates into philosophical discourse.

3

Mnemonics

HYPOMNESIS

Theoretical grammatology, I have argued, is a repetition, a retracing at a
conceptual level, of the history of writing. Its purpose is to disentangle in
that history the nature (or the absence of an essence) of writing from the
ideology or metaphysics of voice which has dominated and restricted writing, in order to reassess the full potential of, and alternative directions for,
a new writing practice.

One of the most basic features of writing, historically, is its status as an
aid to memory, a feature which Derrida discusses at length in "Plato's
Pharmacy." The point of departure for this discussion, of course, is Plato's
apologue, in *Phaedrus,* about the Egyptian god Theuth, the legendary in-
ventor of writing (as well as of geometry, astronomy, and dice). Presented
with Theuth's invention, the king of Egypt, Thamus (or Ammon) passed
this judgment:

> If men learn this, it will implant forgetfulness in their souls; they will
> cease to exercise memory because they rely on that which is written,
> calling things to remembrance no longer from within themselves,
> but by means of external marks. What you have discovered is a recipe
> not for memory, but for reminder. And it is no true wisdom that
> you offer your disciples, but only its semblance, for by telling them
> of many things without teaching them you will make them seem
> to know much, while for the most part they know nothing. (Plato,
> 520)

Socrates expands on this condemnation by comparing writing to painting:

The painter's products stand before us as though they were alive, but
if you question them, they maintain a most majestic silence. It is
the same with written words; they seem to talk to you as though
they were intelligent, but if you ask them anything about what they
say from a desire to be instructed, they go on telling you just the
same thing forever. And once a thing is put in writing, the composition, whatever it may be, drifts all over the place, getting into the
hands not only of those who understand it, but equally of those who
have no business with it; it doesn't know how to address the right
people, and not address the wrong. And when it is ill-treated and
unfairly abused it always needs its parent to come to its help, being
unable to defend or help itself. (521)

The same charges are made today against television as a medium for
popularization of the sciences and humanities, so Derrida's response on
behalf of writing is relevant not only to the philosophical context but to
the context of video education as well.

A review of Derrida's argument in "Plato's Pharmacy" reveals that Plato
is condemning writing not just as "writing-down" but as a whole theory of
the relation of memory to thought. Plato's diatribe against the sophist condemns artifical memory (hypomnesia) in general, including mnemotechnics,
the system of topoi, or commonplaces ("the *tupoi* are the representatives,
the *physical* surrogates of the *psychic* that is absent?") developed for
rhetorical training. Indeed, as we shall see, Derrida's "new rhetoric" is as
much a reanimation of ancient *memoria* as it is of *inventio*. As Derrida
notes, Socrates, in dialogue with the sophist Hippias, who claims universal
knowledge, twice, ironically, forgets to include in his list of Hippias's
accomplishments his mnemotechnics—" 'I have forgotten to mention your
art of memory, which you regard as your special glory' "; " 'Bless my soul,
you have certainly been lucky that the Lacedaemonians do not want to
hear a recital of the list of our archons, from Solon downward; you would
have had some trouble learning it' / *Hippias:* 'Why? I can recite fifty names
after hearing them once.' / *Socrates:* 'I am sorry, I quite forgot about your
mnemonic art' " (*Dissemination,* 106-7).

Plato is attacking, Derrida comments, "not simply recourse to memory
but, within such recourse, the substitution of the mnemonic device for
live memory, of the prosthesis for the organ; the perversion that consists
of replacing a limb by a thing." The sophist sells only "the signs and insig-
nia of science: not memory itself (*mneme*), only monuments (*hypo-
mnemata*), inventories, archives, citations, copies, accounts, tales, lists,
notes, duplicates, chronicles, genealogies, references. Not memory but
memorials." Thus, "insofar as writing *lends a hand* to hypomnesia and not
to live memeory, it, too, is foreign to true science, to anamnesia in its
properly psychic motion, to truth in the process of (its) presentation, to

dialectics. Writing can only *mime* them." The "putting in question of truth" under way today, Derrida adds (and of thought and speech), concerns the history of writing precisely in terms of this debate between sophistics and philosophy regarding what lies properly within, and what outside, memory: "The space of writing, space *as* writing, is opened up in the violent move- ment of this surrogation, in the difference between *mneme* and *hypomnesis.* The outside is already *within* the work of memory":

> We are today on the eve of Platonism. Which can also, naturally, be thought of as the morning after Hegelianism. At that specific point, the *philosophia,* the *episteme* are not "overturned," "rejected," "reined in," etc., in the name of something like writing; quite the contrary. But they are, according to a relation that philosophy would call *simulacrum,* according to a more subtle excess of truth, assumed and at the same time displaced into a completely differ- ent field, where one can still, but that's all, "mime absolute knowl- edge," to use an expression coined by Bataille, whose name will enable us here to dispense with a whole network of references. (*Dis- semination,* 107–8)

The importance of this point—especially the statement clarifying the relationship of (grammatological) writing (hereafter Writing, with a capital) to science or knowledge (that it can only "mime absolute knowledge")— cannot be exaggerated for a comprehension of applied grammatology. For, as Derrida emphasizes, "the opposition between *mneme* and *hypom- nesis* would thus preside over the meaning of writing" (*Dissemination,* 111). "Plato's Pharmacy" could just as well have been entitled "Plato's Mnemonics," keeping in mind that "even though hypomnesia is not in itself memory, it affects memory and hypnotizes it in its very inside. That is the effect of this *pharmakon*" (110). It is worthwhile, then, to review some of the features of the history of artificial memory before discussing the function of mnemonics in grammatology.

PLACE

The recourse to writing as mnemonics in grammatology, as noted above, is an aspect of Derrida's non-Hegelian program. Hegel, that is, argues that to understand a word there is no need either for an intuition or for an image of the referent. We think with words rather than images, he maintains:

> The Ancients' mnemonics, revived a while ago and justly forgotten again, consists of transforming names into images and of degrad- ing thus memory into imagination. The place of memory's force is occupied by a permanent tableau, fixed in the imagination, a tab- leau of a series of images to which is attached an exposition to learn

by heart, a sequence of representations. Because of the heterogeneity of the content of these representations and their permanent images,
and due to the rapidity with which these need to be produced, the
sequence can take place only through tasteless, simple, and perfectly
contingent associations. (*Marges,* 110-11)

Derrida's experimentation with the rebus technique applied to the
proper name and to concepts as names of categories (identification as
descriptions of properties of attributes) engages the problematic of the
function of images in thought precisely at the point at which it inter-
sects with the place of mnemonics in the history of writing. The relation
of the signature as a principle of concept formation to mnemonics may be
seen in this example from Alfred Métraux, presented in *Of Grammatology:*

> "The expression of proper names hardly raises problems when it is
> a question of concrete things, but it puts the imagination of the
> scribe to a hard test if he has to render abstract ideas through pic-
> tography. To transcribe the name of a person called 'highway,'
> an Oglala Indian had recourse to the following symbolic combina-
> tion: strokes parallel to footprints make us think of 'road,' a bird
> painted close to it evokes the rapidity which is evidently one of
> the attributes of 'good routes.' It is clear that *only those who already
> know the names corresponding to these symbols can decipher them.
> On that count, these designs will have a mnemotechnique value.*"
> (334, my emphasis)

The reversal of phoneticization—the reduction of the phonetic in favor of
the ideographic element in writing—which is the goal of grammatology,
takes as its model the principle of rebus writing, both as it appears in the
historical analysis of nonphonetic scripts and (as we shall see) as it is
theorized in psychoanalysis. The problem posed in this regard to applied
grammatology is similar to the one faced by the Oglala Indian in the example cited by Derrida—the development of a mimetics capable of dealing
with the abstractions of knowledge. The history of writing as mnemotechnique offers a solution to this problem.

The only full account of the technique is that given in the *Rhetorica ad
Herennium,* a textbook compiled in Rome (86–82 B.C.—long thought to be
the work of Cicero, though now attributed to the otherwise unknown Corni-
ficius and dedicated to one Herennius),[1] and which was enormously influential throughout the Medieval and Renaissance periods. It contains
what became the stock definition of artificial memory, a procedure for
relating places to images:

> A *locus* is a place easily grasped by the memory, such as a house, an
> inter-columnar space, a corner, an arch, or the like. Images are forms,
> marks or simulacra of what we wish to remember. . . . The art of

memory is like an inner writing. Those who know the letters of the
alphabet can write down what is dictated to them and read out
what they have written. Likewise those who have learned mnemonics
can set in places what they have heard and deliver it from memory.
"For the places are very much like wax tablets or papyrus, the images
like the letters, the arrangement and disposition of the images like
the script, and the delivery is like the reading" [which explains what
Plato meant when he compared painting and writing]. . . . It is essential that the places should form a series and must be remembered
in their order, so that we can start from any *locus* in the series and
move either backwards or forwards from it. . . . The same set of *loci*
can be used again and again for remembering different material. The
images which we have placed on them for remembering one set of
things fade and are effaced when we make no further use of them.[2]

The rules for the images to be set in the places are equally explicit and
detailed, including instructions for both images of things and images of
words. One of the most controversial aspects of the *Ad Herennium* was its
recommendation of the use of "active images" (*imagines agentes*)—striking
images that would make a greater impression on the mind and, hence, last
longer than images formed from banal or trivial things. The effective memory image ought to be disfigured (stained with blood or soiled with mud)
or comic, grotesque, or ridiculous in order to be easily remembered.
Quintillian rejected this advice, as did Plato, we may suppose (keeping in
mind that the mnemonic technique described in the *Ad Herennium* was
known to the sophists with whom Socrates debated). Plato's contempt for
a memory filled with such grotesques is evident in his famous allegory of
the cave (the mind as grotto)—"See also, then, men carrying past the wall
implements of all kinds that rise above the wall, and human images and
shapes of animals as well, wrought in stone and wood and every material,
some of these bearers presumably speaking and others silent"—in which
the contrast between watching the shadows of images in a cave and looking
on nature in the light of day may be understood as another version of the
contrast between artificial and natural memories.[3]

A number of other aspects of mnemonics should be kept in mind as
well. The activation of the memory, for example, was ach-ved by an
imaginary walk through the places with one image located a each site,
spaced at regular intervals along the way. The setting for the places was to be
one familiar to the individual so that the associations (the emotional investment) with the setting (as with the "active images") could serve to
bind the images in place. In short, *one used one's autobiography to think
and write with*—a major point for understanding the status of autobiographical material in Writing—as in the case of the modern mnemonist
described by A. R. Luria:

He would "distribute" [his images] along some roadway or street he visualized in his mind. Sometimes this was a street in his home town, which would also include the yard attached to the house he had lived in as a child and which he recalled vividly. On the other hand, he might also select a street in Moscow. Frequently he would take a mental walk along that street—Gorky Street in Moscow— beginning at Mayakovsky Square, and slowly make his way down, "distributing" his images at houses, gates, and store windows. At times, without realizing how it had happened, he would suddenly find himself back in his home town (Torzhok), where he would wind up his trip in the house he had lived in as a child. The setting he chose for his "mental walks" approximates that of dreams.[4]

The places could include not only landscapes, but familiar people—a group of one's friends lined up in a row—or figures, such as the allegorical figure representing Grammar: "Romberch teaches that we are to remember Grammar with an image—the ugly old woman Grammatica—and her stimulating-to-memory form. We visualize the arguments about her parts through subsidiary images, inscriptions and the like" (Yates, 234). The technique of using the allegorical image of one of the liberal arts as a *locus* was recommended as a means for learning each particular science. The procedure required the combining of memory of things with memory of words, the latter being accomplished by means of an imaginary alphabet, a kind of phoneticized hieroglyphic system made up of birds, tools, and so forth, which images were placed on the figure.

The images for a word or term were generated by techniques similar to those Derrida uses for his rebus or cartouche writing—antonomasia, puns, paragrams. The example given in the *Ad Herennium* involves a line of verse: " '*Iam domum itionem reges Atridae parant*' (And now their home-coming the kings, the sons of Atreus, are making ready)." As one commentator explains, "The images of *Domitius* and *Marcii Reges* (famous Roman family names) represent respectively *domum itionem* and *reges,* while the actors (of popular fame) represent the *Atridae* whose roles they are about to play, and the fact of their being attired the verb *parant.*"[5] "Active images" are used, but the words are recalled in this case (or rather, the images are generated) by the homophonic resemblance of the terms suggested by the scene to the words of the verse.

Memory for words was a more difficult, awkward practice, yet, as Yates notes, combined with memory for things, it served as a hidden generator of much imagery in Medieval and Renaissance works that otherwise (to those unaware of their mnemonic function) seems completely esoteric, secretive. Thinking of the unusual, even surrealistic text that such a procedure might generate, Yates remarks, "What scope for the imagination would be offered in memorizing Boetheius's *Consolation of Philosophy,*

as advised in a fifteenth-century manuscript," whose memorization by
word hieroglyphics would produce the Lady Philosophy coming to life
and wandering, an animated Prudence, through the palaces of memory. An
idea of what such a production might be like may be found in the way
Luria's mnemonist memorized the opening stanzas of *The Divine Comedy*,
the first line of which—*"Nel mezzo del cammin di nostra vita"*—for example, he fixed in this tableau:

> (*Nel*)—I was paying my membership dues when there, in the corridor,
> I caught sight of the ballerina Nel'skaya. (*mezzo*)—I myself am a
> violinist; what I do is to set up an image of a man, together with [Rus-
> sian: *vmeste*] Nel'skaya, who is playing the violin. (*del*)—There's a
> pack of Deli Cigarettes near them. (*cammin*)—I set up an image of a
> fireplace [*kamin*] close by. (*di*)—Then I see a hand pointing toward
> a door [*dver*]. (*nostra*—I see a nose [*nos*]; a man has tripped and, in
> falling, gotten his nose pinched in a doorway (*tra*). (*vita*)—He lifts his
> leg over the threshold, for a child is lying there, that is, a sign of
> life—vitalism. (Luria, 45–46)

The mnemonist's scene displaying the ballerina Nel'skaya, generated as
an image of Dante's verse (the translation into images continues for several
stanzas), provides an emblem of the double band, the new mimesis, so important to grammatology. It demonstrates a writing that functions as an
exact repetition without resemblance; or rather, the resemblance, which
we have already seen at work in other contexts, exists at the level of
words or signifiers only, homophonically, and not at the level of the signifieds or semantic referents. Such is precisely the principle of artificial
memory which Derrida identifies and explores in his theoretical operations.
In the *anamnesic* movement of truth, Derrida notes, truth unveils "that
which can be imitated, reproduced, repeated in its identity"—"it is not the
repeater in the repetition, nor the signifier in the signification. The true
is the presence of the *eidos* signified" (*Dissemination,* 111). Sophistics,
however, "keeps to the other side of repetition":

> What is repeated is the repeater, the imitator, the signifier, the
> representative, in the absence, as it happens, *of the thing itself,* which
> these appear to reedit, and without psychic or mnesic animation,
> without the living tension of dialectics. Writing would indeed be the
> signifier's capacity to repeat itself by itself, mechanically, without
> a living soul to sustain or attend it in its repetition, that is to say, with-
> out truth's *presenting itself* anywhere. Sophistics, hypomnesia,
> and writing would thus only be separated from philosophy, dialectics,
> anamnesis, and living speech by the invisible, almost nonexistent,
> thickness of that *leaf* between signifier and signified. (*Dissemination,*
> 111–12)

Nel'skaya's name recommends her to the mnemonist, then, and not her person, although we may suppose that as an "active image" she carries a certain emotional charge, and thus functions as a kind of Beatrice in her own right, if in an entirely oblique way, showing how an autobiography produces for mnemonics private yet objective terms.

The significance of Plato's comparison of writing to painting emerges out of this demonstration—painting a portrait of an animate model, and writing as a painting of a living word, according to the Greek model of phonetic writing (a model condemning these inscriptions as simulacra three and even four times removed from the truth):

> He who writes with the alphabet no longer even imitates. No doubt because he also, in a sense, imitates perfectly. He has a better chance of reproducing his voice, because the phonetic writing decomposes it and transforms it into abstract, spatial elements. This *de-composition* of the voice is here both what best conserves it and what best cor-rupts it. . . . And no dialectic can encompass this self-inadequation. A perfect imitation is no longer an imitation. If one eliminates the tiny difference that, in separating the imitator from the imitated, by that very fact refers to it, one would render the imitator absolutely different: the imitator would become another being no longer referring to the imitated. (*Dissemination*, 138–39)[6]

Grammatology removes the negative sign from this manner in which the alphabet imitates ("it is good only insofar as it is bad") and applies its ambivalence as a principle of a new practice, as the model of a new mimesis in the service of an experimental pedagogy whose mode is hypomnesic—nonknowledge as rememoration, "a repetition of death and oblivion (*lethe*) which veils and skews because it does not present the *eidos* but re-presents a presentation, repeats a repetition" (135).

The question of mnemonics, in short, rehearses in terms of mimesis the issues of spatialization (topics as places) and decomposition discussed in the previous chapter. Again, psychoanalysis is the supporting discourse, since hypomnesis provides the notion of memory needed to comprehend the function of the unconscious in knowing.

THE MYSTIC PAD

Ancient "Memoria" techniques—images for things and images for words—exemplify the question of special importance in Derrida's new mimesis, the ultimate goal of which is to develop a double-valued Writing, balancing ideographic with phonetic elements. The chief question posed by this project concerns the nature of the ideographic elements (images, pictures, models, metaphors) and the relation between the images and the discursive component of the text. The aspect of mimetic theory most relevant to this problem, as stated in "Plato's Pharmacy," is the fact that "just as painting and writing have faithfulness to the model as their model, the resemblance between painting and writing is precisely *resemblance itself:* both operations must aim above all at resembling" (*Dissemination,* 137). That aspect of mimesis relevant to mnemonics, that is, has to do with the translation process linking verbal and pictorial texts, a process governed by the rebus principle.

The mnemonist's technique, however, because based on a conscious system, is too simple to provide, by itself, the rationale for word-thing relations in grammatology. A more complex notion of memory, and hence a more sophisticated translation procedure, is needed to accommodate psychoanalytic originary remembering, in which the past may *not* be read

> as an *other,* a modified present, a past present, the past of what once
> at least was present, upon some other surface one might once have
> seen arising before one, and which one might still be able to see if
> one were to make the rounds of the theater or of one's memory,
> of the theater of memory (one should read within the layers of *Num-*
> *bers* the sedimentation of all sorts of arts of memory . . . from the
> *Ad Herennium* to the *Ars memoriae* by Robert Fludd, including the
> projects of Giulio Camillo, Giordano Bruno, etc.). (*Dissemination,*
> 308).[7]

Psychoanalytic mnemonics offers a theory capable of dealing with that most extreme form of forgetfulness—repression. The connection between mnemonics and dream writing is suggested by the resemblance of at least one of Freud's models of the mind to the wax tablet of the ancient artificial memory. The model is the "Wunderblock," or "Mystic Writing-Pad," discussed in "Freud and the Scene of Writing." While working out the set of conditions which memory should meet in order to account for his theory of the Unconscious, Freud was casting about for a mechanism that might serve as a model for the psychic apparatus. He first considered optical devices, then hit upon the scriptural metaphor. But none of the conventional means of writing were able to satisfy his conditions until the "Wunderblock" came to his attention:

> A double system contained in a single differentiated apparatus: a
> perpetually available innocence and an infinite reserve of traces have
> at last been reconciled by the "small contrivance" placed "some
> time ago upon the market under the name of the Mystic Writing-Pad,"
> and which "promises to perform more than the sheet of paper or
> the slate." Its appearance is modest, "but if it is examined more close-
> ly, it will be found that its construction shows a remarkable agree-
> ment with my hypothetical structure of our perceptual apparatus."
> It offers both advantages: "an ever-ready receptive surface and

permanent traces of the inscriptions that have been made on it."
(*Writing*, 223)

Freud's elaboration of two systems of metaphors—memory as text or
script and as apparatus or machine, which join finally in the Mystic Pad—
for his theory of memory lends itself admirably to grammatology's search
for a new practice. Freud himself begins his analogy with the hypomnemic
aspect of writing by noting its capacity for preserving traces upon a surface, "the pocketbook or sheet of paper, as a materialized portion of my
mnemic apparatus, the rest of which I carry about with me invisible. I have
only to bear in mind the place where this 'memory' has been deposited
and I can then 'reproduce' it at any time I like" (*Writing*, 222). He further
notes that "auxiliary" apparatuses are usually constituted on the model of
the organ to be supplemented (spectacles, ear trumpets), but in this regard
conventional writing surfaces (paper, slate) do not provide the double system within one apparatus required by the theory of memory—a difficulty
overcome by the Mystic Pad. What the Pad allows to be thought is a writing
surface that preserves *and* erases—that preserves the trace it erases—which
is exactly the way Derrida himself would like to write. The Pad, that is,
already suggests not only the paleonomic strategy of deconstruction but
also a Writing that "takes into account the un-representable" (*Dissemination*, 291), which is capable of miming the duality of form and force
(Destiny, *Moira*, enframing), of presence and what exceeds it:

> To surpass metaphysics, a certain trace must be imprinted in the
> metaphysical text, yet one which points toward a wholly different
> text—not toward another presence or another form of presence.
> . . . The way such a trace is inscribed in the metaphysical text is so
> inconceivable that it can only be described as an effacing of the
> trace itself. The trace comes to be by its own effacement. The trace
> erases itself. The trace is neither perceptible nor imperceptible. [8]

Thus, Freud's theory, including its notion of the Unconscious, suggests a
way of taking into account that which Western thought insistently forgets:
"It is in this way that the difference between Being and beings—that which
has been 'forgotten' in determining Being as presence and presence as the
present—is so deeply concealed that no trace of its remains" (*"Ousia,"* 92).
Enframing (the name of this forgotten difference) involves always the
question of apparatus, of technics and technology, an aspect of the question to which Freud's discussion of psychic apparatus makes an important
contribution.

By lifting the covering-sheet (the wax paper and its celluloid cover) off
the wax slab, the writing vanishes. The surface is clear, but the traces remain in the slab beneath. "Writing supplements perception before perception even appears to itself [is conscious of itself]. 'Memory' or writing is

the opening of that process of appearance itself. The 'perceived may be read only in the past, beneath perception and after it' " (*Writing,* 224). The wax slab is the Unconscious, and the covering sheets represent the "Perception-Consciousness" system. The notion of the "memory trace" as a "path-breaking" or "breaching" on the wax slab of the Unconscious, Derrida remarks, calls for the notion of an originary memory, a conception beyond the capacity of logocentrism. "This impression has left behind a laborious trace which has never been *perceived,* whose meaning has never been lived in the present, i.e. has never been lived consciously. The post-script which constitutes the past present as such is not satisfied, as Plato, Hegel, and Proust perhaps thought, with reawakening or revealing the present past in its truth. It produces the present past" (214), the classic example being the Wolf Man, whose trauma in relation to the primal scene occurs after the event, is delayed and deferred, and is finally a fantasy projected onto the screen of the past.

A feature of Freud's model that helps account for the nonpresence of the trace is the protective celluloid sheet. "Without it the fine waxed paper would be scratched or ripped. There is no writing which does not devise some means of protection, *to protect against itself,* against the writing by which the 'subject' is himself threatened as he lets himself be written: *as he exposes himself*" (*Writing,* 224). Writing is a tool whose *maintenance* (the *"maintenant"*—now—of presence) requires two hands (like the Mystic Pad)—"as well as a system of gestures, a coordination of independent initiatives, an organized multiplicity of origins"; the origin being divided, a double band is needed for registration. "The condition for writing is that there be neither a permanent contact nor an absolute break between strata: the vigilance and failure of censorship. It is no accident that the metaphor of censorship should come from the area of politics concerned with the deletions, blanks, and disguises of writing" (226).

The subject of this writing, then, is not a "master," but is constituted by "a *system* of relations between strata." Thus, the simple communications model of sender-channel-receiver is inadequate for comprehending writing, let alone Writing, for in it, "at the very moment he [the writer] thinks he is directing the operations, his place—the opening toward the present assumed by whoever believes himself capable of saying *I*, I think, I am, I see, I feel, I say (you, for example, here and now)—is constantly and in spite of him being decided by a throw of dice whose law will subsequently be developed inexorably by chance" (*Dissemination,* 298). No wonder, then, that Derrida declares that his texts "could not be of *interest* except if, beyond all ruses and calculations, one is assured that after a certain point I do not know what I am doing, I no longer see that which watches me" ("Crochets," 109). The writer comprehended by the apparatus is put on stage—"the *sociality* of writing as *drama* requires an entirely different discipline" (*Writing,* 227), one that takes into account the "scene of writing" enframing all presentation (the grammatological project).

The dream, as Freud described it, provides a model with which to think through the problems associated with Derrida's double-valued Writing. Displaying a "contra-band" of its own, the dream consists of two tracks: "The dream-thoughts and the dream-content (the latent and the manifest) are presented to us like two versions (*mise en scène*) of the same subject matter in two different languages. Or, more properly, the dream-content seems like a transcript of the dream-thoughts into another mode of expression, whose characters and syntactic laws it is our business to discover by comparing the original and the translation" (*Writing,* 218). Psychoanalysis, in short, is another phase in the history of decipherment, with Freud as the successor to Champollion.

Dream writing, of course, is understood as a kind of hieroglyphics: "*Bilderschrift:* not an inscribed image but a figurative script, an image inviting not a simple, conscious, present perception of the thing itself—assuming it exists—but a reading. 'If we attempted to read these characters according to their symbolic relation, we should clearly be led into error. . . . A dream is a picture puzzle' " (*Writing,* 218). The reversal of phoneticization, which is the fundamental principle of grammatology as Writing, is already available in dreamwork, as theorized in psychoanalysis. Moreover, as Derrida adds, dream writing does not eliminate but subordinates speech: "Far from disappearing, speech then changes purpose and status. It is situated, surrounded, invested (in all senses of the word), constituted. It figures in dreams much as captions do in comic strips, those picto-hieroglyphic combinations in which the phonetic text is secondary and not central in the telling of the tale" (218).

Nor may this pictographic script ever be fully translated into the verbal discourse of the dream-thoughts (which shows one of the main differences between Freud's dream memory and the mnemonic images; or rather, the extraordinary *surplus,* the overdetermination, of the imagery, itself begins to signify in psychoanalysis). There is, however, permeability or continual contamination between the levels of words and images (things): "It must be seen that insofar as they are attracted, lured into the dream, toward the fictive limit of the primary process, words tend to become things pure and simple. . . . But this formal regression could not even succeed, moreover, if words had not always been subject in their materiality to the mark of their inscription or scenic capacity" (*Writing,* 219). Thus, the essential spacing—the ideographic element never fully reduced by phoneticization—upon which the dreamwork "and any formal regression in general can begin to operate" is inherent in the phonic chain and in words from the beginning. It is just this inherent capacity for *mise en scène* or *Darstellbarkeit* that grammatology, following Freud's theory, begins to exploit as

a mode of writing (Derrida's systematic experimentation with agglutina-
tion and deglutination, for example, may be seen to have its point of departure, or at least its rationale, in Freud's observation, regarding the
representational element of spacing, that "if a gap is left between the 'a'
and the 'b' it means that the 'a' is the letter of one word and the 'b' is
the first of the next one"—220).

There is, then, no direct translation available between the verbal and
the rebus scripts in psychoanalytic mnemonics. Against Husserl (and the
phenomenological tradition), who assumes or takes as given the necessary
upsurge of an idea in an individual consciousness, Derrida poses the
Freudian psychical writing, which "cannot be read in terms of any code.
It works, no doubt, with a mass of elements which have been codified in
the course of an individual or collective history. But in its operations,
lexicon, and syntax a purely idiomatic residue is irreducible and is made to
bear the burden of interpretation in the communication between uncon-
sciousnesses. The dreamer invents his own grammar" (*Writing*, 209). There
is no code book available with which to read such a construction; it cannot
be approached in terms of content or signifieds or idealities of meanings,
but only in terms of its materiality, attending to "relations, locations, processes, and differences." As Freud says, "The same piece of content may
conceal a different meaning when it occurs in various people or various
contexts" (*Writing*, 209). Unconscious experience produces its own signifiers in that it produces the significance (status-as-meaningful) of *borrowed*
material (just as thought, in Freud's early, "electrical" model of the mind,
could only retrace facilitations already breached by the drives). The psychic
process, in this respect—the remotivation of residues—resembles the
mnemotechnique.

This operation of psychic writing creates a special condition for the
coming into consciousness of the traces, for the unconscious text "is already a weave of pure traces, differences in which meaning and force are
united—a text nowhere present, consisting of archives which are always
already transcriptions. Originary prints" (*Writing*, 211). The "translation"
into consciousness (into discourse) "is not a transcription, because there is
no text *present elsewhere* as an unconscious one to be transposed or transported. There is no unconscious truth to be rediscovered by virtue of having
been written elsewhere." The translation is "originary," that is, following
the principle of "supplementarity," which characterizes writing's relationship to Western thought—"that which seems to be added as a plenitude to
a plenitude, is equally that which compensates for a lack" (212). Keeping
in mind Husserl's identification of translation with tradition—tradition as
a pure "aether" permitting unrestricted translation of science across the
generations—the consequences for pedagogy of the psychoanalytic model
of translation (adopted by grammatology) are obvious. Psychical writing

"is not a displacement of meanings within the limpidity of an immobile, pregiven space and the blank neutrality of discourse. A discourse which might be coded without ceasing to be diaphonous. Here energy cannot be reduced; it does not limit meaning, but rather *produces it*" (213, my emphasis). This force of production is generated "through the power of 'repetition' alone, which inhabits it originarily as its death [the removal of cathexis is the death of meaning]. This power, that is, this lack of power, which opens and limits the labor of force, institutes translatability, makes possible what we call 'language,' transforms an absolute idiom into a limit which is always already transgressed: a pure idiom is not language; it becomes so only through repetition" (213). For a sign to be a sign, in other words, it must be repeatable, must already be a repetition (hence the mystery of the origin, the paradox of the first sign). Retracing the historical and structural nature of this mystery, grammatology sets up writing's secondarity as the logic of the simulacrum, of the originary ersatz.

ANASEMIA

Part of the interest of Freud's theory of memory for grammatology is his very use of a model (the model as prosthesis for the mind)[9]—both that he uses a model and the specific nature of the model (the Mystic Writing-Pad, like the bobbin of the *fort-da* scene, is a toy). An important aspect of Derrida's new mimesis (repetition as originary translation) will concern the status of models (and of all exemplary material, citations, illustrations) in critical and pedagogical discourse, including especially a formulation of the relation between such discourse and that which it is "about," that which it "represents." The functioning of the analogy of the memory to a toy slate, in other words, opens up the entire problematic of how any knowledge achieves presence: "I continually ask what *must* be done or not be done (for example in reading, writing, teaching, and so on) to find out what the place of that which takes place, is constructed upon (for example the university, the boundaries between departments, between one discourse and another)."[10]

The basic operation in the discourses of knowledge is the metaphor, understood in the broadest sense of the term (referring to the philosophemes of logocentrism and to the metaphorology with which Derrida deconstructs them). In Derrida's new mimesis, the metaphor undergoes a certain transformation itself. Derrida comments, for example, that Freud himself is not using his model in the conventional way:

Freud, no doubt, is not manipulating metaphors, if to manipulate a metaphor means to make of the known an allusion to the unknown.

On the contrary, through the insistence of his metaphoric investment he makes what we believe we know under the name of writing
enigmatic. A movement unknown to classical philosophy is perhaps undertaken here, somewhere between the implicit and the explicit. From Plato and Aristotle on, Scriptural images have regularly
been used to *illustrate* the relationship between reason and experience, perception and memory. But a certain confidence has never
stopped taking its assurance from the meaning of the well-known
and familiar term: writing. The gesture sketched out by Freud interrupts that assurance and opens up a new kind of question about
the metaphor, writing, and spacing in general. (*Writing,* 199)

It is not a question of whether the Mystic Pad is a good metaphor for
representing the work of the psyche, Derrida adds, "but rather what
apparatus we must create in order to represent psychical writing." The
question is not whether the psyche is indeed a kind of text, but "what is a
text, and what must the psyche be if it can be represented by a text"
(*Writing,* 199). The supposedly familiar basis for the comparison thus itself comes into question:

Since consciousness for Freud is a surface exposed to the external
world, it is here that instead of reading through the metaphor in the
usual sense, we must, on the contrary, understand the possibility
of a writing advanced as conscious and as acting in the world (the
visible exterior of the graphism, of the literal, of the literal becoming
literary, etc.) in terms of the labor of the writing which circulated
like psychical energy between the unconscious and the conscious. The
"objectivist" or "worldly" consideration of writing teaches us nothing
if reference is not made to a space of psychical writing. (212)

The vehicle of the conventional metaphor—writing, in this case—is prob-
lematized, becomes as much part of the unknown as the tenor—the psyche.
In fact, there is a reversal of the side from which the representation functions in Freud's analogy—the unknown now problematizes the known,
rather than being appropriated through similitude into the familiar.

Derrida's analysis of the metaphorics in philosophical writing points out
that this reversibility or defamiliarization (akin to Max Black's "interaction") is a potential inherent in the structure of metaphor, a potential
that Derrida intends to radicalize. There are a number of descriptions of
this event in Derrida's essays—for example, this account of the "catastrophic" or "catastropic" metaphor in Heidegger's move to think the
"withdrawal of being" (which "bears on being which is nothing and which
one must think according to ontological difference") as a "withdrawal of
metaphor" ("It bears on language in general")—the effect of which, as
Derrida comments, is to produce a phrasing no longer either proper or
figurative: "Its end would be to state something new, something still un-

heard of about the vehicle and not about the apparent subject of the trope. *Withdrawal-of-Being-or-of-metaphor* would be by way less of leading us to think Being or metaphor than the Being or the metaphor *of withdrawal*, by way of leading us to think about the way and the vehicle, or their fraying" ("Retrait," 23).

Continuing the Heidegger example, demonstrating that there is no "metalanguage," but always another metaphor, Derrida notes what happens when Heidegger defines language as the "House of Being":

> "House of Being" would not operate, in this context, in the manner of a metaphor in the current, usual, that is to say, literal meaning (*sens*) of metaphor, if there is one. This current and cursive meaning —I understand it also in the sense of direction [*sens*]—would transport a familiar predicate (and here nothing is more familiar, familial, known, domestic and economic than the house) towards a less familiar, more remote, *unheimlich* (uncanny) subject, which it would be a question of better appropriating for oneself, becoming familiar with, and which one would thus designate by the indirect detour of what is nearest—the house. Now what happens here *with* the quasi-metaphor of the house of Being, and what does *without* metaphor in its cursive direction, is that it is Being which, from the very moment of its withdrawal, would let or promise to let the house or the habitat be thought. ("Retrait," 24)

The effect is not just that "Being says more about the house than the house about Being"—a simple reversal of the figurative-proper relation— but that the very notion of the proper and familiar is put in question. Nonetheless, as the first step in his two-step deconstructive procedure, Derrida does state that "one must proceed to undertake a general reversal of all metaphorical directions" (*Dissemination*, 81).[11]

The implication of this problematization of the "vehicle" of metaphor (recalling Bachelard's "surrationalism") for Derrida's practice, already noted in his decision to focus on the philosophemes, is to work at the level of the literal (the letter), thus undoing the speculative sublation at the same time that he "unearths" new dimensions of the familiar. Part of his procedure, therefore, is to render explicit the resources available in language, to perform language by letting himself "get carried away" by it, as in the opening of his essay on metaphor, in which he displays the vehicular philosopheme in the concept of metaphor: "*Metaphora* ["*metaphorickos* still designating today, in what one calls 'modern' Greek, that which concerns means of transportation"] circulates in the city, it conveys us like its inhabitants, along all sorts of passages, with intersections, red lights, one-way streets, crossroads or crossings, patrolled zones and speed limits. We are in a certain way—metaphorically of course, and as concerns the mode of habitation—the content and the tenor of this vehicle: passengers, comprehended and displaced by metaphor" ("Retrait," 6). It is clear, then, why Derrida noted that the notion of the "memory trace" in Freud suggested the need for a combined study, "genetically and structurally, of the history of the road and the history of writing" (*Writing*, 214).

Psychoanalysis does, in fact, provide a theoretical strategy enabling Derrida to use the uncontrollable "skid" of this "autobus" as a methodological principle. The theoretical source in this case is the discussion of "anasemia" in the work of Nicolas Abraham and Maria Torok. Anasemia [a problematizing of the meaning of signs—"ana" indicates upward, according to, back, backward, reversed, again][12] is Abraham's term used to describe the vocabulary and concepts developed especially in psychoanalysis in order to cope with the "pathologies" encountered in its practice—as for example in the case of the Wolf Man. A comparison of the Wolf Man with his countryman, Luria's mnemonist, indicates at once the difference between what might be called "classical" versus the "baroque" versions of mnemonics. In both instances it is a question of the "word-thing," a hieroglyphia, a relationship between visual and verbal materials whose composition is governed by homophones.

Moreover, although since its operation is unconscious it may seem to be a case of forgetting, incorporation (as diagnosed in Abraham and Torok's study of the Wolf Man) is in fact a perverse remembering, a refusal to forget or to mourn and give up the "love object." Incorporation (and herein lies its special interest for Derrida) is "antimetaphoric" in its effect, in that the "cryptophoric" subject "reverses" all metaphors, destroys all figures, and treats language only "to the letter," literally.[13] The cryptophor, in other words, inhibits language (as opposed to the process of introjection, which makes metaphor and hence language possible). Normal psychoanalytic techniques are useless in such cases (the Wolf Man never was "cured"), since the symptomatic words, linked to memories of high libidinal value (the shared secret of a desire *fulfilled*), cannot be uttered, are locked away in a crypt:

> He knew how to make from representations afferent to the story so
> well illustrated by his sister [the scene of the father's seduction]
> a crypt within the self. He conserved there, with care, the words of
> a story, truly magical words, because serving at once for denouncing and enjoying. In this way he had them always at his command. To
> have recourse to them it sufficed to take them, in all innocence, in
> a different sense, and to construe—thanks to astute homonymies—a
> completely different scene, not recalling in the least the encrypted
> scene. . . . One of these words would have been the Russian verb *teret*,
> used initially in the sense "to rub" (implied: the penis) and recovered
> for the needs of the case, in a different sense, that of "to wax" [wax—
> the stuff of memory], "to polish." Thus in the new scene, translated

from the old: the penis rubber became the floor waxer. Fetish-image, drawn from a fetish-word in a forgotten sense. (*Ecorce*, 300–301)

The fetish scene of the maid Grusha on her knees scrubbing the floor, then, functioned in the Wolf Man's mnemonics in a way similar to the image of Nel'skaya in the corridor in the mnemonist's hieroglyphia, except that incorporation in the former added a secret third level or crypt controlling the translation between the scene and its discourse.

The word-thing, in the psychoanalytic model, "returns" from the crypt into consciousness by either of two routes—as an image fixed in a symptom or tableau, or as a cryptogram in the strict sense (words activated as puns). The process of the return is ruled by the remotivation of an arbitrary sign, the new motivation deriving from a conjectured memory from the patient's childhood. The decipherment of a cryptophor must address both registers of material (which are themselves indirectly related)—both the principal dream of (silent) rebus scenes (tableaux: the phobogenic dream of the wolves perched in the tree, the erogenic scene of the maid polishing the floor) and the cryptonymy of verbal material:

> It is as though the cryptonymic translation, playing with the allosemes and their synonyms (always more numerous in their open series than is indicated by a dictionary), swerves off at an angle in order to throw the reader off the track and make its itinerary unreadable. . . . It is because of the angular, zigzagging procedure of this cryptonymy, and especially because the allosemic pathways in this strange relay race *pass through non-semantic associations, purely phonetic contaminations,* it is because these associations in themselves constitute words or parts of words which act like visible and/or audible bodies or things, that the authors of the *Verbarium* are hesitant to speak of metonymic displacement here, or even to trust themselves to a catalogue of rhetorical figures. ("Fors," 108, my emphasis)

To decipher the Wolf Man's cryptography, Abraham and Torok had to "invent their own language," even their own genre, a theoretical fiction combining "mathematical rigor" with "fantasy"—thus providing a model for Writing: "The hieroglyphic model at work *everywhere* (it is often evoked in the *Verbarium*) is more and other than an analogical model. It implies, on the one hand, that the ultimate object still remains, even as a 'proper' name or body, a text *to be deciphered* [alluding to Abraham's point that there is no "thing-in-itself," that the phenomenal is itself a symbol, whose conversion into a metaphor is the task of psychoanalysis—*Ecorce*, 394], but it also implies that writing is not essentially verbal or phonetic" ("Fors," 88–89).

Derrida summarizes the anasemic method with three terms representing three elements of anasemia as a discourse: 1. *Narrative:* The anasemic structure describes a story or a fable—narrative or quasi-autobiographical in form—within the concept undergoing anasemic transformation. "The story is described as a path followed backwards by the structure in order to reach all the way back beyond the origin which is nonetheless not in any way a proper, literal meaning." Rather, the origin of (anasemic) sense is non-sense (*Ecorce*, 328). The concept is re-cited in the course of the narrated journey by means of which the text is generated. 2. *Angle:* Anasemia creates an angle within the word itself. The old word is preserved (recalling Derrida's own paleonymy) even while being submitted to a conversion. "A change of direction abruptly interrupts the continuity of the process of becoming explicit and imposes upon it an anasemic angulation." 3. *Sepulcher:* The entire theoretical space is redistributed owing to the possibility of the "loss" or "death" of the subject (the burying of the traumatic un-event in the sepulcher of the Unconscious). "To track down the path to the tomb, then to violate a sepulcher: that is what the analysis of a cryptic incorporation is like" ("Fors," 96-97).[14]

Anasemia constitutes a method for a mode of knowledge (psychoanalysis) whose object of study (the Unconscious) *never appears* (in its own right)—whose nature is to be nonpresent and unpresentable. If the logocentric tradition is founded on the concept of self-presence (identity), then psychoanalysis, as Abraham says, "stakes out its domain precisely on the unthought ground of phenomenology" (the most advanced philosophical system of logocentrism). Psychoanalysis begins with the recognition of the hiatus, the distance that separates the reflecting subject from himself, the "I" from the "me,"—the nonpresence of the self to itself which is the very condition as well as the limit of reflexivity.[15] Because of this "transphenomenal" focus, psychoanalysis is of special relevance to the questions Derrida poses:

> Now how am I to speak of the *a* of differance? It is clear that it
> cannot be *exposed*. We can expose only what, at a certain moment,
> can become *present*, manifest; what can be shown, presented as a
> present, in truth of a present or the presence of a present. However,
> if differance is (I also cross out the "is") what makes the presen-
> tation of being-present possible, it never presents itself as such. It is
> never given in the present or to anyone. Holding back and not ex-
> posing itself, it goes beyond the order of truth on this specific point
> and in this determined way, yet is not itself concealed, as if it were
> something, a mysterious being, in the occult zone of a non-knowing.
> (*Speech,* 134)

Psychoanalysis and grammatology share the problematics of the unknown, then—the impossible project of presenting that which, "being the very condition of discourse, would by its very essence *escape* discourse"

("Fors," 93). Abraham describes how psychoanalysis is able to function
within these linguistically extreme circumstances:

> The language of psychoanalysis no longer follows the twists and
> turns (*tropoi*) of customary speech and writing. Pleasure, Id, Ego
> Economic, Dynamic, are not metaphors, metonymies, synec-
> doches, catachreses; they are, through the action of the discourse,
> products of de-signification and constitute new figures, absent
> from rhetorical treatises. These figures of antisemantics, inasmuch
> as they signify nothing more than going back to the source of
> their customary meaning, require a denomination properly indica-
> tive of their status and which—for want of something better—
> we propose to designate by the coined name of *anasemia.* ("Shell,"
> 20)

Derrida characterizes this "antisemantics," itself a theoretical parallel
to the antimetaphors of incorporation, as a kind of translation—from the
words in ordinary language (for example, writing), to the phenomenological term ("writing"), to Writing in psychoanalytic theory, which "exceeds
the order of the sense":

> A precedence which must be translated in the anasemic relation,
> that one which *goes back* to the source and goes past it, to the pre-
> originary and pre-semantic source. Anasemic translation does not
> deal in exchanges between significations, signifiers and signifieds, but
> between the realm of signification and that which, making it pos-
> sible, must still be translated into the language of that which it makes
> possible, must still be repeated, reinvested, reinterpreted there.[16]

In his introduction to Abraham's essay on anasemia, Derrida explains the
special nature of the figures involved in the translation of the unpresentable. The most prominent feature of the new figure is that, because it must
somehow remark the Unconscious (heterogeneous to consciousness), it
must break with the traditional proportionality of analogy and become
discontinuous, dissymmetrical.

The "shell-and-the-kernel," the example given to illustrate these figure-
less figures, is the very image Freud used to describe the structure of
psychoanalytic representation (the process by which fantasies and drives—
the recto and verso of the apparatus—mediate and bring into relation the
organic and the psychic). At a certain point in the comparison of the mind
to a kernel-and-shell, the analogy breaks off, is suspended (the angle), although the comparison process itself continues, nonmimetically. The
natural referent of the shell-kernel figure—the actual fruit and the laws of
natural space—is interrupted; the figure is retained, but a reversal begins,
such that the thing being explained (in this case, the Ego, with its dual
surfaces, one facing inward, one outward) becomes active, intervenes, forc-

ing a detour in the analogy. One is thus given to understand that the "shell" and the "kernel" in psychoanalysis no longer function like a fruit in nature because the psychoanalytic shell-and-kernel *can never appear:*

> A dissymmetry intervenes between the two spaces of this structure, between the surface of the shell and the depth of the kernel, which, at bottom, no longer belong to the same element, to the same space, and become incommensurable within the very relation they never cease to maintain. The kernel, by virtue of its structure, can never become a surface. "This other kernel" is not the fruit one which can appear to me, to me holding it in my hand, exhibiting it after having shelled it, etc. ("Me," 10)

We encounter here one of the chief reasons why, not just in Derrida but in poststructuralist and deconstructionist writing in general, there has been a resurgence of interest in allegory.[17] Paul de Man, who invokes Walter Benjamin's notion of allegory as a negation of all external reference, of identity, of all attempts to trace the genesis of a meaning to its origins in in an object, is a major example of a critic working with a theory of allegory. To note how allegory challenges the logic of metaphor (symbol), consider de Man's discussion of Marcel's meditation (in *A la recherche du temps perdu*) on Giotto's allegory of charity. De Man first notes a distinction, basic in rhetoric, between the literal and the proper sense of a metaphor. In the example "Achilles is a lion," the literal sense is the real African lion, the figurative sense is Achilles as the lion, and the proper sense is the courage of the lion.[18] The point de Man goes on to make is that

> in a metaphor, the substitution of a figurative sense for a literal sense engenders, by a process of synthesis, a proper sense which may remain implicit, since it is the figure itself which constitutes it. But in allegory, as it is conceived here, one could say that the artist has lost confidence in the substitutive efficacity of resemblances: . . . he states explicitly a proper sense by means of a literal sign which scarcely resembles it and, what is more, represents in its turn a sense which is proper to it and which does not coincide with the proper sense of the allegory. (*Mouvements,* 246–47)

Thus, in Giotto's painting there is a conflict between what is represented literally (the rather unpleasant face of a woman the proper sense of which, taken alone, might be "Envy") and what the artist *says* is meant (Giotto labels the painting *Karitas*). In short, a single allegorical figure engenders two senses—one literal and representational, the other proper and allegorical: between them there is a hostility that results in an aporia, a hesitation that assures misreading. The paradoxical self-canceling effect of literalism (realism, verisimilitude) in allegorical representation is itself the allegory of the undecidability which undermines all meaning in the act of reading anything whatsoever, leaving the reader to consider the significance of the process of writing itself.[19] But while de Man and Hillis Miller have tended to remain fixed at the aporetic moment, Derrida uses its very existence as the justification for a new rhetoric of invention which makes misreading a virtue in the old paradigm and a moot point in the (hypothesized) new paradigm.

Nonetheless, allegory is the mode of representation most adaptable to Derrida's purposes, especially when one realizes that the essential linguistic structure of allegory, according to recent studies, is the pun. Distinguishing the creative, narrative use of allegory from the critic's "allegoresis" ("verticalness, levels, hidden meanings, the hieratic difficulty of interpretation"), Maureen Quilligan calls attention to "the essential affinity of allegory to the pivotal phenomenon of the pun, which provides the basis for the narrative structure characteristic of the genre":

> It might be helpful to remember that the word "symbol," from the Greek *symballein*—to "throw together," means a physical token, the two halves of which form a whole when placed together. It thus has a deep connection with physical phenomena, with *things*. At the same time, the Greek meaning of the term "allegory" preserves a sense of purely social or verbal interaction. If we do not define allegory along with Coleridge as some kind of extended analogy (two halves of meaning which do not fit together very closely, or "organically"), but as a term pointing to the nearly magic polysemy of language itself, we shall see how Coleridge's traditional emphasis on disjunction can be exchanged for a sense of simultaneous, equal significance, a fluctuating figure-ground relationship which contains within it the relations between the two meanings of a single word, as in a simple pun.[20]

Similar to Derrida's neologisms and quasi-concepts (differance, supplement, *pharmakon*) and to his homonymic non-Aristotelianism, the allegorical narrative fosters a radical literalization, focuses on the word as word and on the horizontal connections among words (Derrida's insistence on the excess of syntax over semantics), thus unfolding as "an investigation of the literal truth inherent in words." Freud's attention to word play may be seen in this context as a revival of the operation characterizing all allegory "from Spenser to Pynchon." Allegory, Quilligan argues, oscillates between the metaphorical and literal understanding of words, manifesting the tension between them in order to break the reader's inclination to follow the "plot," the "colorful journey," in the mind's eye, thus forcing the reader to become aware of the truly "literal"—not the actual or lifelike scene depicted, but the "letteral" ("having to do with letters and with reading letters grouped into words"). Not the metaphor of plot (and even less what such a plot might symbolize), but the language itself in terms of sounds and spellings, contains the key to meaning.

The relevance of this theory of allegory to Derrida's program should be evident from what has been shown in earlier chapters, especially its view of personification as "a process which involves the animation of nouns and the close scrutiny of the 'things' embedded within words by etymology and puns" (Quilligan, 115). Thus, Langland in *Piers Plowman,* for example, "centers the radiating structure of the whole poem on a pun," the pun generated precisely by Langland's signature—his first name being William— in the word "will" (164). Quilligan argues that the authors of allegory pose the question, "Do puns reveal the divine design?" in order to *redeem* language, to *stop* misreading finally (64). Here Derrida's use of the punning strategy departs from the intention of the genre, for grammatology pushes beyond the polysemies displayed in Quilligan's analysis to dissemination in order to liberate the allegorical narrative from its ontotheological ideology.

FRAMES

Let me now outline the relevance of the preceding discussion of mne- monics and anasemia to grammatology.

1. The history of mnemotechnics, including the theories of "artificial memory" in classical rhetoric and the "pathological memory" in psycho- analysis, provide (because they share in the opprobrium directed at writing) a context within which to appreciate Derrida's adoption of the homophone as the organizing principle of Writing. Derrida, of course, is not interested in mnemonics or schizophrenic language for their own sake, but as re- sources from which to borrow modes of access to Writing. The rebus device of composing and reading tableaux homophonically (the scene of/as writing), for example, may be used to generate a theoretical discourse from an object of study, working in the mode thus of "originary translation."

Derrida attempts to carry the theory of mimesis, with respect to the relationship between signifier and signified, beyond the opposition im- posed on the debate from Plato to Saussure—between the signs as having naturally motivated (necessary) relations to meanings, and signs as being arbitrary products of convention. Based on the examples of the history of language (the phenomenon of language change, the drift of word spellings, pronunciations, and meanings), of sophistic hypomnesis, and of psycho- analytic studies of disturbed communication—all of which manifest a process of demotivation and remotivation of signs—Derrida proposes a method or systematic practice (harnessing this potential of language to a general science) of the detachment and regrafting of language structure which reopens the entire question of motivation. Derrida broaches the issue in a reading of Saussure, who used the word *"glas"* as an example of a "false onomatopoeia." Saussure's approach is too simplistic for Derrida, the former's point being that *"glas"* (knell) does not really sound like a bell, and that its semantic roots in any case involve not bells but the notion of class. Besides being able to show by a thorough exploration of the allosemes that *"glas"* and "class" are related to "bell," Derrida makes a more general point: " 'Words' can become onomatopoeic, by a functional graft, in whole or in part, by a decomposition or recomposition, detachment or reattachment. But onomatopoeias can also become words ... if the arbitrary and the unmotivated could attain the alleged 'primary character' of such 'authentic onomatopoeias,' why can't a remotivation carry off again the alleged arbitrary?" (*Glas,* 107–8). Derrida's argument finds support in the theory of memory which allows the remotivation of the *loci* or the erasure of the Pad.

In a sense, then, Derrida treats his object of study (whatever it might be) as if it constituted a "found" hypomnemic scene—a scene for which the rebus key has been lost or forgotten, but whose allegorical, nonrepresentational writing (as tableau) remains open to a remotivating translation. He has offered on a number of occasions, as a kind of methodological *"mise en abyme"* of this principle, descriptions or emblems of "writing-reading" as a memory walk (recalling that in "The 'Retrait' of Metaphor," such a walk might be the metaphor of metaphor, "representing itself there as an enormous library in which we would move about without perceiving its limits, proceeding from station to station, going on foot, step by step, or in a bus"—"Retrait," 6).

Alluding, for example, to the grafting of Chinese ideograms to phonetic writing in Sollers's *Numbers,* and to the palimpsest-like structure resulting from the remotivation process (the grafting process itself), Derrida states:

> All this requires that you take into account the fact that, in scratching upon this textural matter, which here seems to be made of spoken or written words, you often recognize the description of a painting removed from its frame, framed differently, broken into, remounted in another quadrilateral which is in turn, on one of its sides, fractured. The entire verbal tissue is caught in this, and you along with it. You are painting, you are writing while reading, you are inside the painting. "Like the weaver, then, the writer works backwards." (*Dissemination,* 357)

The *scene* of the writing, then, includes a specific allusion to a mnemonic hieroglyphics, as indicated in *Glas* in terms of the unicorn tapestry ("La Dame à la Licorne") described in Genet's text. "At first, a pictorial text, representational, iconic, the tapestry, is fastened onto a narrative or discursive text" (*Glas,* 215). The experience of transgression as such—the breaking of a frame, exceeding a limit, crossing or penetrating a frontier or barrier—has something to do with the liaison between words and things and the translation between them: "We advance into a representation, or rather we penetrate without advancing, without breaking through, the surface of an image pinned or sewn into the general thread of the text. Now every penetration, insofar as, with a step, it crosses a merely ideal line, suspends opposition, finds itself confronting no really opposable substance. In that it suspends and traverses, the penetration is never of anything but an image" (*Glas,* 214).

Another reference to a mnemonic discourse, to a text generated by a kind of memory walk through a scene of *loci* and images, may be recognized in *La carte postale:*

> If you reread the post cards I sent you, by the thousands, you will observe perhaps (if you put on them their true value) that everything I wrote there is legendary, a legend more or less elliptical, redundant or translatable *from the image.* From the icon found on the back of the text and its inspection or, in a fashion a bit more perverse, from the image which precedes or follows the sending. I never said anything to you, only transferred that which I saw or believed seen. But first, it is true, there were hours spent in all the shops or museums, selecting that which it was necessary to show you. (*Carte,* 133–34)

The mnemonist called his technique "speculative," although, as Luria noted, it was speculative only in a "literal sense"—"seen with the mind" —seeming thus to Luria to be "almost a pun on the conventional meaning of 'speculative'" ("the abstract reasoning of rationalist philosophy"— Luria, 96). As part of his deconstruction of dialectics, Derrida invokes the same pun in "To Speculate—on 'Freud,'" included in *La carte postale* (to be discussed in the next chapter).

2. The principal anasemic metaphor (one in which, undoing the conventional structure of analogy, the unrepresentable shows itself) in Derrida's essays is the "frame"—alluding to all manner of parerga in the verbal and visual arts (picture frames, prefaces, footnotes, illustrations, everything that is "hors d'oeuvre"). Regarding the function of anasemia, everything Freud (or Abraham and Torok) says about the kernel and the shell, as noted previously, is not by way of analogy or metaphor in the usual sense, but elaborates a vocabulary of relationships capable of treating precisely that which is unknown. Similarly, everything Derrida says about parerga constitutes a way to discuss enframing—that which, never appearing itself, makes appearance possible. The parerga do not represent, are not images of enframing, but they call it to mind. As an example of what is at stake, Derrida finds in Sollers's *Numbers* a text that manages to refer to enfram-

ing. But to do so, "it was necessary to turn to what is outside *our* language in order to signify that incessant extrapresent"—two Chinese ideograms, that is, are interpolated into the writing, one marking, "'something constantly reanimated and unappeased'" and the other, '"being in the process of and precisely'" (*Dissemination,* 310). The question of "place," that is, concerns the "there is" of the "taking place," present only through the "illusions," Derrida says, of statement or utterance:

> What gives the structural necessity to "illusion," "error," and "forgetting," is thus the strange "opening" of this quadrangle, its missing side. The opening *already* goes unnoticed *as* opening (aperity, aperture), as a diaphanous element guaranteeing the transparency of the passageway to whatever presents itself. While we remain attentive, fascinated, glued to *what* presents itself, we are unable to see *presence* as such, since presence does not present itself, no more than does the visibility of the visible, the audibility of the audible, the medium or "air," which disappears in the act of allowing to appear. (*Dissemination,* 314)

Part of the function of Derrida's investigation of parergonal phenomena, then, is to thematize enframing, the functions of the actual, extant "frames" (like the fruit Freud could hold in his hand) being (like the images of objects used by the Oglala Indian to write the abstraction "highway") to *remind* the reader of the question—a device of *memoria*.

To think his way into this transformation of analogy, Derrida, in the essay entitled "Parergon," draws on Kant's *Critique of Judgment* as a guide, which addresses the problem of how the unrepresentable presents itself in the context of a definition of the sublime. Working off of Kant's articulation of the sublime, Derrida defines the notion of the "colossal"—the "almost excessive" or "nearly inapprehensible"—a term designed to call attention to a certain effect of "subjective projection": "This experience of an inadequation of the presentation to itself, or rather, since every presentation is adequate to itself, of an inadequation of the presenter to the presented of the presentation."[21] Kant is talking about a way to "take something in" without understanding it, by joining the concept of measurement (its very inadequacy as a concept) to the infinite, measureless: "Kant allows to introduce itself thus a comparison, place of all figures, analogies, metaphors, etc., between the two orders absolutely irreducible one to the other, absolutely heterogeneous. He throws a bridge across the abyss, between the unpresentable and the presentation" (*Vérité,* 158). This bridge reflects the structure of the bell in *Glas,* used as an anasemic metaphor of the oscillating fetish emotion, the shuttle structuring that text. "But the [fetish] operation is not negative," Derrida declares, "it affirms with a limitless yes, immense, prodigious, inaudible. And it constructs, a sort of solid traverse, to suspend the bell between two towers" (*Glas,* 255). "I write on *la hune,*" Derrida says—"that large horizontal plank of wood from which the bell is suspended"—"between the two." The bell is another piece of hypomnesic apparatus, which functions in terms of the same de-signification process Abraham described in Freud's metaphor of the "messenger" passing between the kernel and the shell:

> Only the *representative,* the mediator between two poles x, seems to
> have conserved a signification, inasmuch as it is a term known by
> comparison with a known relation of mediation. From a purely se-
> mantic point of view psychic representatives, like the symbols of
> poetry, are mysterious messages from one knows not what to one
> knows not whom; they only reveal their allusiveness in a context,
> although the "to what" of the allusion must necessarily stop short of
> articulation. . . . By way of its semantic structure the concept of
> the messenger is a symbol insofar as it makes allusion to the unknow-
> able by means of an unknown, while only the relation of the terms
> is given. ("Shell," 21)

The parergon—that "supplemental out work"—is itself just such a rela-tional structure, designating "a general, formal predicative structure, which one can transport *intact* or regularly deformed, reformed, into other fields, to submit it to new content" (*Vérité,* 64). Derrida's experiment with an epistemology of Writing, based necessarily on hypomnesis rather than anamnesis, working mechanically without the self-presence of living mem-ory, depends upon the relational capacities of items like the parergon and on the history of research into ungraspable experience—like that of Kant on the sublime or Freud on the fetish—for its enabling operations.

OL-FACTORY

It is worthwhile noting the continuity between the epithymics of the chemical senses, developed in the preceding chapter, and the mnemonic approaches explored here, as a way to appreciate the systematic quality of Derrida's program. To reiterate, the problem he confronts involves the theorization of the elements of writing revealed by historical and practical observation, one of these elements being the status of writing as a device of artificial memory. The challenge, then, is to devise a mode of thought, Writing, and pedagogy that functions explicitly according to hypomnesic principles, rather than according to the traditional Platonic anamnesis. The point will be to demonstrate that the features for which writing is tra-ditionally blamed, once liberated from the ideological constraints limiting their exercise, will prove capable of the same virtues of creativity or pro-ductivity formerly reserved to the "genius" of "living memory." While such an approach obviously is in sympathy with the developments of mental prostheses such as "smart computers," it also assumes that Writing continues as a human operation and that the goal of education in a man-machine symbiosis is to explore the specific and irreducibly human resources of intellection needed to direct our technological-scientific ecology.

One of the "defects" of writing is its dependence on recognition—that it is a reminder only, treating of archives and monuments, which it only mimes. A survey of Daniel Sperber's argument in *Rethinking Symbolism*, [22] however, makes explicit the relationship of this feature of writing to the chemical senses. The powerful capacity of the sense of smell, especially ("Internal penetration [into the lungs] through smell," Kant noted, describing smell as "taste at a distance," and the chief means by which filth induces nausea, "is even more intimate than through the absorptive vessels of mouth or gullet"—*Mimesis*, 92), to stimulate memory allows us a further glimpse of the domain Derrida proposes to tap for cognition—the unconscious (recall Freud's relation of repression to smell). The key aspect, for my purposes, of Sperber's theory is his point that the sense of smell *works nonsemiotically,* and as such offers a model (useful in the current shift of the sensorium) for imagining a mode of learning that does not depend on interpretation and decoding of signs.

The quality of olfaction which most lends itself to Derrida's attempt to conceptualize a hypomnesic cognition—based on writing's status as a reminder—is that *while smells may be recognized, they may not be recalled.* One may actively recall the image of a rose, but not its smell. But, Sperber notes, the failure of olfactive memory in the area of direct remembrance is compensated for by the extraordinarily evocative power of smells (which seem to harbor memories the way coral reefs harbor fish), their mnemonic capacity to generate (in the presence of the smell) a metonymic chain of causes and effects associated with the event of olfaction:

> When a smell impinges on the conceptual attention without the
> latter being able to represent it by an analysed description, the mind
> is as it were brought to a standstill by this failure, which it then
> turns into a success of a different order. Unable to find the means
> for describing this information in its stock of acquired knowledge,
> it abandons the search for the missing concept in favor of a sym-
> bolic commentary on its absence, by constructing or reconstructing
> not a representation of the object, but a representation of that
> representation. Thus, the smell only holds the attention in order to
> re-orient it towards what surrounds it. (Sperber, 117)

Although smells are symbols par excellence, giving rise to thoughts of something other than themselves, they have been ignored as a model for a theory of symbol because semiology cannot deal with that which cannot

be coded (the very reason for its appeal to Derrida's search for a nonsemi-
otic epistemology). Rather, the smell functions as a means of *individual*
symbolism (similar to the necessity in mnemonics to select *loci* from one's
autobiography), evoking recollections and sentiments that are withheld
from social communication.

Relevant to Derrida's interest in situations of undecidability, such as
sublimity or fetishism, the symbolic mechanism for which Sperber uses the
olfactory as an illustration functions cognitively precisely when conceptual
representations fail. Symbolism, that is, provides a second—supplementary—
mode of access to the memory in the thought process. "In terms of modern
cognitive psychology, the failure of a sequential process *triggers* [the very
mechanism described in *Dissemination—"le déclenchement"*] a parallel
process, thus inverting the normal order of cognitive processes" (Sperber,
122). Thus, the symbolic mechanism is a "feed back device coupled to the
conceptual mechanism." It supplements direct invocation of concepts, described as constituting an "encyclopaedia" of knowledge about the world,
as distinct from semantic knowledge of the meanings of words, rules, and
categories (the difference between an encounter with a real lion and knowing the meaning of the term "lion"). Symbolic knowledge, however, according to Sperber, concerns not the real lion nor the meaning of the term,
but what is "known" or "believed" about lions (reflecting thus the same
divisions used in de Man's discussion of allegory). It involves, in short, the
kind of knowledge Plato consigned to the category of *doxa* as opposed to
episteme, but which, in Sperber's model, coexists, by virtue of being put in
quotation marks, with the epistemic sciences of the encyclopaedia. The
interaction and interpenetration of the *doxa* and the *episteme,* of course,
are principal interests of grammatology as a science of sciences and as a
participant in the poststructuralist study of the subject of knowledge.

Part of the interest of Sperber's argument is his depiction of ideas or
theories as themselves symbolic—the statement of a doctrine or hypothesis
(Sperber uses Lacan's "The Unconscious is structured like a language" as
his example) is received symbolically, not epistemically, and hence works
by processes of evocation (setting in action metonymic chains of association, for which the response to smell is the chief model) rather than by
direct invocation of the concepts of the encyclopaedia, which alone are
empirically verifiable. Such hypotheses, among which must be counted
those constituting grammatology, are accepted as "true" (heuristically—as
if, why not), although what they imply is not known or understood. The
researcher then supplements this conceptual incompleteness with a search
for the sense of the doctrine or aphorism, to make up for the inadequacy
of the formula to what it evokes in the intellectual imagination. Sperber's
"symbolic" mode supports Derrida's notion of the contribution "literature"
—in the mode of "attending discourse" and "theoretical fiction"—makes

to science: " 'Literature' also indicates—practically—the beyond of every-thing: the 'operation' is the inscription that transforms the whole into a part requiring completion or supplementation. This type of supplemen-tarity opens the 'literary game' " (*Dissemination*, 56).

For Sperber, the symbolic mechanism is "the bricoleur of the mind" working with the debris of concept formation, saving the remains of in-formation not for decoding but for elaboration:

> It is precisely because this information has partly escaped the con-ceptual code, the most powerful code available to humans, that it is submitted to [the symbolic mechanism]. It is therefore not a question of discovering the meaning of symbolic representations but, on the contrary, of inventing a relevance and a place in the mem-ory for them despite the failure in this respect of the conceptual categories of meaning. A representation is symbolic precisely to the extent that it is not entirely explicable, nor expressible by semantic means. Semiological views are therefore not merely inadequate; they hide from the outset the defining features of symbolism. (Sper-ber, 113)

Grammatology, I suggest, works in a similar manner, is a strategy of cognitive evocation, modeled on the effect of olfaction, which, as Sperber describes the operation, puts the elements of the encyclopaedia in quota-tion marks:

> If one says "cunning as a fox" [or, I would add, "the flowers of rhetoric"], an expression which perhaps corresponds to reality, what happens here is that a normal encyclopaedic statement is put in quotes and serves no longer to express knowledge about foxes but something else by means of that knowledge. In other words, sym-bolic knowledge is neither about semantically understood categories, nor about the world, but about the encyclopaedic entries of cate-gories. This knowledge is neither about words nor about things, but about the memory of words and things. It is a knowledge about knowledge, a meta-encyclopaedia in the encyclopaedia and not—con-trary to the semiological view—a meta-language in language. (Sper-ber, 108–9)

Such is the function of the *bite*, the tenterhooks of citation, fundamental to Derrida's principle of iteration or articulation described in the previous chapter as the epithymics of taste.

In the next chapter we shall see how Derrida puts the principles dis-cussed thus far to work in a discourse of knowledge.

4

Models

PICTO-IDEO-PHONOGRAPHIC

The program of applied grammatology which I am outlining takes as its point of departure Derrida's deconstruction of the Book. Derrida's anti-books, at the same time that they work theoretically and thematically to subvert the final obstacle to grammatology—the metaphysics of logocentrism—also demonstrate a certain "graphic rhetoric," the essence of which is a double-valued Writing, ideographic and phonetic at once, which puts speech back in its place in relation to nonphonetic elements. The importance of Derrida's example for an applied grammatology is that it provides a model for articulating in one presentation both verbal and nonverbal materials—the kind of Writing needed for classroom performance and for audio-visual presentation in film and video—in a way, however, that is not dominated by the philosophemes of sight and hearing (theory and voice). As we shall see, audio-visual productions may be written within the enframing of a sensorium reorganized to reflect the contact qualities of the chemical senses.

The first lesson for this future word-thing Writing is derived from the miming, in Derrida's essays, of the "picto-ideo-phonographic" inscriptions of non-Western cultures (*Grammatology,* 90), extending, as Hartman notes, the old "speaking picture" to a three-part composite. Not only was it the case, at least in wall inscriptions, that the Egyptians, for example, used both pictorial and hieroglyphic representations of the same information, but the hieroglyphics themselves were tripartite, including figurative characters (literal representations of objects—quotidian domestic objects or entities reproduced, for all their abstraction, precisely enough to permit the dating of the period in which the script was developed at around 3000 B.C.—Gelb, 215); a symbolic element, expressing abstract ideas by analogical extension of the figurative images; and phonetic characters (figures used exclusively for their sound value).[1]

Derrida similarly elaborates a tripartite script—picto-ideo-phonographic —which, in recent books, consists of the following elements: a discursive commentary (the phonetic level); examples interpolated ("pinned") into the discourse (the ideographic element); and "found" pictorial material (such as the art works "translated" in *La vérité en peinture* or the post card from the Bodleian Library featured in *La carte postale*). At this point an important difference between my approach to Derrida as a grammatologist, and that of the deconstructionist, is clearest: the former emphasizes his model for a new approach to visual-verbal Writing, while the latter emphasizes his analytical strategies (together representing complementary phases of grammatology as an emerging discipline). The purpose of an applied grammatology, that is, is less concerned with the deconstruction of the philosophical tradition (the task of theoretical grammatology—perhaps interminable) than with the grafting of visual items to texts, as executed in *The Post Card*.

Derrida's treatment of the philosophical works which he deconstructs (although the method amounts to a remotivation of the text, stripping away its conclusions while producing alternative directions out of its own structure, similar to the principle demonstrated with the proper name) differs from his stance with regard to works of literature and art, to which, in a sense, he apprentices himself; such works he does not deconstruct but translates, looking toward the discovery of an intermedia Writing. What interests me here is the articulation—the separating attachment—of a critical or pedagogical discourse to the examples it employs, especially when the examples are from "creative" rather than "philosophical" sources.

The ideo- and pictographic elements, then, are given new emphasis in Derrida's program. Every critical and pedagogical presentation, of course, includes the commentator's discourse and the subject matter discussed (similar at the level of the sentence to the utterance-statement relationship). Supplementing this pair, however, constituting a second band of connotation and allegory, Derrida elaborates a series of models, including a reflexive discussion (part of the phonographic element) designating the process by which the other levels interact. The second band has always been employed in academic presentations as well, but only to a very modest extent. Derrida's innovation is to expand this band, giving it at least equal status with the conventionally discursive portions. The value of Derrida's theory, in other words, is not only the dephoneticization he introduces into the essay form but also (for intermedia situations contain-

ing by definition a nonverbal or nondiscursive level of communication) the
particular instruction he provides for the interaction of the phonetic and
nonphonetic elements of Writing.

In this chapter I shall review the lessons of Derrida's theory and practice
for this grafting of discourse to exemplary and pictorial material. This will
be followed in the next chapter by a reading of Derrida's most elaborate
composite production to date—*The Post Card.*

EXAMPLE

The standard dictionary definition of "example," relevant to its function in academic presentations, includes the notion of "a part of something, taken to show the character of the whole" and of "a pattern or
model of something to be imitated or avoided." But to realize what is at
stake here we must keep in mind that the logic of examples is a special case
of concept formation—of relations between the particular and the general,
the sensible and the intelligible. In the Western tradition, the only objects
that *have sense* are those that "fall under" concepts. In contemporary
usage, "a concept is a mental entity, intuited or constructed, expressing a
determinate content of discursively accessible thought. It gives us security
over what we think in a way analogous to the security we derive from the
object that is gripped by the hand" (Rosen, 44). A basic feature of this
understanding of the concept, Rosen adds, is thinking as *having:* "The
notion of 'having' is central in analytical thinking from Plato and Aristotle
to contemporary set theory. A has *b,* whereas *b* belongs to A. This schema
has two main senses. First, we say that a set has members, a function has
values, or an object has properties. Second, we say that a man has knowledge: a knower has a *logos* or a concept of a form or structure. These
senses cannot be the same" (49).

Rosen's point, based on these two senses of having in thinking—as structure and as activity—is to demonstrate the limits of analysis by calling
attention to its forgotten borders, to its dependency on the residues of
intuition which it attempts to exclude. Although it is impossible to have
the concept of "the concept of a concept" (there is nothing to have in any
discursive sense), one is still able to think in this situation, using the
homonymic senses, because, as Rosen argues, "not all senses of 'sense' refer
to concepts."

Rosen's revision of analytic philosophy, opening it to nonconceptual
cognition, is carried even further by Derrida, whose notion of "economimesis" similarly works to break thought's dependency on property
and notions of having. Derrida radicalizes the homonym, as we have seen,
in that his economy dispossesses having by halving it, exploring not only

halving as division, articulation, hinge, but also as jointing in the language of framing: to "halve together" is to join two pieces of wood by cutting from each, at the joint, a portion fitting to that left solid in the other (Derrida's theory of examples is a theory of frames).

Another contextual aspect of the question of the example concerns the relation of taste, as a metaphor or model of judgment, to analytical thought. Judgment is to the concept what the essay is to the book, for, as Victoria Kahn points out, one of the meanings of "essay," etymologically, is "to taste" (the king's food—a risky occupation). *Digestion,* as a metaphor of judgment in the tradition of imitation, was used to suggest the need to *swallow* and *transform* one's predecessors, with the authority of one's judgments resting on the assumption of a universally accessible domain of common sense capable of guaranteeing intelligibility.[2] But from Montaigne to Freud, working against such assimilations, the tendency was not to subsume objects under concepts but to refer them back to pleasure, thus provoking, by this subjectivity, a more or less radical skepticism, leading ultimately to the notion of the unconscious based on a complication of the pleasure principle as unpleasure. The relevant point for now is that an epistemology of taste destroys the validity of examples on which traditional pedagogy depends (their role in concept formation, moving from concrete to abstract, part to whole), because it subverts the intelligibility of common sense. Indeed, as Kahn argues, a critique of exemplarity is best stated in terms of taste, which most readily lends itself to an undermining of the general.

Montaigne, according to Kahn, sets out deliberately to resist any generalization of conclusions from his examples, to disappoint any desire for literal truth, by invoking two *bodies*—his own physical processes and literal "taste," and a "foreign body" of citations from the tradition, contradictory citations supporting every imaginable point of view—the same two bodies Derrida draws on, making his epithymics an extension of Montaigne's skepticism, including his interest in "spitting out" rather than "swallowing": "These remarks [by Montaigne] try not to point beyond themselves to any greater significance. They want to resist translation, sublimation, or incorporation into a system or a comprehensive reading. They are an attempt at purgation, on the thematic level, of the generalizing claim of the example" (Kahn, 1280).

The best-known instance of Derrida's attitude toward the example, involving a literary text, hence an ideographic rather than a pictographic model, is his objection to the way Lacan uses Poe's "Purloined Letter" as an illustration of the "laws and truth" of psychoanalysis. Not only is Lacan's use of the example traditional, but, according to Derrida, that usage violates Lacan's own theories (giving predominance to the signifier) by relying on the theme or content of the story as allegory while ignoring the *framing,* the *mise en scène,* of the narrative form itself. The illustration of a principle of psychoanalysis with an apologue is consistent, Derrida notes, with the conventional philosophical distinction between truth and reality, which allows "the passage of truth through fiction." Lacan's practice, then, remains tied to the orthodoxy of truth as adequation (acquittal of a debt) and as unveiling (of a lack) of truth that commands "the fictional substance from its origin or from its telos, which ultimately subordinates this concept of literary fiction to a rather classical interpretation of *mimesis.*"[3]

Derrida's examples, obviously, will function rather by an anasemically redefined mimesis. Meanwhile, his disagreement with Lacan allows us to glimpse the essence of the problem. Against Lacan's focus on the plot or theme, which suggests the lesson that "a letter always arrives at its destination," Derrida takes into account the framing effects of the narrative, which offer a different, double lesson. First of all, there is the general insight regarding "the paradoxes in the parergonal logic," which "prove that the structure of the framing effects is such that no totalization of the border is even possible. The frames are always framed: thus by some of their content. Pieces without a whole, 'divisions' without a totality—this is what thwarts the dream of a letter without division" ("Purveyor," 99). The logic of the parergon, then, defeats conceptual closure.

More specifically, Derrida notes a "textual drifting off course of the tale's narrative," in part because of the grafts of intertextuality which open the tale to other stories and settings, but also because of the involvement in the tale of the narrator himself, his interest in, even his identification with, Dupin. But Lacan leaves unasked the question, who signs?—the question of the signature: "'The Purloined Letter' is the title of the text and not only of its object. But a text never names itself, never writes: I, the text, write or write myself. It has, lets, or rather brings another to say: 'I, truth, speak.' I am always the letter that never arrives. At the destination itself" ("Purveyor," 100). The problematic of the narrator in literature, as we shall see, applies equally to the author-narrator in academic discourse, making the frame and the signature the same question.

INVAGINATION

Before dealing with the larger question of enframing as signing, I shall take note of the logic of examples which Derrida offers as an alternative to the representational illustration employed by Lacan. It is worth noting that Derrida uses the "loophole" of a figure provided by set theory itself (modern heir of the notion of the concept as a having or belonging to) in order to describe the paradoxical escape of the example from conceptualization. The figure is that which Derrida formulates as "the law of the law of genre":

> It is precisely a principle of contamination, a law of impurity, a parasitical economy. In the code of set theories, if I may use it at least figuratively, I would speak of a sort of participation without belonging—a taking part in without being part of, without having membership in a set. The trait that marks membership inevitably divides, the boundary of the set comes to form, by invagination, an internal pocket larger than the whole; and the outcome of this division and of this abounding remains as singular as it is limitless.[4]

The pocket formed by invagination, accounting for the "enigma of exemplarity," is analogous to the crypt of incorporation as Abraham and Torok described it in the case of the Wolf Man and has the same effect of designification and dispersal on the unity of the concept that incorporation has with respect to the unity of the self.

The invaginating fold or sheathing graphically displays the structure of catastrophic metaphors, a term ("catastropic") that may now be recognized as another borrowing from mathematics, alluding to that division of topology known as catastrophe theory (keeping in mind that, just as Derrida stressed with regard to the comparison of his quasi-concepts to Gödel's undecidability, the reference to topology is "only an analogy" and hence is subject to anasemia). The fold is the simplest of the seven elementary catastrophes—"catastrophe" referring to the event of discontinuity or instability in a system. Derrida's most frequent use of the invagination metaphor, describing the hymenal effect of discontinuity or transformation resulting from his homonyms, is that of turning a glove inside out (which would transform a right-hand glove into a left-hand glove): "One can always, although it is never indispensable, turn the reference like a glove. Pretending to describe this or that, the veils or sails, for example of saliva, the text veils itself in unveiling itself by itself, describing, with the same exhibitionistic modesty, its own texture" (*Glas,* 160).[5]

A glance at a general description of the concerns of catastrophe theory suffices to indicate its relevance to Derrida's interests in boundaries and borderings as they exist in the humanities. "As a part of mathematics, catastrophe theory is a theory about singularities. When applied to scientific problems, therefore, it deals with the properties of discontinuities directly, without reference to any specific underlying mechanism. This makes it especially appropriate for the study of systems whose inner workings are not known."[6] The natural phenomena of discontinuity to which it may be applied include "the breaking of a wave, the division of a cell or the collapse of a bridge, or they may be spatial, like the boundary of an object or the frontier between two kinds of tissue." It is also im-

portant to note, for future reference, that catastrophe theory is not a part
of theoretical physics but of theoretical biology, even "from that part of
the subject which is different in essence from theoretical physics" (Saunders, xi).

The bridge and its potential collapse that concerns Derrida, of course,
is the bridge of analogy, as discussed in Kant's aesthetic of the Sublime:
"The bridge is not *an* analogy. Recourse to analogy, the concept and the
effect of analogy are or make *the bridge* itself. . . . The analogy of the
abyss and the bridge over the abyss is an analogy to say that there ought
to be an analogy between two absolutely heterogeneous worlds, a third
to pass over the abyss, to cicatrize the chasm and to think the gap. In short
a *symbol.* The bridge is a symbol" ("Parergon," 43). Kant's model of
analogy, part of a powerful tradition still operative today, Derrida notes, is
dialectical, based on a certain continuity from the known to the unknown
and from the concrete to the abstract, allowing innovation to occur by
means of proportionality and symmetry. But Derrida is interested in a discontinuous model of innovation and change, one that "produces a silent
explosion of the whole text and introduces a kind of fissure, rather fission,
within each concept as well as each statement," as happens "when the
analogy is weak, the 'quantity of connection' not great enough." [7] In these
circumstances, analogy misleads, becomes frivolous: "A 'stretched' sense
always risks being empty, floating, slackened in its relation with the object"
(*Frivolous,* 133). But the very structure of the sign—its *disposability* in
the absence of the thing—makes frivolity a "congenital breach" in language
(*Frivolous,* 118). The homonym, to be sure, is the most frivolous relation
of all because it produces a crossing with the least "quantity of connection," being an empty repetition of the signifier: "Frivolity originates
from the deviation or gap of the signifier, but also from its folding back on
itself in its closed and nonrepresentative identity" (*Frivolous,* 128). Repetition by itself can produce the effect of invagination.

To help make his point, Derrida uses a "genreless" text by Blanchot,
La folie du jour, which is so singular, Derrida argues, that its title must
designate it like a given name. The invagination or folding explored in this
story, as elaborated at greater length in "Living On: Borderlines," involves
a re-citation of the "beginning" of the story (*recit*) at the end in a way
that blurs the distinction between discourse and quotation:

> Each story is part of the other, makes the other a part (of itself),
> each "story" is at once larger and smaller than itself, includes itself
> without including (or comprehending) itself, identifies itself with
> itself even as it remains utterly different from its homonym. Of
> course, at intervals ranging from two to forty paragraphs, this struc-
> ture of *crisscross double invagination* ("I am neither learned nor.
> . . . A story? I began: I am neither learned nor. . . . The story was

finished! . . . A story? No. No stories, never again.") never ceases
to refold or superpose or *over-employ* itself in the meantime, and
the description of this would be interminable. I must content
myself for the moment with underscoring the supplementary aspect
of this structure: the chiasma of this *double invagination* is always
possible, because of what I have called elsewhere the iterability of
the mark. (*Deconstruction*, 99–100)

Iterability, the sheer possibility of quotation, of repeating, creates the
catastrophic fold in *any text,* giving it the structure of a Klein bottle (in
topology, a single surface "with no inside, outside, or edges. It is formed
by drawing the smaller end of a tapering tube through one side of the
tube and then enlarging the former until it fits the latter")[8] by opening the
inside to the outside: such a text will not have or hold properties any more
than a Klein bottle will hold water. The paradoxical topology of the Klein
bottle (recalling the pots with holes knocked in the bottom found in tombs,
which Kant disqualified from the category of beauty because they manifested a purpose for which they had been rendered useless) represents
grammatology's theoretical conversion of the containers described in some
histories as constituting the origin of writing (referring to the clay spheres,
or *bullae,* filled with tokens representing commodities, whose content later
came to be depicted on the outside by inscriptions, leading finally to the
abandonment of the containers altogether, leaving the inscriptions to function independent of their guarantee—Bunn, 83). The invaginated analogy,
in short, is a deconstruction of the notion of language as a "container"
for ideas.

Another aspect of the invagination which especially interests Derrida
concerns its narrative form: "Double invagination, wherever it comes
about, has in itself the structure of a narrative [*récit*] in deconstruction.
Here the narrative is irreducible. . . . The *narrative of deconstruction in deconstruction*" (*Deconstruction,* 100). No text can refer to something
beyond itself "without becoming double or dual, without making itself
be 'represented,' refolded, superposed, *re-marked* within the enclosure, at
least in what the structure produces as an effect of interiority." Every
text, in other words, places *"en abyme"*—using the "abyss" (of analogy)
now in the idiomatic sense given to it in the terminology of the arts—a
model of itself. *"Mise en abyme,"* a term borrowed from heraldry—a
figure *"en abyme"* is located at the heart of the escutcheon, "but without
touching any of the other figures"—means by analogy "any enclave enter-
taining a relation of similitude with the work which contains it."[9] The
example functions as a kind of figure *"en abyme,"* then, analogous in its
effect to the mirrors placed strategically in certain paintings, rendering
visible what takes place "behind our backs," as in Van Eyck's *Arnolfini
and His Bride,* which includes not just a miniaturization of the scene but

shows *the painter himself,* creating an effect of oscillation between the inside and the outside of the frame (*Dällenbach,* 18, 19).

Thus, the enfolding that most interests Derrida is precisely the interlacing chiasmus of the narrator and the narrative with the "content" of his story or discourse—the very liaison of form and content missing from Lacan's discussion of "The Purloined Letter." Derrida actually provides a diagram (marking his interest in the nonphonetic element of writing) of the structure, an interlacing of two curving lines, recalling the ornamental weave discussed in the section dealing with op writing, described now as "a double chiasmatic invagination of edges" ("Genre," 218). What the example places *"en abyme,"* as we shall see, is the "subject" of knowledge, the signature of the author, jointing life and art, writer and text.

Derrida's strategy with regard to invagination, as he explains in "Living On," is to find a mode of (non)commentary which, like the law of the law of genre, would relate to its objects of study as an excess, the "law of participation without membership, of contamination" ("Genre," 210), modeled on the paradox of the hierarchy of classification in set theory: "This supplementarity and distinctive trait, a mark of belonging or inclusion, does not properly pertain to any genre or class. The re-mark of belonging does not belong. It belongs without belonging, and the 'without' (or the suffix '-less') which relates belonging to non-belonging appears only in the timeless time of the blink of an eye . . . But without such respite, nothing would come to light" ("Genre," 212).

The question he poses, seeking an equivalent status for his discourse, and faced with the problem of a comparison of Blanchot's *L 'arrêt de mort* with Shelley's *The Triumph of Life,* is: "How can one text, assuming its unity, give or present another to be read, without touching it, without saying anything about it, practically without referring to it?" (*Deconstruction,* 80). His procedure will be, he says, to "endeavor to create an effect of *superimposing,* of superimprinting one text on the other," a version of "the double band or 'double bind' of double proceedings" used in *Glas,* for example, which breaks with the conventional assumptions of pedagogy: "One procession is superimposed on the other, accompanying it without accompanying it. This operation would never be considered legitimate on the part of a teacher, who must give his references and tell what he's talking about, giving it a recognizable title. You can't give a course on Shelley without ever mentioning him, pretending to deal with Blanchot, and more than a few others" (*Deconstruction,* 83–84). Or not if one's criteria are those of hermeneutics or semiotics.

The alternative with which Derrida experiments is that of writing as "grafting," as demonstrated in *Dissemination,* in which Derrida's discourse is interlaced with frequent citations from Sollers's *Numbers.* The samples from *Numbers,* however, "do not serve as 'quotations,' 'collages,' or even 'illustrations' ": "They are not being applied upon the surface or in the interstices of a text that would already exist without them. And they themselves can only be read within the operation of their reinscription, within the graft. It is the sustained, discrete violence of an incision that is not apparent in the thickness of the text, a calculated insemination of the proliferating allogene through which the two texts are transformed deform each other, contaminate each other's content" (*Dissemination,* 355).

The relation between citation and discourse, then, is typical of the invaginated "participation without belonging," with neither the novel nor the theory having mastery. *Numbers* is a model to think with rather than a work to be deconstructed, and as such displays and explains itself, thus rendering interpretation and formal description superfluous. Deconstructive criticism, of course, stresses this point but then confines itself to describing how the literary text achieves its reflexiveness, while Derrida moves toward an alternative Writing:

> What is in question here, this time at last, finds itself not displayed
> but given play, not staged but engaged, not demonstrated but
> mounted. . . . Mounted: not in a mechanism that has this time at
> last become visible but in a textual apparatus that gives way,
> gives place, and gives rise, on only one of its four series of surfaces,
> to the moment of visibility . . . in a theatre that takes the un-
> representable into account this time. (*Dissemination,* 291)

The strategy, that is, is not hermeneutic or semiotic, but *dramatic,* a performance of a certain kind:

> The status of its [the theoretical text] relation to *Numbers,* what it
> pretends to add to "that" text in order to mime its presentation
> and re-presentation, in order to seem to be offering some sort of re-
> view or account of it. . . . Just as *Numbers* calculates and feigns
> self-presentation and inscribes presence in a certain play, so too does
> what could still with a certain irony be called "this" text mime
> the presentation, commentary, interpretation, review, account or in-
> ventory of *Numbers. As a generalized simulacrum,* this writing cir-
> culates "here" in the intertext of two fictions, between a so-called
> primary text and its so-called commentary—*a chimera.* (*Dissemination,*
> 294, my emphasis)

Writing in the hypomnemic mode, we recall, can only mime knowledge (its monuments and archives); or it need only mime it in order to generate, by means of translation, something other, the new.

The chimera, reminding us of Derrida's adherence to a theoretical practice of the grotesque, is the emblem of the hymenal betweenness, whose totems include the zoophytic sponge or the unicorn in the tapestry: "The unicorn, the universal antidote, mends all tears and all seams. It is not natural, has no natural place, has perhaps no place, an instantaneously passed frontier between two tissues, two texts, two sexes. This oscillation is my emotion" (*Glas,* 216). The chimera ministers to the graft of Writing in which the pen becomes a knife, in which "it is henceforth prescribed that you clip out an example, and dismember the text" (*Dissemination,* 305). The chimera emblematizes the zone for which catastrophe theory provides the mathematics, and the centaur word-thing of picto-ideo-phonetic Writing provides the language.

PASSE-PARTOUT

Having confined my discussion thus far to the interaction of the phonetic (theoretical discourse) and ideographic (literary examples or images) elements of Writing, I turn now to consider the pictographic element. The image and idiom (the thing and the word both) of the passe-partout (an ornamental mat for a picture; a method of framing in which a piece of glass is placed over a picture and affixed to a backing; a master key) with which Derrida introduces his collection of essays on the visual arts—*La vérité en peinture*—is itself an image of the chimera function. Derrida approaches the problem of grafting discourse to painting by citing a letter in which Cézanne states to Emile Bernard, "I owe you the truth in painting ['*en peinture'*], and I will tell it to you." The clue providing the point of entry into the entire question of word-thing (verbal-visual) connections is the idiom *"en peinture,"* which means not only "in painting" (the painter Cézanne painting the truth) but also "in effigy," alluding to Cézanne *writing* about that truth, telling the truth about the true, a description that "speaks to the imagination" in a kind of "parasitism of language on the system of painting." One illustration of this parasitism, of course, would be the relation between words and images in mnemonic scenes. Derrida's strategy (similar to that used to deal with "the flowers of rhetoric") is to examine the vocabulary or terminology of painting, indeed all words associated with painting (titles of pictures, letters written by painters, catalogs, notebooks, aesthetic philosophy—the archives of painting), as a passkey to the art of painting itself.

The first word-thing he interrogates is the idiom "passe-partout," reflecting the critic's inclination to seek a universal method or passkey that might open every question. The strategy suggests that the object named by the term in its art context might provide, if not a master key, at least a point of entry into the place or topic. The passe-partout as a specific type of framing device, then, "passes throughout" the essays, emblematizing the liminal space between what appear to be a commentary and an original work, indicating that what the collection is about is precisely the relation between theory and example (which can only be displayed indirectly— that which appears in the visible "can no longer be named 'present' except through indirect discourse, in the quotation marks of citation, storytelling, fiction. It can only go out into language by a sort of ricochet"—*Dissemination*, 303).

Derrida's technique is to investigate the function or features of matting, not as an illustration but as a model, to discover in framing an anasemic metaphor of enframing. Describing the mat, Derrida notes that it is generally made of cardboard, with an opening in the middle through which a picture may be seen:

> This picture can, moreover, on occasion, be replaced there by
> another which slides into the passe-partout as an "example." In this
> respect, the passe-partout remains a basically mobile structure;
> but while allowing something to appear, it does not form, neverthe-
> less, *stricto sensu* a frame, rather a frame within a frame . . . it
> plays its card or cardboard *between* the frame, on its internal border
> properly speaking, and the external border of what it displays,
> allows to or makes appear in its empty center: the image, tableau,
> figure, form, the system of lines and colors. (*Vérité*, 17)

The example, that is, rests in its discourse like a picture in its matting (with both circumstances subject to further framing). At one level, we might say that the passe-partout is an anasemic literalization in which theory (based on the philosopheme of sight) and frames have the same purpose—*to mount*, in the sense that the purpose of all parerga, orna- ments, supplements is to put on view.

The relation of discourse to example was also said to be "mounted" in "Dissemination." What happens with respect to this term demonstrates the effect of invagination, which carries an example outside its frame, as described in *Glas*:

> For example (the uniqueness of the example destroys itself, elab-
> orates suddenly the power of a generalizing organ), at the very
> moment when we try to regain control, in a determined text, of the
> work of an idiom, tied to a sequence of proper names and of
> singular empirico-signifying configurations, *glas* names also *classifi-*
> *cation*, that is the inscription in networks of interlaced generalities
> to infinity, in genealogies of a structure such as crossings, couplings,
> switchings, detours, embranchments never depending simply on a
> semantic law or a formal law. (*Glas*, 169)

It is not that the example or idiom (passe-partout in this case) cannot be generalized—it always is, by a process similar to the remotivation of the proper name—but that the operation is not a sublation vertically into a set or concept; rather, it is a horizontal displacement, following a trajectory available in the very structure of language and made visible in the Wolf Man's cryptophors. The linkage governing the generalizing drift or slide, as we know, is the homophone or homonym. Thus matting, which generated "mounting" in its image, becomes an emblem of the copula, a connection and a connector of considerable importance, for, as Derrida notes, exploring the gap between the ontological and the grammatical sense of "to be," the copula marks the opening of language to its outside. It is the chimera or illusion of presence and the present (the privilege of the third person singular form of the verb).[10]

The image of the passe-partout relates further to the discussion in "Dissemination," then, picturing something like the old theatrical organization of page, stage, and theory which is itself put on stage in the scene of writing—the "structural illusion" of representation is retained in the frame of the page or tableau, "proffering its discourse through a kind of 'square mouth'" (Dissemination, 297). The "square" itself, as distinct from whatever appears in the square (a matter of polysemy, open to infinite substitution), precisely marks dissemination, "the obligatory passage through an open surface, the detour through an empty square," of whatever appears, in order to appear—"the column is not; it is nothing but the passage of dissemination" (Dissemination, 351). The square, that is, alludes to the taking place of the present, that to which we can attend, permitting the intersection of meanings (networks, switchings, etc.), which is to say that what is displayed in the square is the is or copula itself as liaison or syntax, a fact that may be written [is] or X, as in "the outside X the inside" (Grammatology, 44) to indicate two things at once: (1) Within its own frame of reference, the is of to be governs all connection, as Derrida notes in citing Heidegger's instructions to write Being. "'The symbol of crossed lines can, to be sure, not be a merely negative symbol of crossing out. Rather it points into the four areas of the quadrangle and of their gathering at the point of intersection. . . . The meaning-fulness of language by no means consists in a mere accumulation of meanings cropping up haphazardly. It is based on a play which, the more richly it unfolds, the more strictly it is bound by a hidden rule'" (Dissemination, 354); (2) "The X (the chiasmus)," Derrida states in "Outwork," "can be considered a quick thematic diagram of dissemination" (Dissemination, 44), suggesting the crisscross liaison of invagination which lies outside of and supplements the copula. Thus, the X conveys at once graphically the forces of polysemy (directed by is) and the force of dissemination, with the status of the mark also as erasure connoting the difference between the two. In Numbers and in Derrida's simulacrum of it, "the powers of the 'est' ["is"] are not simply canceled out. They are enumerated. Account is given of them by situating them, framing them. . . . The present indicative of the verb 'to be,' the tense of the great parenthesis and of the fourth surface, is thus caught up in an operation that divides it by four. Its predominance is properly discarded—that is, (s)played—(drawn and) quartered by being framed on all (four) sides" (*Dissemination*, 352).

Two forces are at work in the anasemic analogy, therefore—the copula and the chiasmus. On the one hand, the copula, "the 'is,' which is 'Being' as an indication of presence, procures this state of calm, this consciousness of ideal mastery, this power of consciousness in the act of showing, indicating, perceiving, or predicating" (*Dissemination*, 352). On the other hand, the chiasmus of dissemination "endlessly opens up a *snag* in writing that can no longer be mended, a spot where neither meaning, however plural, nor *any form of presence* can pin/pen down the trace. Dissemination treats—doctors—that *point* where the movement of signification would regularly come to *tie down* the play of the trace" (*Dissemination*, 26).

"Mounting," finally, itself describes a manner of copulation (to extend the law of genre to the scene of engendering which, Derrida insists, is part of the term in French), in particular copulation a tergo, from the back, the position of the parents in the Wolf Man's primal scene. The weaver, too, it must be recalled, works from the back. As does Derrida. There is such a thing, that is, as "frame-work" (like dreamwork). The frame *works*, in effect, produces invagination whose law is the logic of parerga—"a certain repeated dislocation, a regulated deterioration, irrepressible, which makes the frame in general break, collapses it sidelong into its angles and joints, turns its internal edge into its external, taking account of its thickness, allowing us to see the tableau from the side of the canvas and the wood" (*Vérité*, 85–86).

FETISH

Given that Derrida's (phonetic-theoretical) discourse works in the place of the passe-partout, the next step is to consider how the items mounted in this frame—the examples (as opposed to the discursive subject matter)—function. There are two kinds of items placed on display and put to work—verbal images (part of the ideograph), such as the "umbrella" in *Spurs*, and visual art works, such as the drawings by Adami in "+R"—both occupying the "second band" of Derrida's textual chimera.

I noted previously that the examples are placed *"en abyme,"* bringing what lies "outside" the scene inside—specifically, the writer-painter's signature. The examples shown in the passe-partout, then, function like the stage mirror described in "Dissemination"—a mirror "turned to the back of the stage," a mirror "whose tain lets 'images' and 'persons' through, endowing them with a certain index of transformation and permutation" (*Dissemination*, 314). They function this way because the mounted items have the status, for whoever selects them, of fetishes (adding thus cathexis to the autobiographical motivation of the *loci* used in mnemonics). The examples Derrida mounts are models of this fetish function.

An interesting instance of the exemplary status of Derrida's examples, one in fact falling between the verbal image and direct translation of a visual work, is that of the shoes (as things and as a title for one or several Van Gogh paintings) elaborated in "Restitutions." The ratio among the picto-ideo-phonetic elements of Writing is manifested in this essay, which, as clearly as any in Derrida's corpus, works with two bands—one straightforwardly discursive (remarking the debate between Meyer Schapiro and Martin Heidegger with respect to the interpretation of a painting by Van Gogh), and the other an exploration of the shoe as a graphic model for an alternative to the hermeneutic and formalist criticisms under discussion in the first band (the bands are not here literally separated as they are in *Glas*, "Tympan," or "Living On: Borderlines"). The point on which the debate focuses—a disagreement over to whom the shoes in the painting belong (whether to a city dweller, perhaps Van Gogh himself, or to a peasant farmer, perhaps a woman)—itself displays the notion of conceptual property which Derrida intends to deconstruct.

The shoes also signal another theme central to Derrida's logic of examples—fetishism—shoes being among the most fetishized objects, according to Freud, "who speaks more strictly of the fetishism of the shoe. In the first part, or the first movement, of his 1927 essay on 'Fetishism.' The genealogy of the fetish he proposes at that time (as the substitute for the woman's or mother's phallus) accounts, according to him, for the privilege accorded to the foot or the shoe."[11]

That the shoe is a classic fetish suggests the question of the motivation in general of any object-choice. In order to account for the way each critic projects onto the shoes his own ideology (Schapiro's urban Jewishness, Heidegger's rural Romanticism), Derrida notes the need to explain why each one chose that particular object, that type of painting or painter—the problem of the exemplariness of the exemplary model, the identification of the critic with the "object" of study. In Derrida's view, "the projection operates in the choice rather than in the analysis of the model" (*Vérité*, 420, 421). The example, therefore, may fulfill its normal explanatory function even while it folds back on itself, reflecting the "subject" of knowledge as well. Heidegger is instructive here of something Derrida himself suggests in his asymptotic approach to Shelley's "Triumph of Life," in that Heidegger (for a time, at least) talks of peasant shoes generally, with the "celebrated tableau" being introduced as an example of this example, and for which a mere drawing on the blackboard would suffice as pictogram: "and therefore: a light touch, a very brief contact, indeterminate enough to engender almost any discourse" (*Vérité,* 365-66).

Derrida's own analysis proceeds by an inventory of the properties or attributes of the shoe as a *kind* of thing (a topos in painting and a concept), using it as a support for a theoretical question similar to the way Freud used the Mystic Writing-Pad. Thus, the shoe models, or serves as mirroring screen for, Derrida's notion of invagination: "The 'form' of the shoe has another privilege: it systematizes the two types of object defined by Freud: elongated, solid or firm on one surface, hollow or concave on the other. It—*ça*—turns itself inside out—like a pair of gloves" ("Restitutions," 10).

The most important attribute of the shoes, or of those represented in the paintings, for the model is that they have *eyelets* (apropos of theory as sight) and laces, depicted, notably, as unlaced. "By this word interlacing [*entrelacement*] we understand at least three things: (1) the interlacing of the lace with itself, (2) that it is partially laced (inter-laced as one says ajar [*entreouvert*] for that which is not completely open), (3) and finally that the figurer of the interlacing is interlaced with the figured, the lacing with the laced" (*Vérité,* 385). The lacing movement is another model of the shuttle, the oscillating rhythm or vibration of superimposition which is the syntax of all Derrida's articulations, including the relation between discourse and examples.

What the lacing calls to mind for Derrida is an alternative to structuralism, which he wryly dubs "stricturalism." For while the detachment and reattachment that concern Heidegger and Schapiro (echoing debates about the demotivation and remotivation of words or phonemes) displays a dialectical logic—their arguments are exactly or diametrically opposed—what interests Derrida is the differance articulating the argument, and especially the way each calls upon the same example to support his half of the case. Unlike a dialectic, which cuts and sutures, *stricture* offers a logic of the double bind (imaged by the chiasmatic crisscross of the laces—that they may be both tied and untied, tightened or loosened) showing that the shoes are neither attached to any person nor unattached (*Vérité,* 389). Stricture as a notion enables Derrida to think about the example (the way its properties direct the dynamics of an argument) in *other* terms than those provided in the debate: "To think *otherwise* does not imply that one thinks without any relation or in a simple relation of transformation altering current or philosophical thought, but rather according to another relation of interlacing which is neither reproduction nor production transformative of a given material" (*Vérité,* 403).

It is not that the example does not *represent,* in a manner of speaking, but that it does so by the logic of the parergon, which "perverts all part-whole relations," generating a supplement or surplus of evidence (Derrida takes the same example used in the debate and generates from it the logic

for an entirely different question, thus obliquely refuting the conclusions
drawn from the example by the two critics). The shoes are not an allegory
of painting, as the "old language" would put it, Derrida states, but rather,
the detachability of the shoe from the person (like a fetish from its origin)
marks the detachability of the painting from reference. The shoes *mark*—
avoiding "say," "show," "represent," "paint," while resonating with
"marcher" (to walk), *"marges"* (margins) and *"marché"* (market)—this
statement announcing the example's function as a "representation-placed-
in-the-abyss" (*mise en abyme*): "This is a tableau, we are the painting in
painting [*en peinture*] . . . these laced lines form the 'frame' of a tableau
which appears to enframe them. We, the shoes, are larger than the frame
and the incorporated signature" (*Vérité,* 392). The shoes, an example
functioning *"en abyme,"* "enlarge suddenly excessively," Derrida adds,
"one can put everything in them." The sudden shift of "size"—the *"taille"*
of de-tail—demonstrates the effect of invagination—and of fetishism.

An analysis of any of the items mounted in Derrida's passe-partout discourse (including the passe-partout itself) would reveal a similar effect—
the expansion out of bounds, the abounding, of a commonplace (including
in this term the sense of domestic, familial, familiar as well as of "topos")
item, image, or thing into a theoretical model, marking not any particular
polysemy of themes but the narrative process of the example as such in its
operation of chiasmatic invagination. The matchbox, *drawn* (the "idea" as
plastic art) from Genet's text, with its "drawer-like" invagination (discussed both in *Glas* and in "Cartouches"), is one example. The umbrella
(in the statement "I have forgotten my umbrella," cited in Nietzsche's
notebook) is another, with its dual properties modeling the double function of style: "The style-spur, the spurring style, is a long object, an oblong
object, a word, which perforates even as its parries. It is the oblongi-
foliated point (a spur or a spar) which derives its apotropaic power from
the taut, resistant tissues, webs, sails and veils which are erected, furled
and unfurled around it. But, it must not be forgotten, it is also an umbrella" (*Spurs,* 41).

I would call attention for now especially to the nature of the examples
Derrida develops—like the things that provided the images for the first
hieroglyphic letters, they are simple, quotidian items—as well as to the
very fact that he does elaborate them as models, although the movement
or direction of the explanation is anasemic, demotivating and remotivating.
The things are not offered as models of any particular position but as
models of the invention process itself, productive and restrictive at once,
of any exemplarity whatever.

The "lowliness" of the objects used as examples—alluded to in the
homonym *"bas"* ("low" and "sock")—suggests a point of departure for a
further comment on the example as fetish. As Derrida remarks in the mid-

dle of his argument, "As in the process of fetishism, everything is the business and economy of detail, of the *"détaille"* (*Vérité,* 374). The play on
"tail" as size (*"taille"*), echoing the mounting a tergo of the fetish scene, is
also part of the discussion of the colossal in "Parergon." That the detail or
example might be immeasurable is suggested by the question Derrida poses
to Kant's third *Critique:* "If phenomenalization is going to be admitted,
why should the sublime be the absolutely large rather than the absolutely
small?" (*Vérité,* 155). The colossal, mediating the move from the sublime
to fetishism, from Enlightenment aesthetics to psychoanalysis, interlaces
the two effects: The equivalent of the absolutely large (grand), whose effect in aesthetics was to be frozen in stupefied wonder, is in psychoanalysis
the confrontation with the absolutely small, the "little thing" as fetish,
whose effect threatens castration, bringing one up short in the face of the
medusa (being "medusa-ized"). "Such a decision is a castration," Derrida
says of the selection of examples, not by way of condemnation, but as
descriptive of the nature of writing as incision or tear, "the 'operation' of
reading/writing goes by the way of *'the blade of a red knife'* " (*Dissemination,* 301).

The fetish manifests the shift of the commonplace to the singular, part
of the reversible exchange between the idiomatic and the universal that
characterizes exemplarity, since the fetish is an object "addressed" to an
individual (the example will not work for everyone). In short, the fetish
displays the signature effect. As Derrida emphasizes at several points
throughout *La vérité en peinture,* the parergonal structure and the signature effect are the same topic, both opening out into a new mimesis which
imports into linguistics

> all the questions and all the codes of questions which develop around
> the effects of the "proper name" and of the "signature," removing
> in the course of this effraction all the rigorous criteria of a framing—
> between the inside and the outside, the tableau and the thing . . .
> and if mimesis has it that the internal system of language does not
> exist or that one never uses it or that at least one never uses it
> without contaminating it and that this contamination is inevitable,
> therefore regular and "normal," constituting part of the system
> and of its functioning, making up part of it, which is the whole, mak-
> ing it a part of a whole which is larger than it. (*Glas,* 109)

The relation of the signature effect to the fetish object may be seen in
"Signéponge." Derrida finds Ponge's signature especially instructive, since
Ponge takes the side of the proper (in order, like Genet, to appropriate
objects), analogized as the "clean," against the "disgusting" (the *vomi*).
What disgusts Ponge is not "the dirty" but "the soiled," the proper which
has been affected, which usually happens (in his poems) "by liquid means"
(the liquid "L" of *Glas*), which must then be absorbed or sponged up with

linen or tissue, termed a "mass of *ignoble* tissues" ("Signéponge," 127). The interest of such "abject objects" is that they "become the very example of non-value, of nothing or next-to-nothing, the no matter what of cheap things, the anonymous or nearly so in the crowd of little things" (*Digraphe,* 20). The effect of such lowly things is a reversal from cheap to priceless (the colossal oscillation), from insignificance (being so unremarkable) to absolute rarity, from arbitrary to necessary, thus marking the signature with its effect. Moreover, Derrida stresses that Ponge is talking not about an example or concept of tissues, or towels, but the "here and now," dated and signed, encountered in his bathroom, "this" absolute one, hence singular. To signify oneself in the insignificant (outside of sense or concept), Derrida suggests, is to sign ("Signéponge," 127). The antonomasia of signing, then, as a part of the exemplarity of the impossible object, has to do with "something which, in the proper, in the structure itself of the proper, produces itself only in passing into its other, in putting itself in-the-abyss, to invert itself, contaminate itself, divide itself" ("Signéponge," 122).

Grammatology, working from the perspective of fetishism, must find a way to write of abject effects. "How to do it without simulacra to set up something?" Derrida asks, "by shams, fetishes, pastiches" (*Glas,* 51). The example, vehicle or auto of the text "as a whole," is an ersatz, a prosthesis. Prosthesis is a surgical term, meaning a therapeutic device, "which has the purpose of replacing by an artificial preparation an organ which has been removed totally or in part" (*Glas,* 136). The circumflex accent mark, the mark that transforms Genet into *genêt,* is the wound marking the detached (detachable) phallus: "The signature is a wound and there is no other origin for the work of art" (*Glas,* 202, 207). The fetish works not on the scale [the scales of judgment] of the pyramids, then (Kant's example of the Sublime), but of the circumflex: "The circumflex with which he adorns himself is a kind of chief [*"chef,"* in heraldry, the upper part of an escutcheon] or a sham headgear [*"couvre-chef"*]. It is sewn in place of a living wound which signs" (*Glas,* 211).

The text itself limps (the shoes do not fit), moves with the aid of a prosthesis; that is, with the grafts, described as "parentheses" (mentioned also as one form of invagination) (*Glas,* 136; *Dissemination,* 327). The brackets of the parentheses ("crochets") also refer to a "crochet hook." The crocheted text (a matrix of interlacing) simulates the "most subtle article of fetishism," according to Freud, "that of the pubic sheath worn like a bathing suit which conceals absolutely the genital organs and therefore the difference between the genital organs" (*Glas,* 253). The generalized fetishism resulting from this undecidability escapes from the representational logic of strict fetishism, which implied a "substitution" for the "thing itself." In Derrida, the fetish and castration are removed from the representational ideology that constrains these notions in psychoanalysis (the phallus as a decidable center in a certain fantasmatic organization). In grammatology the distinction between thesis and prosthesis becomes undecidable.

Moreover, the texture of Writing is a prosthesis not so much for the mind but for the genitals (not for the consciousness but for desire). Marshall McLuhan and many other commentators have considered communications technology to be an extension of the relevant sense (eyes and ears). But from the point of view of grammatology, concerned with the Writing that directs the enframing of technology, there is a more fundamental relationship involved: Writing as prosthesis for the genitals. Derrida learns from Freud that the apparatuses and machinery in dreams "stand for the genitals (and as a rule male ones)" (*Writing*, 229). Grammatology mounts a practice for overcoming the investments that have thus far limited the evolution of writing: "'As soon as writing, which entails making a liquid flow out of a tube onto a piece of white paper, assumes the significance of copulation, or as soon as walking becomes a symbolic substitute for treading upon the body of mother earth, both writing and walking are stopped because they represent the performance of a forbidden sexual act.'" We know from Derrida's elaboration of the hymen as a "quasiconcept" that Writing in the coming epoch should be more vaginal than phallic—or at least invaginated.

TRANSDUCTION

The other kind of item placed in Derrida's passe-partout is visual art, constituting the pictographic element in Writing. The essays on Adami and Titus-Carmel in *La vérité en peinture,* in other words, are not commentaries but "participate without belonging" to their subject matter, which is in turn *incorporated* (not introjected) into Derrida's discourse as found object, making a collage, the fragmented whole of which bears (bares) Derrida's signature. "Certainly, I would not have consented to perform a discourse upon, along side or beneath these coffins without avowing the desire to put myself in them in my turn, irrepressibly, compulsively, 127 times at least, *to inscribe my name on the cartouche*" (*Vérité,* 218). There seems, in fact, no other way to account for Titus-Carmel's work, Derrida emphasizes, remarking that it "remains without example" (it counts and accounts for itself 127 times).

The Pocket Size Tlingit Coffin (subtitled *Of Lassitude Considered as a Surgical Instrument*), as described by Titus-Carmel himself, is the generic title under which are gathered 127 drawings of a single "model." The model is a mahogany box of "modest" dimensions (10 X 6, 2 X 2, 4 cm):

"The bottom of the box is covered by a mirror and, from one part to the other of its two widths have been placed two buttresses serving as rests for a willow oval, wrapped on two portions of the perimeter with synthetic grey fur. The oval is, moreover, sustained by a lacing whose ties, crossing the walls of the box at six points, knot around a kind of key, falling freely all around the little hardwood coffin. A thin (fibre)glass plate, fixed by four minuscule brass screws, closes the ensemble" (*Vérité,* 215). Accompanying the model and the drawings of it made from every angle is a written document consisting of twelve propositions, which elliptically explain the history and structure of the coffin. These supplementary inscriptions have the status of a cartouche—the title of Derrida's article ("Cartouche"), recalling both the elliptical or oblong figures on Egyptian stele enclosing the hieroglyphs of the proper name and the space framed by scrollwork on an escutcheon.

The relationship that exists within the *Tlingit Coffin* between the sculpture (the three-dimensional object) and the 127 drawings of it emblematizes or marks the relationship of Derrida's text to its object of study ("model"). The model "does not belong to the line of which it makes a part" but is heterogeneous to it (*Vérité,* 216). Derrida's own discourse similarly "touches nothing," leaves the reader or viewer alone with the work, "passes beside it in silence, as another theory, another series, saying nothing about what it represents for me, nor even for him" (*Vérité,* 217). The object is left "in its crypt" to find its way into discourse by the same detours opened up by the Wolf Man's cryptophors.

Unlike Heidegger, who declared that art "speaks," Derrida insists on the muteness of the series, or on its capacity to work without concept, without conclusions, coming to inhabit discourse the way the death drive does, without calling attention to itself, yet submitting the "master" to its service: "Such would be the de-monstration. Let us not abuse the easy wordplay. De-monstration proves without showing, without evidencing any conclusion, without entailing anything, without an available thesis. It proves according to a different mode, but proceeding with its step of demonstration [*pas de demonstration*] or non-demonstration. It transforms, it transforms itself, in its process rather than advancing a signifiable object of discourse" (*Carte,* 317). The series of drawings de-monstrates the problem of order and representation in the relation of examples to models.

Derrida's own text relates to his object of study the way the drawings relate to the hardwood box, an "example" chosen because, like *Numbers,* it exposes exposition. The little coffin, being itself a "work" made by an artist rather than something "natural," does not have a privileged position in the series. Derrida calls it not a model, example, or referent but a "paradigm"—an artificial model fabricated, resulting from, a certain *techne* (it is not clear whether the drawings are plans for, or reproductions of, the model). And yet the special status of the paradigm is that it has an extra dimension—no two-dimensional drawing can capture it fully. "The little [paradigm] will have been constructed like a crypt, to guard jealously its secret at the moment of the most extensive exposition" (*Vérité*, 225). But this cryptic quality is the status of all objects, things, especially "little" things, which suggests to Derrida that the way to translate the ensemble into discourse in the way made available by Abraham and Torok in their *Verbarium* of the Wolf Man. The technique that enabled the Wolf Man to utter his crypted scene or name involved the alloseme, the generation of terms out of a set made up of the semantic family of a given word, including all synonyms, antonyms, and homonyms.

The strategy for composing a verbal track to accompany or frame the *Tlingit Coffin* is to let the *Coffin* defend itself on its own (the example as enigma), while concentrating on the generation of a "contingent" of terms —cartouche, paradigm, article, duction, contingent itself, and so forth— which are processed in a way parallel to the way Titus-Carmel runs through 127 variations in his drawings of the paradigm, "putting them in perspective, turning them about in every sense (direction) by a series of swerves [*écarts*], variations, modulations, anamorphoses," finally stopping after a predetermined number of pages, creating the same effect of contingent necessity or arbitrary motivation as the series of exactly 127 drawings (*Vérité*, 229). The anagram and the homonym operate on the lexicon the way anamorphoses operate on representational perspective, thus furthering Derrida's solicitation of theory as sight. Part of the tactic is to mime the sequence of dated drawings by composing as if in a journal, with dated entries (whose dates overlap, it is worth noting, those of the post cards in *La carte postale*), each day's entry constituting a variation on a theme. Such is the logic of the simulacrum as translation, as a verbal imitation of a "mnemonic scene," that is, of a fetish (the *Tlingit Coffin* being a representation of a fetish of the Tlingit Indians).

Having dubbed the coffin a "paradigm," then, Derrida invents his discourse out of the allosemes of the model term: "To enclose oneself with all the family of *paradigm*" (*Vérité*, 225). On the one hand, there is *paradeigmatizô*, having to do with "proposing something as a model" but also with setting or making an example of someone: "The *Coffin*'s story has to do, perhaps, with a condemned example, not with a condemnation in order to set an example, nor of an example of condemnation, but of an (exemplary) condemnation *of the example*: damned paradigm. To death" (*Vérité*, 226). On the other hand, there is *paradeiknumi*—"to show *beside*, put on display, distribute, attribute, the latter suggesting 'tribute.' "

The association of the artist's style with "to draw" leads to a collection of terms such as *tire, tirer, tiroir, tirage, trait*, including puns like those in

English on drawing as pulling and sketching, drawers, drawing out, and so
forth. Further, "he induces precisely *duction,* and even 'ductus,' the idiomatic trait of style." The *ductus* is the equivalent of a signature, all the
more compelling because of its proximity, in its final syllable, to *Titus.*
Ductus prompts the search for words *ductile* enough to describe the paradigm, but all are found wanting, including all the terms associated with
production, deduction, and so forth, leaving as an exception *traduction*—
translation, whose special application here as miming may be indicated by
borrowing the untranslated spelling in English. Derrida's science employs
neither deduction nor induction, but transduction.

> Another instance of the technique worth noting concerns "parergon"
> itself: The topology of the cartouche sublates what I have analyzed
> elsewhere under the rubric *parergon* (the supplement of the outwork
> in the work). Briefly, a series which I truncate here: the paradigmatic
> coffin, the patron, the parricide to which it gives rise. The parergon,
> the tour de force, the strength of stroke, in this case: to reduce the
> paradigm, the model or "parangon" (this word has long awaited its in-
> sertion in this topic) in place of the parergon. In the same series,
> the *pharmakon.* (*Vérité,* 254)

In this meeting in a series of *parergon* and *paragon,* of *example* and *model,*
the oppositions of particular-general, inside-outside are displaced.

The relation of parergon and paragon, constitutive of Derrida's textual
chimera, are marked in another work by Titus-Carmel, *La grand bananeraie
culturelle,* a series consisting of one real banana—the model—which gradually decomposes, wilts, turns black as the days pass, and a quantity of
imitation or artificial bananas, all alike. The real banana is part of the series
and part of reality (another reality) at the same time, as manifested by its
decomposition. The real banana is in the maternal position, Derrida explains, the "natural phallus" of the banana being in the mother's position
because its responsibility, its priority in the series, is evident—hence, it
marks the effect of de-monstration, a silent showing. The cartouche, on
the other hand—the title, signature, documents—is in the paternal position,
paternity (as Freud noted) being "always inferred from a sentence, from a
declaration in the form of a judgment. Because paternity may not be perceived or touched" (*Vérité,* 254). Thus, when the artist-father (the logos is
son of the father, with models and examples falling under the father-son
relation) declares that the paradigm is the source of the drawings, the
signature effect problematizes his statement, putting him always in the
position of the Cretan liar. The cartouche recites the truth only to give rise
to conditions of doubt, and so enters into the series as one simulacrum
among others. But the chimera is both mother and father—the picto-ideo-
phonographic Writing states and de-monstrates: "From now on you will

have to read the *'est'* in this *écarté* or this *écart* [gap] (*'écart:* a term of
heraldry. One quarter of a shield divided into four parts. The principal
arms of the house are placed in the 1st and 4th *écart,* that is, the two in
the upper half of the shield; in the lower two are the arms obtained by
marriage or from the maternal line'), in which the West as a whole is
separated from itself" (*Dissemination,* 352). The field as a whole produces
a double bind in which what is said interlaces with what is shown. The cartouche inscribed beside the shield creates a paradigm effect, the truth
effect of the proper name, the aura of the corpse in its tomb, of the Tlinget
chief.

The motivated quality of Derrida's choice of the *Tlingit Coffin,* which
hinges upon his association of that work with certain aspects of *Glas*
(especially the kinship of Genet's matchbox to the coffin), is even more
pronounced in the other word-thing essay in the collection, entitled "+ R
(par-dessus le marché)," dealing with the drawings of Adami. Adami made
several drawings related to *Glas* in *Derrière le miroir,* one of which reproduces or counterfeits the signature "J. Derrida" with the "da" cut off.
The drawing—representing a fish, hooked and "drawn" half out of the
water, itself shown as a drawing in a spiral notebook, lying open, displaying handwriting along with the sketch—so captures the spirit of Derrida's
contemporary hieroglyphics that he baptizes the work "Ich,"[12] or "I"
(among other things), feeling upon seeing it "as if I was read in advance,
written before writing, prescribed, grasped, trapped, caught" (*Vérité,*
178). It is the feeling of confronting one's fetish. The other drawing,
actually executed on both sides of a sheet, representing front and back
(one side the drawing of a back of a painting), Derrida dubs "Chi," and
calls the ensemble "Chimera."

Motivated by Adami's drawings addressed to *Glas,* Derrida sets out, as
he terms it, to translate (*transduct*) Adami's drawings in turn. The traditional media and genre distinctions between the two bodies of work
collapse into a double-valued Writing: "formal writing, discursive writing,
picto-ideo-phonogram" (*Vérité,* 182). Adami's studies for *Glas* in no way
constitute illustrations, in the first place because there is no notebook-
fish scene in *Glas,* although the drawing does convey the apparatus of the
double band (the spiral binder of the chiasmatic interlace) and the inside-
out logic of the "argument of the sheath." Rather, "Ich" performs its own
operation such that it "signs the absolute reverse or back side of a text, its
other scene," making visible or allowing to be seen "death, that which
[*Glas*] could not exhibit itself." "Ich," therefore, functions with respect
to *Glas* the way the Bodleian post card functions in *La carte postale*—
together (text and "card," with *"carte"* being the anagram of *écart* as
gap, swerve, square, or quarter of a shield) they are recto and verso of a
double scene, verbal and nonverbal, modeling the structuration and

stricturalism of the new Writing: both are structured according to the chiasmus of double invagination of works that do what they say by exposing their own exposition. "Ich" does not resemble or represent *Glas,* then, but "dislocates, dissociates, disjoints, shifts, truncates, interrupts the exposition in *Glas,* yet reassembles and shows *Glas*'s unexposed side. . . . X, the letter of chiasmus, is *Chi,* in its usual transcription. I call thus this other scene, pursuant to if you like the anagrammatic inversion of *Ich,* or of *Isch* (the hebraic man). Pronounce it *qui* or *khi,* aspirating or rasping a bit, with an extra *r* through the throat, almost *cri.* But one can try out various languages and all the sexes (for example *she*)" (*Vérité,* 189).

The principle of the anagram or paragram is, in fact, the mode of transduction Derrida uses to invent a simulacrum of the drawings. Transduction guides Derrida in his return, in turning back upon and hooking Adami with his own line, interlacing their presentations across media, as indicated in the title, "+ R." "To transpose, or to put it another way, to betray the function or the phase of the stroke in Adami, when he operates 'to the line,' let drop the gl, to treat with tr" (*Vérité,* 195). To transduct line to letter, Derrida proposes to adopt the rhythm of the tr phonex[13] in order to write about Adami in the same way that he used the gl phonex in *Glas.* He invents his theoretical narrative thus by accumulating words with tr (in the *key* of tr, based on the "r" in *Chi*)—*"train, trait, trajet, trampe, tresse, trace, trajectoire, transformation, transcription, traduction."*

But, Derrida adds, do not mistake the work with syllables or sounds for a return to logocentrism, reabsorbing space into voice, painting into philosopheme, as in a form of hypercratylism. What is involved in the technique, rather, is hypomnesis, giving the lead to the artificial memory in writing, setting to work the tr in a computerlike search of vocabulary, keyed not for meanings, but for the drawn letters.

And then *tr* does not represent, does not imitate anything, it only imprints one differential trait, therefore more an unformed cry, it no longer remarks the lexicon . . . *tr* lends itself to analysis. Like any transformable conglomerate. Decompose the *tr,* run variations on its atoms, operate substitutions or transfers, rub out like Adami when he draws. In a first tableau, keep at first the double consonant, efface such and such bar of the *t,* replace it by traits of another consonant. For example *f* (almost the catastrophic reversal of *t*) but it could be, for another voyage, *b, c, d, g, p, v.* Retain the same *r,* you will have then, with the variation in *fr,* disengaged a + *r effect.* Consonant + r, and in drawing the +, you will have cited, along the way, all Adami's crosses. The progress of the red crosses especially, the hospital insignias, the fantastic ambulance men marking at once war and peace, the undecidable neutrality in the topography of political Europe. (*Vérité,* 199)

This passage is the best account available in Derrida of a drawn writing, taking the letter as a line, divisible (against the prejudices of phonocentrism), letting the semantic or representational effects fall where they may. *Glas,* Derrida notes, was written similarly with the + *L effect,* thus calling attention to the fact that Adami's drawings relate to *Glas* (as its verso) the way *r* relates to *l*—they are complementary or antithetical consonants, such that where one is absent the other occurs more frequently, becoming a dominant (Roback, 237). The cross, of course, marks in the plus sign the chiasmus, designating the stricture of articulation upon which Derrida's entire strategy rests.

The lesson for grammatology in this essay has to do with the relation in the word-thing, which exists at two levels—within Adami's art works themselves and in the relation of these works to Derrida's discourse (already described as transduction). Adami's drawing "The Portrait of Walter Benjamin" provides an example of the former level, a drawing that Derrida refers to, because of its extreme condensation, as the "hieroglyph of a biography, theory, politics, and allegory of the 'subject'" (*Vérité,* 206). Adami's "hieroglyphic" technique (manifesting Derrida's systematic research into all forms, ancient and modern, of written pictures or drawn words) consists of the exploration of certain details, extracting detachable fragments—typewriter, eyeglasses, and so forth—as metonyms (or prostheses) of the portrayed figure, thus giving these items the status of monumental fetishes. Recalling Benjamin's own theory that photography, with its capacity to make visible what is hidden from the unaided eye, constitutes a psychoanalysis of the visible world, Derrida remarks: "The sample of the enlarged detail is dependent in any case on both a cinematographic and psychoanalytic technique. These two powers, two techniques, two situations, another of Benjamin's demonstrations, are indissoluble. One and the same mutation" (*Vérité,* 209).

This statement by Derrida suggests (a major consideration for an applied grammatology) that the best method now available for extending grammatology, for putting it to work, includes film (or video) theory and practice as well as psychoanalysis. We may observe in the film context that the notion of frame enlargements of photographs—the "blow-up" is a homonym for the blow-up associated with deconstructive or disseminating dehiscence. The blown up detail, the "close-up," a corollary of the reversals of invagination and the colossal, is a feature of the example placed *"en abyme,"* as in this close inspection of the matchbox whose apparatus Derrida points to as a model of invagination: "The matchbox has this in particular that it does not open, like so many other little coffers, along the articulation of a hinge. Here, for once, *one* box opens or closes by sliding into another, which is none other than itself. One box open at the top fits into another box, the same, open at two ends, at the extremities. A hermetic closure composes the two openings, it composes itself of two. The box decomposes itself—into two independent boxes" (*Vérité*, 259). The same microscopic, magnifying glance is applied not only to objects— matchbox, umbrella, post card—but also to verbal material, in essays that often take as their point of departure nothing more than a parergonal bit from a major work (a footnote from Heidegger, a journal entry from Nietzsche, a line from one of Hegel's letters).

Having reviewed now the chiastic relationships that exist within the picto-ideo-phonographic chimera, along with Derrida's procedures for presentation on two bands—de-monstration for the maternal quarters of the field, transduction for the paternal quarters—I shall turn to an analysis of Derrida's practice of Writing in *The Post Card*. The use of the post card is the most elaborate instance yet of the incorporation of the pictographic element in Derrida's Writing. What remains to be clarified in the following discussion is the relationship of Derrida himself to the examples he chooses. The selection of the *Tlingit Coffin* (compared to the box of matches which Genet described carrying in his pocket—an aspect of "Cartouche" which I did not develop) and the *"Chimère"* drawings (explicitly addressed to Derrida) was motivated by Derrida's association of them with his own texts, notably *Glas*. Rather than making any attempt to explain or comment on the works formally or hermeneutically, Derrida borrowed them for his own composition. Like the images in mnemonics, the pictorial element in Writing is "autobiographical"—the examples choose the writer but then are remotivated as models of the exemplification process as such. They demonstrate, in the maternal position, what Derrida is unable to say in his discourse, showing *"en abyme"* the back side. Just how Derrida signs his models will be the subject of the next chapter.

5

Speculation

LETTERS

he Post Card is a collection in four parts (the same "squared" structure used in *Dissemination* and *La vérité en peinture*—the four quarters, with *carte* being an anagram of *écart* and *trace*)—three essays on psychoanalysis, "differing among themselves with regard to length, circumstances, style, and date," including "Spéculer—sur 'Freud,'" "Le facteur de la vérité," and "Du tout,"[1] along with "Envois," described as "the preface to a book which I never wrote" (echoing a classic definition of the essay as a genre).[2] "Envois" is a non- or antibook, then, whose "memory" persists, Derrida says, in the three essays: "It would have treated what has to do with the post office, with posts in all genres, in the manner of psychoanalysis, less in order to attempt a psychoanalysis of the postal effect than to refer to a singular event, Freudian psychoanalysis, to a history and to a technology of the courier, to some general theory of the dispatch and to everything that by some telecommunications pretends to be destined" (*Carte*, 7).

Like *Glas, The Post Card* has two "tracks," "columns," or "bands." One consists of the reproduction of an engraving depicting Socrates and Plato, taken from the frontispiece of *Prognostica Socratis basilci*, a thirteenth-century English fortune-telling book by Matthew Paris (signaling the homonymic *moira* effect linking Destiny and destination). The reproduction (also printed on the cover—"do not forget that everything began with the desire to make of this image the cover of a book"—*Carte*, 268) folds out, so that it may be kept in view on the right-hand side of the pages

125

(Genet's position in *Glas,* the column of images or figural intuition, the zone of the + R effect) while reading the large batch of separately dated "letters" said to be transcribed from a correspondence carried out on the backs of post cards imprinted with this reproduction. To the four pieces of the collection Derrida grafts elsewhere two more essays (although "Envois" is in principle infinitely expandable): "Télépathie," a group of cards supposedly misplaced and later recovered, and "D'un ton apocalyptique adopté naguère en philosophie," Derrida's address at the Cerisy-la-Salle colloquium devoted to his work.[3]

The text is further divided, in that what we are given is one side of a correspondence (the part signed "Derrida"), but no replies. Nor is the correspondence complete (although it is concluded, covering a two-year span, dated 3 June 1977 through 30 August 1979; or through 17 November 1979, if you include the blurb on the back cover, signed J. D., speaking to the potential reader with the familiar you—*tu*—used to address the "beloved" in the letters). Some of the letters (cards) were burned, we are told, deleted according to a secret calculation, their place in the sequence marked by a gap (*écart*) of fifty-two spaces. All these divisions function at one level to violate the unity, closure, or completeness that characterizes the traditional Book. At another level, keeping in mind that "Envois" is proffered as "a retrograde love letter, the last one of history" and that the ruse of the preface alludes explicitly to Rousseau's famous novel, the cuts transfer the castration theme of the *New Héloïse* from the signified background (Abelard) to the foreground of the signifier (writing with a knife).

As a "preface" to a study of Freud and psychoanalysis, "Envois" mimes the famous transferential correspondence Freud carried on with Fliess— the self-analysis marking the "origin" of psychoanalysis, of which only Freud's letters survive (published in expurgated form), and which ended with a picture post card of the Temple of Neptune, Paestum, inscribed, "Cordial greetings from the culminating point of the journey. Your Sigm." The experiment also puts into practice an interest Derrida has had for some time in the letter as a philosophical genre—given the undecidability of its statements owing to the informality and autobiographical component of the form, what status do letters written by philosophers have in the discourse of knowledge? He dramatizes the question by reviewing the scholarly controversy regarding the authenticity of Plato's letters. "Speculer—sur 'Freud' " is a close reading of *Beyond the Pleasure Principle* from the perspective of Freud's letters, on the order of the connections noted in *Glas* between Hegel's letters concerning his family life and his philosophical theories.

The feature that makes the letter exemplary of the logocentric era (a synonym for "postal era") is that it is addressed and signed, directed or destined (*"Destinataire"* = addressee). We take for granted the postal institution, thinking of it simply as a service, a technology extending in its history from the runners of ancient times to the modern state monopolies using airplanes, the telex, and so forth: "And with its *tekhnè* it implies a great number of things, for example, identity, the possible identification of senders and receivers" (*Carte*, 72). The entire history of the postal *techne* rivets "destination" to identity. The technology of identification (postal networks, telephone exchanges) can in turn serve as a model for exploring our theories of the self—as in Freud's use of the "messenger" as an anasemic metaphor for communications between the Unconscious and the Conscious. At another level, the question of the "destiny" and destining of the proper name is raised—to what extent, in the problematics of identity, does the name-of-the-father destine one's life? How does "Freud" sign psychoanalysis (emblematized in the fortune-telling book, recalling the earlier discussion of *Moira*, but also alluding to Freud's hypothesis that fortune telling is a phenomenon of "thought transference")?[4]

Identity in all its aspects (truth and being) is the ideology of the postal principle. But what becomes of this ideology in the current epochal shift, to which the radical change in communications technology makes a major contribution? Can Poe's "Purloined Letter," Derrida asks—especially with respect to the relations among the "police," psychoanalysis, and the epistle—be adapted to the new media? The telephone conversations frequently mentioned in "Envois" allude to Freud's description of telepathy as a kind of "telephonic conversation" (*New Introductory Lectures*, 54). Does the telephone, and all telecommunications, threaten literature as much as telepathy, as Freud explained, threatened psychoanalysis? The epochal shift does entail certain consequences for the knowledge disciplines: "The end of a postal epoch is without doubt the end of literature" (*Carte*, 114). "A whole epoch of the said literature, if not all, cannot survive a certain technological regime of telecommunications (the political regime is secondary in this respect). Nor philosophy, nor psychoanalysis. Nor love letters" (*Carte*, 212).

Such predictions or prophecies, Derrida stresses, are made problematic by the intersection of "ends" with the notion of "closure." For there is always a remainder, something extra left *poste restante* (the archive or encyclopedia of culture), for those who realize that the postal is not finally a transcendental principle equatable with the era of being. From the deconstructive point of view, the essence of the postal is not that letters *arrive* (the functionalist view, shared by Lacan) but that they sometimes *fail to arrive*. In terms of spacing rather than destiny, "the post is nothing but a 'little fold,' a relay to mark that there is never anything but relays" (*Carte*, 206). In other words, the *techne* concerns enframing, the production of images by whatever means, which is to say that the *techne* itself cannot "end" or "arrive at its completion," since it is what allows anything at all to become present or appear. *Techne* (is) differance (*Carte*, 206-7). The grammatologist (and the academic humanists of the future) studies enframing, not "literature." Literature does not end, but the classification "literature" becomes irrelevant.

AUTOGRAPHY

"Envois" interrogates the effect of the letter—the interaction of identity and knowledge—in terms of Derrida's own proper name. It could be subtitled "Speculate—on 'Derrida,'" complementing the monograph-length "Speculate—on 'Freud.'" In fact, the main drama, or tour de force, of this text is the "action by contact" that finally joins these two signatures—"Derrida" and "Freud"—through a sequence or series of terms, like the one linking parergon to paragon, which, following the laws of electro-magnetism (as an analogy), can carry a signature effect to any distance through the medium of language. The pretense of coding, the secret names and mysterious clusters of alphabetical letters ("EGEK HUM XSR STR"), allude finally to the secret of Derrida's signature disseminated in the text. The post card and the signature (proper name) share the character of being both readable—the post card circulates, its message exposed to anyone who looks, but, whether because of the excess or poverty of the message, it is meaningless (without interest) to all but the recipient: "What I love about the post card is that, even in an envelope, it is made to circulate like an open but unreadable letter" (*Carte*, 16). The laconic (Lacanic?) quality of the message, combined with the historical circumstance associating the official adoption of the cards with the war of 1870 (the army needed a way for soldiers to communicate with their families without divulging information useful to the enemy), makes the post card an emblem of the nature of writing: "Writing is unthinkable without repression. The condition for writing is that there be neither a permanent contact nor an absolute break between strata: the vigilance and failure of censorship. It is no accident that the metaphor of censorship should come from the area of politics concerned with the deletions, blanks, and disguises of writing" (*Writing*, 226). The association of writing with repression—writing as a stylus with shaft and veils, which thrusts and parries, which reveals and conceals, functioning inevitably within the domain of light and "heliopolitics"—in psychoanalysis, legitimates grammatology's turn to mnemonics and epithymics. For, as Freud notes in a letter to Fliess, explaining "deferred action," "To put it crudely, the current memory stinks just as an actual object may stink; and just as we turn away our sense organ (the head and nose) in disgust, so do the preconscious and our conscious apprehension turn away from the memory. This is *repression*."[5] This gesture, *turning away as if from a disgusting odor,* is the very motion of speculation, as we will see.

Everything that can be said of the post card applies also to the signature. There is also a censorship that binds the writer to writing: "We are written only as we write, by the agency within us which always already keeps watch over perception, be it internal or external. . . . In order to describe the structure, it is not enough to recall that one always writes for someone; and the oppositions sender-receiver, code-message, etc. remain extremely coarse instruments" (*Writing*, 226-27). Derrida returns to this problem in "Envois," to investigate the operation this time with his own signature. The framing that Lacan ignored in his seminar on "The Purloined Letter," the question of the narrator so developed in literary criticism, is now foregrounded not only in terms of Freud's relation to speculation in *Beyond the Pleasure Principle* but Derrida's as well: "I am in this book Plato, Ernst, Heinele, etc." (*Carte*, 59). I noted earlier that the subject of knowledge relates to his examples as to a fetish. The question to be investigated now is how Derrida inscribes his own name on Freud's cartouche.

The problematic that Derrida introduces here in terms of the post card (its message so banal, so trivial, as to seem unanalyzable; its existence so ubiquitous and "abject" as to render it conceptually invisible) he discussed earlier in terms of an "umbrella"—the umbrella (the circumflex as headgear) as proper name (in the illuminated scene, the proper names "Plato" and "Socrates" are placed above the heads of the respective figures "like an umbrella") (*Carte*, 18).

> My discourse, though, has been every bit as clear as that "I have forgotten my umbrella." You might even agree that it contained a certain ballast of rhetorical, pedagogical, and persuasive qualities. But suppose anyway that it is cryptic. What if those texts of Nietzsche (such as "I have forgotten my umbrella") and those concepts and words (like "spur") were selected for reasons whose history and code I alone know? What if even I fail to see the transparent reason of such a history code? At most you could reply that one person does not make a code. To which I could just as easily retort that the key to this text is between me and myself, according to a contract where I am more than just one. But because me and myself are going to die . . . our relation is that of a structurally posthumous necessity. (*Spurs*, 137)

In Derrida's theory, writing is by definition "posthumous," it "lives on," is always an "untimely meditation." Such is the lesson of one sense of "post." Another "post" directs the strategy of the letter as a disguised "self-address" (the essay being, in Montaigne's definition, a love letter to oneself). Derrida writes the post cards to himself (the code is between me and myself) by means of "apostrophe"—"Thus I apostrophize . . . (the man of discourse or of writing interrupts the continuous linkage of the sequence, suddenly turns toward someone, indeed some thing, he addresses himself to you" (*Carte*, 8). And in Derrida's homonymous style, the apostrophe is also the mark used with the reflexive verb in French and is the mark of possession in English, representing thus the gap that both requires and makes possible self-reflection, the gap of the postal relay.[6] Apostrophizing, Derrida mimes Nietzsche's "last man," the last philosopher (in the problematic of ends), who declares in his soliloquy, "With you, beloved voice, with you, last breath of the memory of all human happiness, allow me still this commerce of a single hour . . . for my heart loathes believing that love is dead; it does not support the shudder of the most solitary of solitudes, and it obliges me to speak as if I were two" (*Fins*, 465). In the epochal shift, that is, voice passes away along with the postal.

Part of the strategy of the experiment conducted in "Envois" may now be recognized. Derrida, tracking down the effects of identity ("Even if I feign to write [on the post card or on the marvelous telemachine] and no matter what I say about them, I seek above all to produce effects"—*Carte*, 124), places himself in the position of censor in the psychic economy, thus performing in a kind of psychoepistle the metaphorical description of an Unconscious-Conscious communication. Part of his purpose, given that grammatology is a boundary science and a science of boundaries, is to explore the notion of the "boundary idea": "Repression does not take place by the construction of an excessively strong antithetic idea, but by the intensification of a 'boundary idea,' which thereafter represents the repressed memory in the processes of thought. It may be termed a 'boundary idea' because on the one hand it belongs to the conscious ego and on the other hand forms an undistorted portion of the traumatic memory" (*Origins*, 154–55). The metaphorics of this network articulating the primary and secondary processes includes not only the kernel-shell model with the messenger running betweeen but also the notion of trace itself, which evokes as its analogy the entire history of roads. Hence, many of the letters carefully record Derrida's travels, coming and going (*da/fort*) on his lecture tours ("I resemble a messenger of antiquity . . . and I run to bring them news which ought to remain secret"—*Carte*, 12), playing also on the theme of the "legs" (legacy) of Freud. The censor's function, of course, is not to prohibit communication but only to disguise it—the secret is public.

The public aspect of the secret (the secret dramatized in "Envois" is the "identity" of the addressee) picks up a topic developed previously in "Signature Event Context," which poses as a limit-case, testing the theory of iterability, a circumstance that would prove that writing is productive even when cut off from all its origins or ends:

> Imagine a writing whose code would be so idiomatic as to be established and known, as secret cipher, by only two "subjects." Could

we maintain that, following the death of the receiver or even of both partners, the mark left by one of them is still writing? Yes, to the extent that, organized by a code, even an unknown and non-linguistic one, it is constituted in its identity as mark by its iterability, in the absence of such and such a person, and hence ultimately of every empirically determined "subject." This implies that there is no such thing as a code—organon of iterability, which could be structurally secret. ("Signature," 180)

The possibility, repeatedly mentioned in "Envois," that one or both of the correspondents may die, either by suicide or in an accident, alludes to this limit case. The narrative approach itself, the autobiography/fiction of the love letters, may be recognized as the tale required by anasemia to expose obliquely, as if by ricochet, the scene of writing.

By positioning himself in the place of the censor, Derrida hopes to be able to work both scenes of the double science at once. A major shortcoming of philosophy (and of the discourses of knowledge in general), according to Derrida, is its failure to realize that the text must be signed twice. Putting their confidence in the copyright and the proper name, "each philosopher denies the *idiom* of his name, of his language, of his circumstance, speaks by means of concepts and generalities necessarily improper" ("Signéponge," in *Digraphe,* 123). To sign requires more than simply affixing the name to a text. Rather, one must literally inscribe the signature *in* the text (one does, in any case). "It will be necessary for me to sign, that I sign and for that that I do like another, like him (Ponge in this case), that is, that I give to my text an absolutely proper, singular, idiomatic form, therefore dated, framed, bordered, truncated, cut off, interrupted" (*Signéponge,* 119).

This second order of the signature renders the relationship of the subject to knowledge more rather than less enigmatic. Thus, we find Derrida's proper name at the head of his text, at the break between the foreword and the "preface" (ironically entitled "envoy," the genre of closings), like a protective umbrella: "Worn out as you are with the movement of the poets and the psychoanalytic movement, with all that they authorize in matters of sham, fictions, pseudonyms, homonyms, or anonyms, alleviated, familiarized by the fact that I assume without detour the responsibility for these *envois,* for those which remain or no longer remain, and in order to give you peace I sign them here with my proper name, Jacques Derrida" (*Carte,* 9–10). The undecidability of such statements, thoroughly established in "Limited Inc," extends to remarks in interviews as well, such as the one in which Derrida declares that "what I write, one quickly sees, is terribly autobiographical. Incorrigibly."[7]

What Derrida wishes to expose is the truth effect of the signature, of the "I" who appears to speak, by displacing the opposition between pre-text

and text, life and art, thus problematizing our understanding of the way a
text "exits [exist] *into* the real," as in this discussion of Lautréamont who,
through a simulacrum of prefacing, takes up a hybrid position "that has
already ceased being part of the preface and *doesn't yet* belong to the
'analytic' part" (*Dissemination,* 36): "Dissemination question: what 'is
going on,' according to what time, what space, what structure, what becomes of the 'event' when 'I write,' 'I place beside me an open inkstand
and a few sheets of unspitballed paper,' or 'I am going to write,' 'I have
written': about writing, against writing. . . . What's the story with this
autography of pure loss and without a signature? And how is it that this
performance displaces such force in going without truth?" (*Dissemination,*
41). There is only one way to research such a question—by opening oneself to an autograph hunt for one's own signature.

D-E-R-R-I-D-A

The Post Card is an especially valuable addition to Derrida's theory,
since it clarifies the deconstruction that "autobiography" is submitted to
in autography. It continues, that is, the poststructuralist concern for the
place of the subject of knowledge. As noted earlier in discussions of Ponge
and Genet, Derrida's autograph involves a turn, like the apostrophe,
which transforms the proper name into a thing, into a rebus. But if this
turn or descent carried Ponge into the realm of the sponge and Genet into
the field of flowers, "Derrida" is nothing so substantial. "I have, in other
texts, devised countless games, playing with 'my name,' with the letters
and syllables *Ja, Der, Da.* Is my name still 'proper,' or my signature, when,
in proximity to 'There, J. D.' (pronounced, in French, approximately Der.
J. D.), in proximity to 'Wo? Da.' in German, to 'her. J. D.' in Danish, they
begin to function as integral or fragmented entities, or as whole segments
of common nouns or even of things?" ("Limited Inc," 167).

Derrida mentions several times that his decision to write "on" figures
such as Freud and Heidegger includes unconscious as well as theoretical
motivation (the "object" of study is always also a "boundary idea," a
"love-object"). The *da* in Freud's *fort/da* and in Heidegger's *Dasein* contain part of Derrida's name, giving those respective theories a certain
connection, aleatory yet necessary by force of the "after effect," with
Derrida's autobiography ("here Freud and Heidegger, I conjoin them in
myself as the two great phantoms of the 'grand epoch' " (*Carte,* 206).

Given that "the signature of the proper name can also play the role of
a cache (sheath or fleece) to conceal another signature" ("Crochets," 112),
it is never finally possible to decide who or what signs. This characteristic
of the theory is itself part of Derrida's signature, which, besides the *Der*

and *Da* of designation (playing on de-sign, in all senses), also includes another location—"Derrière: every time that word comes first, if it is written therefore after a period with a capital, something in me brings me to recognize therein my father's name, in golden letters on his tomb, even before he was in it" (*Glas*, 80). But this "behind" is also anatomical, "posterior," indicating that Derrida's name is implicated in one of the most famous "recognition" scenes of psychoanalysis—the Wolf Man's obsession with the housemaid, viewed from behind, on her knees scrubbing (making proper), a fetish derived from the primal scene of the parents having sex a tergo. "Everything is always attacked from the back [*de dos*], written, described from behind [*derrière*]. A tergo" (*Glas*, 97). Derrida's *derrière* signs here the framing of narrative, as in his analysis of the narrator's position in "The Purloined Letter": "There are only ostriches, no one escapes being plucked, and the more one is the master, the more one presents one's rear. This is the case of whoever identifies with Dupin" ("Purveyor," 76).

Reversing his initials, as pronounced in French, reveals another basic term of Derrida's theory within his signature—*"déjà"* (the always *already*). The *already* and the *behind* reinforce one another: "I am already (dead) signifies that I am *behind*. Absolutely behind, the Behind which has never been seen full face, the Already which nothing has preceded, which therefore conceived and gave birth to itself, but as cadaver or glorified body. To be behind, is to be above all—separated from symmetry. I retrench—behind —I bleed at the bottom of my text" (*Glas*, 97).

The *derrière* is in the master trope of "Envois" which, Derrida states, has to do with "turning the back" (*"tourner le dos"*—turning tail, taking flight, turning over, as well as *giving the cold shoulder,* an act of scorn or disdain). "To turn my back on them while pretending to speak to them and take them as witness. This conforms to my taste and to what I can bear from them. To turn over the post card (what is Socrates's back when he turns his back on Plato—a very amorous position, don't forget—? That is also the back of the post card . . .). The word 'back' [*dos*] and all the families which stir behind it, beginning from behind [*derrière*]. There (da) is behind, behind the curtain or the skirts of the cradle, or behind oneself" (*Carte*, 192).

To avoid playing the ostrich, Derrida turns his back in another way, as censor at the frontier of the Unconscious, letting the forces of disguise and iterability work, transforming his text into a Rosetta stone—hieroglyph and vulgate at once. "Envois" dramatizes this tension and at the same time introduces a new attitude toward knowledge into academic writing: against the traditional model of research (the drive to find out and declare a truth —put into question by Nietzsche and Freud), Derrida proposes instead an elaboration of enigmas rendering all conclusions problematic: truth gives way to secrets, closure to undecidability. He proposes a writing oriented toward stimulation or provocation rather than information, a pedagogical writing to raise questions rather than a scientific discourse giving answers. "As for 'learned' letters, you know, you alone, that I have always known how at least to make use of knowledge to distance the curious . . . I do not use ordinary language, the language of knowledge, to adorn myself or to establish my empire, but only to efface all the traits, neutralize all the codes" (*Carte*, 88–89). "Derrida," then, has the status of the post card (openly hermetic) or of the umbrella (open and closed).

Part of the lesson of autography for the academic writer is not only that the discourse of knowledge is motivated by desire (a common point from Plato to Freud), but that we write *for ourselves, to ourselves*, in a secret code interlacing information for others and surprises for ourselves. Like a post card, the discourse of knowledge has two sides. If psychoanalysis taught us how to *read* both sides of the card, grammatology aspires to *write* on both sides.

"The *Derrière* and the *Déjà* protect me, render me unreadable, shelter me in the verso of the text. I am not accessible, readable, visible, except in a rear-view mirror. All the rhetorical flowers in which I disperse my signature, in which I apostrophize and apotrope myself, read them as forms of repression" (*Glas*, 97). To write from the position of censor is to attempt to think directly from the superego and the conscience[8] ("I am your terrorizing 'superego' "–*Carte*, 18). And what this agency cannot accept is divulgence: "What there is of divulgence in the slightest publication, the most reserved, the most neutral, I still find inadmissible, unjustifiable—and especially r–i–d–i–c–u–l–o–u–s, a priori comical" (*Carte*, 89). The new autobiography (autography) has little to do with confession or expression, then, as if, in any case, it were possible so easily to brush aside the guard at his post: "You are the name, or the title of all that I do not understand. That which I can never know [*connaître*], my other side, eternally inaccessible, not unthinkable at all, but unknowable, unknown—and so lovable. On your subject, my love, I can only postulate" (*Carte*, 160). This name, or title, is "Derrida."

Reversing the usual situation in which the author unwittingly reveals himself while attending to the presentation of information, Derrida, as censor, organizes the information according to the dictates of the name. In this process, with all its safeguards, a quantity of material typical of conventional autobiography is published, but with another purpose, that of prosthesis—the autobiographical information as *loci*, mnemonically remotivated in the service of current research. We are presented with a memory (but whose?): "I was just over four years old, easy to calculate, my parents were at the far end of the garden, myself alone with her on what we called the veranda. She slept in her cradle, I recall only the celluloid baby which burned in two seconds, nothing else (neither of having lit it myself nor of the least emotion today, only my parents who came running" (*Carte,* 270). Such fragments no longer function normally, since they belong to "Derrida," not Derrida: "I can always say 'that is not me'" (*Carte,* 255) being caught up, enframed, in the narrative fiction. The "auto," that is, does not function at the level of such content. Yet such material is included as part of the experiment, since the effects of the censor are more clearly discernible when it is partially relaxed, as it is when dreaming (Laplanche and Pontalis, 66). By noting what it allows to pass, what is excluded comes to a kind of negative shape.

The superego, according to Freud, is constructed "'on the model not of its parents but of its parents' superego; the contents which fill it are the same and it becomes the vehicle of tradition and of all the time-resisting judgments of value which have propagated themselves in this manner from generation to generation'" (Laplanche and Pontalis, 437). Here is the question of "telepathy," of the ghost (the psychotic incorporates his parent's trauma), relevant to the theme of tradition, with whose continuity Derrida proposes to interfere. Keeping in mind that censorship (repression) is directed not against the instinct as such but against its signs or representations (and not against perceptions but memories), Derrida, performing as censor, comes upon an image of his signature, an image whose structure and effect is the organizing experience of "Envois," having as well, together with the post card bearing it, the status of model.

When Derrida sees the post card in a display case in Oxford's Bodleian library, it affects him the same way he reacted upon seeing Adami's *"Chimère"* drawings, the way Grusha on her knees affected the Wolf Man. There is an "apocalyptic revelation" or recognition scene: "Socrates writing, writing before Plato, I always knew it, it remained as a photographic negative to be developed after twenty-five centuries—in me of course . . . Socrates, the one writing—seated, bent over, scribe or docile copyist, Plato's secretary. He is in front of Plato, no, Plato is *behind* [*derrière*] him smaller (why smaller?) but standing up. With extended finger he has the air of indicating, designating, showing the way or of giving an order—of dictating, authoritative, magisterial, imperious" (*Carte,* 14).

The importance of the scene is that it de-monstrates, with one stroke, the truth of tradition: "Everything in our bildopedic culture, in our encyclopedic politics, in our telecommunications of all kinds, in our telematicometaphysic archive, in our library, for example the marvelous Bodleian, everything is constructed on the protocolary charter of an axiom, which one could demonstrate, display on a card, a post card of course, it is so simple, elementary, brief, stereotyped" (*Carte,* 25). The axiom is that Socrates comes before Plato—the order between them is the irreversible sequence of heritage. But what Derrida recognizes in Matthew Paris's image reversing the traditional relationship (the *derrière* and designation [*da*] of his signature), which makes the scene "terrorizing" as well as apocalyptic (a "revelation")—catastrophic, in short—is that his signature is implicated in the postal principle itself. That is, even while the postal era believes the proposition of an irreversible heritage (father to son, speaker and logos), its practice is just the reverse, exactly as the post card shows. The post card—as a means of communication marking the operation of an institution of identity, and also the engraved scene—is an image of *teleology*. This recognition is all the confession we get in "Envois," but it alerts us to the possibility that, just as Nietzsche, with his philosophy of affirmation, of saying Yes to the Eternal Return, was working *against* the dictates of his proper name, which in Slavic is associated with "nullity" and "negation" (yet these terms do describe the way he is received—Roback, 78), so too is Derrida working against the "destiny" that links him with teleology. At the same time, the *derrière* signs the fundamental structure of grammatology, for the situation in which dictation "comes from behind," another example of which, in the other tradition, has Jesus dictating to John the Baptist (by the intervention of an angelic messenger), as described in "Of an Apocalyptic Tone," is the scene of writing as such: "But by a catastrophic inversion here more necessary than ever, we can as well think this: as soon as we no longer know very well who speaks or who writes [commenting on the dispatches on dispatches to which John responds], the text becomes apocalyptic. And if the dispatches [*envois*] always refer to other dispatches without decidable destination, the destination remaining to come, then isn't this completely angelic structure, that of the Johannine Apocalypse, isn't it also the structure of every scene of writing in general?" (*Fins*, 471).

F–R–E–U–D

The issue Derrida explores in terms of *Beyond the Pleasure Principle* summarizes everything that has concerned me thus far and states the conditions of an applied grammatology:

> The speculator recalls himself, but we cannot know whether this "himself" can say "I, me, myself." . . . This is why, if we must have recourse here to the autobiographical, it must be in an entirely new way . . . it will force us to reconsider the whole topography of the *autos*, the self. . . . *Beyond the Pleasure Principle* is thus not an *example* of what we believe we already know under the name of auto-biography. It writes the autobiographical, and, from the fact that an "author" recounts something of his life in it, we can no longer conclude that the document is without truth value, without value

as science or as philosophy. A "domain" opens up in which the "inscription" of a subject in his text is also the necessary condition for the pertinence and performance of a text, for its "worth" beyond what is called empirical subjectivity. (*Psychoanalysis,* 135)

To see how Derrida signs Freud (to discover the autography in his choice of subjects, his own status as "participant observer"), we must first consider how Freud signs psychoanalysis.

In working with the destiny of names or the fortune of words, we are in the domain of "Semitic nomocentricity": "A characteristic difference between the Greeks and the Jews lies in the fact that while the former emphasized action and process, most of their mythology revolving around transformation, the latter were constantly inquiring into the origin of the name, seeking its rationale.... While we say 'true to type,' the Jews would say 'Like his name, like him'" (Roback, 59). Name effects are a major element in psychoanalysis, of course, and "Freud" itself is often cited as an example of the destiny of a name (often, during Freud's lifetime, as a joke or insult), since, by antonomasia, *"die Freude"* means pleasure and is closely associated with *"die Lust,"* after which Freud names his chief principle. Hence, in focusing on *Beyond the Pleasure Principle,* Derrida is deliberately studying Freud's effort to confront the destiny of his signature (in fact, as Derrida shows, Freud makes every effort to defend the pleasure principle against all rivals, such as Jung with his archetypes).

There are many other examples in history of a "genius" following the dictates of the name. Roback lists a large number of examples, one being Michelangelo, in that *Buonarotti* means "he who *files* well, who is a good polisher" (Roback, 71). Considerable work has been done on "Freud," beginning with Freud's own observations, noting, for example, with respect to a certain incident, its frequent confusion with *"Freund"* (friend) (*New Introductory Lectures,* 72). Robert Pujol, describing Freud's signature in his study of Leonardo, notes that the *Sieg* in Sigmund is the equivalent of *Vinci,* both meaning "conqueror" (it was Freud's childhood ambition to imitate the "conquistadors"[9]). The "Joconde," or *Mona Lisa,* means *"freudig,"* or joyous, and so forth (*Fins,* 189–92). Nicholas Abraham observed, studying the case of Little Hans, an association in the patient's mind of "Freud" with *"Pferd"*—the horse of his obsession—which enabled Freud to cure the patient (*Ecorce,* 442).

Derrida's analysis in "Speculate—on 'Freud,'" while it does much else besides, is a major addition to this line of research and accounts at the same time for his own signature. The jointing term, stricturing the entire countersigning scene, following the macaronic translation principle of the Rosetta stone, is *"froid"*—cold: the essay could be called "Speculate—on 'froid.'" A certain coldness is to Freud what the sponge is to Ponge, or the flower to Genet, or the *derrière* to Derrida. It is surprising that the connection has not been made before, since it accounts for Freud's signature on "psychoanalysis"—as a term, rather than as content (pleasure, etc.). The Greek word for "soul" from which the "psyche" of "psychoanalysis" derives is *psuche:* "To the naturalistic Greek, *psuche* was but a cold breath, a gust of wind, which remains after life is gone, as its twin word *psuchos* (frost, chill) indicates" (Roback, 142). Not just "breath," as is well known, but a *cold* breath informs "psyche."

Roback adds that the *ps* phonex in Greek is predominant in words "of an opprobrious nature"—(*pseudo* = false, *psogos* = shame, *psolos* = soot, and so forth, collecting semantic families in a way similar to Mallarmé's *English Words*)—"what *ps* is for the Greeks, the *shm* sound is for the Jews, viz. one of contempt" (Roback, 142). That Derrida's *"tourner le dos"* is defined as a gesture of contempt, not to mention that its English equivalent is "giving the cold shoulder," marks Derrida's signature in "psychoanalysis" and "Freud" both. The gesture of contempt is fundamental to "Derrida," not only because "showing the rear" has to do with more than the "ostrich" position, being, as anthropologists have noted, nearly a universal gesture of contempt, but because the physiological gesture required to pronounce *Da,* as noted in the "voco-sensory" theory of motivation which Derrida plays with in *Glas* (the theory that word meanings are motivated by the articulatory movements required to make the sounds of speech, hence bodily writing), is to extend the tongue (Roback, 109, 141, 172). To pronounce *Da* is to stick out the tongue (in a concealed way), another gesture of contempt, similar to Roland Barthes's statement that "the Text is that uninhibited person who shows his behind to the *Political Father.*"[10]

Derrida's interest in the "abject" level of analysis, however, is to discover how, or if, such arbitrary matters become motivated, accepted, how the contingent becomes the necessary. Thus, in his analysis of *Beyond the Pleasure Principle,* which he reads as if it were a theory of speculation, Derrida finds that the gesture controlling Freud's speculative procedure is precisely the gesture of coldness present in both their signatures. To appreciate this point requires a review of Derrida's argument.

Psychoanalysis epitomizes autography, being a mode of knowledge, a generalized truth, and an institutionalized science constructed out of an idiomatic memory technique of an individual—it is, Derrida says, "the science of Freud's name." In its simplified form, the question Derrida asks is "how an autobiographical writing, in the abyss of an unterminated auto-analysis, could give *its* birth to a world-wide institution." (*Carte,* 325). The entry point into this question, drawing on the parergonal logic of the example, is the famous anecdote in which Freud recalls observing his grandson playing a game with a bobbin on a string. Freud himself refuses to "speculate" on the significance of the recollection because of its "unscientific" nature. But Derrida shows that the bobbin example functions as a "de-monstration," without concept, that the progress of reasoning followed in the pages of *Beyond the Pleasure Principle* repeats the structure of the anecdote, reflecting the throwing away and retrieval of the bobbin in the oscillation of its argument. Relevant to our earlier discussion of the example *"en abyme,"* Derrida notes here that "the story he reports seems to place the writing of the report into an abyss structure," and he adds this caveat:

> I have never wished to overuse the abyss, nor above all the abyss structure. I have no strong belief in it, I distrust the confidence that it, at bottom, inspires, and I find it too representational to go far enough, not to *avoid* the very thing into which it pretends to plunge us. What does the appearance here of a certain *mise en abyme* open on, and close around? This appearance is not immediately apparent, but it must have played a secret role in the fascination that this little story of the reel exerts upon the reader—this anecdote that might have been thought banal, paltry, fragmented. (*Psychoanalysis,* 120)

Nonetheless, the relation between the example and its discourse (the problematic of models, which is the topic of this chapter) is the organizing question of the essay:

> In every detail we can see the superposition of the subsequent description of the *fort/da* with the description of the speculative game, itself so assiduous and so repetitive, of the grandfather in writing *Beyond the Pleasure Principle.* It's not, strictly speaking, a matter of superposition, nor of parallelism, nor of analogy, nor of coincidence. The necessity that links the two descriptions is of a different sort: we shall not find it easy to give a name to it, but it is clearly the main thing at stake for me in the sifting, interested reading that I am repeating here. (*Psychoanalysis,* 119)

The anecdote of the bobbin is both theoretical and autobiographical (the distinction becomes problematic), autobiographical not only in the usual sense of its setting in Freud's personal experience but in the sense that it images Freud's writing—it performs the scene of writing. Freud's case is especially interesting because the movement of the bobbin (the round trip) is the image not only of the zigzag stitch sewing anecdote to theory but the image of Freud's relation to the psychoanalytic movement as an institution (and here is the reversal of teleology, the aftereffect of beginnings as ends). Freud plays with his theory the way the grandson plays with the bobbin. The grandson in effect dictates to Freud, a reversal or tautology that extends from Freud's biological family to his psychoanalytic (institutional) family—as cybernetics suggests, the forces at work in organisms and in organizations are the same. In both instances relationships (among people and ideas) are governed by the *fort/da* movement of repulsion and attraction (incorporation, introjection) that is a feature of survival, of the instinct to "live on." Thus, Freud's speculations on the pleasure principle become intelligible in the context of his concern over the succession in the institution he hoped to build (the "cause and effect" enframing order of "science" becomes fused with "cause" as mission and transmission).

The methodology used for the analysis of the interaction between idiom and science, private and public, particular and general, is the juxtaposition of what Freud *says* in his theories and what he *does* in his writing (the basic procedure of deconstruction). The result is a reaffirmation or a reminder, of the basic dilemma of the study of things human—the observer is part of the observation: "What happens when acts or performances (discourse or writing, analysis or description, etc.) make up part of the objects they designate? When they could give themselves as an example of that very thing about which they speak or write? One certainly does not gain thereby an autoreflexive transparence, on the contrary" (*Carte,* 417). Every example, every model, every theory, in other words, is a "boundary idea," folded back on itself, fetish and concept, prosthesis and thesis at once. This condition of thought, lending every problem the structure of a Klein bottle ("The borders of the whole then are neither closed nor open. Their trait divides itself and the interlaces no longer undo themselves," Derrida says of Freud's struggle to resolve the question of the life-and-death drives in the pleasure principle, adding in a footnote that this structure is that of "the chiasmatic double invagination of borders"—417) and makes any resolution (any analytic tying up) of a speculative problem (specular, because of the mirroring *"mise en abyme"*) impossible.

The kind of speculation de-monstrated in *Beyond the Pleasure Principle,* then, is nondialectical, works without conclusion, synthesis, or concept, is without genre. Thus, it reinforces the program of *The Post Card* as a whole, which is to call attention to the inescapable metaphoricity of philosophy and the human sciences. Freud entered reluctantly into the speculative process, first translating an observation ("whether outside of, or already within, language") into a *description* in language. Then this translation had to be translated into the language of theory, the schemas for which had to be borrowed from an extant science in order to be receivable. The interest of this enframing process for Derrida concerns the way each of the steps opens knowledge to speculation, effaces the distinction between sensible and intelligible, aisthesis and episteme, thus permitting or ensuring entry of the researcher's predilections into the process. Derrida groups all the terms related to this specularity—transition, transportation, transgression, transference, and so forth—under the term "transfer" (metaphor), by which is meant all the networks having to do with "correspondences, connections, switchings, of a traffic and sorting of semantics, postal railway without which no transferential destination would be possible" (*Carte,* 409).

Freud himself, recognizing the dangers of intuition and remaining suspicious of philosophy, decided *not to conclude.* His response to the paradox of *Unlust,* of unpleasure (disgust, the death principle) was to leave it *ungelöst (Carte,* 416), unresolved—a homophonic relation that is Derrida's clue to the lesson contained in *Beyond the Pleasure Principle* and to Freud's signature as well: "The only possible solution: *a cold benevolence,* indifferent (*ein kühles Wohlwollen*) to the results of our own efforts of thought" (407). Derrida makes no effort to elaborate his discovery, introducing it *only as an adjective ("une bienveillance froide"),* [11] even as a translation of Freud's own description of his suspensive, floating, provisional stance, preferring instead to stress Freud's new speculation as an alternative to the old conceptual dialectic. Freud models, beyond the opposition and contradiction of Hegelian speculation, a new principle of *rhythm,* emblematized by the going and coming (*"ida y vuelta,"* the *ida* suggesting that Derr*ida* signs the *fort* as much as the *da*) of the *fort/da* bobbin on the interlacing string. The *froide* is only mentioned, because Derrida employs the signature effect not as an end in itself but as a discovery procedure, as a research device suggesting the point of entry into a topic. Just as the "edge" or "border" (*Kante*) suggested that the *Critique of Judgment* would best yield to the topic of parerga, so did the *froide* indicate that *Beyond the Pleasure Principle* would open along the line of a certain coldness. It is, moreover, written in the key of *ps,* from "Envois" (which means postscript) to the phonex magnified in the monogram of Plato and Socrates (P.S.) (just as *Glas* is written in the key of *gl*). The liaison in the subtitle— *From Socrates to Freud and Beyond*—is motivated thus by the *ps* which signs not only Plato and Socrates but *PSychoanalysis, Freud, froide, cold, indifference, contempt, repression (turning away as if from an odor), Derrière, tourner le dos, fort/da, Da, Derrida.* Such is the chainmail, the network or grid of action by contact, the force of the signature moving along the telephone wire which strictures the reading of *Beyond the Pleasure Pinciple* by *Derrida* in particular.

POST CARD

As for the post card itself, it is another exemplary example, a model, like the shoe, the umbrella, the matchbox, the abject objects of the contraband within the picto-ideo-phonographic Writing, de-monstrating in their utter simplicity the verso of discourse. What this card shows is teleology and its overcoming, representing as it does all the material of spacing and parerga which conceptualization excludes or demotes to the status of "the didactic preface, the 'synthetic exposition,' the 'frontispiece,' the façade one sees from the front before penetrating further, the picture engraved on the cover of the book" (*Dissemination*, 36).

The image encountered in the Bodleian emblematizes teleological "return inquiry." Indeed, part of the interest of "Envois" is that it is an experimental version of an analysis presented in Derrida's first book—the introduction to Husserl's *Origin of Geometry*. One of the principal points made in this early book concerns Husserl's notion of *Rückfrage*, translated as "*question en retour*," or "return inquiry," which Derrida discusses in terms of the same postal metaphor used in *The Post Card*: "Like its German synonym, return inquiry (and *question en retour* as well) is marked by the postal and epistolary reference or resonance of a communication from a distance. From a received and already readable *document*, the possibility is offered me of asking again, and *in return*, about the primordial and final intention of what has been given me by tradition. The latter, which is only mediacy itself and openness to a telecommunication in general, is then, as Husserl says, 'open . . . to continued inquiry' " (*Geometry*, 50). The tele, or postal, analogy—the metaphorical focus of Derrida's analysis—involves a relational zigzag motion of circulation, the same movement remarked in Freud's *fort/da* and Heidegger's *Dasein.*

Tradition and translation, Derrida notes, are two aspects of the same possibility (*Geometry*, 72). According to the postal principle, tradition and translation consist of an idealized communication. For example, "the Pythagorean theorem," Husserl states, "indeed all of geometry, exists only once, no matter how often or even in what language it may be expressed. It is identically the same in the 'original language' of Euclid and in all 'translations' " (72). The model of language for Husserl is the objective language of science. "A poetic language, whose significations would not be *objects*, will never have any transcendental value for him," Derrida notes (82). Husserl conceives scientific language to be (ideally) univocal. "It thus keeps its ideal identity throughout all cultural development. It is the condition that allows communication among generations of investigators no matter how distant and assures the exactitude of translation and the purity of tradition" (101–2).

For Husserl, then, "the *primordial* sense of every intentional act is *only* its *final* sense, i.e. the constitution of an object (in the broadest sense of these terms). That is why only a teleology can open up a passage, a way back toward the beginnings" (*Geometry*, 64). His method, the return inquiry, always begins with "the sense as we now know it." Thus, despite sedimentation (and because of it, following a model of research as archeology), one can "restore history to its traditional diaphaneity." Tradition, in this teleological view, is the "aether" of historical perception (49). Husserl's science is one that counts on its ability to be able to say the *same,* to repeat itself in a continuity that anticipates every change in "science," no matter how radical or revolutionary. The history of such a science entails the notion of "horizon"—"the always-already-there of a future, a kind of 'primordial knowledge' concerning the totality of possible historical experience"—a unity anticipated in every incompletion of experience, thus making the a priori and the teleological (the beginning and the end) coincide (117).

Much of Derrida's work over the years has been an attempt to expose and overcome teleology and its twin, the drive of the proper, as evidenced, for example, in his adopting from psychoanalysis the technique of anasemic reversal, which, in this context, may be recognized as a parodic mime of return inquiry. Derrida argued against Husserl that in the transmission of a tradition (understood as a kind of telecommunication), "noncommunication and misunderstanding are the very horizon of culture and language" (*Geometry,* 82). Against Husserl's endeavor to reduce or impoverish language in the interests of univocity, Derrida (setting his future course) poses the example of James Joyce, who exploited equivocity: "To repeat and take responsibility for all equivocation itself, utilizing a language that could equalize the greatest possible synchrony with the greatest potential for buried, accumulated, and interwoven intentions within each linguistic atom, each vocable, each word, each simple proposition, in all wordly cultures and their most ingenious forms" (102). Following Joyce's example (in *Finnegans Wake*), translation would not simply pass from one language into another on the basis of a common core of sense but would pass through all languages at once, cultivating their associative syntheses instead of avoiding them.

In *The Post Card* Derrida explores the equivocity in tradition, as manifested in the postal metaphor. He shifts his attention, in other words, to the possibility that a letter might *not* be delivered (the discontinuity disruptive of tradition), thus remotivating the model, studying it from the side of dysfunction. "It is necessary that I make (practically, effectively, performatively), but for you, my sweet love, a demonstration that a letter can always—and therefore ought—not ever arrive at its destination" (*Carte,* 133). The proof is simple at the level of the theoretical model—the postal system—requiring only the designation of the dead letter office. The division within the French psychoanalytic movement, split into factions quarreling about the "correct" interpretation of their science—the subject of "Du Tout" (the last essay in the collection)—is proof at the institutional level.

The possibility that a letter might go astray, ignored by Husserl and denied in principle by teleology, is a phenomenon to be celebrated as an extension of that detour called "life": "It is good that this is the case, it is not a misfortune, it is life" (*Carte,* 39). Derrida renders himself unreadable (emblematized in the secret and the burning of the correspondence), precisely in order to affirm life. What the postal institution labels the "dead letter office," Derrida calls the "division of living letters" (*Carte,* 136). It is worth noting that the title of the seminar in which Derrida originally investigated the questions treated in "Speculate—on 'Freud' " was "Life Death," involving on the one hand the problematic of biology, genetics, epistemology, and the history of the life sciences (readings of Jacob and Canguilhem, among others) and on the other hand a consideration of Nietzsche and of Heidegger's reading of Nietzsche (*Carte,* 277). The nature of speculation concerns reproduction in terms of a kind of sociobiology (cybernetics and the information theories that accompany the new communications technology)—the tendency of species and institutions to reproduce themselves as the same (like the truths of Husserl's ideal science) and yet to evolve and change along the way. The immediate question for Derrida has to do with rival theories of pedagogy or of creativity as "semination" (the seminars in- or dis-): "The Life of the Concept is a necessity that, in *including* the dispersion of the seed, in making that dispersion work to the profit of the Idea, *excludes* by the same token all loss and all haphazard productivity. The exclusion is an inclusion. In contrast to the seminal differance thus repressed, the truth that speaks (to) itself within the logocentric circle is the discourse of what *goes back to the father"* (*Dissemination,* 48).

The application of this Hegelian reproduction of the Concept would be something like Husserl's scientific classroom. Its opposite would be the apocalyptic jeremiads of the prophets, who scattered their aphoristic seeds abroad without address. The difference, Derrida says, is between telling and foretelling, between "proofs" and "metaphors." From the point of view of grammatology, of course, the opposition is an alliance of "enemy brothers." Derrida, rather, is interested in the articulation that joints these attitudes: "What do they together exclude as the inadmissible itself?" (*Fins,* 462). The same debate between the philosophic and the poetic continues today, Derrida notes in calling attention to Kant's attack on the "overlordly tone": "Not to take sides or come to a decision—I shall do no such thing—between metaphor and concept, literary mystagogy and true philosophy, but for a start to recognize the ancient interdependence of these antagonists or protagonists" (458-59).

Derrida's point also has to do with information theory, which describes information in terms of novelty—the more redundancy, the less information. Novelty in this conception is negentropic, counters the tendency to run down, wear out. But in Derrida's practice of the simulacrum, sheer repetition itself generates the new, opens the gap of novelty. To transform the postal principle there is no need to find some original or novel position outside, elsewhere. Following the steps of deconstruction, rather, Derrida shifts the polarity of teleology as a concept, replacing destiny with chance —the luck, for example, that brought to his attention Matthew Paris's fortune-telling book. His strategy in general is sabotage—"leaning on a well-placed lever to force a disconnection, derailment, a ringing off, to play with the switching and to send elsewhere, to reroute" (*Carte,* 174). We can appreciate here why Derrida attempted to write from the position of censor, the superego, since according to psychoanalysis it is the censor that forces the detour. Repression is precisely that which disturbs the logos of technology, the classic order of cause and effect, of original and copy in representation, the clearly defined order of sequence in the presentation of evidence or of inheritance. "Repression subverts the logic implicit in all philosophy: it makes it so that a pleasure can be—by the Ego—experienced as displeasure. This topical differentiation is inseparable from Repression in its very possibility. It is an ineluctable consequence of differance, of the structure of 1, 2, 3, in a *differing from self.* It is not easily describable in the classic logos of philosophy and it invites a new speculation" (309).

The immediate application of this new speculation is to overcome the desire of the professors to *conclude,* to render a question inert through resolution, to reduce the tension of a problem or an interpretation to the nirvana state of zero pressure by designing a decided meaning. It is important to clarify Derrida's relation to these professors. We must remember that this gadfly is apostrophizing, talking to himself, first of all. His proper name, for one thing, is inscribed on the two postmasters of the modern post age. The very drive of the proper whose effects he interrogates in the theory of the signature is the movement of two postal concepts signed with the *Da.* "The movement of propriation recurs in the *Da* of *Sein* and the *Da* of *Dasein.* And the existential analytic of *Da-Sein* is inseparable from an analysis of the distancing and the proximity which is not so foreign to that of the *fort/da*" (*Carte,* 381). Given the involvement of his own name in the very syllable of identification, Derrida is in a privileged position for the exposure of signature effects. Moreover, in keeping with the rhythm explored in *Beyond the Pleasure Principle,* Derrida himself suspends all conclusions (does not desire to replace the conclusions of others with his own). Thus it is not possible, he notes, to decide whether he is for or against the postal principle. And the enigmatic effect of his presentations, so rigorously irresponsible, is more provocative than any rival conclusion could be. The "end" of his essay on the apocalyptic tone, for example, interpolates what must be in the reader's mind: "But what are we doing, you will still insist, to what ends do we want to come when we come to tell you, here now, let's go, 'come,' the apocalypse, it's finished, that's all, I tell you this, that's what happens, that's what comes" (*Fins,* 478). We are waiting, that is, still. The effect of such suspensions is precisely the effect of all apocalyptic revelations, always postponed to the future, still to come, which makes this genre the revelation, if not of the truth of truth, at least of the scene of writing as such (468). The lesson—a text that performs more than it says.

SCRIPT

Derrida's strategy with regard to the content as well as the demonstrative manner of his presentation is similar to a fundamental procedure of science education—the use of a model to work through complex, inaccessible phenomena by means of simple, concrete, accessible objects or images. In this case, the complexities of logocentrism are condensed into nothing more than a post card ("everything is constructed on the protocolary charter of an axiom, which one could demonstrate, display on a card, a post card of course, it is so simple, elementary, brief, stereotyped" —*Carte*, 25). The entire discourse of "Envois" is a transduction of the card, drawing on it the way the text of "+ R" drew on Adami's pictures. The illuminated scene is a mnemonic image ("I always knew it, it remained as a photographic negative") "developed" by the new chemical philosopheme— "This is the darkroom of that writing force where we developed pictures that 'I' and 'you' will never have had anything but the negatives of" (*Dissemination*, 326), because "we" are always seen (put in the scene of writing) by that which we see, explain, designate, attend (to).

There is one innovation that transforms Derrida's procedure from traditional pedagogy into grammatology—anasemia: the direction of the metaphor (following the insight of the Bodleian card) is (catastrophically) reversed, to begin with, and then displaced. Derrida acknowledges that his operation could be misunderstood when he remarks that Heidegger would no doubt accuse him of extending the metaphor of the post card beyond its reach, even of building a metaphysics of the post card. But to prohibit metaphoricity on these grounds, Derrida says, assumes that the card is being used simply as a figure, image, or trope of "being," when just the opposite is the case: "But to accuse me, prohibit me, etc., one must be naïvely certain of knowing what a post card is or what the mail is. If on the contrary I think the postal and the post card from the side of being, of language, and not the inverse, etc., then the post is no longer a simple metaphor, it is, as locus of all transfers and of all correspondences, the "proper" possibility of all possible rhetoric" (*Carte*, 72-73). The comparison is directed toward the post, the postal is dependent on *being* (understood grammatically, rather than ontologically—the "is" or "there is" [*il y a*], the syntactical liaison of the copula, supplemented by the hymen of differance, introduces telecommunication). In no longer treating the postal as a metaphor of the dispatch, message, or destiny of being, Derrida adds, one is able to take into account what happens in language, thought, and science, "when the postal structure takes a leap, *Satz,* if you like, and poses itself or posts differently" (such as the shift from Book to electronic media).

With this reversal the vehicle (auto) or analogical thinking is itself explored and expanded—a kind of grammatological Maoism, in which the tenor ("superstructure" of the metaphor—*being*—turns back on the significance of the vehicle—base). This operation exposes the teleological circulation of the concept which pretends that sublation works by raising the sensible into the intelligible. One result is the realization that the use of communications technology is a concretization of certain metaphysical assumptions, consequently that it is by changing these assumptions (for example, our notion of identity) that we will transform our communicational activities. Writing offers an alternative to the way current theory of communication programs the network.

Derrida's experiment with the vehicle (auto-) is deconstructive in that it shows how, out of the richness of detail available in the familiar model, an entire system of thought different from the accepted system may be devised on the basis of *excluded,* "accidental," or *irrelevant* features. "Envois," for example, suggests a view of the human condition based on the chance possibility that a letter may *not* arrive (a dysfunctionalism). The model of the post card is elaborated by the presentation of a quantity of documentary material alluding to all aspects of the mail, the process of mailing, the museum of postal history in Geneva, and so forth. Thus he makes of the card, as he says, "an allegory" (*Carte,* 121); for the accumulation of documents and naturalistic details, as Angus Fletcher notes, is a basic device of allegory: "The belief that icons of any kind can have the 'power of the word' is no doubt at the base of the naturalistic type of allegorical fiction. Such fiction builds a whole world out of documentary detail, which at first appears intended solely to inform the reader, but which on second view appears intended to control the reader" (294–95). Fletcher adds that in their emergent phase all sciences rely on allegory. Grammatology, of course, intends not to control readers but precisely to expose the allegorical effect in theoretical writing, the feeling of the secret encrypted in didactic propositions.

Derrida's theoretical grammatology offers for application not just a version of how to visualize a given philosopheme but a comprehensive mode of presentation equally adaptable to pedagogical or popular media. *Glas* (especially if one includes as its post card the *"Chimère"* graft) stated and de-monstrated a model for verbal-visual Writing of the kind that is required in intermedia situations such as the classroom or television. The double column text that is conventional for video (film) scripts—one column for verbal discourse, one for the visual (figural) track—is simulated in *Glas,*

miming a "machine" (apparatus) that "can not be managed like a pen"—
"the machine adapts itself to all the progress of Western technology (bel-
lows, acoustics, electronics)" (*Glas,* 250). In book form, the two tracks of
Glas are spatially distributed, allowing only analytic access to the two
scenes ("one must pass from one signature to the other, it is not possible
to put a hand or tongue on both at once" (285). In intermedia productions, of course, the two tracks or bands play at once. In this context the
point of Derrida's insistence on the separation and the independence of
the frame and the example (accompanying one another without touching)
may be recognized as a formula for the relation of the audio and the video
tracks.

The theory of Writing posed in *Glas,* in short, exceeds the Book, shows
off the limitations of the Book and of the pedagogical procedures modeled
on the Book's conceptual structure. Similarly, a principal feature of "Envois," extending the "organography" (written for the organs) of *Glas,* is
the way it continually points beyond itself to an intermedial presentation.
We are told that the image on the post card becomes a kind of mime by
means of a collage technique—with a certain art of recomposition the scene
on the card "is capable of saying everything": "It suffices to manipulate—as
they do themselves anyway (tricks, sleights of hand, intrigues)—to cut out,
glue, and set going or parcel out, with hidden displacements and great
tropic agility" (*Carte,* 121). With the "découpage" technique the scene on
the card is modified, giving it the status of a "modified readymade." The
modifications include coloring the card, writing on it, adding or subtract-
ing pieces or figures, and so forth.

It soon becomes apparent that "Envois" is a book in the process of becoming a (film or video) *script*—"This will be our little private cinema"
(*Carte,* 193)—Writing as scripting. The discourse refers also to a quantity
of other "supports" used in the correspondence—films, cassettes, drawings,
photographs. Finally the decision is made to "burn" all these materials,
preserving only the words and the card. But the words continually remind
the reader of their "legendary" status, of their function as title for a visual
trace. "Envois," it is true, is a "conceptual" script in that the collages, etc.,
are—Borges fashion—mentioned without being enacted. In this respect,
appropriate to theoretical grammatology, Derrida allies himself with those
avant-gardists who perform theory as a kind of visual art, drawing out the
specular from the speculation. These conceptualists, from the Futurist
movement to the present day (On Kawara is one example), have used the
post card as an art medium, part of a systems aesthetic in which mailing
the card activates social sculpture.

As if reading a screenplay, then, we are given directions concerning the
video portion of the broadcast. The filmed version of the narrative would
include, for example, animation sequences, using the card cutouts (think

of how this is done in *Monty Python's Flying Circus*), such as the one suggested involving the names "Plato" and "Socrates" inscribed over the heads of the figures, designating "Socrates" as the one writing: "There is a gag in this image, silent cinema. They have exchanged their umbrellas, the secretary took the boss's, the largest one, you noticed the capital of one, the small letter of the other. Followed by a feature-length intrigue" (*Carte*, 18). Another source of visual material providing the images for the video track would be the books of photographs documenting the lives of Heidegger and Freud which are mentioned in the text, including the description of scenes of Freud with his daughter, or Heidegger with his fiancée, to be modified by découpage, of course. The drama of the theoretical narrative itself, with its various journeys and settings in the academic world, should also be evoked, including the scene of the professors jogging in the cemetery at Yale, not to mention the apocalyptic visit to the Bodleian library, the pilgrimage to Freiburg, the postal museum, and so forth.

APEIRON

Derrida's running commentary on the post card is a deliberately wild hermeneutic. Mocking the ethnocentric assumptions of the return inquiry, which always begins in the known present and assumes continuity forward and backward, Derrida interprets the iconography of the post card according to modern gestural codes rather than according to medieval conventions. Based on the gestures and positions of the two figures, Derrida speculates (parodically) that Plato may be riding a skate board or may be a train conductor preparing to board, may be riding in a gondola or pushing a wheelchair or baby carriage (in short, that he is enacting all transfers). The proper names of Plato and Socrates are put in play as a monogram, linking them in terms of the S-P or P-S combinations (phonexes) with abbreviations relevant to the theme—"postscript," "subject and predicate," "primary and secondary processes."

In the course of his "delirious" speculation (close in spelling to the unbinding of *"délier"*) Derrida inserts the "correct" interpretation of the original emblem provided by a specialist scholar. According to the expert, the meaning is quite evident, simple: "It is necessary to read verbally the miniature. Socrates is in the process of writing. Plato is next to him, but is not dictating. He points with his index finger toward Socrates: there is the great man. With his left index finger he attracts the attention of the spectators, which one must imagine to the right of the philosopher who writes. He is thus subordinated, a smaller size and with a more modest hat" (*Carte*, 186). No need to choose between the "delirious" and the "scientific" opinions, Derrida notes, since one is just a more elaborate

version of the other. The effect of setting the starkly conservative explanation of the expert next to the cornucopia (the new "mimesis" as *copia*, an
economy of surplus, flowing discourse) of "Derrida's" ravings ("the icon is
there, vaster than science, the support of all our fantasms") is to demonstrate the drive of the proper within the academic book. The strategy is
similar to the one used in "Restitutions" in which Derrida, countering the
argument between Heidegger and Schapiro over to whom the shoes in Van
Gogh's paintings belong, points out that it is not clear even that the shoes
are a *pair*, that they "belong" together, let alone that they are "detached"
from any body.

Ever since his first book, Derrida has been trying to alter the academic
attitude toward fact, to begin to question the "exemplariness" of fact, to
encounter fact rather in its wild singularity, which silently shows Being
itself (as he put it in his early statement, shifting soon to B̶e̶i̶n̶g̶ or differance) under the negativity of the *apeiron* (*Geometry*, 151-52). The
apeiron is the zone of the "invisible column" of enframing whose "square
mouth" gives to appearance the copula:

> It is unique and innumerable like what is called (the) present. The
> unique—that which is not repeated—has no unity since it is not
> repeated. Only that which can be repeated in its identity can have
> unity. The unique therefore has no unity, is not a unit. The unique
> is thus the *apeiron*, the unlimited, the crowd, the imperfect. And
> yet the chain of numbers is made up of uniqueS. Try to think the
> unique in the plural, as such, along with the "unique Number that
> cannot be another." You will witness the birth of *"millions of
> tales"* and you will understand that one and the same term can
> germinate twice—a germinate column—disseminating itself in over-
> production. "O crossroads . . . O marriage, marriage! [*O hymen,
> hymen*]." (*Dissemination*, 365)

The *apeiron* is the unlimited, the indefinite, the undecidable, outside
the furthest sphere of *ouranos* (the furthest limits of the universe), as in
Anaximander's notion of "an infinite supply of basic substance 'so generation and destruction do not fail.' "[12] We can appreciate why Derrida professes his admiration for Plato's *Philebus* in *The Post Card* (it also supplies
the Platonic text for "The Double Session"), for it was the prominence of
the *apeiron* in *Philebus* that, we are told, assured its continued use as a metaphysical principle in the subsequent Platonic tradition. The *apeiron* is
Derrida's alternative to the *aether* of tradition. Against the transcendental
reduction's ideal of tradition as the "repetition of the *same*," of history as a
transparent medium and translation as univocity, Derrida proposes to
capitalize on the equivocity and consequent errors and accidents that send
all dispatches on a possible detour to the dead letter office.

All the references to telephone conversations and the telephone exchange recorded in "Envois" (even the bobbin's thread is compared to a telephone line) suggest the model of tradition as subject to all the effects of electronic transmission (in the postal era, now reaching closure, the document itself is transmitted, as opposed to an electronic transformation of the message into pulses/drives), foremost among which is noise and interference: "The chronological vector of history brings the progressive disaggregation of the idea," Michel Serres remarks. "This disaggregation is not a forgetting pure and simple (how to define this forgetting?), but simply a continual weakening of the idea by successive communication. The history of ideas is this telephone play which gives at reception information as deformed as the chain of communication is long."[13]

Derrida joins Serres in advocating a "philosophy of transport," of science as a network of continuous exchanges, borrowings, and transfers of models and methods which confounds classification and specialization and in which invention is best described, Serres says, as an *ars interveniendi* —or even as *transduction*.[14] To make a point similar to Serres's, Derrida stresses the *received* character of dispatches (of any message whatsoever) with consequences that he exposes in *Glas* or *The Post Card* by means of his découpage of the apocalyptic genre. "We see there: 'The Gospel and the Apocalypse violently severed, fragmented, redistributed, with blanks, displacements in accents, lines skipped or shifted around, as if they reached us over a broken-down teletype, a wiretap within an overloaded telephone exchange'" (*Fins*, 474). With respect to "revelations" as the genre of the scene of writing, Derrida adds, "So John is the one who already receives some letters through the medium of a bearer who is an angel, a pure messenger. And John transmits a message already transmitted, testifies to a testimony that will be yet that of another testimony, that of Jesus; so many sendings, *envois*, so many voices, and this puts so many people on the telephone line" (469–70).

In the new *invention* or *ars interveniendi*, interference or mistaken switchings is not an obstacle but a creative tool. The example from the history of science which would best illustrate this grammatological approach to tradition as communication (rather than as production), as transduction (rather than as reduction) (Serres), would not be the "Pythagorean Theorem," used by Husserl, but the "post card" sent from Galileo to Kepler in August, 1610, inscribed with the following cryptogram: "SMAISMRMILMEPOETALEUMIBUNENUGTTAURIAS."[15] Recognizing it as an anagram, Kepler translated it into five Latin words— *"salve umbistineum geminatum martia proles"* (Greetings, burning twins, descendants of Mars)—which he understood to mean that Galileo had observed that Mars has two moons. Galileo, however, actually meant the message to read, *"altissimum planetam tergiminum observavi"* (I have observed that the highest of the planets (Saturn) has two moons"). The interest of the paragrammatic mistranslation is that the sense intended is referentially wrong (with his primitive telescope Galileo mistook Saturn's rings for moons), while the interpreted sense is referentially correct. Mars does have two moons, although they were not observed until 1877. The sense of the aleatory is a principal interest of grammatology, which seeks to harness this capacity much the way other phenomena observed first in their natural state (fire, flight) have been artificially reproduced by science and technology.

Writing no longer adheres to the "Model of the Book": "The Model Book, doesn't it amount to the absolute adequation of presence and representation, to the *truth* (*homoiosis* or *adequatio*) of the thing and of the thought about the thing, in the sense in which truth first emerges in divine creation before being reflected by finite knowledge?" (*Dissemination,* 44). Dissemination, and grammatology, operate within a different mode in which knowing and knowledge are oriented not by the *results* as after-effect, known in advance and to which presentation must conform, but to creativity, innovation, invention, change: "The adventurous excess of a writing that is no longer directed by any knowledge does not abandon itself to improvisation. The accident or throw of dice that 'opens' such a text does not contradict the rigorous necessity of its formal assemblage. The game here is the unity of chance and rule, of the program and its leftovers or extras. This *play* will still be called *literature* or *book* only when it exhibits its negative, atheistic face (the insufficient but indispensable phase of reversal" (*Dissemination,* 54). The mark of this excess is the cross— the + of the *apeiron,* always more, the "extra nothing," "the beyond the whole, beating out the rhythm of both pleasure and repetition" (*Dissemination,* 57)—or the X, apropos of *Numbers:* "They remain undecipherable precisely because it is only in your own representation that they ever took on the aplomb of a cryptogram hiding inside itself the secret of some meaning or reference. X: not an unknown but a chiasmus. A text that is unreadable because it is *only* readable. Untranslatable for the same reason" (*Dissemination,* 362).

Grammatology, then, does not so much interpret models as Write with them. The model in science, that is, is yet another incarnation of hieroglyphics. "The symbols used for electronics since the beginning of this century parallel the development of the pictograms of ancient languages," R. L. Gregory notes. "At first the symbols were realistic drawings of the components. Within a few years the electronic 'pictograms' became simpler: the emphasis was placed on the functionally important features of the components, while the outward shapes were lost . . . each symbol is a kind of abstract cartoon."[16] Similar developments, relating to the use of "model" in a more general sense, occurred in other sciences as well— Gregory mentions the "orrery" as a physical model of selected features of the solar system, although he adds: "Models are a kind of cartoon-language. Just as the pictographs of ancient languages became ideograms for expressing complex ideas—finally expressed by purely abstract symbols as pictures become inadequate—so such models become restrictive. They give way to mathematical theories which cannot be represented by pictures or models" (152). Tied as he is to a representational theory of models, Gregory fears that human perception may prove an obstacle to survival, unable to adapt to "non-sensory data, and the resulting non-perceptual concepts of physics."

From Derrida's point of view, Gregory's concerns and his view of the inevitable mathematicization of language are of a piece, are corollaries of logocentrism, and ignore the alliance of the earliest pictograms with the most recent mathematical graphics in terms of spacing. Nonetheless, Gregory's view of the model as a hieroglyph is an important clue to the direction to be followed by grammatological research. Bunn's semiotic study of models echoes Gregory's analogy, considering the model as a tool *contemplated as hieroglyph* of the world (as a synecdoche) instead of applied to its specific end (the tool—any object, in fact—becomes language, or better, writing, by remotivation). The model, Bunn explains, *performs the complementarity of the philosopher and the prophet* (the theme of Derrida's essay on the "Apocalyptic Tone"), because of the "rhythm" (John Dewey's term) governing its use—to test and explore, to record and prophesy at once (159). Hence, the appropriateness of an emblem of teleology being the frontispiece for a fortune-telling book. The importance of the connection of scientific models to hieroglyphs is that, as we have seen, hieroglyphics is the mode of inscription providing the guiding thread for the evolution of grammatology from its historical through its theoretical to an applied phase. Grammatology in its next phase will Write with models as well as model the scene of writing.

PART II

Post(e) – Pedagogy

Jeder Mensch ist ein Künstler

—Joseph Beuys

Today, how can we not speak of the university?

—Jacques Derrida

6

The Scene of Teaching

EDUCATION

Greph. In part I of this book I was concerned with defining the model of Writing available in Derrida's texts which might furnish a practice for applied grammatology. My argument is that applied grammatology will be characterized by a picto-ideo-phonographic Writing that puts speech back in its place while taking into account the entire scene of writing. Now, in the second half of the book, I will attempt to clarify the pedagogical principles associated with applied grammatology. The question to be posed has to do with the pedagogical rationale for the Writing described in part I, a rationale more accurately termed "post(e)-pedagogical," in order to indicate that it is both a move beyond conventional pedagogy and a pedagogy for an era of electronic media (with *poste* meaning in this context television station or set). My purpose in this chapter is to open the question of the nature of the educational presentation (the manner of the transmission of ideas) adequate to a poststructuralist epistemology and to air some of the rhetorical and polemical notions relevant to a pedagogy of general writing.

Does Derrida have a pedagogical theory? Edward Said suggests that perhaps he has nothing else but a pedagogy. Discussing Derrida's contribution to the anthology *Politiques de la philosophie,* entitled "Où commence et comment finit un corps enseignant" (one of the Derrida's most explicit expositions of his ideas about education), Said acknowledges the political character of Derrida's insistence that teachers in state-run institutions have a special responsibility for understanding the system by which ideas are mechanically passed on from teacher to student and back again. But Said adds that Derrida's deconstructive technique and his undecidable counter-concepts give sovereignty to the teacher, requiring knowledge of nothing outside the text, and hence are easily teachable, in contrast with Foucault's extrinsic historical archeology, which is difficult to teach (the implication being that Foucault's procedure is superior—"Textuality," 700–702).

A different view of the question is that of the discussants participating in the seminar on teaching at the Derrida colloquium, *Les fins de l'homme*, who indicated that Derrida does not have a pedagogy but that he encourages others to imagine (and then enact) what a deconstructive teaching might be like (*Fins*, 653). Derrida's own discussion of teaching, of course, offers the best point of departure for my purposes.

Derrida participated in the formation of a *"groupe de recherches sur l'enseignement philosophique"* (*GREPH*), which became active in 1974.[1] The group was formed in response to a proposed reform (the "Haby" reform) of the French system which would reduce the amount of philosophy taught in the schools and limit philosophy as a school subject to the last year of secondary work. Considering this reform to be an attack on philosophy by the state, a number of philosophers (or professors of philosophy) called for a complete review of the place of philosophy inside and outside the institutions of learning, and of the relation in general of education to the state. Participants in the group that formed in response to this challenge, catalyzed by Derrida's discussion of the reform in several articles, attempted to "elaborate a new problematic and to propose untried forms of intervention." The image that soon arose of *GREPH*, according to the group's own account, was that of a very politicized movement, committed to the idea that there was no "natural" age (a physiological "age of reason") preferable for and appropriate to the study of philosophy. Philosophy, rather, should be organized progressively like most other school subjects, beginning in the primary grades. Their politics, that is, was addressed principally to the educational institution and called into question the grid that divides the university into a set of disciplines and specializations.

In their working paper, the group proposed a number of questions to direct the professors toward self-scrutiny. The guiding question concerned the link between philosophy and teaching in general: Is there an essential indissociability between the didactic and the philosophic (regardless of content area)? This question opened a number of suggested topics for study, covering every aspect of the educational enterprise from the composition of exam questions to the political ideology of the institution as such. Among these topics, the one that informs my own project is, "the study of the models of didactic operation legible, with their rhetoric, their logic, their psychology, etc., within *written* discourses (from the dialogues of Plato, for example, the Meditations of Descartes, Spinoza's Ethic, the Encyclopedia or the Lessons of Hegel, etc., up to the so-called philosophic works of modernity)" (*GREPH,* 434). The written discourses I am examining for their didactic import, of course, are Derrida's own texts.

My purpose is not to impose, by way of description or commentary, a set of views or practices onto Derrida's theories, claiming that what I have to say accounts for his views. Rather, the relation of my book to Derrida's texts is similar to that which Foucault describes as his relation to Nietzsche: "For me, the people I like, I utilize. The only mark of recognition that one can show to a thought like that of Nietzsche is precisely to use it, to deform it, to make it grate, creak. Then, if the commentators say that it is or is not faithful, is of no interest."[2] In any case, Derrida wants no disciples and denounces them in advance. Moreover, he has recently begun to address himself directly to educational questions, so there is no need to speak for him (a situation that still leaves open, however, the question of the didactic operation legible in his discourse). Noting that his essay in the *Politiques* collection is his first direct statement on education, Derrida remarks:

> After around fifteen years experience teaching and twenty-three years of public employ, I am only beginning to interrogate, exhibit, criticize systematically (. . . it is the systematic character that matters if one does not want to content oneself with a verbal alibi, cavillings or scratchings which do not affect the system in place . . . ; it is the *systematic* character which matters and its *effectiveness,* which has never been attributable to the initiative of one person, and that is why, for the first time, I associate here my discourse with the work of the group engaged under the name of GREPH), I begin therefore, so late, to interrogate, exhibit, criticize systematically—with an eye toward transformation—the confines of that in which I have pronounced more than one discourse.[3]

He adds that "deconstruction has always had a bearing in principle on the apparatus and the function of teaching in general" and that its application to philosophy is just one stage of a "systematic trajectory" (64-65).

In an interview given in the fall of 1975, Derrida explains that his hesitation to apply his deconstruction "publicly" to the institution (as opposed to the "privacy" of his teaching practice) was that the only effective criticisms of the university to date had been mounted from positions he was in the process of deconstructing (working his way toward understanding how to avoid the dialectical pitfalls of such critiques), while the strategies of the avant-garde tradition (to which he is sympathetic) had proven to be entirely ineffective (consisting largely of dialectical inversions). Once having decided to take up the implications of deconstruction for an institutional critique, which, as he explains, applies not only to content but especially to the *scene* of teaching—to the institution as a political organization, including its support structure (the apparatus of presses and

journals), in short, to the power relations of the knowledge industry—
Derrida commits himself to strategic alliances with the extant modes of
cultural and ideological criticism and with certain aspects of avant-garde
practice. The entry point of his deconstruction, that is, is the (clandestine,
but nonetheless "violent") introduction of heterogeneous forces into the
"teaching body" in order to deform and transform it, taking the risk that
such forces might be reappropriated or be unreceivable: "The unreceivable
—that which takes at a determined moment the unformed form of the unreceivable—can, even should, at a determined moment, not be received at all,
escape the criteria of receivability, to be totally excluded, which can take
place in broad daylight, even while the unreceivable product circulates from
hand to hand" ("Crochets," 104–5)—reflecting the open and closed structure de-monstrated in Derrida's models (umbrella, post card, matchbox).

The nature of a Derridean pedagogy, mixing the operations of traditional and unreceivable modes of criticism, poses certain paradoxes that
raise problems for an applied grammatology. One way to locate the question, in order to recognize its conventional side, is to relate it to the ancient
argument between philosophers and sophists, dialecticians and rhetoricians,
between philosophy and poetry, the modern form of which is the issue of
the "two cultures" (as in the C.P. Snow-F.R. Leavis controversy).[4] The
debate involves the distinction between knowing the truth (discovered
dialectically) and presenting this truth, once known, in a way that would
convince or persuade others (rhetorically). When it became apparent in the
work of the sophists that artistic presentations could persuade in the absence of truth, philosophy broke with literature, the consequences of
which are still with us today and whose history may be traced in the for-
tunes of the two styles—the plain (scientific) and the rhetorical (literary).

It is predictable that deconstruction displaces this opposition, but the
application of such a formula to a practice is not unproblematic. The paradox operating here, to put it bluntly, is that while Derrida's texts appear
to be among the most difficult and esoteric works of our time, they nonetheless call for a program or practice that can only be described as a popularization of knowledge. To appreciate the latter aspect of Derrida's work
requires that we keep in mind his involvement with *GREPH* and with the
Estates General of Philosophy. One of the principal goals of the Group for
Philosophic Teaching, that is, is to extend the teaching of philosophy to
earlier levels of schooling. The chief problem for such an undertaking is to
find ways to teach philosophy "philosophically" to young people. More
recently, as discussed in the context of grammatology's move beyond the
book, the same problem was posed by the Estates General of Philosophy,
but with regard to extending philosophy to the media, particularly television. The problem in this case is to communicate with the general public,
rather than with school children, but the challenge of how to present the

essentials of the humanities to a nonspecialized and "untrained" public in a way that involves "real knowledge" (the classic dilemma of "vulgarization") rather than mere spectacle is the same.[5]

In this respect, the problem of the "preface," discussed in "Outwork," is identical with the problem of pedagogy in general—of a communication between a teacher (the one who is supposed to know) and a student (the one who thinks he is supposed to learn what the teacher knows). Everything that Derrida says apropos of the deconstruction of the preface applies equally to the pedagogical discourse, with the student being in the position of the reader of a text about which as yet he knows nothing.

Such is the problem to which Hegel addressed himself in his famous prefaces, discussed by Derrida in "Outwork": "'A preliminary attempt to make matters plain would only be unphilosophical, and consist of a tissue of assumptions, assertions, and inferential pros and cons, i.e. of dogmatism without cogency, as against which there would be an equal right of counter-dogmatism. . . . But to seek to know before we know is as absurd as the wise resolution of Scholasticus, not to venture into the water until he had learned to swim' " (*Dissemination,* 47). The preface in its traditional usage, epitomized by Hegel, reflects the dilemma of the dialectical attitude confronted with the necessity of rhetoric in order to bring its "inside" into communication with its "outside"—the world of ordinary language. Hegel "resolved" the dilemma by means of teleology, which, drawing on all the Hegelian values of negativity, sublation, presupposition, ground, result, circularity, etc., as Derrida notes, determines the preface as a postface by a semantic *aftereffect:* "Hegel is thus at once as close and as foreign as possible to a 'modern' conception of the text or of writing: nothing precedes textual generality absolutely. . . . But Hegel brings this generalization about by saturating the text with meaning, by *teleologically* equating it with its *conceptual tenor,* by reducing all absolute dehiscence between writing and wanting-to-say, by erasing a certain occurrence of the break between *anticipation* and *recapitulation*" (20).

The problem that Hegel wishes to efface is that of the relation of the order of inquiry to the order of exposition (*Darstellung*). Hegel, typifying the bias of logocentrism, imagines or idealizes a writing in which "there would be no more discrepancy between production and exposition, only a *presentation* of the concept by itself, in its own words, in its own voice, in its logos" (*Dissemination,* 30–31).

But Marx, representing an alternative that is of interest to grammatology, takes into account the gap between the two orders (inquiry and presentation). In Marx's prefaces, "the development is so little modeled upon a law of conceptual immanence, so hard to anticipate, that it must bear the visible marks of its revisions, alterations, extensions, reductions, partial anticipations, plays of footnotes, etc. The *Preface* to the first

edition of *Capital* (1867) exhibits, precisely, the work of transformation
to which the earlier 'presentation of the subject-matter' has been submitted, the quantitative and qualitative heterogeneity of the developments,
and the entire historical scene in which the book is inscribed" (*Dissemination,* 34).

Derrida's own strategy, going beyond Marx, who still retained the speculative order of truth which makes presentation a (mere) supplement to
inquiry, is to exploit the strange qualities of the simulacrum: "While pretending to turn around and look backward [the gesture of teleological return inquiry], one is also in fact starting over again, adding an extra text,
complicating the scene, opening up within the labyrinth a supplementary
digression, which is also a false mirror that pushes the labyrinth's infinity
back forever in mimed—that is, endless—speculation. It is the textual
restance of an operation, which can be neither opposed nor reduced to the
so-called 'principal' body of a book" (*Dissemination,* 27).

We are dealing, in short, with the logic of the supplement, or originary
translation. Derrida begins the displacement of dialectics by foregrounding
it in a presentation that always *exceeds* its concept ("Dissemination, soliciting *physis* as *mimesis,* places philosophy *on stage* and its book *at stake"*
—*Dissemination,* 53). However complicated the principle, the practical consequences are simply stated—every pedagogical exposition, just like every
reading, adds something to what it transmits: "There is always a surprise
in store for the anatomy or physiology of any criticism that might think it
had mastered the game, surveyed all the threads at once, deluding itself,
too, in wanting to look at the text without touching it, without laying a
hand on the 'object,' without risking—which is the only chance of entering
into the game, by getting a few fingers caught—the addition of some new
thread. Adding, here, is nothing other than giving to read" (63). It is not
surprising that a pedagogy committed to change rather than to reproduction would seize upon the irreducibility of the medium to the message
(apropos of education as a form of communication) as the point of departure for its program (to be discussed further in terms of the pedagogical
mise en scène).

The Age of Hegel. Another version of the lag between inquiry and presentation (the postal relay of representation) which a new pedagogy must
confront is caused by the generally conservative nature of the educational
institution. Michel Serres defines the problem as the disparity between a
recent epistemology (which is thoroughly interdisciplinary, based on the
free exchange of concepts across all fields of knowledge) and an older
pedagogy (which is highly specialized): "Exchange is the rule, even if it is
not total: importation and exportation which mark, in my sense, the end
of the era of specialists. The learned community is henceforth polyglot.

The more one goes towards pedagogy, transmission, the more one goes towards specialty: socio-political frame, ecological space; the more one goes towards invention, the more one encounters exchange and translation" (*L'interférence,* 27).

The implication of Serres's epistemology is the collapse of the disparity now separating inquiry and presentation (as transmission), not in the sense of the Hegelian sublation of presentation, but as a transmission that is itself invention, inquiry being nothing other than a repetition of the discourse of (other) sciences—a supplementary repetition: "For the scholar himself, mobility becomes the secret of discovery. If the progress of sciences is multiplicative, of complication and application (in the sense of putting into correspondence), the *ars inveniendi* loses its mystery—and genius its aura of sacralization—to become *ars interveniendi:* multiplication of interferences, and the establishment of short-circuits. To invent is not to produce, but to translate" (*L'interférence,* 65). As noted previously in the discussion of the *apeiron,* Derrida shares Serres's epistemology, at least as a strategy appropriate to the deconstruction of the post-age (the strategy of switchings and misdirected letters—correspondence—in *The Post Card*).

Part of Derrida's program is relevant to Serres's assessment of the lag between pedagogy and invention: "But what interests me the most," Derrida remarks, "is to try to limit a certain delay: for example between the work on and against the institution and, on the other hand, that which I perceive as the most advanced place of deconstruction of a philosophic or theoretic type" ("Crochets," 113). It is necessary, he argues, to bring educational practice into line with contemporary epistemology—to help pedagogy negotiate the same paradigm shift that altered the arts and sciences at the beginning of our century, leaving pedagogy behind in the age of Hegel.

Derrida's analysis of the place of pedagogy in Western thought is a corollary of his analysis of writing in general. Everything that he says about the bias against writing in logocentrism applies as well to pedagogy, understood as a representation and communication that models itself after the Book. Teaching in the age of Hegel or the post-age, thus, has a retrospective, rather than a prospective, function, Derrida states, and operates by a semiotic logic: "Teaching delivers signs, the teaching body produces (shows and puts forth) proofs [*enseignes*], more precisely signifiers supposing knowledge of a previous signified. Referred to this knowledge, the signifier is structurally second. Every university puts language in this position of delay or derivation in relation to meaning or truth" (*Politiques,* 76). The assumption guiding a semiotic pedagogy is that "the professor is the faithful transmitter of a tradition and not the worker of a philosophy in the process of formation" (76), with the latter notion—*the classroom as a place of invention rather than of reproduction*—being the attitude of grammatology.

To continue the association of Derrida's discussion of pedagogy with his deconstruction of writing, it is worth noting that he characterizes teaching in the age of Hegel as "dictation" (*Politiques,* 82), which is to say that his analysis of the scene on the Bodleian post card, depicting Plato "dictating" to Socrates (in "Derrida's" wild reading), is relevant to the scene of teaching. Indeed, Derrida finds Hegel's teleology (the return inquiry of the postal relay) and his speculative dialectic at work within his educational thinking. Specifically, the point of departure for the essay that Derrida contributed to the *GREPH* volume, entitled "The Age of Hegel" (playing on the homophone linking "age" as "epoch" to "chronological age"), is a letter in which Hegel, at the age of fifty-two, describes himself at the age of eleven learning philosophy at school. The anecdote of the philosopher describing himself, with hindsight, in a period before he was a philosopher (already Hegel, but not yet "Hegel"), represents for Derrida the structure of teleology. "One will have understood nothing of the age (for example of Hegel) if one does not think first the conceptual, dialectical, speculative structure of this *déjà-pas-encore* [already-not-yet] (*GREPH,* 74).

One of the fundamental issues here concerns the status of such recollections (like Freud's recollection of his grandson playing with the bobbin on a string). In the anecdote Hegel is using himself as an example in making an argument for teaching philosophy in the *lycée*—the *already* is the image of himself in the past (the past self fulfilling its destiny, linked continuously with the present); the *not-yet* is that what he is doing at age eleven is memorizing definitions, not yet speculating (doing philosophy like the author of the letter). This already-not-yet structure is the model of the world's oldest pedagogy, Derrida adds: "revelation, unveiling, truth discovered of the already-there in the mode of the not-yet, socratic-platonic anamnesis sometimes revived by a philosophy of psychoanalysis" (*GREPH,* 78). The scene in the letter stages the question of the two memories, also— Hegel remembering with satisfaction his prephilosophic exercises of hypomnemic memorization. Translated into pedagogy, however, Hegel's lesson is that philosophy can and should be taught as early as possible (Hegel is everyone—an attitude that *GREPH* itself finds attractive), but it can only be taught unphilosophically: not ready for the "speculative idea," pupils were to be taught *prescriptively* (an attitude that *GREPH* opposes). Part of Derrida's point is to remind his colleagues of the history of the question that concerns them most—the age at which a person might begin to study philosophy philosophically—given that the concept of age itself arises in the "age of the concept" (the age of Hegel). Simply to extend traditional philosophy to a wider audience is not the solution to the erosion of the humanities in a media age. Rather, new ways of "doing" philosophy must be explored: "If philosophy has in effect an 'irreplaceable function,' is it because nothing can replace it in case of its decease? I believe rather that it replaces itself always: that will be rather the form of its irreplaceability. That is why the struggle is never simply for or against *the* philosophy, the life or death, the presence or absence, in teaching, of philosophy, but between forces and their philosophical solicitations, within and outside the scholarly institution" (458).

To make this point, Derrida uses a study by Canivez on "the condition of the professor of philosophy up to the end of the nineteenth century" (*Politiques,* 75). The interest of this strategy is that it provides a sense of what the general assumptions were about teaching in "the age of Hegel," drawing not just on Hegel's views but on the reception of his theories in the profession in general. In order to provide a glimpse of the Hegelian pedagogy, I would like to reproduce a version of this strategy by citing a work, published at the end of the last century, that gives a sympathetic survey of Hegelian education. One lesson of such a review is that Hegel's pedagogy has survived, continues to live on, just as has his dialectic.

Regarding the question of the "age" proper for learning philosophy, the state system against which *GREPH* is protesting has determined that the individual will encounter philosophy in the period Hegel labels "Youth" (the other periods being "Child" and "Man," with "Old Age" set aside as of no interest to educators). Derrida and his colleagues assume that the state fears philosophy because it motivates the individual to want to change the established system. But for Hegel, it is not philosophy but simply one's youth that prompts rebellion against the state:

> The peace in which the child lives with the world is broken by the youth. And precisely on account of this persistent appeal to the Ideal the youth bears the appearance of having a more exalted aim and a greater generosity of soul than has the man engrossed in mere transitory interests. On the other hand it is for the youth to discover that it is precisely the man of affairs who in freeing himself from his own subjective or merely individual fancies and visions of far-off unattainable "Ideals" has merged himself in the concrete Reason of the actual world and has come to put forth his energies for that world.
>
> To this self-same end, indeed, the youth himself must come at last. . . . And it is precisely in the carrying out of this, his *immediate* aim, that the youth becomes a man, and discovers at last the futility of his projects for revolutionizing the world.[6]

The teacher's task is to help the student face the crisis, even tragedy, of the descent from his Ideal into what seems an "inferno of Philistinism" by helping him recognize this descent as "nothing else than the necessity of Reason."

Another way to describe this process by which the rebellious student is assimilated into the quotidian of the community is as the *Aufhebung* of the individual into the species. "'With the school begins the life of universal regulation, according to a rule applicable to all alike. For the individual spirit or mind must be brought to the putting away of its own peculiarities, must be brought to the knowing and willing of what is universal, must be brought to the acceptance of that general culture which is immediately at hand'" (Bryant, 38).

The teacher's role in the Hegelian system is that of model and authority, a concrete embodiment of the ideal self with which the student must identify (from Socrates to Freud and beyond, transference is an important element in the pedagogic effect). "In the theoretical aspect of the child's education the teacher is an authority whom he must follow, and that in the ethical aspect of his education the teacher is a model whom the child must imitate" (Bryant, 68). As for the pupil, "all his power assumes the form of *intent attention.* And this is as much to say that for the time being he merges all his interest in the indications given him of what is going on in the mind of the teacher. Without being aware of it, he becomes an intent psychological observer. And the direct aim which actuates him in this is to develop in his own mind what he discovers as taking place in the mind of the teacher. . . . But this, clearly, is nothing else than *Imitation*" (94).

Several other points of this Hegelian pedagogy are worth noting in order to clarify the position that *GREPH* opposes. The means of instruction in a Hegelian system is (exclusively) language: "An image as such can represent only a particular and isolated fact or object; on the other hand, relations, totalities, multiplicities, exist in truth only for the thought-aspect of consciousness, while thought, properly speaking, can unfold into concrete realization only in and through language" (Bryant, 111). "It is precisely for this reason that language constitutes not only the earliest subject-matter, but also at every stage, the predominating medium of education. . . . All other appliances find their highest values in this: that the knowledge of them is raised to its highest term through description of them in words, through command of them rendered exact by explanation of the relation of part to part in words" (115). Accompanying this privileging of verbal discourse (as opposed to Derrida's interest in a picto-ideo-phonographic Writing) is the view that "properly speaking, the human voice gives utterance to what is innermost in the individual consciousness. What the individual is, he infuses into his voice" (117).

Finally, for the Hegelian, the most universal and noblest of all the means of cultivating the mind is "the thoroughgoing study of grammatical forms" (Bryant, 136). The ultimate goal of this program is to develop the mind to maturity, understood as the subordination of sensation and perception to thought, resulting in a capacity for true observation. These powers of observation are meant to be put to work in Science (104-5). The goal of education for science shows the extent to which the Hegelian system fused with the ideal of a positivist education. Auguste Comte also offered a version of the "Ages of Man"—theological (fiction), metaphysical (abstract), and scientific (positive)—and, like Hegel (and a certain Freud, as Derrida says), promoted the ideal of the "Age of the Adult"—the practical grown-up who is rational and reconciled to the real—as the proper end of education. In the tradition of Bacon, and the Encyclopedists before him and the logical positivists after him, Comte sought a unification of knowledge through science, which would result from developing a unified (purified) language.

Even if recent history (the aftermath of the student protest of the sixties) seems to testify to the accuracy of the Hegelian model, we are nonetheless, and for reasons generated by the entire spectrum of knowledge, approaching the end of the positivist era and the closure of its ideal of a scientific education (part of the task of grammatology is to assist and hasten this closure), and with it perhaps will come the closure of all thinking in terms of ends, of teleology. Michel Foucault is one of the educators beginning to think this closure. Trying to "visualize the manner in which this truth within which we are caught, but which we constantly renew, was selected, but at the same time, was repeated, extended and displaced," Foucault lays out an outline of the "ages" of education:

> I will take first of all the age of the Sophists and its beginning with Socrates, or at least with Platonic philosophy, and I shall try to see how effective, ritual discourse, charged with power and peril, gradually arranged itself into a disjunction between true and false discourse. I shall next take the turn of the sixteenth and seventeenth centuries and the age which, above all in England, saw the emergence of an observational, affirmative science, a certain natural philosophy inseparable, too, from religious ideology—for this certainly constituted a new form of the will to knowledge. In the third place, I shall turn to the beginning of the nineteenth century and the great founding acts of modern science, as well as the formation of industrial society and the accompanying positivist ideology. Three slices out of the morphology of our will to knowledge; three staging posts in our philistinism. [7]

Foucault notes that he is able to undertake this analysis precisely because we have moved, are in the process of moving, to a new will to knowledge, which in turn entails a new educational model. The task of applied grammatology is to investigate the question of this new model. The ideal of an educated person held by a given era, as Derrida points out, is always predicated on the basis of a theory of truth. "Through all these specific determinations," Derrida states, alluding to the same history of education

Foucault outlines, "one finds the same schema, the same concept of truth, of truth of the truth linked to the same pedagogical structure" (*GREPH*, 78), that structure being the Socratic-Platonic dialogue (the S–P phonex analyzed in *The Post Card*). Is it possible to imagine an education in which this dialogue and its valorization of "living memory" would not be the ideal? What might be the ideal of an educated person proposed by a post-structuralism that puts in question the very notion of truth, in which the claims of truth to objectivity and neutrality are exposed as effects of an apparatus of power? It would be a mistake to try to answer this question prematurely. Nor is my introduction to applied grammatology anything more than a gathering of some of the elements that may contribute to the phrasing of this question. But what has been cited as the Hegelian model of education gives an idea of what the new model will *not* be.

Against Reproduction.   The shift in the paradigm of education which I am investigating may be summarized as a shift away from the exclusive dom-ination of mind (intellect as verbal discourse—the focus of "intent atten-tion" in Hegelian instruction) to a mode that includes the body (desire and the will to knowledge), a shift with important implications for instructional method. Derrida's deconstruction of Western metaphysics, applied to the classroom, begins with an attack on the predominance of the voice and the word in the Hegelian model in order to put speech back in its place. "All teaching in its traditional form, and perhaps all teaching whatever," Derrida says, referring to the concept of translation apropos of teaching method, "has as its ideal, with exhaustive translatability, the effacement of language. The deconstruction of a pedagogical institution and all that it implies. What this institution cannot bear, is for anyone to tamper with language. . . . It can bear more readily the most apparently revolutionary ideological sorts of 'content,' if only that content does not touch the borders of lan-guage and of all the juridico-political contracts that it guarantees. It is this 'intolerable' something that concerns me" (*Deconstruction*, 93–95).

The direction that the pedagogical transformation might take is already apparent in this citation, reminiscent as it deliberately is of the way Mal-larmé and the modernist poets (whom Derrida cites as the initiators of theoretical grammatology) tampered with (touched) language. Briefly put, the emergence of a postmodernized education (the entry of education into the contemporary paradigm) can be facilitated by a retracing of the paths (facilitations) already breached by the experimental arts of this century. Keeping in mind the idea that a grammatological pedagogy is designed to close the gap between current theory and an outmoded practice, the new education will find in the arts a major reserve or resource for technique. The logical place to look for an example of a practice already adequate to Derrida's theory (which, after all, is not "futuristic" but is an effort, educationally speaking, to catch up) is the experimental arts (which is why my book includes a discussion of Joseph Beuys).

To appreciate the deconstructive strategy adopted by Derrida—its practical value in the context of education—it is helpful to review a current assessment of the educational institution within which grammatology must operate. The essential point of modern social analyses of education is that education is a device of power and control whose chief purpose is to reproduce the dominant values of society and to legitimize the authority of the state (finally, of the class structure). The difference between current assessments and nineteenth-century views like those summarized above is that the association of education with state power and its advocacy of the ideals of universalism and nationalism are now perceived as problems rather than as objectives. In this vein, for example, Foucault discusses the relationship between discipline and punishment in terms of a correspondence between the functions of the educational and the penal systems.[8]

One of the most concise analyses of education as an instrument of class power (the kind of strategy with which Derrida is willing to temporarily ally himself) is *Reproduction in Education, Society, and Culture,* by Pierre Bourdieu and Jean-Claude Passeron. Derrida has stated several times that his deconstruction must be undertaken from *within* the institution, and a reading of Bourdieu and Passeron, showing the extent to which the university depends on and reproduces the forces of state power, shows why this approach is necessary. The error of the avant-garde, Derrida says, is to imagine that the system has an "outside." Given the universality of the model of *Universitas,* which puts every university by definition into a compromising negotiation with powers of a particular state, whether the state is Nazi or Socialist, etc., Derrida decides that "to want to make way *immediately* for the other of *Universitas,* that can just as easily ally with determinable forces ready to take control of the State and the University. Hence the necessity, for a deconstruction, to not abandon the terrain of the University at the moment when it apprehends itself in its most powerful foundations. Hence the necessity to not abandon the terrain to empiricism and therefore to no matter what forces. Hence the political necessity of our alliances" (*GREPH,* 106).

Bourdieu and Passeron's reading of the situation makes explicit the situation to which Derrida refers. According to them, pedagogic action is by definition authoritative; it is in its very nature a kind of symbolic violence. Therefore, all nonrepressive educational theories from Rousseau through Freud (to Reich and Marcuse) are finally utopian and are violent in their very illusion of being nonviolent. The conclusion that all such utopian pedagogies eventually self-destruct (being self-contradictory) would seem to be verified by the failure of the nonrepressive experiments in many universities in the wake of the student protest movement. It is reasonable, then, that *GREPH* should proceed more cautiously, selecting as one of the central problems for educational reform the study of the "pedagogical effect," especially considering that Bourdieu and Passeron contend that this effect depends on and requires authority and legitimacy in order to function at all. Harold Bloom's discussion of the scene of instruction, in which the Oedipal forces of rivalry with the father and the Freudian defense mechanisms at work in the family romance in general, are to be found, is relevant to this research as well.[9] Derrida's attempt to write *with* the censoring mechanism of the superego (in *The Post Card*) should be understood in this same context.

The task Bourdieu and Passeron undertake is "to establish what an institution must be in order to be capable of producing the institutional conditions for the production of a habitus at the same time as misrecognition of those conditions."[10] Indeed, the system works *because* of a misrecognition on the teacher's part of the source of the authority involved. The professor works within an ideology of academic freedom—an illusion of autonomy (the inside/outside structure)—which is strongest when the teacher is paid by the state. In this view, the notion of a critical university staffed by state employees is simply utopian. Its deception is cruelest when the teacher pretends to set aside authority (as in the experiments of the sixties), because the authority that generates the pedagogical effect derives not from the educational system itself, nor from the knowledge professed or possessed by the teacher as expert, but is delegated by the state.

One of the consequences of this point which I wish to pursue concerns Bourdieu and Passeron's analysis of pedagogy as communication—the real focus of my topic. The key issue has to do with the status and function of language in the educational situation. The receivability of the pedagogic message depends upon a homogeneity in the pupil's environment uniting the home and the social environment with that of the school (which is why Derrida suggests the introduction of unreceivable and otherwise heterogeneous materials into the school text). The general point Bourdieu stresses is that there is a direct correlation between social origin and academic performance, a class function of the educational system which the ideology of legitimacy disguises. What interests me in this analysis is the identification of the privileging of a literate and verbalizing relationship to language in the schools as a feature of bourgeois hegemony—"the structural affinity between teaching in the humanities and bourgeois primary pedagogic action [referring to the home and social environment]" (*Reproduction*, 50); in short, the problem of the culturally disadvantaged child.

On the way toward articulating the poststructuralist model of an educated person, it is worth noting Bourdieu and Passeron's assessment of the kind of person who thrives in the current system: "Thus, all university norms, those which preside over the selection of students or the co-option of colleagues as well as those which govern the production of lectures, theses and even purportedly scientific works, always tend to favor the success, at least within the institution, of a model type of man and work, defined by a double negation, i.e. brilliance without originality and heaviness without scientific weight, or, if you will, the pedantry of lightness and the coquetry of erudition" (*Reproduction,* 202).

Any attempt to tamper with this model must consider that it is the nature of disciplinary and specialist organization to be homogeneous—to exclude any practice that does not reproduce the legitimacy of the system. For this reason, Bourdieu and Passeron say, teaching comes to resemble a priestcraft ritualizing an original prophecy. The teacher is indoctrinated to believe he can only repeat a message rather than produce one himself. And, as Derrida remarks in his introduction to Warburton's study of Egyptian hieroglyphics (Warburton being one of the initiators of historical grammatology), "The political question of literati, of intellectuals in the ideological apparatus, of the places and stockages of writing, of caste-phenomena, or 'priests' and the hoarding of codes, of archival matters . . . all this should concern us."[11] Indeed, the condition of the academic essay today resembles the status of Egyptian hieroglyphics in Warburton's time —originally intended (in their ancient context) for public communication, even for popular (politico-religious) messages, they became indecipherable, esoteric, unreceivable, and hence occult as the ability to read them was lost. Warburton's insight (preparing the way for the final decipherment by Champollion)—that the hieroglyphs were meant to be read by the public— reflects Derrida's view that any code is iterable. That the key to a given code was lost or hidden is not in itself the problem, since this possibility constitutes the structure of writing. The catastrophe is the second veiling, which covered over the first, which made the effect of concealment invisible, allowing people to forget the original encrypting and accept the power of the priests and scribes as natural: "Naturally destined to serve the communication of laws and the order of the city transparently, a writing becomes the instrument of an abusive power, of a caste of 'intellectuals' that is thus ensuring hegemony, whether its own or that of special interests: the violence of a secretariat, a discriminating reserve, an effect of scribble and scrypt" ("Scribble," 124).

The effectiveness of the teaching message, according to Bourdieu and Passeron, is due precisely to something like the effect of the scribes' scribble and not to the properties of the message itself. Pedagogical communication is not reducible to the formally defined relations of communication (sender-receiver), much less to the explicit content of the message. For in addition to whatever conscious symbolic mastery is conveyed, the educational process also communicates an implicit pedagogy, transmitting a kind of "total" knowledge of a cultural code or style by means of the apprentice's identification with the person of the master (as in the Hegelian model), who, to a large extent, has himself unconsciously internalized this style (*Reproduction*, 47–48). The resultant paradox is that pedagogic communication is able to perpetuate itself, even when the information transmitted tends toward zero. Here, then, is an assessment of classroom dialogue which puts in question the primacy of verbal discourse in education:

> The confident use that teachers make of the university idiom is no more fortuitous than students' tolerance of semantic fog. The conditions which make linguistic misunderstanding possible and tolerable are inscribed in the very institution: quite apart from the fact that ill-known or unknown words always appear in stereotyped configurations capable of inducing a sense of familiarity, magisterial language derives its full signifcance from the situation in which the relation of pedagogic communication is accomplished, with its social space, its ritual, its temporal rhythms; in short, the whole system of visible or invisible constraints which constitute pedagogic action is the action of imposing and inculcating a legitimate culture. (*Reproduction*, 108)

In Bourdieu and Passeron's view, then, professorial discourse—the literate mastery of the word—prevents learning, alienates the student, and condemns the teacher to "theatrical monologue and virtuoso exhibition" even while maintaining the fiction or farce of dialogue. Pedagogical discourse has become hieroglyph in the worst sense—that of the mystified and fetishized symbol *prior to the epistemic break of the historical grammatologists.*

THEATER

Mise en scène. Poststructuralism tends to share Bourdieu and Passeron's analysis of pedagogic communication but not their pessimism about the inevitability of the situation. There is agreement that the most significant aspect of pedagogic communication is finally not the message but the "medium," understood in the largest sense as the scene of teaching in the environment of the university. Writing in the *GREPH* anthology, Bernard Pautrat explains the new orientation: "The discourse of the master is inseparable from the unconscious *mise en scène* of the discourse, of its embodiment [*"mise en corps"*] in the body of the master" (*GREPH*, 271). Pautrat's response to the insight into the importance of the scene of teaching is to turn to a pedagogy of the body, of the material reality of the teacher and his setting. Pautrat's interest in the peculiarities and idiosyncrasies of the professor's idiom that seduces the student into discipleship (the desire to imitate) is typical of the poststructuralist concern for the singular and the anomalous, in contrast to the Hegelian focus on the universal. Truth, in Pautrat's view, is an affair of the body, an effect or event that has its own character distinct from the definitions of truth applicable to knowledge as discourse. If the teacher (man or woman) inevitably tends toward the place of the father overseeing the logos (his son), the Oedipal situation (and with it the whole theoretical system of psychoanalysis) will prove relevant to pedagogy. The paradox Bourdieu and Passeron note regarding the perpetuation of a pedagogic communication that conveys no real information can be explained, using psychoanalysis, in terms of the unconscious investments, the pleasures and perversions and drives, that motivate all parties to the exchange (transference and countertransference).

The model of discipleship encouraged under the Hegelian system—the identification with and reproduction of the master's style (now understood as the gesture of a singular body rather than as the representation of universal ideas)—finally undermines the critical goals of the philosophical message, since the least thoughtful relationship to knowledge is discipleship. The new pedagogy, then, must attempt to do away with the undesirable pedagogical effect of discipleship precisely because it generates disciplines and authorities.

The new methodology of instruction, Pautrat suggests, will shift from an exclusive concern for the knowledge comprehended through verbal discourse to include the "lived" relation to the "scene of instruction," whose operations are submitted to the same deconstruction applied to the Book (the complicity between the Book and pedagogic communication). The new imperative is to replace the purely intellectual, distanced, neutralized transmission of information (the ideological image of pedagogical communication) with a paradoxical technique of affective knowledge. How is this to be done?

> It will be necessary one day to begin to use fully these margins of the professor's discourse, the place, the size of the audience, the sexual division, the disposition of the bodies, all that without which there would not even be a philosophic discourse. It is necessary to change scenes, if one thinks that the scene, by the complexity of its entreaties in which it plays, short of and beyond the gesture alone, the voice alone, is even to signify elsewhere, otherwise than in the intellect alone, the truth to be communicated. *A good scene is always worth more than a long discourse* in order to reveal the reality of exploitation, the reality of sexual difference, because it tends to take from behind the intellectual defenses, the very ones which entrust truth to the intellect alone without practice and without force. (*GREPH,* 276, my emphasis)

Pautrat calls this pedagogy paradoxical because it attempts to teach the "unteachable *relation* to truth," something that can only be approached, if at all, by an inventive use of the scene of teaching, bringing into play the *mise en scène* of the classroom.

The question Derrida poses in this context is, "What is a teaching body?" (*Politiques,* 87). The pedagogical effect of mastery, the magisterial effect, occurs by means of the (illusion of) the teacher's excentricity to the scene: "The excentricity of the teaching body, in the traditional topology, permits at once the synoptic surveillance covering with its glance the field of taught bodies . . . and the withdrawal of the body which only offers itself to sight from one side" (88). In short, a body becomes magisterial only by exercising a "stratified effacement" of itself ("before or behind [*derrière*] the global teaching corps, the student body, or the socio-political body"), adopting the neutral tone and the plain style of "science" which "makes disappear by a sublime annihilation all that in the visage cannot be reduced to the speakable and the audible" (89). Against the traditional topology of educational space, Derrida proposes to expose all exposition—the programs and strategies of all questioning which are by definition inaccessible to individual and conscious, representable control—placing himself *more* than in the center: "A center, a body at the center of a space exposes itself on all sides, uncovers its back, lets itself be seen by what it does not see" (99), which is what Derrida was doing with his signature in *The Post Card* (the two other bodies to be included in the teaching body, he states at the conclusion of "Un corps enseignant," are the words "Jacques Derrida" with which he signs the article).

Reproduction and its dependence on transference and identification, then, may be countered by exercising the signature effect. Derrida looks not only to Freud and Marx (Pautrat's choice) for a model for an enactment of the signature effect in the classroom but also to avant-garde theater, especially as couched in the theories of Mallarmé and Artaud. The central problem for poststructuralist education—*how to deconstruct the function of imitation in the pedagogic effect*—resembles the efforts of modern artists in all media to find alternatives to "mimetologism." Artaud's theater of cruelty interests Derrida because it "announces the very limits of representation": it is theater that is not representation but "life itself."

Especially important in this context is Artaud's emphasis on the *mise en scène* at the expense of verbal discourse. I will pay close attention to Derrida's description of Artaud's theater of cruelty because it constitutes an outline of a procedure available for the enactment of a poststructuralist teaching in which, as Pautrat noted, a scene is always better than a discourse. It may be, then, as Bourdieu and Passeron said, that the classroom is inevitably a theater. But the grammatological classroom will at least be an avant-garde theater, which is to say that the new pedagogy will benefit from the recent history of avant-garde performance art, the general effect of which is to erase the stage and transform the neutrality and distance separating actor and audience, master and pupil. The weakness of the avant-garde up to now is that it tried to break cleanly with social institutions rather than deconstructing them. Therefore it became a pedagogy without a school, a situation that applied grammatology will change by bringing together or interlacing science and art.

The essential feature of Artaud's theory relevant to pedagogy is the demotion of speech, reversing the history of theater in the West, which has used *mise en scène* (and all aspects of staging and spectacle) merely to illustrate the verbal discourse (just as writing has been categorized as merely the representation of speech). Speech, it is stressed, will not disappear from theater (or from the classroom), "but will occupy a rigorously delimited place, will have a function within a system to which it will be coordinated" (*Writing*, 239). Two aspects of Artaud's notion of *mise en scène* essential for an application to pedagogy are made clear in Derrida's discussion:

1. Representation as such is not, any more than is speech, to be totally rejected, but only transformed or deconstructed. To name a *mise en scène* released from servility to text and the author-god would require, Derrida says, "a play upon all the German words that we indistinctly translate with the unique word 'representation'":

> The stage, certainly, *will no longer represent*, since it will not operate as an addition, as the sensory illustration of a text already written, thought, or lived outside the stage, which the stage would then only repeat but whose fabric it would not constitute. The stage will no longer operate as the repetition of a *present*, will no longer *re*-present a present that would exist elsewhere and prior to it, a present whose plenitude would be older than it, absent from it, and rightfully capable of doing without it: the being-present-to-itself of the absolute Logos, the living present of God. Nor will the stage be a representation if representation means the surface of a spectacle displayed for spectators. It will not even offer the presentation of a present, if present signifies that which is maintained *in front* of me. Cruel representation, if representation signifies, also, the unfolding of a volume, a multidimensional milieu, an experience which produces its own space. (*Writing*, 237)

Such too will be the mode of representation in the grammatological classroom, in which the old model of tradition as translation is understood to mean "transduction" or "originary translation."

2. The theater of cruelty demands a new theatrical writing that, when Derrida describes it, amounts to a definition of grammatological writing as well. "And what of this new theatrical writing? This latter will no longer occupy the limited position of simply being the notation of words, but

will cover the entire range of this new language: not only phonetic writing and the transcription of speech, but also hieroglyphic writing, the writing in which phonetic elements are coordinated to visual, pictorial, and plastic elements" (*Writing,* 240). With an analogy that he says "requires patient meditation," Derrida compares Artaud's "hieroglyphic" writing with Freud's description of dreamwork. "Present in dreams, speech can only behave as an element among others, sometimes like a 'thing' which the primary process manipulates according to its own economy. 'In this process thoughts are transformed into images, mainly of a visual sort; that is to say, word presentations are taken back to the thing-presentations which correspond to them, as if in general the process were dominated by considerations of representability (*Darstellbarkeit*)' " (*Writing,* 241).

Mime.   A useful text for determining the nature of the performance needed in the scene of teaching is Derrida's discussion of Mallarmé's "Mimique," the latter extracted from *Sketched at the Theatre,* an aesthetics of mime based on Paul Margueritte's solo performance, *Pierrot Assassin of His Wife.* [12] It is worth noting, considering Freud's use of popular culture (the toy slate, the rebus picture-puzzles [13] and the jokes, etc.), that Margueritte's piece was a new interpretation of the popular comic figure of the *commedia dell'arte* and that the publicity given to his performance contributed to the Pierrot revival that was an important part of European Modernism (Gerould, 103-4). In short, Margueritte's Pierrot and "Mimique" designate an important element in the history of performance art.

Margueritte's innovation was to create a modern Pierrot—tragic and neurotic rather than comically sympathetic. The extremity of the character, "horrible, mysterious and fatal," may also be compared with psychoanalysis in that the drama he performs—the acting out of the (possible?) murder of his wife by tickling her to death—has been related to the abreaction theater of psychotherapy. The most relevant part of Derrida's discussion (in "The Double Session") to pedagogy has to do with the theory of mimesis operative in Mallarmé's mime, keeping in mind that both hypomnesis and the simulacrum (significant strategies for Derrida) imply that one should only mime knowledge. Derrida's reading of "Mimique" suggests some of the features of a mime performance that might be adaptable to applied grammatology.

In *The Post Card* Derrida remarked that the post-age, with its detour or return inquiry of truth, extends from Plato's *Philebus* to *Beyond the Pleasure Principle* (and beyond). The interest of Mallarmé, accounting for his status as an initiator of theoretical grammatology, is that his mimesis explicitly breaks with the paradigm of truth which has controlled representation and education from Socrates to the present. Even Freud never quite relinquished the Platonic notion of "living memory," for example. In anamnesis the order of memory and of imitation are the same: the thing imitated is always before the imitation. The ontological notion on which this order is based is that a discourse on what *is* the *real* (a decidable logos) is possible, which distinguishes between the being-present and appearance. It goes without saying in this ontology that the imitated is more real, truer, superior to the imitator because it is prior. However often this order may be reversed throughout history, the absolute discernibility between the imitated and the imitation, and the anteriority of the former over the latter, have never been displaced.

The interpretation of mimesis historically has preserved this order—the order of cause and effect, of truth—whether in the mode of *aletheia* (revelation) or *adaequatio* (correspondence). In both modes of truth, the representation effaces itself in bringing to appearance the *physis* (essence of life) of the imitated: "It is in the name of truth, its only reference—*reference* itself—that *mimesis* is judged, proscribed or prescribed according to a regular alternation" (*Dissemination*, 193). Derrida argues that Mallarmé's essay makes thinkable a different mimesis, one that not only reverses the order of the relation (anamnesis itself does too with its notion of "the future as a returning past present," as does teleological return inquiry) but that displaces the distinction altogether. "Mimique," in effect, is an example of double invagination at work, in that it does what it says by the operation of a certain syntax giving words an undecidable status: "Reference is discreetly but absolutely displaced in the workings of a certain syntax, whenever any writing both marks and goes back over its mark with an undecidable stroke. This double mark escapes the pertinence or authority of truth: it does not overturn it but rather inscribes it within its play as one of its functions or parts" (*Dissemination*, 193). Like speech, then, truth is not excluded but is put in its place, inscribed in a more general system whose principle is the quotation mark. Knowledge mimed is science in quotation marks, no longer insight, but *in cit*ation.

The significance of the mime's silence is that, although his gestures are not merely spontaneous, they do not follow any prior verbal discourse: "His gestures, his gestural writing (and Mallarmé's insistence on describing the regulated gesture of dance or pantomime as a hieroglyphic inscription is legendary), are not dictated by any verbal discourse or imposed by any diction. The Mime inaugurates; he breaks into a white page" (*Dissemination*, 195). Like dreams, or the theater of cruelty, the Mime is a metaphor for Writing, signifying not only the subordination of speech but the silent working of differance. Moreover, the body itself becomes a kind of hieroglyph—"The white page and the white paint of the pale Pierrot who, by simulacrum, writes in the paste of his own make-up, upon the page he is." Thus, the Mime "must *himself* inscribe *himself* through gestures and plays of facial expressions. At once page and quill, Pierrot is both passive and active, matter and form, the author, the means, and the raw material of his mimodrama. The historian produces himself here" (*Dissemination*, 198). In this performed autography, the identity of representer and represented should not be mistaken for the authenticity of something like Rousseau's orator, "who represents only himself," as opposed to the actor, "who effaces himself and is lost in his hero" (*Grammatology*, 305), since this is the very opposition being deconstructed.

Like Freud, whose speculations were shown to perform the movement of the bobbin game, so too does Mallarmé perform in his text an auto-writing that simulates the Pierrot example. Pierrot's performance imitates an action that may or may not have taken place in the past. It is an action presented without taking place; that is, it is a fiction. The relation of the theory presented in "Mimique" to the actual performance of *Pierrot* is similarly fictional (and here is the real interest of the piece for Derrida), in that it is based, as Derrida shows at length, on Mallarmé's *memory* of a performance that he quite likely never even saw and that took place several years prior to the writing of the piece. Mallarmé's "reference," rather, was to a book written by Margueritte, which itself has a complex, intertextual history (such that finally it is impossible to determine the exact nature of what Mallarmé was working with when he produced his theory).

The point of Derrida's analysis, which follows the logic of the supplement, is to show that both Margueritte's performance and "Mimique" are closed and open at once, that they both involve a double writing—one that refers only to itself, and one that refers indefinitely to other texts. The structure of this combination is the *graft* (collage), whose principal effect, as a heterogeneous entity, is the problematization of all referentiality and all inside/outside oppositions. The effect of a double scene with undecidable reference is to escape the categorizations of truth which historically have restricted the notion of mimesis. If the text imitates nothing, it cannot be measured in terms of adequation. Nor is it a present unveiling of the "thing itself" in the "here and now."

The new mimesis, rather, utilizes the logic of the ersatz, the prosthesis, the simulacrum—an originary imitation:

> There is no simple reference. It is in this that the mime's operation does allude, but alludes to nothing, alludes without breaking the mirror. . . . This speculum reflects no reality; it produces mere "reality-effects." . . . It is a difference without reference, or rather a reference without a referent. . . . Mallarmé thus preserves the differential structure of mimicry or *mimesis,* but without its Platonic or metaphysical interpretation, which implies that somewhere the being of something that *is,* is being imitated. Mallarmé even maintains (and maintains himself in) the structure of the *phantasma* as it is defined by Plato:

the simulacrum as the copy of a copy. With the exception that there
is no longer any model, and hence, no copy. (*Dissemination,* 206)

The "Mallarméan" strategy for escaping Platonism and the dialectic, taken
up in turn by Derrida, is not an "impatient" reversal nor a "leap outside"
(neither of which can succeed) but a patient, discrete displacement, by
means of the simulacrum, of Platonism and Hegelianism, a barely perceptible difference of a veil (hymen) or leaf passing between them (the difference noted elsewhere between the signifier and the signified, in the
distinction between sophistics and dialectics).

Spacing. It may be possible now to formulate a preliminary, partial statement about the nature of a grammatological pedagogy. To begin with, it
takes up the problem of spacing—the reversal of the phoneticization process, giving new importance to the nonphonetic element of writing, putting
speech back in its place (a principal theme of the manifesto in *Of Grammatology*)—not at the micro-level of differance or the gap of articulation,
the level most frequently invoked in deconstructionism, but at the macro-
level of *mise en scène.* An application of grammatology to teaching, in
other words, involves a rethinking of the "space" in which the discourse
of ideas takes place. Given that grammatological presentations are neither
reproductions of reality nor revelations of the real, it is clear that grammatology *involves a displacement of educational transmissions from the
domain of truth to that of invention.* And the space of invention is to be
understood specifically in the rhetorical sense as referring to the topics,
places, *loci* collected in the commonplace books compiled during the
Renaissance. Invention in this rhetorical tradition—an extension of the
tradition of artificial memory (discussed in chapter 3), with the hypomnemic resource shifting, because of the invention of printing, from mental space to the pages of commonplace books [14]—is not a matter of "genius"
or originality but of searching through the places or topoi to find materials
for one's own text. The grammatological classroom, then, functions (metaphorically) in the manner of hypomnesis. We can imagine it as a kind of
living tableau, as if the "Pygmalion" story could be applied to the mnemonic
example Frances Yates cites from Peter of Ravenna (the principles of
grammar being memorized by placing images associated with the lesson
onto the allegorical figure of Grammatica, an old woman with a knife); the
models or examples discussed earlier (in this mnemonic scene brought to
life in the classroom), such as the Mystic Pad, the shoe, and so forth, are
like the hieroglyphic alphabet used to "write" on the "place"; and the
performer-Mime is the allegorical figure itself. *Memoria,* in other words,
as much as *inventio,* is an important aspect of the new pedagogy (which,
like the new rhetoric, does not simply return to the old tradition but carries
some of its principles into a new dimension).

The context just referred to helps to clarify what Derrida means to say perhaps in his own descriptions of the Mime's performance (or at least clarifies a possible extension of his descriptions to the classroom). I am thinking especially of the statement at the conclusion of "The Double Session" (remarking an idea that informs a number of his essays) that "the crisis of literature takes place when nothing takes place but the place, in the instance where no one is there to know" (*Dissemination*, 285). Many other passages could be drawn on to fill out this notion, such as the following: "This 'materialism of the idea' is nothing other than the staging, the theater, the visibility of nothing or of the self. It is a dramatization which *illustrates nothing*, which illustrates *the nothing*, lights up a space, re-marks a spacing as a nothing, a blank: white as a yet unwritten page" (*Dissemination*, 208). My argument is that what we are meant to discern (able to discern) when nothing takes place but the place is precisely the places and commonplaces (based on an analogy with the commonplace books, although we have other ways to generate materials now, such as computers and all our hypomnemic technology) to be utilized for invention.

A major challenge to the teaching performance in a classroom space conceived of as a metaphor of *inventio* is *how* to show the places taking place. I should note first, in approaching this question, that the solicitation of *theoria, eidos,* and *idea* outlined in chapter 2 is of fundamental importance to a new pedagogy, since we normally think of pedagogy as a communication or transmittal or transference of ideas. As Derrida points out, relevant to the effect of his new mimesis on the idea, "The stage thus illustates but the stage, the scene only the scene; there is only the equivalence between *theater* and *idea*, that is (as these two names indicate), the visiblity (which remains outside) of the visible that is being effectuated" (*Dissemination*, 209). Theory and theater are undergoing the same deconstruction, so that representation at either level is displaced from a "natural" to an "artificial" mode of repetition: " 'Re-presentation': theater does not show 'things in themselves,' nor does it represent them; it shows a representation, shows itself to be a fiction; it is less engaged in setting forth things or the image of things than it is in *setting up a machine*" (*Dissemination*, 238, my emphasis).

As I stressed in part I, the machine of hypomnesis is the repetition of signifiers rather than signifieds, operating on the principle of the homophone and the homonym. The idea put to work hypomnemically is not the signified concept, then, but the letters/phonemes of the word itself, which are set free to generate (or may be read in this way) conceptual material *mechanically* by gathering into a discourse terms (with all their baggage of signifieds) possessing these letters (similar to the + L and the + R effects). This artificial technique of invention, to draw on another pun, relates to mimesis not as copy but as *copia*—the love of abundance (*apeiron*) which characterized the Renaissance. Pedagogically, the commonplace books were used precisely to teach the student how to acquire an abundance of matter, as in *De copia* by Erasmus, which taught how to make themes "ample and verbose" and "delighted in eloquence and copiousness more for its own sake than for persuading a judge in forensic causes" (Lechner, 178).

Copia operates with the sign of the cross, chiasmus or plus, as is indicated by the structurality of the place of invention, which Derrida characterizes as the folds of a fan (recalling the intercolumnar spacings of mnemonics). The signifieds or themes of Western thought in all their polysemic richness are disseminated like so many *images agentes* on the series of folds (places):

> The blank or the whiteness (is) the totality, however infinite, of the
> polysemic series, *plus* the carefully spaced-out splitting of the
> whole, the fanlike form of the text. This *plus* is not just one extra
> valence, a meaning that might enrich the polysemic series. And
> since it has no meaning, it is not *The* blank proper, the transcenden-
> tal origin of the series. This is why, while it cannot constitute a
> meaning that is signified or represented, one would say in classical
> discourse that it always has a delegate or representative in the
> series. (*Dissemination*, 252)

All the themes of whiteness and blankness in Mallarmé's poetry *re-mark*, then, this supplementary valence, such that, when one wishes to put into the frame the taking place of the places, what emerges is "the very movement and structure of the fan-as-text"—"all this in the movement of a fan" (*Dissemination*, 251). The opening and/or closing of the fan ("the polysemy of 'blanks' and 'folds' both fans out and snaps shut, ceaselessly") is compared to the "waves" of the "watery moiré pattern" (a silk print). Not a method but a "marching order," as Derrida describes the machine of spacing, the interlacing movement of chance and necessity *brings into contact the moiré movement with memory,* thus linking his places with the tradition of hypomnesis: "For example, consider the duels among the *moire* [watered silk] and the *mémoire* [memory]" (*Dissemination*, 277), not to mention, he adds, a whole series or chain of other terms generated by the o-i-r complex or constellation. Such is the operation of the + L effect, the plus of *copia* or abundance, which also explains why an example can always exceed the model, since both examples and models—as in the series of drawings associated with the paradigm of the *Tlingit Coffin*—are articulated by the spacing (fanlike) motion of dissemination.

Mallarmé also uses the language of dance to characterize the textual movement, which suggests that the Mime-pedagogue might borrow from certain aspects of modern dance—those aspects that have influenced performance art—for ways to articulate the spacing of places.

> While designating the dancer's pirouette as a cipher or hieroglyphic,
> it also enciphers the sign "pirouette," which it causes to pirouette
> or turn upon itself like a top, this time designating the movement of
> the sign itself. . . . In this way, the pirouette, like the dancer's
> pointed toe, is always just about to pierce with a sign, with a sharp
> bit of nothing, the page of the book or the virginal intimacy of
> the vellum. And hence the dance of the signifier cannot be said to
> confine itself simply to the interior of a book or an imagination.
> (*Dissemination,* 240)

The dance refers to the undecidable syntax of Mallarmé's texts, whose
motion is modeled in all the analogies having to do with writing as walking, pathbreaking, the marching orders and roadwork of the machine. Thus,
when the paradoxical syntax of a text like "Pas" (on Blanchot) is encountered—drawing on the same ambiguity that informs *plus* in French,
"the decisive, undecidable ambiguity of the syntax of 'any more' [*plus de*]
(both supplement and lack)" (*Dissemination,* 274)—a reversal of the analogy between syntax and dancing helps to decipher what is taking place.

The *foot* that was absent, detached, or present as a phantom in the essay
on Van Gogh's shoes ("Restitutions"), alluding also to "foot" as the metrical unit of verse (measure, and hence size—the colossal—as rhythm), is
set in motion in "Pas" in the shuttle between *pas* as step and *pas* as negation (*ne pas*). A phrase like *"pas d'au-dela"* (undecidable between a "step
beyond" and "no beyond") perfectly states the simulacrum of movement
in the space of writing (the taking place of the place itself, which goes nowhere).[15] The "step" that does not walk, in the syntax explored in "Pas,"
recalls the language of choreography and suggests that what is involved
here might be easier to dance than to explain or describe: "This non-sense
or non-theme of the spacing that relates the different meanings to each
other (the meaning of 'blank' or 'white' along with the others) and in the
process prevents them from ever meeting up with each other cannot be
accounted for by any *description"* (*Dissemination,* 252–53). But a glance
through a grammar of dance verifies that much of Derrida's terminology
used to discuss syntactical movement also carries choreographic meanings
(as he himself suggests in *Of Grammatology* when he extends writing to
include all manner of inscription). As one classic text on this topic notes,
French is the international language of dance terminology, so the choreographic associations with *pas* require no Rosetta stone.

The useful aspect of this analogy is that in classic choreography dancing
is described in linguistic terms: the dance "positions" are "vowels"; the
simple movements are "consonants"; compound movements are "syllables";
steps are "words"; a series of steps (sequences) constitutes "sentences";
combinations of sequences are "paragraphs." Tracing (apropos of the
trace) denotes an *indication* of movement, the lines of movement on the

floor, without any transfer of weight, that is, without taking a step. A step without a step is quite possible in dance, in short, and is the very thing that constitutes the trace in dance. For that matter, the *"pas pas pas"* produced out of Blanchot's syntax (in "Pas") could be something like the Mime's notorious "walking in place"—*"pas sans pas."* In any case, dance lives within the *fort/da* or go-and-come law of gravity, according to which every jump, spring, or throwing motion is followed inevitably by a *tombe* or a *chute*—a falling back.[16]

Sovereignty. Artaud's theater of cruelty or Mallarmé's Mime are not to be carried over directly into the classroom, of course, but represent analogies for thinking through the relationship of idea to theater in the new pedagogy. Such analogies may suggest strategies for breaking with the master-disciple (Hegelian) structure of reproduction which informs current practice. I have argued that this break repeats the break with mimesis and representation experienced in other dimensions of the modern paradigm shift, a comparison that helps account for the peculiar introduction to *La vérité en peinture*—the allusion to Cézanne's letter promising the "truth in painting," although Cézanne himself is not discussed in any of the essays in the collection. By mounting Cézanne momentarily in the passe-partout of his discourse, Derrida alludes to the revolution in the visual arts which followed upon Cézanne's discovery that what he was painting were not landscapes but (literally) pictures, not mountains and houses but triangles and rectangles; hence, that the measure of a good picture was not its representational qualities but its formal design.

Painters have always had to balance the demands of representation and design, but Cézanne's insight has the structure of a gestalt shift, a shift of attention from figure to ground, which reorients the total conception of a practice. The equivalent shift in pedagogy would be to pass from occasional scholarly reports of instances when what was taught was not "the truth" but what was "receivable" (such as Walter Ong's book on Ramus showing how simplified primers for introducing boys to Scholastic logic played a major role in the shift from Medieval to modern logic by rendering superfluous the Scholastic complexities),[17] to pass from that to a systematic foregrounding of the pedagogic effect itself, independent of its content. The result of this shift of attention in the classroom would not be a non-representational pedagogy but something more Duchampian—the establishment of a new *relation* of pedagogy to knowledge or science.

The postmodernizing of pedagogy is based on the recognition that knowledge in and of the humanities is precisely a knowledge of enframing, of media and *mise en scène* understood not as a representation of something else but as itself a mode of action in the cultural world. The conclusion to be drawn from this recognition could be summarized by the axiom that has transformed the natural and human sciences as well—the observer participates in the observation; the organization and classification of knowledge are *interested* activities. The immediate lesson of this situation for a grammatology involves the reunion of the "two styles" (dialectical and rhetorical, plain and poetic), as in Derrida's conjunction of Freud and Artaud: the special writing in the theatre of cruelty, that is, produces "dreams calculated and given direction, as opposed to what Artaud believed to be the empirical disorder of spontaneous dreams. The ways and figures of dreams can be mastered. . . . In the theatrical treatment of dreams, 'poetry and science must henceforth be identical' " (*Writing*, 242).

As may be seen in Derrida's study of Bataille (an important model for the non-Hegelian relationship to knowledge), poetry (meaning any non-scientific use of language) and science will both be put to work. Translated into the classroom, double (art-science) discourse will consist of knowledge or science as information enframed by a *mise en scène* responsible for exceeding and breaking the mastery of the knowledge discourse. Roland Barthes's attitude typifies the new relationship between science and art, joined in one presentation. In this new "intellectual art," he explains, "we produce simultaneously theory, critical combat, and pleasure; we subject the objects of knowledge and discussion—as in any art—no longer to an instance of truth, but to a consideration of *effects.*"[18] The idea is that "one plays at science, one puts it in the picture—like a piece in a collage" (Barthes, 100). In his own case, Barthes often played with linguistics: "You use a pseudo-linguistics, a metaphorical linguistics: not that grammatical concepts seek out images in order to express themselves, but just the contrary, because these concepts come to constitute allegories, a second language, whose abstraction is diverted to fictive ends" (124).

The strategies involved in the inscription of science into the scene of writing and of teaching is treated in the essay on Bataille ("From Restricted to General Economy: A Hegelianism without Reserve"). Bataille's example is important because, as Derrida remarks, Bataille attempts in his texts to achieve an attitude called "sovereignty," explicitly opposed to Hegel's "Lordship" or mastery, his strategy being the exercise of "heterology," a mode of writing that avoids the homogeneity of scientific and philosophic discourse (Derrida's interest in maintaining the independence of the frame and the examples, and his introduction of "unreceivable" materials into the passe-partout, are extensions of "heterology"). Bataille's relevance is that he worked on a way to *say* the inadequacy of speech, even of all representation, a project that shows why Pautrat said the new pedagogy would have to be "paradoxical." The risk in talking about silence (as any teacher must do, and for which the operations of the Mime are an analogy) is that a meaning might be given to that which does not have one (and this fall back into discourse is also a return to Hegelianism). To control this risk, sovereignty (a precursor of deconstruction) betrays meaning *within* meaning, betrays discourse *within* discourse, by choosing words, like "silence" itself, that "make us slide." "In order to run this risk within language, in order to save that which does not want to be saved—the possibility of play and of absolute risk—we must redouble language and have recourse to ruses, to stratagems, to simulacra. To masks" (*Writing,* 262-63). Sovereignty, in short, resides in the "night of the secret" rather than in the clear light of explanation. Similarly, a teaching that counters the master's assertions, his effort to find out and conclude, will exploit the enigma that hides and provokes. The purpose of the enigma is to foreground the pedagogical effect in its pure form, acknowledging and exposing the paradigm of "truth as a woman," in which truth poses as something hidden. Mnemonically, the figure of this truth is "Baubo"—the hieroglyph of truth placed on the genitals of the figure Grammatica.

The heterology of Bataille's "sliding words," or the paleonymics of Derrida's deconstruction, are achieved by a new style that interlaces the styles of art and science into a unique relationship:

> An absolutely *unique relation:* of a language to a sovereign silence which *tolerates no relation,* tolerates no symmetry with that which tilts itself and slides in order to be related to it. A relation, however, which must rigorously, *scientifically,* place into a common syntax both the subordinated significations and the operation which is nonrelation, which has no signification and freely keeps itself outside syntax. Relations must scientifically be related to nonrelations, knowledge to unknowledge. "The sovereign operation, even if it were possible only once, the science relating objects of thought to sovereign moments is possible" (*Méthode de méditation*). "Henceforth, an ordered reflection, founded on the abandoning of knowledge, begins" (*Conferences*). (*Writing,* 264)

The word "science" here, however, "submits to a radical alteration: without losing any of its proper norms, it is made to tremble, simply by being placed in relation to an absolute unknowledge," amounting to the "absolute excess of every *episteme*" (*Writing,* 268). It might be written "science plus," or "science + L," giving "scilence."

The most important aspect of sovereignty for pedagogy is that it inscribes knowledge in a space that science cannot master or dominate and that defies reproduction, thus reversing the usual order and direction of knowledge gathering. Current scientific discourse is organized by a "relation oriented from the unknown to the known or knowable, to the always already known or to anticipated knowledge." But general writing (sovereignty) reverses this direction (similar to Abraham's anasemia), since it is only a relation to nonmeaning. Hence, "the known is related to the unknown, meaning to nonmeaning"—a movement, Derrida says, that can only be sketched in the "poetic image," since unknowledge can never be described, but only its effects registered (*Writing*, 270-71).

Sovereignty, in other words, is another way to express the situation of the subject of knowledge—unknowledge as the will to knowledge, the desire to know that we forget about but that enframes the information we gather. The idea in a grammatological classroom is treated in terms of Freud's notion of "boundary ideas"—conscious ego and traumatic memory at once. The purpose of Derrida's double science is to learn to analyze other texts and to write one's own, with regard to both bands, to work both scenes at once.

An example of a text that performs this double operation is Wittgenstein's *Philosophical Investigations*. The importance of this work as "science"—its impact on modern philosophy of language—goes without saying. What is rarely remarked, however, because it has not been read at the level of its examples (the effect of double invagination), is that *Philosophical Investigations* is also an intensely dramatic personal document in which, we might suppose, Wittgenstein worked through a self-analysis (similar to Freud's letters to Fliess, loaded with boundary ideas that served nonetheless to found psychoanalysis as a system of knowledge), which enabled him to avoid the suicide that claimed his brothers. I do not wish to undertake a full analysis of the text in these terms here, but only to point out the way in which the examples, read in the light of this biographical information (the suicides endemic in his family), tend to form a narrative independent of the logical discourse in which they are mounted.

The epistemological problems Wittgenstein poses here are relevant in any case to the examination of the pedagogical effect—for example, when he states: "The grammar of the word 'knows' is evidently closely related to that of 'can,' 'is able to.' But also closely related to that of 'understands.' ('Mastery' of a technique)." [19] To which he adds:

> But there is also *this* use of the word "to know": we say "Now I know!"—and similarly "Now I can do it!" and "Now I understand!"
>
> Let us imagine the following example: A writes series of numbers down; B watches him and tries to find a law for the sequence of numbers. If he succeeds he exclaims: "Now I can go on!"—So this capacity, this understanding, is something that makes its appearance in a moment. (*Investigations*, 59)

When reading both sides of this text, the exclamation "Now I can go on!" means not only that a student has learned how to perform an exercise *in the absence of a concept* ("But if a person has not yet got the *concepts*, I shall teach him to use the words by means of *examples* and by *practice*"—*Investigations*, 83)—the level relevant to the question of the teaching "effect"—but also that Wittgenstein himself is able to survive, *live on*, understood in association with a system of examples which chooses to approach the feeling of understanding by analogy with such mental states as "depression" and "pain." He could have investigated the question of "the meaning is the use" with any term, but he chose "pain": " 'But I can (inwardly) undertake to call THIS 'pain' in the future.' " "You learned the *concept* 'pain' when you learned language" (*Investigations*, 93, 118). Similarly, in asking after the nature of images, he states: "How do I know that this color is red?" (*Investigations*, 117). That on the second band this red is associated with blood may be seen in this bizarre example: "I see someone pointing a gun and say 'I expect a report.' The shot is fired.—Well, that was what you expected; so did that report somehow already exist in your expectation? . . . Was the thing about the event that was not in the expectation too an accident, an extra provided by fate?—But then what was *not* an extra? Did something of the shot already occur in my expectation?" (*Investigation*, 130). After dwelling on the gunshot, the very next example, the next number in the text, takes up the question of the color red, as if to say that the red spot he has been thinking about is the effect of the gunshot: " 'The red which you imagine is surely not the same (not the same thing) as the red which you see in front of you; so how can you say that it is what you imagined?'—But haven't we an analogous case with the propositions 'Here is a red patch' and 'Here there isn't a red patch'? The word 'red' occurs in both; so this word cannot indicate the presence of something red" (*Investigations*, 130). And he adds soon after the example of "two pictures of a rose in the dark" (*Investigations*, 141), hinting at the way blood looks black when it is spilled in real life.

Grammatology, then, is interested in the relationship between idiom, the "unique" situation of the individual (Wittgenstein's life situation, which included the temptation to commit suicide), and the general principles of a science with which the individual chooses to interact. Nor is there any necessary cause-and-effect order in this relationship, in Derrida's approach (which would imply the subordination of one ingredient to the other), but only a chiasmatic interlacing. Gerald Holton poses a similar study of the "correspondence between the personal style and the structure of the laws of nature themselves" in his *Thematic Origins of Scientific Thought*. As Holton points out, "science" refers to two quite distinct activities:

> One is the private aspect, science-in-the-making, the speculative, perhaps largely nonverbal activity, carried on without self-consciously examined methods, with its own motivations, its own vocabulary, and its own modes of progress. The other is the public aspect, science-as-an-institution, the inherited world of clarified, codified, refined concepts that have passed through a process of scrutiny and have become part of a discipline that can be taught, no longer

showing more than some traces of the individual struggle by which it had been originally achieved.[20]

Grammatology is committed to a pedagogy that will shift its focus from the latter to the former aspect of science—that will collapse discipline into invention. Holton agrees with this approach in that, in drawing out the educational consequences of his studies of the personal styles of major scientists (one consequence being the abandonment of specialized disciplines), he notes that discovery is accessible to rational inquiry, including the use of psychology (the problem of how an individual discovery is made) and the sociology of knowledge (how the discovery gets accepted).

How might this new pedagogy actually be performed? In the next three chapters I shall discuss three examples of educational practice, each already fulfilling a major aspect of Writing, which indicate by their very existence, not to mention their extreme success, that applied grammatology is not simply a utopian ideal.

7

Seminar:

Jacques Lacan

We have already seen in a number of contexts the extent to which grammatology uses psychoanalysis and the notion of the unconscious in order to challenge the metaphysics of presence and of the self-conscious subject. Psychoanalysis is equally important in the application of grammatology to pedagogy, for it provides a resource for dealing with one of the principal difficulties facing this experiment. To reiterate, the strategy of Writing is not to eliminate speech, representation, science, or "truth" from academic discourse, but to put them in their place, to break their dominance by bringing them into balance with a nonverbal element that is not associated with the virtues of classicism—clarity, simplicity, harmony, unity. The practical question, then, is *how* to talk, lecture, mount a discourse in a grammatological classroom. One of the best models available upon which to base a new pedagogical discourse is Jacques Lacan's seminars, of which at least five volumes (of the twenty-four listed as forthcoming) have been published.

While it is true that Lacan's phallogocentric ideology is unacceptable to Derrida (as noted earlier with respect to Derrida's critique of the seminar on "The Purloined Letter" in "The Purveyor of Truth"), it is equally true that the presentational strategies Lacan used in his famous seminars, attended on occasion by Derrida, Barthes, and many other important French intellectuals, are compatible with grammatological Writing—that a grammatologist could use Lacan's technique the way Mallarmé, according to Derrida, used mimesis: retaining its structure while abandoning its reference.

In fact, Derrida Writes the way Lacan lectured, with the double science and the contra-band being a version of Lacan's "double inscription"—both address and draw on the resources of the conscious (secondary process, discursive, logical) and the unconscious (primary process, non-sense) mind, combining in one operation the scientific with the poetic.

Lacan was working in a specific set of circumstances which do not apply to grammatology directly. He introduced his nonmagisterial style into the classroom as a necessary corollary of his attempt to teach psychoanalysis—to undertake the formation of analysts—as a university course. His project was doubly controversial. There were those who thought that psychoanalysis as a special mode of knowledge could not be separated from a personal analysis (the clinical context). But those who thought that analysis could be taught in the university argued that it should be taught in a scholarly and abstract manner, like any other discipline. Lacan, however, as Sherry Turkle explains, insisted that "only the theory constitutes the science, and only the science is subversive as a new epistemology, a new way of knowing."[1] As for the manner of presentation, although Lacan wanted to move into the university in order to work more closely with linguists and mathematicians who could help formalize psychoanalysis into mathematical statements—mathemes—he also rejected the abstract academic tone for a style based on the peculiarities of the clinical situation, a style that he explicitly characterized, in contrast to the "classical" tone of the university, as "baroque."

Lacan's project is applicable beyond the context of psychoanalysis as a discipline, of course, as may be seen in Shoshana Felman's remark that the notion of "transference" ("the acting out of the reality of the unconscious"), by which the analytic situation functions, applies not only to therapeutic communication but wherever there is interlocution—especially in teaching.[2] Felman cites in this vein Freud's statement that at least three activities are formulated with the "mirage" of transference—psychoanalysis, government, and education. In short, one way to discuss the pedagogic effect would be to investigate the phenomenon of transference and countertransference comparatively, juxtaposing the analyst-patient relation with that of the teacher-student.

Lacan himself, seeking a style that would enable him to translate into the classroom what psychoanalytic experience reveals to the analyst, tried to take into account, and to counter, the effects of transference (the identification of the patient with the analyst—and vice versa—which is also the basis of the master-disciple relationship in teaching: another reason why Lacan's model is of interest to grammatology). Felman characterizes Lacan's pedagogical style as "ironic," although part of the irony, it must be said, is that whatever the usefulness of his strategies for breaking with the Hegelian model of mastery, Lacan himself was an authoritarian and an intellectual terrorist, as is evident, for example, in Turkle's account of his administrative tyranny over the School of Psychoanalysis ("The Freudian Field") at Vincennes (the experimental university established outside Paris in the wake of the May 1968 student protests). Nonetheless, the Lacanian pedagogy manifested in the seminars offers several important lessons for applied grammatology, especially considering that Felman, along with other commentators, describes his lecture style as the equivalent of Artaud's theater of cruelty or Mallarmé's poetry—the same models invoked by Derrida.

Even more appropriate than the Mime's silence as a metaphor of putting speech back in its place is the silence of the analyst, which, when translated into pedagogy, involves the replacement of the master's assertions and explanations with a set of oblique, apotropaic interventions, in a style that Felman describes as a kind of "writing in black and white, using shadow as well as light." In any case, the analytic situation is the prototype of working with unknowledge, with the mirage of transference being precisely that the analyst is "the subject who is supposed to know," although in reality the analysand alone "knows" (but cannot remember).

To appreciate Lacan's performance, we should keep in mind his audience, which included not only "majors" (apprentice analysts and others with a similarly direct interest in psychoanalysis) but also a crowd of philosophy professors and other intellectuals. This group presented a mix of those who knew too much about theory and those who knew very little. That Lacan managed to satisfy both groups (he comments at one point that nothing he could do seemed to scare them off) establishes his presentational mode as a laboratory for developing a discourse that is at once popular and learned—a major goal of grammatology. His occasional remonstrances with respect to the attitude of the class (only half had read "The Purloined Letter" the day he discussed it) reveal something about his pedagogical effect: "We find ourselves before this singular contradiction—I don't know if it should be called dialectical—that the less you understand the better you listen. For I often say to you very difficult things, and I see you hanging on my every word, and I learn later that some of you did not understand. On the other hand, when one tells you simple things, almost too familiar, you are less attentive. I just make this remark in passing, which has its interest like any concrete observation. I leave it for your meditation." [3]

"Difficulty" is essential to Lacan's epistemology, as we shall see, and is the direct result of several assumptions about the communication of psychoanalytic knowledge. He stresses, along with many other modern theorists, that "there is no metalanguage," no means to say the truth about truth, although he does believe that truth can be *shown* in what it speaks of. Therefore, he adds, analysis turns to other means· "Is it necessary to say that we must acquaint ourselves with other modes of knowledge than that of science, when we have to deal with the epistemological drive?"[4] His list of these other modes reveals his conception of psychoanalysis as a comprehensive discipline, synthesizing the humanities and the human sciences, as he says, comparing it to the Medieval notion of "liberal arts." Noting Freud's own list of subjects which should be included in psychoanalysis as a university discipline—"besides psychiatry and sexology, we find 'the history of civilization, mythology, the psychology of religions, literary history, and literary criticism' "[5]—Lacan continues, "For my part, I should be inclined to add: rhetoric, dialectic in the technical sense that this term assumes in the *Topics* of Aristotle, grammar, and, that supreme pinnacle of the aesthetics of language, poetics, which would include the neglected technique of the witticism." Moreover, "this technique would require for its teaching as well as for its learning a profound assimilation of the resources of a language [*langue*], and especially of those that are concretely realized in its poetic texts" (*Selection,* 82–83), which is to say that a pedagogical discourse must begin to take on some of the density of poetry—hence its difficulty.

The difference in the educational backgrounds of his audience is not a problem for Lacan's pedagogy, finally, considering that he is not concerned with the transmittal of information. Rather, his purpose is to bring about the very conjunction of pedagogy and invention discussed in chapter 6. "There is in every knowledge once constituted a dimension of error, which is to forget the creative function of truth in its nascent form" (*Le moi,* 29). Thus, the more one knows in a field, the greater the risk of falling into the error of relying on predigested materials. Psychoanalysis, however, situates itself precisely at the level of origination rather than of institutionalization. "What we discover in analysis is at the level of *orthodoxa.* Everything that operates in the field of analytic action is anterior to the constitution of knowledge, which does not prevent us while operating in this field from constituting a knowledge of it" (*Le moi,* 30). Like Derrida, who is interested in exploiting the way ordinary language contaminates all attempts at system or classification, Lacan locates the strength of his discipline at the source of error of science, "since every science arises out of the manipulation of language which is anterior to its constitution, and that it is in this manipulation of language that analytic action develops."

The pedagogical effect Lacan himself wishes to achieve corresponds to the grammatological evocation of unknowledge. Reflecting on the problematic nature of teaching, that teachers' mistakes are not due to an ignorance of "subject matter" (but of the "subject" of knowledge, the one who knows), Lacan remarks, "That led me to think that there is no true teaching except that which manages to awaken in those who attend an insistence, that desire to know [connaître] which emerges only when they themselves have taken the measure of ignorance as such—the extent to which it is, as such, fecund—and also on the part of the one who teaches" (Le moi, 242). At the level of unknowledge—or of the unconscious— everyone in his audience is equal, a level that he addresses by means of a "double inscription": "Is our reason so weak that it cannot recognize itself on equal terms in the mediation of scientific discourse and in the primary exchange of the Symbolic object, and that it cannot rediscover there the identical measure of its original guile?"[6]

Lacan, following Freud, stresses that the real cannot be apprehended or investigated except through the intermediary of the symbolic. In this view, based on Freud's "energy" or "electrical" model of the mind (outlined in the early Project for a Scientific Psychology), in which all conceptualization and judgment can only retrace the paths of thought previously breached by the drives of desire (that one in a sense reasons with desire), it is wrong to pose a firm distinction between the inner and the outer worlds. Rather, the human world, joining libidinal (inner drives) experience with cultural information (outer perceptions), "is not closed, but open to a host of extraordinarily varied neutral objects, objects even which have nothing more to do with objects, in their radical function as symbols" (Le moi, 125). This assumption suggests the possibility of communicating with students in a way similar to that used with patients: "For [the symbol] to induce its effects in the subject, it is enough that it makes itself heard, since these effects operate without his being aware of it—as we admit in our daily experience, explaining many reactions of normal as well as of neurotic subjects by their response to the symbolic sense of an act, of a relation, of an object. There is therefore no doubt that the analyst can play on the power of the symbol by evoking it in a carefully calculated fashion in the semantic resonances of his remarks" (Speech, 58).

These resonances may be evoked in two ways, at least, one being by means of the sound of language itself (the exploitation of homophones, the level at which Lacan prefers to work, to be discussed later with respect to lalangue), and the other the presentation of nonverbal materials (relevant to Lacan's pedagogical, if not to his clinical practice). In general, both modes are used to bring into play "unconscious thought," involving the activation of what Derrida described as hypomnesis, as opposed to the "living memory" or anamnesis:

> The unconscious is that chapter of my history which is marked by
> a blank or occupied by a falsehood: it is the censored chapter. But the
> Truth can be found again; it is most often already written down else-
> where. That is to say:
> —in monuments: this is my body—that is to say, the hysterical nucleus

of the neurosis where the hysterical symptom reveals the structure
of a Language and is deciphered like an inscription which, once recovered, can without serious loss be destroyed;
—in archival documents also: there are my childhood memories,
just as impenetrable as are such documents when I do not know their
source;
—in semantic evolution: this corresponds to the stock of words and
acceptations of my own particular vocabulary, as it does to my style
of life and to my character;
—in traditions as well, and not only in them but also in the legends
which, in a heroicized form, transport my history;
—and lastly, in the traces which are inevitably preserved by the distortions necessitated by the linking of the adulterated chapter to the
chapters surrounding it, and whose meaning will be re-established by
my exegesis. (*Speech,* 21)

All of these "external" resources may be drawn on—"mimed," Derrida
would say—in a double inscription in order to say "something else," to provoke the desire to know and the desire to investigate this desire itself.

I shall turn now to the examination of one seminar—*Encore,* given during the academic year 1972-73—(while continuing to refer for purposes of
comparison to other texts as well) for a more specific description of Lacan's
pedagogical style. My purpose throughout will be not to seek a full psychoanalytic rationale for the style but to focus on those aspects of it which
are relevant to a grammatological Writing.

ST. THERESA

Keeping in mind that the book to which I refer is the transcript of a
seminar, we can see that Lacan's presentation bears a significant resemblance
to Derrida's picto-ideo-phonographic Writing. The cover of *Encore* (but we
should imagine a print displayed in the classroom)—a reproduction of
Bernini's sculpture, *The Ecstacy of St. Theresa*—recalls the illustration used
on the cover of *The Post Card.* In both cases, the visual work provides the
organizing image of the discourse, not to be interpreted but to serve as a
point of departure for working through a theoretical problem.

The other published seminars reflect the same procedure. The cover of
volume 2 displays a detail from Mantegna's *Calvary,* showing Roman
soldiers rolling dice for possession of Christ's robe; the cover of volume 11
displays Holbein's *The Ambassadors,* which includes a death's head in
anamorphic perspective at the bottom of the scene. These pictures (the
discussion of which Lacan introduces in each case at approximately mid-
term) have a dual purpose. In the first place, alluding allegorically to the
theme of the seminar, they provide a concrete point of reference for the

discussion of certain principles. An excerpt from the session dealing specifically with the work, selected by the editor and printed on the back cover, identifies the substance of the ostensible theme and signals the possibility of reading the seminar as a "legend" for the picture. Here, for example, is the blurb for *Encore:*

> You have only to go see in Rome Bernini's statue to understand
> at once that she is coming [*jouit*], Saint Theresa, no doubt about it.
> And what is she enjoying? It is clear that the essential testimony
> of mystics is precisely to say that they experience it, but they know
> nothing about it. These mystical ejaculations are neither babblings
> nor verbiage, which is in short what one could read at best. At the
> very bottom of the page, note—add there the *Ecrits* of Jacques Lacan,
> because it is of the same order. What was tried at the end of the
> last century, in Freud's day, what was sought, all these good men in
> Charcot's entourage and others, was to reduce the mystical to a
> matter of fucking [*foutre*]. If you look close, it is not that at all. That
> pleasure which one experiences and knows nothing about, isn't
> that what sets us on the path of ex-sistence? And why not interpret
> one aspect of the Other, that of God, as supported by feminine
> bliss? [7]

The other function of the image is mnemonic, providing a reminder in association with which the year's work may be more readily recalled. This aspect is most evident in the first seminar, because in it Lacan did not use an art work as the hinge figure. Rather, at the close of the final session, he distributed to each of the students a small figurine representing an elephant (hence, the cover of that volume bears a photograph of an elephant). My interest in this function of the image, of course, relates to the mnemonic property of Writing, so I have to remark that the figurine represents memory as such, as in the saying that someone has a memory like an elephant. The figurine alludes to a specific part of the year's discussion, when Lacan refers to elephants while making a point that, with the entry into language, the symbol emerges and becomes more important than the object which it names:

> I have already repeated it so many times. If you do not get it into
> your head. . . . The word or the concept is nothing other for the
> human being than the word in its materiality. It is the thing itself. It
> is not simply a shadow, a breath, a virtual illusion of the thing, it
> is the thing itself. Reflect for a moment in the real. It is a fact that
> the word *elephant* exists in their language, and that the elephant
> enters therefore into their deliberations, that men have been able to
> take with respect to elephants, before ever touching them, resolutions much more decisive for these pachyderms than anything else
> that happened to them in their history . . . before anyone ever raised
> toward them a bow or a rifle. [8]

The figurine, then, reminds the student of the power of the word to affect the real, an observation that he formulated elsewhere in challenging the distinction between the "conjectural sciences" (like psychoanalysis) and the "exact" (mathematical) sciences: "For experimental science is not so much defined by the quantity to which it is in fact applied, as by the measurement it introduces into the real" (*Selection*, 74). His pedagogy, too, is an "intervention," rather than a reproduction.

Even while he is introducing these and other images into his discourse, Lacan declares that he has little faith in them, which is part of his strategy for avoiding magisterial effects and the "idolatry" of fixed "recipes." Nonetheless, he remarks that "models are very important. Not that it means anything—it intends nothing. But we are like that—it is our animal weakness, we need images. And, lacking images, it happens that symbols do not appear" (*Le moi*, 111).

The problem, then, is to discern how the image of Bernini's ecstatic saint functions in Lacan's discourse. Knowing in principle that it is a metaphor in a double inscription, we may begin with a definition of the double question posed in the seminar, one aspect of which concerns "knowledge" of something, and the other the "subject" who knows. The question Lacan set for the year's research is directed both "outward," to a general question about which psychoanalysis as a science claims to know something (human sexuality), and "inward," to his own relationship to the process of knowing. The image of Saint Theresa emblematizes both questions, or both aspects of this question, as Lacan indicated (in the legendary excerpt) when he placed his collection of essays, the *Ecrits*, on the side of the mystic's pleasure, an analogy that hints at what is taking place in the course. We should keep in mind, too, that the statue functions as a mnemonic image for something that will not be understood at the time of the seminar, but as an aftereffect. The image, that is, carries the student through the "time of understanding," the delay of *"Nachträglichkeit"* in the Freudian model of mind, which suggests the relevance to Lacan's teaching of his own advice with respect to the reading of Aristotle: "If Aristotle is not so easily understood, because of the distance which separates us from him, it is just that which justifies my telling you that to read does not obligate one to understand. First it is necessary to read" (*Encore*, 61). Or, as he cautions after inscribing a chart on the blackboard, "avoid understanding too quickly" (74).

The "objective" task posed for the year's work is to take up the question that Freud left aside when he hypothesized that the libido is *only* masculine. The question is: *"Was will das Weib?"*—what does the woman want? (*Encore*, 75). Lacan rephrases the topic on several occasions, stating, in his provocative way, that there is in fact no sexual *relationship* (that sexual bliss is not a sign of love): "This matter of the sexual relation, if there is a point from which it could be clarified, it is precisely from the side of the ladies, to the extent that it is by the elaboration of the not-all [*pas-tout*] that a path might be breached. This is my true subject this year, behind the *Encore,* and is one of the senses of my title. Perhaps I will manage thus to bring out something new about feminine sexuality" (54).

Lacan mentions here a feminist whom he had angered by the presumptuousness of this question and whom he put off even more by suggesting she come back the next day when he would explain everything to her. Part of Lacan's effect, in any case, involved such baitings and provocations in the interest, it seems, of deliberate misunderstanding. For as he says of his chart, "it does not appear to me to be exemplary, except, as usual, for producing misunderstandings" (*Encore, 73*). Stephen Heath's critique of *Encore* represents the consequences, if not of understanding too quickly—too easily or readily—then of responding to only one side of Lacan's double inscription. Heath takes the year's theme ("what does the woman want?") and its relation to the image of Saint Theresa literally, straightforwardly.[9] Bringing to his reading of *Encore* two preoccupations of his own—sexual politics and cinema—Heath, like a gentleman coming to the aid of an insulted lady, denounces Lacan's sexism (while apologizing as a male who probably has no business talking about feminine sexuality either). Heath's point is well taken, in that, like Derrida's critique, it calls attention to the metaphysical and phallogocentric stricture of Lacan's insistence on working within the formula of "truth is a woman" (even though Lacan adds here—"for a man"). Heath's cinematic interest, however, leads him to assume that Lacan is interpreting Bernini's statue and that he is doing so in a way that ignores the problematics of seeing (the link with cinematic viewing): "What is striking," Heath complains, "is [Lacan's] certainty as to what the statue means" (Heath, 52). For Heath this certainty suggests that Lacan is appealing to "the direct evidence of an image," to the immediacy of seeing which elides sexual difference. Heath goes on to give a useful analysis of Lacan's statements about feminine sexuality in *Encore* and an intelligent discussion of voyeurism and fetishism in the fascination of the cinematic image, thus ignoring both the symbolic operation of the image and the other major question posed in the double inscription.

IGNORANCE

The other topic researched in the seminar is Lacan's ignorance with respect to the first question, *"Was will das Weib?"* From the point of view of grammatology the second question is more interesting, since it foregrounds Lacan's pedagogical performance. Lacan's purpose, in this context, is less to come to any conclusions about feminine sexuality than it is *to demonstrate the nature of psychoanalytic knowing as such*—the special perspective of psychoanalysis on science as an activity. The question is posed as follows: "How is a science still [*encore*] possible after what one could call the unconscious?" (*Encore*, 95). This question in fact informs Lacan's program in general, as could be shown with citations from almost any one of his texts: "You see the emergence of a double questioning. If we can couple psycho-analysis to the train of modern science, despite the essential effect of the analyst's desire, we have a right to ask the question of the desire that lies behind modern science."[10] As that comment suggests, the primary question concerns the analyst's participation, at the level of desire, in the questions he poses: "I may even seem to have been saying the same thing myself in my teaching recently, when I point straight out, all veils torn aside, and in a quite overt way towards that central point that I put in question, namely—*what is the analyst's desire?*" (*Concepts*, 9). What does the analyst (like woman) want?

Because Lacan develops a pedagogy that puts this question on stage, placing himself in an exemplary way in the position of the analysand rather than of the analyst,[11] his teaching is especially important as a resource for grammatology's search for a nonmagisterial style. The assumption on which Lacan bases his performance is shared by Derrida: "Analysis distinguishes itself from all that which has been produced in discourse until now, in that it states this, which is the snag in my teaching, that I speak without knowing. I speak with my body, and that without knowing. I say thus always more than I know" (*Encore*, 108). His knowledge, or rather his teaching, resembles St. Theresa's bliss, in that both are produced in the absence of (self) knowledge. Lacan says of his teaching, relevant to this condition, "It is not so much on the *I* that the accent should be placed, to know about what *I* can proffer, but on the *from*, that is on that from where it [ça] comes, this teaching of which I am the effect" (30).

This condition has a direct bearing on the status of the question, "what does the woman want?"—the question of feminine sexuality, which Lacan poses in fact in terms of the relation between the sexes—love. What gradually emerges from session to session of the seminar is that Lacan is exploring the relation between love and knowledge. The problem is that "there is a relation of being which cannot know itself. It is that structure which I interrogate in my teaching, to the extent that this impossible knowledge is thereby forbidden" (*Encore*, 108). Placed in this context, Lacan's use of the metaphor "truth is a woman" takes on a different tone: "I do not know how to take up, why not say it, with truth—any more than with woman. I have said that each one, at least for the man, was the same thing. It amounts to the same embarrassment. It so happens that I have a taste for one as much as for the other, despite everything one says about it" (108).

These citations reveal that, far from being an image of his object of study, interpreted as giving evidence apropos of feminine sexuality, St. Theresa emblematizes Lacan's own condition, that in observing his teaching performance we are witnessing something like the ecstacy without knowing of the mystic. To pose the presence of desire within his own discourse exposes "la *bêtise*" (stupidity, nonsense), Lacan notes: "My mere presence in my discourse, my mere presence is my stupidity," and he adds that, whereas other discourses flee *bêtise*, analytic discourse seeks it out, seeks the *sublime* of stupidity (*Encore*, 18–19). We can say, then, that Lacan posed the question *"Was will das Weib?"* precisely because it is the most extreme version possible of an impossible question, impossible because the woman's bliss represents for Lacan the impossible knowledge of the Other. By setting such a question for the seminar, *Lacan turns the research back on himself,* delineating all the more clearly the special features of psychoanalytic knowing.

Encore teaches the love of knowledge, couched in the specific terms of the desire of the subject of knowledge and presented in a way intended not just to *tell* about this passion (designated actually as the "passion of ignorance"), *but to instill it, stimulate it, in the audience.* All pedagogy takes as its goal the fostering of the love of knowledge, if not of wisdom, but psychoanalysis is privileged in this respect, since it is nothing less than a knowledge of love, such that love and knowledge come together in it in a powerful way. "To speak of love, in effect, one does nothing but that in analytic discourse" (*Encore,* 77). And what the analytic discourse conveys, according to Lacan, "is that to speak of love is in itself bliss," with the Pleasure Principle itself being an example of the merger of love and science. Lacan even declares at one point that "we must, this year, articulate what is there as a pivot of all that is instituted in the analytic experience—love" (40).

The aspect of love most important for the seminar, for psychoanalysis as a university subject, is the love of knowledge, which accounts for Lacan's description of what he takes to be the underlying theme of the course:

> I have spoken some of love. But the pivot-point, the key to what I have put forward this year, concerns what there is of knowledge in it, the exercise of which I have stressed represents nothing but a bliss [*jouissance*]. (*Encore,* 125)

Moreover, the character of pedagogy in the seminar is designed to provide the experience of knowledge as bliss, based on Lacan's hypothesis about their interdependence:

> Knowledge is worth exactly as much as it costs, of how much of one's own flesh is invested in it, that it be difficult, difficult in what way? —less in its acquisition than in its enjoyment. There, in delight, the

conquest of this knowledge renews itself each time that it is exercised, the power that it gives remaining always turned towards its bliss.

It is strange that that has never been highlighted, that the sense of knowledge is entirely there, that the difficulty of its exercise is that which raises that of its acquisition. (*Encore,* 89)

Part of the lesson of the liaison of bliss and knowledge is always to include in science the desire of the subject. The behaviorist experiments of the rat psychologists, for example, are interesting not in terms of the rats' behavior, Lacan says, but in terms of the scientists' behavior—their relation to the labyrinths they build (*Encore,* 129). In short, the irruption of the unconscious into science opens knowledge to enigma. The method Lacan devises to work with this enigma represents his greatest affinity with Derrida's Writing and provides a model for using speech in the classroom, for lecturing in a way that puts speech back in its place.

LALANGUE

The homonym and the homophone are as essential to Lacan's pedagogy as they are to Derrida's Writing (and herein lies the usefulness of the seminars as a resource for an applied grammatology). When he declared the special focus of psychoanalysis to be the desire of the subject of knowledge, accompanied by a pedagogy that introduced his own desire—the action of the unconscious, of his *bêtise*—into the scene of teaching, Lacan was not setting up an impasse nor an aporia for the research subject, but simply creating the conditions that constitute the starting point for the psychoanalytic mode of knowledge. This mode, as I mentioned before, operates not according to the anamnesic principle of self-consciousness, "living memory," or introspection, but by means of hypomnesis and the repetition of the signifier. We have already discussed this distinction as it appears in Derrida, but Lacan has his own formulation of it, as for example when he says that he is going to submit to the test of the signifier "a certain number of *dires* [sayings] of the philosophical tradition"—to interrogate how the *dires* of Aristotle and Freud traverse one another on the question of bliss (*Encore,* 25, 57)—with *dires* being the anagram of *désir* (desire).

Following Freud's lead (the conjunction of science and pleasure in the formulation of the Pleasure Principle), Lacan sets in motion his own merger of love and knowledge by asking if the term *"jouissance"* itself knows something. At one level, he is asking if the Other knows—what the mystic knows, or what the woman knows. The problem, in fact, is less one of knowledge than of pedagogy—the transmission of knowledge, for the real issue is what the mystic or the woman is or is not able to *say* about what is known, keeping in mind always that Theresa, woman and mystic at once, is a metaphor finally for unconscious thought. Lacan is not researching mysticism, nor even (although this point is not as obvious) feminine sexuality, but the activity of the unconscious in language. Lacan offers a "formula" with respect to this issue (his procedure often being to begin a lesson with an aphoristic or condensed formulation dealing with the matter of a given session): *"The unconscious is that the being* [l'être], *in speaking, delights, and,* I add, *wants to know nothing more about it.* I add that that means—*knows nothing at all" (Encore,* 95). Freud's formula, Lacan says, was "there where it speaks, it enjoys," recalling Lacan's own formula—the unconscious is structured like a language—both of which point to the way psychoanalysis cut the Gordian knot of the "inaccessibility" of the unconscious—of dreams and all related phenomena—by focusing its investigation on the *parlêtre,* the speaking being (equating *l'être* with the letter, *la lettre).* Thus, when Lacan says that the unconscious knows nothing, he adds that "the unconscious has revealed nothing to us about the physiology of the nervous system, nor about the functioning of binding, nor about premature ejaculation" (104). Given this situation, in order sometimes to escape "the infernal affair," Lacan jokingly notes that he resorts to certain techniques of Zen teaching—to respond to questions with a bark: "ça!"

But as a teacher, one of whose assumptions is that he says more than he knows, Lacan is not content to remain at the level of religion in any form. Rather, he adopts a manner of speaking ("Theoretical models," Max Black states, "whether treated as real or fictitious, are not literally constructed: the heart of the method consists in *talking* in a certain way")[12] which allows language to say what it knows, or allows the unconscious to show itself in the play of language. The procedure is based on the discovery through analysis "that there is a knowledge which does not know itself, a knowledge which supports itself in the signifier as such" (giving rise to the use of metaphors drawn from the experience of mystics to describe the effect of receiving these "messages") *(Encore,* 88).

The locus of this knowledge is indeed the Other ("the unconscious, which I represent to you as that which is inside the subject, but which can be realized only outside, that is to say, in that locus of the Other in which alone it may assume its status"—*Concepts,* 147), from whence it must be taken: *"il est à prendre."* In other words, the signifier teaches here that to learn *(apprendre)* requires this taking *(à prendre)* and also that this acquisition, as noted earlier, is more valuable the more it costs (joining *appris* with *mis à prix). Jouissance* (bliss) refers, then, to a fourth level of "sense," the four levels being sense, non-sense, common sense, and *"jouis*-sense."[13] The sense of psychoanalysis as it is usually understood is its critique of sex, Lacan explains. But this sense reduces to a "non-sense" in the sweet nothings exchanged between lovers. At the level of "common sense," this pleasure has to do with jokes, laughter, suggestive remarks, and the like. Still another level, the one that interests Lacan in *Encore,* carries the insistence of desire in the chain of signifiers, productive of homonyms and puns, and called, in this context, *jouis-sens.* The technique, ultimately, is derived from this comment to Fliess in one of Freud's letters, anticipating his joke book: "It is certainly true that the dreamer is too ingenious and amusing, but it is not my fault, and I cannot be reproached with it. All dreamers are insufferably witty, and they have to be, because they are under pressure, and the direct way is barred to them" (Freud, *Origins,* 297).

In alerting his class to the existence of this level of sense, Lacan makes liberal use of puns, the point being that the pun itself tells him, in a sense, how to proceed, as for example when he confronts the impossible question *"Was will das Weib?":* "It is here that I play on the pun [*équivoque*]. The impossible knowledge is prohibited, censored, forbidden [*interdit*], but it is not if you write it conveniently *l'inter-dit,* it is said [*dit*] between [inter-, *entre*] the words, between the lines. . . . It is a question of showing the tendency of this putting-into-form, this metalanguage that is not one, and which I make ex-sist. About that which may not be demonstrated, something true nonetheless can be said" (*Encore,* 108). This dimension of the between, this interdimension of reading between the lines, to be associated with Derrida's hymenal betweenness (*entre-antre*), opens up a new dimension of knowledge called the *dit-mension* (a pun on the *dit*—said, spoken —which could be rendered in English by means of the other syllable, the mention in di-mension, with the *di* suggesting the double inscription of the pun—di-mention). This di-mention, in which the signifier exercises its effect, is also the dimension of *bêtise,* the stupidities which may now be understood as referring to the incessant puns in the lectures. "The signifier is stupid [*bête*]," Lacan remarks, and, in the pun, engenders "a stupid smile" which, he hastens to add, is the grin of angels, at least those that can be seen in the cathedrals, including Bernini's angel. They smile so, he suggests, because they are "swimming" in the supreme signifier (which is, after all, the phallus). The angels, that is (like the one standing over Theresa in the statue) carry no messages, and to this extent, "they are truly signifiers." He stresses the signifier "because it is the basis of the dimension ["which should be written *dit-mension*"] of the symbolic, which alone the analytic discourse enables us to isolate as such" (24–25). Bernini's statue, in short, provides no evidence for what is at issue in *Encore,* because, as an image, it exists at the level of the Imaginary, which is dependent on sense perception. But *Encore* is not a seminar about the Imaginary—and here is the source of Heath's misreading (*The Four Fundamental Concepts of Psychoanalysis,* which *is* about the Imaginary, would be a more useful point of departure for his cinematic concerns)—but about the Symbolic and the "sense" of di-mention (what Derrida discussed as spacing). The association of this mode of knowledge, taken at the level of the pun, with bliss (like that pictured in the statue) is justified by Lacan's description of what takes place: "It is because there is the unconscious, that is *lalangue* in as much as it is by cohabitation with it that a being defines itself called the speaking being, that the signifier can be called to make a sign" (130).

This cohabitation of the subject with *lalangue,* producing the speaking being called a human, is a kind of copulation productive of bliss. Something is touched, a dimension reached through the di-mention, which is akin to sexual bliss in its fundamental contribution to human reproduction (in the form of the repetition which constitutes identity), akin but supplementary—not sexual (the mystics, too, however, use sexual metaphors for what they know), but on the order of love, which, Lacan stresses, is a relationship having nothing to do with sex. The term introduced here to further the investigation is *lalangue,* written in one word, which Lacan uses to distinguish his interest in language from that of linguists and structuralists. *Lalangue* has nothing to do with communication or dialogue but is a presentational mode of a different sort: "Lalangue presents all sorts of affects ["its effects are affects"] which remain enigmatic. These effects are those which result from the presence of lalangue to the degree that, as knowledge, it articulates things which go much further than what the speaking being supports in a stated knowledge. . . . The unconscious is a knowledge, a know-how of lalangue. And what one knows how to do with lalangue surpasses by far what one is capable of accounting for in terms of language" (*Encore,* 127).

Jean-Claude Milner has written a book on *lalangue,* based apparently on the paper he gave at a session of the *Encore* seminar (*Encore,* 92), student papers and guest lectures being as much a part of Lacan's practice as of any other professor.[14] Milner's topic is "the love of language"—taking up Lacan's question of the scientist's desire by asking about the "love" that motivates people to become linguists. He reminds us that not only is language teachable (indeed, linguistics has no social basis as an activity except in the university), but that it is the vehicle of all other possible teaching. Psychoanalysis supplements conventional pedagogy, which tends to forget language or assume its transparency and secondarity, by asking what language itself knows. Milner approaches this question, as does Lacan, by alluding to Saussure's study of the anagrams in "saturnian" verse. Saussure, showing that the phonemes in these Latin poems are paired and selected according to the anagram of a name linked to the narrative sense of the verse, assumed that the ordering principle could be attributed to a secret knowledge. But, Milner remarks, Saussure was never able to prove his hypothesis (indeed, he never published any of these studies), partly because the anagrams turned up in every verse he examined, ancient or modern. In these anagrams, then, philology faced a phenomenon it could not account for, having to do with the material intersection of language with the real.

The anagram, that is, far from being illusory, touched precisely on a fundamental reality of language—the homophone. Because of the irreducible and material nature of its reality, the homophone (and all the odd figures of association it makes possible) has a function of excess, an *"en plus,"* related to Derrida's chiasmatic plus: "This function of excess we call lalangue" (Milner, 92-93). "It is always possible to valorize in any locution a dimension of the non-identical: it is the pun and all that it includes, homophony, homosemy, homography, everything that sustains double meaning and speaking in hints, incessant tissue of our interviews" (18). Milner describes these figures of association (*lalangue*) as being those that linguistics excludes from language in order to achieve closure and establish itself as a science, representing only certain approved chains or sequences such as etymology, diverse paradigms, derivations, transformations, and so forth.

Why Lacan mentioned that *lalangue* is that which causes a language to be termed one's "mother tongue" is explained in this comment: "This register is nothing other than that which absolutely distinguishes one language from every other one: a singular mode of making puns, there you have what makes a specific language. By that, it becomes a collection of places, all singular and all heterogeneous. . . . By that it also makes itself substance, possible matter for fantasms, inconsistent ensemble of places for desire" (Milner, 22). Derrida's discussion of the difficulty and the importance of translation is based on this same feature of the particularity of the homophones to a given language, although both Derrida and Lacan (and psychoanalysis in general) take advantage of the macaronic possibility of using puns that cross between language—hence they both admire James Joyce: *"Finnegans Wake,"* Lacan says, "is very much that which is closest to what we analysts, thanks to the analytic discourse, have to read—the slip" (*Encore,* 37).

As for the desire of the linguist, Milner defines it by reversing the "scientific" explanation of *lalangue,* which suggests that it is caused by or is the effect of the "Indo-European" origin of modern languages. But Indo-European is itself an effect, generated by a speculative knowledge, Milner says, reflecting the desire of the linguists to write *lalangue* itself. This interaction between a "real" and a "fantasmatic" language is not a problem, from Milner's perspective, but a condition or necessity of research which we are only beginning to acknowledge and exploit. Following Lacan, Milner proposes the ideal of a new academic writing based on these points: "that no one is master of lalangue, that the real insists therein, that finally lalangue knows. Then, if the linguist does not lack a certain tact, he could

accomplish to a degree a scholarly writing in which coincide rule and *Witz*"
(Milner, 133).

MATHEME

The style Milner calls for is similar to what Derrida has in mind when he
notes that "the reading or writing supplement must be rigorously prescribed, but by the necessities of a *game,* by the logic of *play,* signs to
which the system of all textual powers must be accorded and attuned"
(*Dissemination,* 64). In short, as we shall see in Lacan's development of this
style, *lalangue* does not consist of saying just "anything at all," but only
what the homophonic principle permits. The strategy of rule and *Witz,*
then, is systematically to exploit the witticism in the context of a specific
problem—in this case, the question set is "what does the woman want?"
Lalangue comes to his assistance, Lacan remarks, "not only in offering me
a homonymy, of *d'eux* [them] with *deux* [two], of *peut* [can, is able to]
with *peu* [little, few], take for example that *il peut peu* which is there for
us to use for something—but simply in permitting me to say that one *âme*
[souls, using *âme*—soul—as a verb, conjugated like the verb to love, *amour*].
J'âme, tu âmes, il âme. You see that only writing serves us here, even to
include *jamais j'âmais* [*jamais* = never]" (*Encore,* 78). Lacan concludes
from this exercise that the existence of the soul may be put in question by
proposing that it is an effect of love (that the soul is contained within the
conjugations of *amour*).

The extent to which the verb "love" contains the "truth" of the human
subject may be seen in one of Lacan's charts graphing the four positions of
the subject, each represented by a letter:

> I begin with *A,* the radical Other [*Autre*], the real pole of the sub-
> jective relation, to which Freud attached the death drive. Then you
> have the *m,* the *moi* [ego] and the *a,* the other who is not an other
> at all, since it is essentially coupled with the *moi,* in an always reflex-
> ive, interchangeable relation—the *ego* is always an *alter-ego.* You
> have here *S,* which is at once the subject, the symbol, and also the
> *Es* [Id, It, Ça]. The symbolic realization of the subject, which is
> always a symbolic creation, is the relation which goes from *A* to *S.*
> It is sub-jacent, unconscious, essential to every subjective situation.
> (*Le moi,* 370)

The interesting point here, besides the relevance of these elements to the
project in *Encore,* is that the relation of *A* to *S,* of the Other to the Subject (the relation explored in *Encore*), Lacan declares, "must pass always
by the intermediary of its imaginary substrata, the *moi* and the *autre,*

which constitute the imaginary foundations of the object—A, *m, a,* S" (*Le moi,* 371). The graph, in other words, spells *amas,* the Romance conjugation of "you love."

Lacan's discourse abounds with puns instructive in the matter of love. He goes so far as to say that "it has been clear for some time that university discourse should be written *uni-vers-Cythère* [one-toward-Cytherea], since it should propagate sexual education" (*Encore,* 47), alluding to Baudelaire's "Voyage to Cythera": "In your island, O Venus! I found standing only a symbolic gallows where my image hung. . . . Ah! Lord! give me strength and courage to look upon my heart and body without disgust!"[15] The seminar's title refers to this body—*en-corps,* embodiment—as well as a number of other things (such as trying again to say what has not yet been understood). The various versions of his "graphicization" (a term used to avoid the precise mathematical meaning of "graph"), such as the four positions represented by A, m, a, S, for example, take note of "the correspondence which makes of the real an opening between semblance (appearance), resulting from the symbolic, and reality such as it is supported in the concreteness of human life—in that which determines that the *encore-à-naître* [still to be born, referring to what one anticipates in or expects from the sexual experience] will never give anything but the *encorné*" (*Encore,* 87). One sense of *encorné*—to gore—alludes again to *Cythère,* to the grotesque image in the poem of the hanged man disemboweled and castrated (by fierce birds of prey). But the term also means "cuckold," to give horns, and by extension of this context, to be horny— the recurrence, the return, encore, of sexual desire; the failure of the sexual act to satisfy the demand for love.

What comes into play in the analytic situation is the subject's most fundamental desire, the "want-to-be," of which an individual's specific desires—the desire to be an analyst, a student's career choice, for example —are but manifestations, substitute objects (the object *a*), similar to the account of being in relation to Being in Existentialism. Not this account of the themes in the analytic situation, but the manner in which Lacan presents his hypotheses, based on the psychoanalytic view of the unconscious as structured like a language, is the focus of the lesson for grammatology. Lacan, that is, uses mathematics as an analogy for the kind of writing that will enable him to learn something from and about the unconscious.

Derrida, too, is interested in mathematics as an example of a writing that breaks with phoneticization and explores a dimension independent of voice. Derrida and Lacan are similar in their effort to extend the reach of language at the level of *lalangue* into a dimension closed to conventional philosophical language.

A grammatology that would break with this system of presuppositions ["the resistance to logical-mathematical notation has always been the signature of logocentrism and phonologism"] must in effect liberate the mathematicization of language, and must also declare that "the practice of science in fact has never ceased to protest the imperialism of the *Logos,* for example by calling upon, from all time, and more and more, nonphonetic writing." Everything that has always linked *logos* to *phone* has been limited by mathematics, whose progress is in absolute solidarity with the practice of a nonphonetic inscription. About these "grammatological" principles and tasks there is no possible doubt, I believe. But the extension of mathematical notation, and in general the formalization of writing, must be very slow and very prudent, at least if one wishes it to take over *effectively* the domains from which it has been excluded so far. It seems to be that critical work on "natural" languages by means of "natural" languages, an entire internal transformation of classical notation, a systematic practice of exchanges between "natural" languages and writing should prepare and accompany such a formalization. . . . The effective progress of mathematical notation thus goes along with the deconstruction of metaphysics, with the profound renewal of mathematics itself, and the concept of science for which mathematics has always been the model. (Derrida, *Positions,* 34–35)

Having written a formula on the blackboard—$a/S_2 \rightarrow \$/S_1$—to note the relations among the Imaginary, the Symbolic, and the Real, Lacan remarks, "Their writing itself constitutes a support which goes beyond speech [*parole*] without going outside the effects themselves of language" (*Encore,* 86). This writing is valuable with respect "not to truth which pretends to be all, but that of the half-spoken [*mi-dire*], that which is distinctly on guard against going as far as an avowal." He wants to retain the effect of language but without the message, the signifier detached from the signified (like Mallarmé's mimesis without reference).

In his testimonial contribution to an anthology on the experimental university at Vincennes, Lacan explained that only the analytic discourse did not take itself for the truth, that it taught nothing, worked with the singular rather than the universal, and therefore excluded the effect of domination.[16] In introducing this discourse into the university, he added, he did not intend to try to overcome the antipathy of the analytic versus the university discourse (the former originating from the position of the object of desire, the latter from that of knowledge without a subject), but to exploit it. Whatever materials he might introduce into this situation, "trying to teach that which does not teach anything," would be inadequate (abject, Derrida would say), hence, "any object would suffice and always presents itself poorly. That is to say it is necessary to correct it. Mathematics serves this purpose: to correct the object. It is a fact that mathematics corrects and that what it corrects is the object itself. Hence my reduction of psychoanalysis to the theory of sets" (*Vincennes*, 91). The "object" in this context can refer only to the "object *a,*" the substitutable and substitute object of desire.

Whether Lacan intended his mathematical formulations to be taken literally or figuratively is a matter of some debate (as Sherry Turkle notes, 182). On several occasions, however, Lacan did take the trouble to refute the famous article, "The Unconscious: A Psychoanalytic Study," by Jean Laplanche and Serge Leclaire,[17] in which they extend Lacan's formula of the metaphor—$F(S/S)S \cong S(+)s$—into a full formalization, treating the bar (as written in Saussure's division between the signifier and the signified) as a fraction sign. The problem with this complete formalization is that it suppresses part of Lacan's purpose for using formulas. "There is between the signifier and the signified, another relation which is that of the effect of meaning. Precisely at the point at which it is a question, in metaphor, of marking the effect of meaning, one can absolutely not, therefore, without taking certain precautions, and in as bold a way as has been done, manipulate this bar in a fractional transformation—which one could do if it were a question of a relation of proportion" (*Concepts*, 248–49).

In *Encore*, in any case, it is clear that Lacan is working in terms of analogy. The mathemes here are phrases formulated at the level of *lalangue*, hence enigmatic, homophonic, aphoristic, yet precise. Lacan's presentation of these phrases throughout the course, building a kind of theoretical drama or plot which develops suspensefully from original ambiguity to the final, completed pun, reveals what he means when he says that his teaching strategy is to place himself in the position of the analysand. That is not to say that he literally performs a transferential analysis before the class, nor even, as Turkle suggests, that his presentation is "designed to provoke the listener or the reader into a self-analytic experience" (148), but that, in working with *lalangue*, he generates a series of sentences, organized around the year's theme, which is a simulacrum of the analysand's discourse, thus forcing the class into the position of the analyst listening for the resonances of the unconscious in the patient's monologue.

The formulas Lacan disseminates in his discourse are not meant to replace natural language but to supplement it. "Language [*langage*] includes considerable inertia, which one sees in comparing its functioning to the signs called mathematics, mathemes, uniquely from the fact that they transmit themselves integrally. One has absolutely no idea what they mean, but they transmit themselves. It remains the case nonetheless that they do not transmit themselves except with the aid of language, due to which the whole affair limps" (*Encore*, 100). Such is the condition of pedagogy—"Mathematical formalization is a matter of the written, but which subsists only if I employ to present it the tongue [*langue*] I use" (108). Lacan's formalization, then, takes place both at the level of the algorithm and the holophrase, distinguishing his "conjectural" science from the traditional "exact" sciences (a distinction he assumes is disappearing). "This science which reduces the real to a few little letters," Lacan states, referring to the formulas of Newton and Einstein, "will appear without doubt in the unfolding of the ages as an astonishing epic [*épopée*] and also will thin out perhaps as an epic with a slightly short circuit" (*Le moi*, 344).

These statements indicate that Lacan's project is not to carry psychoanalysis over into the domain of the natural sciences but to borrow from mathematics a certain model of writing. This distinction is especially clear in *Encore*, with its juxtaposition of formulas and phrases (from *lalangue*), both applied to the task of distinguishing the passion of ignorance (which functions in the relation between the Symbolic and the Real, joining language and the body) from the passion of love (which functions in the relation between the Symbolic and the Imaginary, in the communication between two speaking beings). The distinction Lacan wishes to establish between his strategy and mathematics has to do with *lalangue*. Explaining that one learns something about the economy of bliss only "by essentially contingent means," Lacan adds, "the analytic knack will not be mathematical. It is just because of this that the analytic discourse distinguishes itself from scientific discourse" (*Encore*, 105).

The formula that Lacan seeks, that is, is not couched finally in numbers but as a kind of holophrase, a "kernel of non-sense" to be isolated in the subject, constituting something like a signature. Lacan praises Laplanche and Leclaire for their discoveries in this vein as much as he blamed them for their misunderstanding of his mathematical analogy, referring to the case of an obsessional neurotic patient for whom Leclair proposed "the so-called *Poordjeli* formula, which links the two syllables of the word *licorne* [unicorn], thus enabling him to introduce into his sequence a whole chain in which his desire is animated" (*Concepts*, 250). The non-sense phrase, *Poordjeli*, condensed from a number of longer utterances, functions like a formula governing all the repetitions in the obsessive discourse. Psychoanalytic interpretation, Lacan remarks with respect to this example, "has the effect of bringing out an irreducible signifier. One must interpret at the level of the *s*, which is not open to all meanings, which cannot be just anything, which is a signification, though no doubt only an approximate one. What is there is rich and complex, when it is a question of the unconscious of the subject, and intended to bring out irreducible, *non-sensical*—composed of non-meanings—signifying elements" (250).

The formula or signature (*Poordjeli*, but Lacan also goes on to discuss the Wolf Man's case as an example of research into "what signifier—to what irreducible, traumatic, non-meaning—he is, as a subject, subjected") will be singular, determined by the contingency of the individual's history. But what can be formalized in mathematical terms is the repetition itself, which constitutes the subject's "portrait": "The sameness is not in *things* but in the *mark* which makes it possible to add things with no consideration as to their differences. The mark has the effect of rubbing out the difference, and this is the key to what happens to the subject, the unconscious subject in the repetition."[18] At the level of the mark, the subject may be described by analogy with number theory, the genesis of numbers by the formula $n + 1$. Lacan is concerned specifically with the numerical genesis of two. "The question of the two is for us the question of the subject, and here we reach a fact of psychoanalytic experience in as much as the two does not complete the one to make two, but must repeat the one to permit the one to exist. This first repetition is the only one necessary to explain the genesis of the number, and only one repetition is necessary to constitute the status of the subject" ("Inmixing," 191).

This genesis of the subject in the repetition of a signifier is an important aspect of the lesson in *Encore*, although Lacan draws on several other properties of mathematics as well for the formal operation of *lalangue*. For example, mathematical operations are conducted formally, without dependence on the intuitions of experience, similar to the play that produces new terms by means of the homophone. Indeed, the special status of the letter in mathematics is comparable to the manipulations of spelling in anagrams, portmanteau words, agglutinations, and so forth—the shifting of a letter in a math formula or in *lalangue* changes everything. Finally, however, the comparison is an approximation used for effect. After noting the difference between an alphabet letter and a Chinese character, Lacan states: "The letters that I issue here have a different value from those which come out of set theory. The usage made of them differs, and yet—this is its interest—it is not without a certain relation of convergence" (*Encore*, 37).

LOVE

The convergence of *lalangue* with set theory is best seen in a review of the formula-phrase actually developed in *Encore*. The seminar in the year preceding *Encore*, Lacan mentions, dealt with the question of the One, organized by the phrase "*Y a d'l'Un.*" The one has to do with the "first"— the master—signifier: "I would ask you to consider the logical necessity of that moment in which the subject as X can be constituted only from the *Urverdrängung*, from the necessary fall of this first signifier. He is constituted around the *Urverdrängung*, but he cannot substitute anything for it as such—since this would require the representation of one signifier for another, whereas here there is only one, the first" (*Concepts*, 251). Lacan is discussing in this citation the Wolf Man, whose pathology consists of this blockage of the sequence of signifiers. But in *Encore* Lacan takes up the question of two, the number of love.

"Love is impotent, even if it be reciprocal, because it ignores that it is nothing but the desire to be One, which leads us to the impossibility of establishing the relation of them [*d'eux*]. The relation of them who?–two [*deux*] sexes" (*Encore,* 12). The condition of human sexuality, the division into two sexes, is obviously central to psychoanalysis in general, as well as to Lacan's formulas, with one of his more interesting apologues–a story of man as a broken egg, an *"hommelette"*–being addressed to this context. Love, expressed in the phrase "we are but one," is the signified attached (in ignorance) to the sexual relation. But Lacan stresses that "love never made anyone exit from himself." It is at just this point, however, that set theory becomes useful: "Set theory bursts in by posing this–we speak of the One for things which have among themselves strictly no relation. Put together objects of thought, as one says, objects of the world, each one counts as one. We assemble these absolutely heteroclite things, and we give ourselves the right to designate this assemblage by a letter" (46). It is not enough to say that these letters merely *designate* the collections. Rather, the letters *make* the collection, Lacan states, adding that the unconscious "is structured like the collections which in set theory are like letters."

Lacan plays several variations on these themes, but in the final session of the term he completes two formulations he had been developing through-out the year. I will not attempt to explain the full meaning of these formulas, limiting myself instead to a description of the aspect most relevant to grammatology, namely, as Lacan put it, "to discuss what can be the function of the written in the analytic discourse" (*Encore,* 30). For this purpose it suffices to see that he exploits *lalangue,* to see how he plays with phrasing, since it is this usage in itself, and not its themes, that gram-matology might borrow.

The first example involves the translation from an apparently mathe-matical formula to a formulation in *lalangue,* having to do with the genesis of the subject. The formula is: $S_1 (S_1 (S_1 (S_1 —S_2)))$. *Lalangue* permits him, he says, to write the S_1 (which we already know can mean the Id, pronounced *Es* in German) as *essaim* (S-un, or S-one), meaning "swarm." The S_1, designating the master-signifier in the unconscious, is "one-among-others," an "element" in a system–the unconscious structured like a lan-guage, that is, as a system of non-sense elements brought into relationship by their difference each from the other–so that there is never just one signifier but a crowd or swarm of signifiers constituting a language or a subject.

Continuing the translation, Lacan explains that the S_2 can be understood as a question—*"est-ce d'eux que ça parle?"*—is it of them that it speaks? (with puns on "S" as *"est-ce"* and "two," *"deux,"* as *"d'eux"*). The point of the formula is to bring together or designate a transfer from S_1 to S_2, as in this sentence: "This S_1 of each signifier, if I pose the question *is it of them that I speak? [est-ce d'eux?]* I will write it first in its relation with S_2." Lacan further explains, "The S_1, the swarm [*essaim*], master-signifier, is what assures the unity, the unity of the copulation of the subject with knowledge. It is in lalangue, and not elsewhere, to the extent that it is interrogated as a language [*langage*], that the existence disengages itself of what a primitive linguistics designated by the term 'element.'. . . The S_1 would be in relation with the S_2 in as much as it represents a subject" (*Encore,* 131). In short, the letter formula is another version of Lacan's basic formula-phrase—"a signifier represents a subject for another signifier."

The other principal formula of the seminar is the phrase *"cesser de ne pas s'écrire"* (ceasing to not write itself), referring to "the fashion in which the so-called sexual relation—become there relation of subject to subject, subject in as much as it is nothing but the effect of unconscious knowledge —ceases to not write itself" (*Encore,* 131-32), which is the definition of the contingency of a sexual relation. Against the formula of *contingency* Lacan poses the formula of *necessity,* the necessary—that which *ne cesse pas de s'écrire* (never ceases writing itself). That there can be no existence of the sexual relation in the spoken dimension, *le dire,* the interdiction that forces psychoanalysis to work with the di-mention of *lalangue,* is indicated by a double negative combining the phrases of contingency and necessity, the sexual relation being that which *ne cesse pas de ne pas s'écrire* (never ceases not writing itself)—the impossible. The shifting play of the negative among these phrases is precisely what writes, in *lalangue,* the character of love:

> Isn't this to say that it is solely by the affect which results from this
> gap ["the exile of the speaking being from the sexual relation"]
> that something is met with, which can vary infinitely at the level of
> knowledge, but which, one instant, gives the illusion that the sex-
> ual relation ceases not writing itself?—illusion not only that some-
> thing articulates itself but inscribes itself in each one's destiny,
> by which, during a time of suspension, that which would be the
> sexual relation finds in the being who speaks its trace and its means
> of mirage. The displacement of the negation, from the *cesse de ne
> pas s'écrire* to the *ne cesse pas de s'écrire,* from contingency to neces-
> sity, is the point of suspension to which all love attaches itself. (*En-
> core,* 132)

The destiny and drama of love, then, Lacan states—the experience two contingent bodies have of feeling *meant* for each other—may be written in the movement of the negative, and not only there but also in the punning emergence of necessity out of the negation: from not ceasing (*ne cesse pas*) to necessity (*nécessité*). With this conjunction, the students are given the final piece of a formulation that Lacan had been building, in between digressions, during the entire semester.

One of the chief lessons of Lacan's discourse for a nonmagisterial pedagogy is its exploitation of linguistic and symbolic devices, addressing the class in the poetic mode of evocation as well as in the scientific mode of assertion. "In this regard, we could take note of what the Hindu tradition teaches about *dhvani,* in the sense that this tradition brings out that it is proper to the Word to cause to be understood what it does not say" (*Speech,* 58). It so happens that, according to Lacan, the tradition illustrates the point with a love story (about a girl who cleverly gets rid of a Brahmin whose unexpected arrival had threatened to prevent her meeting with her lover). Referring to the analyst's ability to evoke effects in the unspoken dimention, Lacan remarks (continuing the mathematical analogy), "The *primary* character of symbols in fact brings them close to those numbers out of which all the others are compounded, and if they therefore underlie all the semantemes of language, we shall be able to restore to the Word its full value of evocation by a discreet search for their interferences" (59).

We have already seen this effect in the examples of the Bernini image and in the formulations of *lalangue,* but there remains one other major image to discuss.

KNOTS

The other major image mounted in *Encore* is based on topological geometry, especially the diagrams associated with knot theory. A number of the diagrams are included in the book (during his American lecture tour, Turkle reports, Lacan spent hours drawing borromean knots, made of interlocking circles, on the blackboard before each lecture—(235), recalling Derrida's interest in the shoelaces, the bobbin string, and other images of interlacing topologies as analogies for the textual operation. The use of topological references, like the selection of an emblematic art work, makes *Encore* a typical example of Lacan's seminar style. The central problem in *Encore,* from my point of view, has to do with the specific use of these two elements—the sculpture depicting an angel with an arrow standing over St. Theresa, and a set of knot diagrams. The grammatological assumption (supported by Lacan's own principle of symbolic, as well as homophonic, evocation) is that Lacan is writing by means of the articulation of these two images, that they constitute the pictorial component of a picto-ideo-phonographic hieroglyph, with each level relating to the other in a supplementary, rather than complementary, way.

Like the other elements in Lacan's performance, the knots are part of a double inscription, functioning on several levels at once. In order to read what Lacan writes ("In your analytic discourse, you assume that the subject of the unconscious knows how to read"—*Encore*, 38), keeping in mind the principle of the delayed time of understanding ("The good part of what I recount is that it is always the same thing. Not that I repeat myself, that is not the issue. It is that what I said previously acquires its meaning later"—36), we may exercise some of Lacan's own suggestions regarding the fundamentals of analytic discourse: "But we learn that analysis consists in playing in all the multiple keys of the orchestral score ["read both vertically and horizontally at the same time"] which the Word constitutes in the registers of Language and on which depends the overdetermination" (*Speech*, 55). As Turkle explains, apropos of the double inscription of the knots, "For Lacan, mathematics is not disembodied knowledge. It is constantly in touch with its roots in the unconscious. This contact has two consequences: first that mathematical creativity draws on the unconscious, and second, that mathematics repays its debt by giving us a window back to the unconscious" (247).

The place to begin considering what it is possible to see through this example-window (seeing as knowing involves the interaction of the Imaginary with the Symbolic, the ego with the unconscious—Lacan's version of autography: "The subject passes beyond that window pane in which it always sees, mingled, its own image"—*Le moi*, 209) is Lacan's own statements about knots in *Encore*. He states that he is using mathematical formalization as a model (*Encore*, 118)—specifically, as a model with which to research the effect of writing in analytic discourse (hence, its interest for grammatology). The model works in at least two ways, both of which contribute to the use of mathematics as a way to go beyond speech without giving up the effect of writing.

"Writing," according to Lacan, "is a trace in which is read an effect of language. It is what happens when you scribble something" (*Encore*, 110). Pointing to a knotted loop drawn on the blackboard, Lacan suggests that it could be a letter in an unknown script. A letter may be thought of as a flattened knot, one difference between handwriting and a topological diagram of a knot being that the two-dimensional space of writing involves intersecting lines, while the three-dimensional space of knots (to which the diagram refers) involves lines that overlap. That the writing effect of knots might be read is evidenced by the anagram relating "to read" (*lire*) with "to tie" or "to bind" (*lier*)—"*lier* and *lire* have the same letters, please note" (109). But whatever is inscribed on the board—whether diagram, formula, or phrase—makes little difference, Lacan says, since (in a pedagogic setting) all require a discursive supplement to make them receivable.

At the same time, they pull language into the di-mention, coaxing it to say what exceeds it.

The other way in which the knots go beyond speech is by constituting a direct transcription of the formulations of *lalangue.* "Why did I introduce the borromean knot [last year]? It was to translate the formula *I demand of you*—what?—*to refuse*—what?—*what I offer you*—why?—*because that is not it*—*it,* you know what that is, the object *a.* The object *a* is without being. It is the lack presupposed by a demand, which may be situated only by metonymy, that is, by the pure assured continuity from the beginning to the end of the sentence. A desire without any other substance than that which the knots themselves assure" (*Encore,* 114). The object *a,* mediating the relation with the Other, the cause of desire, satisfies the genital drives in the bliss of reproduction *en-corps.* The borromean knot, consisting of a series of interlocking circles or loops, manifests the relation between syntax and desire as binders.

The borromean knot "can serve to represent for us that metaphor, so widespread, to express that which distinguishes language usage—precisely the chain" (*Encore,* 115). Thus, this knot de-monstrates the same point Lacan made with the formula passing from S_1 to S_2 ("it is not for nothing that at our meeting before last I brought here to illustrate it [the master-signifier, the One] a piece of string, such that it makes the ring by which I began to interrogate the possible knot with an other"—131), as well as his use of the legend of Don Juan, who had his women one by one, an apologue illustrating, Lacan claims, woman's view of male sexuality. At one level, then, the borromean knot remarks Lacan's theory of the unconscious structured like a language, operating hence according to the rhetorical devices of metonymy and metaphor, with the knot being a metaphor of this metaphor itself—the knot as writing, in its function of tying and binding. This metaphor obviously is of considerable interest to grammatology:

> The telling, or re-telling, of stories in the time before writing was in-
> vented, was sometimes accomplished with the mnemonic device
> of knots tied on a string. . . . The device has lasted to the present, for
> example, among some Roman Catholics, who refer to their prayer
> beads as a "rosary," and some Buddhists. The next step probably was
> to have a particular knot, or combination of knots, represent a spe-
> cific word, type of event, or quantity. When they were invaded by
> Europeans in the sixteenth century, the Inca Indians had a system for
> writing numbers and other information in knotted strings called
> *quipus.* The earliest forms of pictographic writing had the direction
> of reading signs ordered "as if" on a string, in order to establish
> the proper sequence. . . . In a metaphoric sense, writing is the placing

of alphabetic knots on a string. DNA and RNA, the chemical bases
of life, use a similar method of amino acid "knots" in a "rope"
of protein. [19]

To see how the borromean knot specifically translates (as Lacan claims)
the formula *ce n'est pas ça* ("that is not it") requires that we look further
into what the knot is capable of evoking in all of its registers. For one
thing, in a metaphor that combines the notion of the unconscious structured like a language with the archetype of the unconscious as a labyrinth,
the knot in some mythologies represents the labyrinth of the human condition (which has to be untied). [20] Lacan's "that is not it," that is, refers
also to the behaviorist account of pleasure and pain. Against behaviorists
who "make a little labyrinth for rats," Lacan argues that we cannot learn
how speaking beings know by studying beings that do not speak (rats).
Not the rat in its labyrinth, but the *ratage* (failure) of desire to find satisfaction, registered in the knots of syntax (the labyrinth of *lalangue*), is
Lacan's focus. Inevitably, the knot is the "not": the phrase "that is not it"
—stating the fundamental division in the subject between love and sex,
truth and the real (experienced when the bliss obtained is other than the
bliss expected)—gives rise, Lacan suggests, to the original experience of
negation. "It is the speaking body in as much as it cannot succeed in reproducing itself except thanks to a misunderstanding of its bliss. That is
that it does not reproduce itself except thanks to a *ratage* [failure] of what
it wants to say . . . [which is] its effective bliss" (*Encore*, 101, 109). "I
spoke of the rat a moment ago—that is what it was a question of," Lacan
states, referring to this *ratage* (133). Thus, he takes over and remotivates
even the image of the behaviorist rat, become an emblem in this context of
the knot in writing, and the not-written. The knots in writing (the borromean knot as the chain of signifiers) and the displaced negation creating the illusion of love (as in the formula *ne cesse pas*, etc., agglutinated
as *nécessité*) are versions of the same condition, with love and writing both
being effects of language (44–45).

Lacan, however, does not confine himself to tying or drawing the knots.
He also proposes at least one action or event: "The true problem, the general problem, is to make it so that with a given number of string loops,
when you cut one, all the others without exception be free, independent"
(*Encore*, 112). This question, from the point of view of Writing and of
dhvani, turns our focus away from the knot as such to the cutting of the
knot. How is this cutting to be read? It is, in the first place, at one level, a
direct reply to the initial question of the seminar—*"Was will das Weib?"*
That this is so may be seen in the fact that the question "what does the
woman want?" is repeated (after a long absence from the discussion) on
the same page and preceding, by a few lines, an allusion to the cutting of
the knot (115). In this way the two principal images mounted in the dis-

course—St. Theresa and the borromean knot—are brought together as question and response.

If the class recognized at the time the articulation of these two images, its first association would most likely come at the level of *doxa,* "common sense" or popular "wisdom," whose response to the question "what does the woman want?" is—politely—to get married (tying the knot refers to the marriage ceremony); crudely—to get fucked (cutting the knot refers to breaking the hymen). The knot, like the *pharmakon,* has in this context an undecidable value: "It is significant that knots and strings are used in the nuptial rites to protect the young couple, though at the same time, as we know, knots are thought to imperil the consummation of the marriage. But ambivalence of this sort is to be found in all the magico-religious uses of knots and bonds" (Eliade, 112). But Lacan has already stated explicitly that he rejects the early psychology that reduced sublimity to copulation— "that is not it." In any case, to stop our reading at this level, reading the seminar as a kind of sexist joke, would simply repeat Heath's mistake of limiting Lacan's discourse to sexual politics (without denying that Lacan's metaphor of truth as a woman is indeed phallogocentric).

SHAMAN

There is a knowledge or a knowing of and in the body which has nothing to do with sexual relations, but with transference (determining the unconscious as the discourse of the Other—one of Lacan's most famous formulas). Transference, Lacan says, must be treated like a knot, topologically, to discern the position or place from which the Other speaks: "Whether or not we treat it as a Gordian knot remains to be seen" (*Concepts,* 131). Alexander the Great, of course, cut the knot of King Gordias rather than trying to untie it—sometimes understood as an act of analytic rationality. But Lacan tends to approach the riddle of transference (the enactment of the unconscious) with a more Eastern attitude, puzzling over his "loops of string in an attempt to think about the body and psyche at the same time" (Turkle, 246).

The knot has something to do with the relation to the Other and with the drives of life and death. In exploring this articulation further I shall keep in mind Lacan's view that, even if there is no metalanguage, neither is there any prediscursive reality ("Each reality founds itself on and defines itself by a discourse"—*Encore,* 33), which indicates that the place to look for the significance of the knots is in cultural symbolism rather than in a phenomenology of the body. Moreover, the issue concerns not phallic bliss but the other one, the bliss of speaking, having to do thus with the function of the knot in Lacan's pedagogical discourse—the subject of the seminar. My purpose is not to interpret Lacan's intentions but to offer a version of what may be read in the seminar.

St. Theresa, obviously, is a mystic as well as a woman, and the implied question at this level is "what does the *mystic* want?" which might be generalized into a question about the desire of God. In fact, while explaining *lalangue* to Noam Chomsky during the visit to MIT, Lacan first wrote on the board the pun central to *Encore—Deux, D'eux—*and then in one corner of the board wrote *Dieu,* God ("pronounced only slightly differently"—Turkle, 244). The word "Dieu," if not the word of God, appears in *Encore*'s *lalangue* several times: the term *l'Etourdit (étourdir* = to stun, to astound) is mentioned, for example, with the "dit" syllable spelled out by itself—"d, i, t"—which would be pronounced (letter by letter) as the word *déité,* deity (the other bliss, the bliss of the Other, has to do with a correspondence between speaking and God, of being in communication with the gods) (*Encore,* 20). "The Other as place of the truth, is the only place, although irreducible, which we are able to give to the term of the divine being, of God [*Dieu*] to call him by his name. God is properly the place where, if you will permit me the play, *le dieu—le dieur—le dire* [passing from "god" to "words" or "statements"] produces itself. *Le dire* [statements] make God" (44). Theology (including the writings of such mystics as St. Theresa), like History, "is made precisely to give the idea that it has some meaning" (45), which leads Lacan to pose the question of the effect of writing as such. His project is to show that the "love letter" (always including the pun with *l'être,* being) and theology both are addressed with respect to the Other, the place of speaking, a conjunction manifested most clearly in the sexual metaphors of mysticism and the religious metaphors of courtly love (both alluded to in *Encore*).

It suffices for my purpose to indicate that the religious theme is one of the seminar's topics in order to open the question of what cutting the knot means at this level. Perhaps the most I can say, considering that *ficelle—*"string" or "cord," which is the term Lacan uses, as in *ronds de ficelle,* the title of the chapter in which the knots are discussed—also means "trick" or "stage trick," is that, like the shoelaces in Derrida's "Restitutions" (*The Truth in Painting*), the borromean knot represents an exemplary example. The knot, that is, is an example showing how any example whatsoever functions in Lacan's pedagogy—that he manipulates his class by means of the example (having an effect of puppet strings), with the cutting of the knot so that all the loops fall free having the status of a magician's stage trick, like pulling knotted scarves out of his mouth. Magicians, as Eliade reports, "are supposed to enchant their victims by means of cords and knots."[21]

The theme of this particular example allows me to continue this line of thinking, because the rope trick—a description that might fit Lacan's use of knotted strings and topological diagrams in his class—is a characteristic feature of shamanistic practice. Lacan has been accused not only of sexism but of practicing a kind of shamanism (a term used by his opponents as a synonym for imposter). For a psychoanalyst to be compared with a shaman, however, is not an insult, given the historical accuracy of the comparison (as a number of studies have shown, the therapeutic techniques and results are similar in both practices, even if the cosmologies are different).[22] The shaman's power derives specifically from his special relationship with death—his ability to "detach" his soul from his body temporarily (without having literally to die) and thus journey to the land of the dead and return—which bears a resemblance to Lacan's account of the analyst's position in the clinical situation: "This means that the analyst intervenes concretely in the dialectic of analysis by pretending he is dead, by cadaverizing his position as the Chinese say, either by his silence when he is the Other with a capital O [*Autre*], or by annulling his own resistance when he is the other with a small o [*autre,* the object *a*]. In either case, and under the respective effects of the symbolic and the imaginary, he makes death present" (*Selection,* 140).

To justify pursuing this analogy, however, I should note that Lacan himself makes some allusion to the relation between psychoanalysis and shamanism. Actually he refers more frequently to other related traditions in which the rope trick is a commonplace—Buddhist and Indian mysticism. The allusion to shamanism in *Encore* amounts to nothing more than mentioning Siberia (the locale in which shamanism originated historically). The reference comes, nonetheless, in a particularly rich sequence: *"La nuée* ["cloud," or figuratively a shower or swarm, as in the *essaim* of S-one] *of language*—I express myself metaphorically—*makes writing*. Who knows if the fact that we are able to read the streams which I look at on Siberia as metaphorical trace of writing is not tied—*lier* and *lire* have the same letters, please note—has something which goes beyond the effect of rain?" (*Encore,* 109). He could refer to any region on the map, but he chooses to name Siberia. And "cloud" (*nue*), besides the fact that it puns on knot (*noeud*), is also quite important in the context of the rope trick, as we shall see in a moment.

Lacan's discussion of the borromean knot could be said to carry at the level of *lalangue* a certain echo of the Bororo, the people studied by Lévi-Strauss, whose essays on shamanism (comparing it to psychoanalysis) are relevant. Lacan, of course, based his structuralist psychoanalysis on the model of Lévi-Strauss's application of linguistics to anthropology; his specific reference to the Bororo also contributes to the analogy between magical and clinical (analytic) thinking: "The ego [*moi*], imaginary function, intervenes in psychic life only as symbol. One uses the ego the way the Bororo uses the parrot. The Bororo says *I am a parrot*, we say *I am me* [*moi*]" (*Le moi*, 52).

Siberia and the Bororo are merely signifiers offering a place to graft the shamanistic rope trick to the borromean knot. In *Ecrits* ("Science and Truth"), however, Lacan does explicitly relate his principal question—the desire of the subject of knowledge, the subjective drama of the scholar or scientist—to the shamanistic subject, in that in magic and psychoanalysis alike, truth may function as "cause" (with the shaman in his rituals and the analyst in the transference actually lending their bodies as support for the process of understanding—870-71).

Whatever the status of the relation between psychoanalysis and shamanism, Lacan could evoke, by means of an analogy of the knot and its cutting with the shamanistic rope trick, a certain symbolic significance relevant to the theme of his seminar. The two basic features of the rope trick, common to all the variations found in European legends, are: "(1) that magicians cut up either their own limbs or someone else's, and afterwards put them together again; and (2) that conjurers, male or female, climb ropes and disappear into the air" (Eliade, *Mephistopheles*, 163). Read as metaphors of Lacan's technique, the first trick might simply refer to a classical mode of rationality: "We will follow the technique of the art of dialogue," Lacan stated in his first seminar. "Like good chefs, we have to know which joints, what resistances, we will encounter" (*Techniques*, 9). In this sense, cutting the knot in the right place so all the links come loose is like the cook carving the joints properly—both are analogies for resolving the transference and achieving the cure. Similarly, the second trick—disappearing up the rope into a cloud, as it is sometimes described, methodologically resembles Wittgenstein's admonition (also referring to the difficulty of talking about being in language), at the end of the *Tractatus*, to throw away the ladder of his argument once it had been climbed. As Eliade notes, the image takes several forms:

> The tree-climbing of the shaman is, essentially, a rite of ascension into Heaven. And it is significant that in traditional Indian imagery, the climbing of a tree symbolizes both the possession of magic powers and metaphysical gnosis. We have seen that the conjurer of *Suruci-Jataka* climbs a tree with the help of a magic rope, then disappears in the clouds. This is a theme of folklore which is also to be found in learned texts. The *Pancavimsha Brahmana*, for example, speaking of those who climb to the top of the great Tree, states that those who have wings—that is to say *those who know*—succeed in flying, whereas the ignorant, having no wings, fall to the ground. (*Mephistopheles*, 178)

Read in this context, Lacan's appropriation of Saussure's example—*Tree*, the word and the concept-image, exemplifying the signifier and the signified—to elaborate his own stylistic approach (in the "Agency of the Letter in the Unconscious") takes on added importance.

> I have only to plant my tree in a locution, climb the tree, even project on to it the cunning illumination a descriptive context gives to a word; raise it so as not to let myself be imprisoned in some sort of *communiqué* of the facts, however official, and if I know the truth, make it heard, in spite of all the *between-the-lines* censures by the only signifier my acrobatics through the branches of the tree can constitute, provocative to the point of burlesque, or perceptible only to the practised eye, according to whether I wish to be heard by the mob or by the few. (*Selection*, 155-56)

Those who climb the tree and have wings are the ones who know, in this tradition. The beings with wings in *Encore,* of course, are the angels, represented in the Baroque churches, Lacan says, with beatific smiles suggesting *bêtise*—the knowledge that does not know itself. The "shutters" that close off bliss, and that it is the task of analysis to open, can only be apprehended by "strange insights": "*Etrange* [strange] is a word which can be decomposed—*l'être-ange* [angel-being]" (*Encore,* 14). The *bêtise* of the angels, identifiable with Lacan's own *bêtise* displayed in *lalangue* by which he is able to say more than he knows, indicates that in Bernini's sculpture, taken as an emblem of the analytical situation, the analyst's position is that of the angel, and the analysand's that of St. Theresa. For in analysis, the analyst is not the one who knows (although the illusion that he does know creates the condition of transference): "The analyst's position ought to be that of an *ignorantia docta,* which does not mean learned, but formal, which can be, for the subject, forming" (*Techniques,* 306).

Granting that the perspective I am exploring might authorize a consideration of the borromean knot as the shaman's cord, the question remains as to what the cord might evoke. As Eliade explains, in Indian speculations, in which there is abundant use of images of cords and threads, "the cosmic cords (that is to say, the winds) hold the Universe together, just as breath holds together and articulates the body of a man" (*Mephistopheles,* 170). If the shaman's cord is the breath of life, then Lacan's strings signify nothing less than the *psuche* or *psyche,* the cold breath or the soul in the term "psychoanalysis," which is to say that *mythology supports Lacan's use of knot theory as a model for the psyche.*

As for the cutting of this cord, Eliade continues: "When, at the end of the world, the ropes of the winds are cut, the Universe will fall apart. And since 'it is by the air, as by a thread, that this world and the other world and all beings are strung together . . . they say of a dead man that his limbs have become unstrung'—, for it is the Air (the breath) that binds them like a thread" (*Mephistopheles,* 170-71). As that which binds body to soul, earth to heaven, the string, being cut, becomes an image of death and, finally, of destiny—including the destiny of "election," of the call to be a shaman, signaled in this tradition by a thread falling from heaven. In Greece and ancient Europe, as well as in India, the (invisible) cord "served to symbolize the human condition in general, destiny, the web of temporal existence, and consequently 'servitude' " (187).

The images, then, are ambivalent, expressing, as Eliade explains, both a "privileged position" of living in "communication with the Creator" and a "tragic situation," being "the prisoner of a fate, bound by 'magic' or by one's own past" (*Mephistopheles,* 176). Psychoanalysis, too, takes human destiny and the human condition as its subject, as Lacan indicates in this epigraph, citing Leonardo Da Vinci, in "The Agency of the Letter in the Unconscious": "O cities of the sea, I behold in you your citizens, women as well as men tightly bound with stout bonds around their arms and legs by folk who will not understand your language" (*Selection,* 146). And what the subject discovers through the intermediary of the analyst, Lacan explains, "is its truth, that is its signification which takes up in its particular destiny those givens which are proper to it and which one could call its lot" (*Le moi,* 374). Beyond the pleasure principle there exists the Symbolic order—"The death drive is nothing other than the mask of the symbolic order" (375). Destiny in analysis is the repetition (the chain of signifiers originating from the master-signifier, represented by the bor- romean knot, which means that the knot is a formulation of the death drive) that reveals the image imprinted on the subject, "that image which most certainly he knew as human essence since it provokes passion, ex- ercises oppression, which reveals its features to (the analyst's) look. These features he discovers in a family portrait" (*Ecrits,* 84).

There is something disgusting, grotesque, in the image of destiny, re- calling Derrida's concern with the *vomi.* Lacan makes this point by referring to the same image Derrida discussed several times[23]—that of M. Valdemar (in Poe's short story) suspended between life and death, his body dis- integrating after uttering (in an uncanny voice) the phrase "I am dead." Valdemar's dissolution (an image of the subject's decomposition in analy- sis) represents the "brutal" apparition of "the figure impossible to look at directly which is in the background of all the imaginations of human destiny" (*Le moi,* 270). Freud's own experience with such an image is re- ported in the dream of Irma's injection (the one he claimed unlocked for him the secret of dreams), in which, upon looking into his patient's (Irma's) mouth, the dreaming Freud saw deep in her throat "a frightful spectacle" —secret of hidden flesh, associated with the genitals, of course, but in the region of the Adam's apple, called in French "the knot." As we know from *Encore,* this image indeed remarks the impossible—the genitals in the throat implying a conjunction of the two blisses, the phallic and the other one, of the word.

The second episode of the dream concludes not like the first, with an image conveying disgust, but with a formula—the formula of trimethyla- mine (a substance produced by the decomposition of sperm and having the odor of ammonia). And what Lacan says about this formula, after writing it out on the blackboard for the class to see—taking the meaning of the dream of Irma's injection to be, just as Freud claimed, not any specific theme, but the secret of dreams, of how dreams mean—could be applied to Lacan's own use of mathematical inscriptions (his lectures being the simulacrum of a dream as well as of the analysand's discourse): "Like an oracle, the formula gives no response to anything whatever. But the man- ner itself with which it is stated, its enigmatic, hermetic character, is the response to the question of the meaning of dreams. One could model it on the islamic formula—*there is no other God but God.* There is no other word [*mot*], no other solution to your problem, than the word" (*Le moi,* 190).

Like Freud's dream, Lacan's use of knots is reflexive, finally, exemplary of the evocative mode of transmission appropriate for psychoanalysis, and for a pedagogy, like that sought by grammatology, based on the lesson of psychoanalysis. Eliade suggests, in fact, that the real value of the shaman's stage tricks, the manipulation of cords and knots as part of a spiritual exercise, is precisely to provoke thought:

> But it is above all the cultural function of the rope-trick—or, to be more exact, of the archaic scenarios which made it possible—that seems to us important. . . . From this point of view, the rope-trick— like all other displays of magic—has a positive cultural value, for it stimulates the imagination and reflection, one acting on the other, by the questions and problems that it raises and, ultimately, by putting the problem of the "true" reality of the World. . . . In dif- ferent contexts the thread or cord is capable of suggesting different shades of meaning. It is of course the chief function of exemplary images that they invite, help and even force a man to think, to define his ideas, continually to discover new meanings, and to deepen and develop them. It is highly significant that the image of the cord or thread plays a principal role in the imaginary universe of primitive medicine-men and in the extra-sensory perceptions of modern men, as well as in the mystical experience of archaic societies, in Indo-European myths and rituals, in Indian cosmology and phi- losophy, in Greek philosophy. (*Mephistopheles,* 186, 188)

The lesson of Lacan's seminar for applied grammatology is just this use of models—of pictures and puns—to provoke thought, working through a

double intervention ("The analyst operates on the two registers of intellectual elucidation by *interpretation,* of affective manoeuvre by *transference"—Ecrits,* 85). Love involves not just *l'amour* in the transference
that informs the educational, as much as it does the analytic, situation, but
le mur (wall—Lacan has written *l'amur*), the wall of language. Do not just
put on the "leaden shoes of pedagogy" in this situation, Lacan urges, referring to traditional didacticism, but rather, "You can make use [of this
mur du langage] in order to reach your interlocutor, but on condition that
you understand, from the moment that it is a question of using this wall,
that both you and he are on this side, and that you must aim to reach him
along it, like a cue-shot along the cushion" (*Speech,* 151).

In the next chapter we shall see another version of this ricochet (and
theatrical cue) in the shamanism of Joseph Beuys.

8

Performance:

Joseph Beuys

Lacan provided an example of how to lecture in a way adaptable to applied grammatology. What we need now is an example of how to perform in a grammatological classroom in a way that fulfills the possibilities outlined in Derrida's notion of the Mime, including the use of mnemonics and models. Examples of what an applied grammatology might be like—of a picto-ideo-phonographic Writing put to work in the service of pedagogy—are already available in the intermedia practices of certain avant-garde artists. Contemporary movements such as conceptual art, performance art, and video art may be considered from our perspective as laboratories for a new pedagogy, since in these and other movements research and experiment have replaced form as the guiding force. "Now, as art becomes less art," Allan Kaprow maintains, "it takes on philosophy's early role as critique of life."[1] In short, there is a general shift under way, equally affecting the arts and the sciences, in which the old classifications organizing the intellectual map into disciplines, media, genres, and modes no longer correspond to the terrain. The organizing principle of the current situation is the collapse of the distinction (opposition or hierarchy) between critical-theoretical reflection and creative practice. Derrida's promotion of a fusion between philosophy and literature is just one symptom of this hybridization. One lesson of these circumstances, which have increased the normal disparity in the schools between invention and pedagogy, is that models for reform are as likely (perhaps more likely) to be found outside as inside our own discipline.

It is not possible in the space of one book, of course, to survey all the pedagogical materials and procedures available in the intermedia arts. Rather, I shall focus on one example of an artist-pedagogue—Joseph Beuys —to examine in detail one version of Writing beyond the book. My point in discussing Beuys in the context of grammatology is not to suggest that he represents a norm for a new pedagogy but that, in his very extremity, he demonstrates more clearly than anyone else the full implications and possibilities of Writing. Working in the spirit of Foucault's observation— that in our era the interrogation of limits has replaced the search for totality[2]—I find in Beuys someone who is as extreme, as singular, as exemplary in the field of performance art as Derrida is in philosophy. To- gether they form a paradigm that may serve as a point of departure for a new pedagogy.

I should orient my approach to Beuys as explicitly as possible, given the potential unfamiliarity of his work (at least for students of literature and criticism). Beuys has been widely discussed in art journals as perhaps "the greatest living European artist of the post-war period."[3] Having received considerable attention from the popular media in Germany (including lengthy appearances on television and a cover story in *Der Spiegel*), he has become there the symbol of avant-garde art, the way Andy Warhol was for a time in the United States.[4] An international art dealer who ranks the hundred leading contemporary artists according to market factors (sales, showings, etc.) rated Beuys number one in 1979, replacing Robert Rausch- enberg.[5] In other words, Beuys is anything but a marginal figure.

Outside of Germany, Beuys is perhaps best known in the United States. His one-man show at the Guggenheim Museum in New York, 1979, marked his third visit here. As Caroline Tisdall reports, Beuys's first visit consisted of a lecture tour to New York, Chicago, and Minneapolis (winter 1973). He spoke of his *Energy Plan for Western Man,* which contained his ideal of "Social Sculpture": "First of all the extension of the definition of art be- yond the specialist activity carried out by artists to the active mobilisation of every individual's latent creativity, and then, following on from that, the moulding of the society of the future based on the total energy of this individual creativity."[6] Reminding his audience that humanity is still evolv- ing and that, as "spiritual" beings, our thought, will, and emotions take an active part in (and are themselves altered by) the dynamics of change, Beuys described how we must link our "organic instinctive feeling powers to our thinking powers,"—"our vision of the world must be extended to encom- pass all the invisible energies with which we have lost contact" (Tisdall, 37).

The second visit, a "one week performance on the occasion of the opening of the René Block Gallery, New York, May, 1974," was designed to extend and present in a dramatic form this Energy Plan. Entitled "I

like America and America likes me," the Action consisted of Beuys shar-
ing a caged room in the Gallery with a coyote for three days:

> The action as such began when Beuys was packed into felt at Ken-
> nedy airport and driven by ambulance to the gallery. In the gallery in
> a room divided by a grating a coyote was waiting for him. The
> Texas wolfhound represents pre-Columbian America, which still
> knew the harmonic living together of man and nature, in which
> coyote and Indian could live with one another before they were both
> hunted down by the colonialists. During the action Beuys was at
> times entirely covered in felt. Out of the felt only a wooden cane stuck
> out. One is instinctively reminded of a guardian, a shepherd. Beuys
> talked with the coyote, attempted to find an approach to him, to es-
> tablish a relationship. From time to time Beuys rang a triangle which
> he carried around his neck. Sounds of a turbine from a tape recorder
> disturbed the atmosphere, bringing a threatening nuance into the
> play. Fifty copies of the "Wall Street Journal," the leading economic
> newspaper, lying strewn about the floor, completed the environ-
> ment. The coyote urinated on the newspapers.[7]

As for the Guggenheim exhibition, Beuys himself took "creative responsibility" for the organization and display, making it not just a presentation (in fact, a retrospective of his career) but "an autonomous work of
art that validates already existing objects," although many of the objects
originated in performance pieces and hence were not intended to stand
alone as "art objects." Beuys placed the following statement in the introduction to the catalogue:

> My objects are to be seen as stimulants for the transformation of the
> idea of sculpture, or of art in general. They should provoke thoughts
> about what sculpture *can* be and how the concept of sculpting can
> be extended to the invisible materials used by everyone: *Thinking
> Forms*—how we mould our thoughts or / *Spoken Forms*—how we shape
> our thoughts into words or / SOCIAL SCULPTURE—how we mould
> and shape the world in which we live: *Sculpture as an evolutionary pro-
> cess; everyone an artist.* That is why the nature of my sculpture is
> not fixed and finished. Processes continue in most of them: chemical
> reactions, fermentations, colour changes, decay, drying up. Every-
> thing is in a *state of change.*[8]

My interest in Beuys, similar to my interest in Lacan, concerns not his
ideology or themes so much as his strategies of presentation, his Writing,
his Style as itself an idea. There is no concern for "influence" in either
direction in my discussion. Derrida did visit the Guggenheim exhibition,
choosing to *ascend* the museum's famous spiraling ramps. After climbing
from station to station (as the display sectors were called), Derrida remarked

to his son Jean that the exhibit experience replicated nicely the "Stations of the Cross."[9] In any case, placing Beuys's work in the context of grammatology has the virtue of addressing at least one of the problems associated with the reception of his work, which is that commentators thus far have tended to confine themselves to descriptions of his work, venturing by way of explanation little more than paraphrases of Beuys's own statements. But, as Lothar Romain and Rolf Wedewer stress in calling for analyses that bring to bear other categories and contexts, Beuys's interviews and lectures do not constitute interpretations but exist at the same level as, even as part of (verbal extensions of), the art.[10] Not that this chapter is an interpretation, either, since I am interested in borrowing some of Beuys's procedures exactly as he explains them (I want to learn from him, not account for him). The fact that Beuys's Actions lend themselves so readily to grammatological terms—indicating the convergence at a theoretical level of two radically different idioms—I take as evidence supporting the feasibility and fruitfulness of a "general writing."

My argument will be guided by the principle of the post card—I have found in Beuys's works more post cards (he does in fact use the post card as a medium) for Derrida's texts, providing the verso for the texts' recto, similar to Derrida's own discovery with respect to Adami's drawings or Titus-Carmel's *Tlingit Coffin.* My approach to Beuys, then, will be in terms of Derrida's principles, performing the transition from a theoretical to an applied grammatology. The following list, anticipating the more specific discussion in the rest of the chapter, indicates the areas of relationship between Derrida's theory and Beuys's performance:

1. *Teaching.* A shared point of departure is each man's status as a professor of a specific discipline within the traditional academy— Derrida as professor of the history of philosophy at the *Ecole normale superieure* in Paris, Beuys as professor of sculpture at the Academy of Art in Düsseldorf. Their educational projects, however, extend well beyond the boundaries of their respective disciplines and institutions, not only in the direction of interdisciplinary theory and intermedia practice (the Cerisy-la-Salle colloquium, for example, included workshops exploring the implications of Derrida's texts for philosophy, literature, education, politics, psychoanalysis, and the visual arts) but also to organizations designed to intervene deconstructively in the educational system as a whole— *GREPH* and the Estates General of Philosophy in Derrida's case, and the Free International University for Interdisciplinary Research in Beuys's case.

2. *Creativity.* Summarized in the term *apeiron,* Derrida's theory of Writing is an *inventio,* a new rhetoric of invention. Translated into

a pedagogy, Writing becomes a research into creativity, into all processes of innovation and change. Beuys's sculptural practice similarly constitutes not only a self-reflexive theory of sculpture but also a theory of the very notion of creativity as such in all human productivity, as indicated in his slogan, "everyone an artist."

3. *Models.* Derrida's exploration of a new hieroglyphic writing, supplementing verbal discourse with ideographic and pictorial elements, is practiced by Beuys on a scale ranging from the abject to the colossal. The point is not simply that Beuys's works include objects and images, since the same could be said of any visual artist, but that his objects are specifically models, employed in a kind of allegorical writing.

4. *Mime.* Derrida's account of the "teaching body," in conjunction with his discussion of the Mime and the theater of cruelty, offers a theory of performance which corresponds to Beuys's performance art. Beuys's object-models are generated as elements of Actions, performance Events, or "rituals," in which Beuys mimes both science and mythology in a didactic exploration of the creative process. In both cases, theater and theory merge into one activity (which perhaps could be dubbed "theorter").

5. *Autography.* The question of the place of the subject of knowledge, which informs Derrida's work and poststructuralism in general, is especially complex because it includes a "deconstructed self," decentered, disseminated, a condition or status manifested in Derrida's notion of the signature. The place and function of the deconstructed self is especially important to the new pedagogy in which the teacher must sign for the lessons. Beuys's use of shamanism offers a way to de-monstrate the autographical character of poststructuralist, postmodernist knowing—idiomatic and impersonal at once—since the shaman draws on the most subjective, private areas of experience for his handling and treatment of public affairs and objective problems. The shaman, to use Lacan's terminology, is an example of the embedding of the Imaginary (one's personal mythology) in the Symbolic (the system of language and culture).

Fortunately, two excellent, thorough surveys of Beuys's *oeuvre* are available in English (Tisdall's catalogue for the Guggenheim exhibition and the chronologically organized survey by Adriani, Konnertz, and Thomas), so there is no need for me to enter into a general description of his career. Nonetheless, before discussing specific examples, I would like to point out at least some of the features of Beuys's program which are relevant to grammatology.

SHAMANISM

The most salient feature of Beuys's work is his adoption of shamanism as his presentational mode and even as his lived attitude. Beuys is unusual in this respect only because of the extent to which he has integrated his art and his life into the shaman's role. The artist as shaman, however, turns out to be descriptive of a major trend in modern art, beginning with the "primitivism" of the early modernists (Gauguin, Picasso) and extending through to contemporary "abreaction" and "ritual" modes of performance and body art (Vito Acconci, Dennis Oppenheim). Whether or not there is any connection between this shamanistic tendency in the arts and the much-disputed "tribalizing" effect of the electronic media (as described by McLuhan) is a matter of conjecture. More immediately relevant is the proposition that "performance," if not shamanism itself, "the unifying mode of the postmodern, is now what matters."[11] So says Michel Benamou in his introduction to the volume collecting the proceedings of an international conference on performance. "One might ask," he states, posing the question that motivated the conference, "what causes this pervading need to act out art which used to suffice by itself on the page or the musuem wall. What is this new presence, and how has it replaced the presence which poems and pictures silently proffered before? Has everything from politics to poetics become theatrical?"

The strategic paradox of the shamanistic performance most significant for the contemporary shift is its displacement of the subjective-objective, private-public opposition. Thus, what may seem to be the apotheosis of egotism and narcissism is in fact something quite different. As Jack Burnham notes, we are confronted with a situation in which, "as our mythic structure deteriorates, the archetypes vanish and it is the trials and psychodramas of the individual that provide us with our sense of direction . . . At this most crucial and sensitive point the artist focuses upon the primal aspects of his own creative motivation."[12] But these psychodramas are not the romantic or expressionist glorifications of the self that they might appear to be. Rather, as Burnham explains in a comment that is relevant to the educational research implicit in the decompositional, oral writing of *Glas,*

> Various forms of post-painting and post-sculpture now being practiced by artists relate to the earliest stages of infant development. Here, first attempt at interpersonal relationships, measuring of spaces, exploring the body, making discrete and random piles of objects, and other preverbal activities mirror the artist's striving to reach the seat of the unconscious itself. Just as alchemists understood the return of chaos (mental oblivion) as an essential part of the Great Work, the role of the shaman in ritual activity was to neutralize

and realign the individual ego, replacing it in part with a balanced and complete superego. In a parallel fashion, we are witnessing the destruction of signature art as artistic behavior becomes increasingly archetypal and ontological. (Burnham, 154)

The essence of the paradox has to do with a shift in the interaction between the particular and the general. As noted earlier in the case of mnemonic systems, in shamanism the personal self is used as a vehicle for a knowledge practice and is not explored for its own sake.

Roland Barthes provides an interesting perspective on the relevance of shamanism to the poststructuralist effort to displace the old categories of self in a way that is particularly relevant to grammatology. Questioning the historical passage of "to write" from a transitive to an intransitive verb, Barthes argues that the best definition of the modern "to write" can be found in *diathesis,* the linguistic notion of voice (active, passive, middle), "designating the way in which the subject of the verb is affected by the action."

> According to the classic example, given by Meillet and Benveniste, the verb *to sacrifice* (ritually) is active if the priest sacrifices the victim in my place for me, and it is middle voice if, taking the knife from the priest's hands, I make the sacrifice for myself. In the case of the active, the action is accomplished outside the subject, because, although the priest makes the sacrifice, he is not affected by it. In the case of the middle voice, on the contrary, the subject affects himself in acting; he always remains inside the action, even if an object is involved. The middle voice does not, therefore, exclude transitivity. Thus defined, the middle voice corresponds exactly to the state of the verb *to write:* today to write is to make oneself the center of the action of speech [*parole*]; it is to effect writing in being affected oneself; it is to leave the writer [*scripteur*] inside the writing, not as a psychological subject (the Indo-European priest could very well overflow with subjectivity in actively sacrificing for his client), but as the agent of the action. [13]

In contemporary experimental writing, "to write," Barthes argues, has become a middle verb, establishing a new status for the agent of writing: "The meaning or goal of this effort is to substitute the instance of discourse for the instance of reality (or of the referent), which has been, and still is, a mythical 'alibi' dominating the idea of literature. The field of the writer is nothing but writing itself, not as the pure 'form' conceived by an aesthetic of art for art's sake, but, much more radically, as the only area [*espace*] for the one who writes" (166). In the middle voice, then, nothing takes place but the place (space).

It is worth noting that Derrida explicitly relates the betweenness of differance with the middle voice:

> And we shall see why what is designated by "differance" is neither
> simply active nor simply passive, that it announces or rather re-
> calls something like the middle voice, that it speaks of an operation
> which is not an operation, which cannot be thought of either as
> a passion or as an action of a subject upon an object, as starting from
> an agent or from a patient, or on the basis of, or in view of, any
> of these *terms*. But philosophy has perhaps commenced by distribut-
> ing the middle voice, expressing a certain intransitiveness, into the
> active and the passive voice, and has itself been constituted in this
> repression. (*Speech*, 137)

Beuys's exercise of the shaman's position, operating in the middle voice, provides a frame within which philosophy may be rethought.

The distinction between the active and the middle voice (illustrated in the classic example by a ritual situation) reflects the distinction between priestcraft and shamanism as rival modes of spiritual activity: the institutional representative versus the nomadic medicine man. Barthes himself makes explicit the connection of his theory of the subject in writing with shamanism in his essay "The Death of the Author," in which the "shaman" is opposed to, or designated as the alternative to, the "author": "In primitive societies, narrative is never undertaken by a person, but by a mediator, shaman or speaker, whose 'performance' may be admired (that is, his mastery of the narrative code) but not his 'genius.'"[14] Certain modern writers, Barthes says, have attempted to recover something like the shaman's position, against that of the "author," who joins his person to his work: "For Mallarmé, as for us, it is language which speaks, not the author: to write is to reach, through a preexisting impersonality—never to be confused with the castrating objectivity of the realistic novelist—that point where language alone acts, 'performs,' and not 'oneself'" ("Death," 8). Derrida uses Mallarmé to make a similar point, of course, and now we can see that the shaman, working in the middle voice, is another example of what is involved in Writing.

Shamanism, to give a general definition, is the self-cure of a deep depression by the use of psychic techniques (trance states induced by monotonous rhythms, for example) that enable the individual to gain control over his unconscious imagery.[15] This self-healing in turn gives the shaman the power to heal others, his principal function in a primitive community being that of doctor. Freud's self-analysis, constituting the origin of psychoanalysis, resembles in certain respects the experience of the shaman's calling. Derrida's focus on the emergence of psychoanalysis as a domain of knowledge, the model problem for grammatology as a science of science (especially in *La carte postale*, for which Freud's letters to Fliess, by means of which Freud enacted the therapeutic transference, provide the organizing reference), indicates the usefulness of shamanistic performances as a dramatization of grammatology's concern. The question posed in "Spéculer—sur 'Freud' "—"how an autobiographical writing, in the abyss of an unterminated auto-analysis, could give *its* birth to a worldwide institution" (*Carte,* 325)—reflects the fundamental problem of poststructuralism: the status of the subject of knowledge, of the specific relation of idiom to system in the process of knowledge.

Claude Lévi-Strauss, comparing shamanism and psychoanalysis, identifies the aspect of his articulation which is most relevant to applied grammatology. Grammatology's interest in both pscyhoanalysis and shamanism as models for a new pedagogy (specifically, in the practices of Lacan and Beuys as exemplary figures) has to do with the peculiar mode of communication they developed in order to address a register of comprehension other than the rational intellect (without, at the same time, neglecting the latter). Both practices, that is, share a similar manner of manipulating symbols. The similarity becomes especially apparent, Lévi-Strauss notes, in the therapeutic techniques developed to treat schizophrenics who are not reachable with the talking cure originally advanced for the treatment of neurotics.

> Actually the therapist holds a dialogue with the patient, not through the spoken word, but by concrete actions, that is, genuine rites which penetrate the screen of consciousness to carry their message directly to the unconscious ["carried out not by a literal reproduction of the appropriate behavior but by means of actions which are, as it were, discontinuous, each symbolizing a fundamental element of the situation"]. Here we again encounter the concept of manipulation, which appeared so essential to an understanding of the shamanistic cure but whose traditional definition we must broaden considerably. For it may at one time involve a manipulation of ideas and, at another time, a manipulation of organs. But the basic condition remains that the manipulation must be carried out through symbols, that is, through meaningful equivalents of things meant which belong to another order of reality.[16]

Lévi-Strauss is convinced that shamanism may be as useful for "elucidating obscure points of Freudian theory" as psychoanalysis is for helping to understand the shamanistic cure. In our present state of comprehension, one seems to be the inverse of the other—"In the schizophrenic cure the healer performs the actions and the patient produces his myth; in the shamanistic cure the healer supplies the myth and the patient performs the actions." But if Freud's intuitions about the ultimate biochemical nature of psychopathology (supported by recent discoveries of chemical imbalances in the physiology of schizophrenics) are accurate, even these differences in practice will be insignificant, since both cures will function according to a set of homologous structures which "in aggregate form we call the unconscious." Lévi-Strauss's description of this set corresponds to Lacan's distinction between the Imaginary and the Symbolic:

> For the preconscious, as a reservoir of recollections and images amassed in the course of a lifetime, is merely an aspect of memory. . . . The unconscious, on the other hand, is always empty—or, more accurately, it is as alien to mental images as is the stomach to the foods which pass through it. As the organ of a specific function, the unconscious merely imposes structural laws upon inarticulated elements which originate elsewhere—impulses, emotions, representations, and memories. We might say, therefore, that the preconscious is the individual lexicon where each of us accumulates the vocabulary of his personal history, but that this vocabulary becomes significant, for us and for others, only to the extent that the unconscious structures it according to its laws and thus transforms it into language. (Lévi-Strauss, 198–99)

Grammatology, then, can learn from Lacan and Beuys about how to mount a practice that moves between preconscious (Imaginary) and unconscious (Symbolic) registers, keeping in mind that the conditions that shape psychoanalysis also shape contemporary adaptations of shamanism, such as that undertaken by Beuys, so that Beuys and Lacan are in roughly the same position relative to Lévi-Strauss's advice: "The modern version of shamanistic technique called psychoanalysis, thus, derives its specific characteristics from the fact that in industrial civilization there is no longer any room for mythical time, except within man himself. From this observation, psychoanalysis can draw confirmation of its validity, as well as hope of strengthening its theoretical foundations and understanding better the reasons for its effectiveness, by comparing its methods and goals with those of its precursors, the shamans and sorcerers" (Lévi-Strauss, 200).

THE CALLING

As for Beuys himself, aside from his childhood fantasies about Genghis Khan (he carried a cane with him everywhere and imagined himself to be a nomad herdsman), his first encounter with shamanistic practice was as patient rather than as "doctor." A pilot on the eastern front in the Second World War, Beuys's dive bomber crashed in a wilderness area of the Crimea (one of the five times he was injured or wounded during the war). Tartar herdsmen discovered him in the wreckage, buried in the snow, and cared for him for over a week before he was transported to a German hospital. " 'I remember voices saying *Voda* (Water), then the felt of their tents, and the dense pungent smell of cheese, fat and milk. They covered my body in fat to help it regenerate warmth, and wrapped it in felt as an insulator to keep the warmth in'" (*Beuys*, 16-17). Tisdall adds that "it is true that without this encounter with the Tartars, and with their ritualistic respect for the healing potential of materials, Beuys would never have turned to fat and felt as the material for sculpture," as he did in the 1950s and 1960s, although, as she stresses, by that time the materials are not merely autobiographical allusions but are "elements of a theory to do with the potential and meaning of sculpture" (to be discussed later).

The war years as a whole, and this incident in particular, resulted ultimately in a personal crisis, culminating in a nervous collapse (deep depression) lasting from 1955 through 1957. The illness in retrospect may be recognized as one of the elements traditionally associated with the shaman's calling. "This crisis was very important for me," Beuys later noted, "because everything, truly everything, was put in question. It was in the course of that crisis that I decided, with energy, to research all that in life, art, science was the most profound. I was already prepared for it by my earlier work but this was to be an entirely different theory of art, science, life, democracy, capital, economy, liberty, culture" (Vadel, 15). This global reorientation, Beuys added, is "closely linked to what people call an individual mythology," involving not only the discovery of a new theory but also "what would be defined later as features of a shamanistic initiation" (15).

Up to and through the period of crisis, Beuys made many drawings related to his experience (including the extensive notes made during the war on the landscape, people, and customs of the region in which shamanism originated). These drawings are the equivalent in his self-healing process of Freud's letters to Fliess (and of Freud's "Egyptian dream-book," about which Freud said in one of his letters, "It was all written by the unconscious, on the well-known principle of Itzig, the Sunday horseman. 'Itzig, where are you going?' 'Don't ask me, ask the horse!' At the beginning of a paragraph I never knew where I should end up. It was not written to be read, of course—any attempt at style was abandoned after the first two pages"— *Origins*, 258). Beuys's drawings, too, are a mode of research in which, like Freud, Beuys laid the foundations for an institution while exploring his own psyche. Describing his impulse to draw, Beuys states:

> With me, it's that certain questions—about life, about art, about
> science—interest me, and I feel I can go farthest toward answering
> them by trying to develop a language on paper, a language to
> stimulate more searching discussion—more than just what our present
> civilization represents in terms of scientific method, artistic method,
> or thought in general. I try to go beyond these things—I ask questions,
> I put forms of language on paper, I also put forms of sensibility, in
> tention and idea on paper, all in order to stimulate thought.[17]

It is worth noting in this context that Beuys, as a young man, wanted to study the natural sciences, especially the life sciences, but that he was discouraged by the specialized, narrow manner in which these sciences were taught.

The drawings deserve attention because their themes and structures provided the resources for his later performances, many of which amount to an enactment of his drawings. They exemplify the purely graphic element of Writing (a drawn writing), the exercise of which brings into appearance a dimension of knowing that is the equivalent in the visual arts of *lalangue.* In the preface to the catalogue of an exhibition of Beuys's drawings, with a title that echoes Derrida's interest in the apotropaic—*The Secret Block for a Secret Person in Ireland*—the curator remarks that "for Beuys drawing has been a way of thinking, or a *thinking form*" (in an interview in the same catalogue Beuys states, "When I speak about thinking I mean it as *form.* People have to consider ideas as the artist considers sculpture: to seek for the *forms* created by thinking"). The curator's assessment of the forms developed in the collection indicates the extent to which Beuys's program parallels Derrida's hieroglyphic project to extend language into a general writing. "The widening of language is the key to the process of change in thinking, and for Beuys the widening of language came through drawing. Drawing becomes a way to reach areas unattainable through speech or abstract thinking alone: to suspend all notions of the limits or limitations of a field so that it encompasses everything. The *germination point* of all the later thinking appears in the drawings."[18]

Like Derrida's texts, Beuys's drawings break the "laws of genre" ("Beuys's contribution to the history of drawing is as individual as it is unique—he has gone beyond the bounds of drawing as we know it").[19] Part of the powerful effect of the drawings is that they achieve a mixture of rigor and play like that which Derrida promotes in scholarship. He uses a great variety of techniques, but most of all it is the unusual nature of his materials that fascinates: "pencil and paint, rabbit's blood and pieces of fish, phosphorus and iron chloride, milk and furniture stain, gold enamel, silver leaf and fruit remains have been used in a seemingly infinite number of permutations. And the surfaces he draws on are just as diverse—envelopes, book covers, pages from newspapers or notebooks or ledgers, wallpaper, corrugated cardboard, silver foil, wax-paper, normal paper" (Simmen, 86)—lists that read almost like a combination of Derrida's categories of the abject and the *vomi* (all the glutinous liquids associated in *Glas* with the "+ L" effect). Collage and the exploitation of chance effects, needless to say, are part of the strategy: "His procedure is a delicate probing of these materials, and they respond by revealing their poetic possibilities. This is particularly true of the used and worn things he chooses." Beuys's technique, then, can be thought of as an analogue of the metamorphosis of terms in Derrida's "decomposition"—"Pencil and paint for Beuys are aids to meditation about destruction and things destroyed. . . . Things often seen, often overlooked undergo a metamorphosis" (Simmen, 87).

In 1961 Beuys was appointed Professor of Sculpture at the Düsseldorf Academy of Art, beginning the phase leading to the full realization of his calling, for at this time his personal trajectory intersected with certain international tendencies in the arts. Düsseldorf, in any case, was becoming a major center of avant-garde activity, being the home of Group Zero (led by Otto Piene and Heinz Mack), the German rival of the French *Groupe de Recherche d'art Visuel (GRAV)*. Beuys met and began to work with members of an international group active in Düsseldorf—Fluxus—which counted among its most active participants George Maciunas, Nam June Paik, Charlotte Moorman, Wolf Vostell, George Brecht, Dick Higgins, Emmet Williams, Daniel Spoerri, and John Cage (*Beuys,* 84). Fluxus sponsored "events" in a number of European cities, events that took the form of "Happenings," or experimental, Neo-Dada concerts.

As Tisdall notes, this concert element—the unconventional musicianship involved—is what most interested Beuys in Fluxus, sound being for him an essential sculptural material (noise, music, language). Beuys's very first Action (the term he prefers to "performance"), performed 3 February 1963, lasted only twenty seconds: "I dashed forward in the gap between two performances, wound up a clockwork toy, two drummers, on the piano, and let them play until the clockwork ran down" (Tisdall, 87), although it should be added that the next night he performed the much more complex "Siberian Symphony, section 1."

In this avant-garde company Beuys developed his ritual format, which has made him famous, tending first to favor provocation, and later meditation, as his dominant mood. He had by this time adopted a permanent costume, marking his denial of the distinction between art and life, including his felt hat (the magic hat, which is part of the traditional shamanistic garb) and a flight vest (alluding both to his biography—his service as a pilot in the war—and the shaman's power of flight, the "technique of ecstacy" in Eliade's definition).[20] The flight vest itself indicates the special point of interest for grammatology in this aspect of Beuys's work—the convergence in his objects of autobiographical and mythical dimensions. Reserving for later a detailed discussion of his actions and theories, I would like for now to take note of Beuys's own statements of intention regarding these two components of his work—the autobiographical, related to psychoanalysis; the mythological, related to shamanism. Their conjunction in Beuys's Actions provides one version of the position of the subject in knowledge.

The point I wish to stress is the similarity of Beuys's intention, with respect to shamanism, to the program of grammatology, designed to *exceed* science (not to oppose it as such). "So when I appear as a kind of shamanistic figure, or allude to it, I do it to stress my belief in other priorities and the need to come up with a completely different plan for working with substances. For instance, in places like universities, where everyone speaks so rationally, it is necessary for a kind of enchanter to appear" (*Beuys,* 23).

In his interviews Beuys often mentions shamanism and psychoanalysis together as strategies for addressing the general public in a way that is at once educative and therapeutic—his intention is to use these two forms of discourse and styles of knowledge as pedagogies. "It was thus a strategic stage to use the shaman's character but, subsequently, I gave scientific lectures. Also, at times, on one hand, I was a kind of modern scientific analyst, on the other hand, in the actions, I had a synthetic existence as shaman. This strategy aimed at creating in people an agitation for instigating questions rather than for conveying a complete and perfect structure. It was a kind of psychoanalysis with all the problems of energy and culture" (Vadel, 18). Beuys stresses that he is interested not in providing solutions in the form of scientific or pseudo-scientific theories, nor in transmitting information, but in stimulating thought—"I am much more interested in a type of theory which provokes energy among people and leads them to a general discussion of their present problems. It is thus more a therapeutic methodology" (17). This intention parallels the pedagogical aim of grammatology to stimulate creativity.

Psychoanalysis and shamanism, each in its own way, is a knowledge of death. *Beyond the Pleasure Principle,* for example, in which Freud speculates on the life and death drives, is the tutor text of "Spéculer—sur 'Freud,'" for some of Lacan's most important theories (he devotes his second seminar to it), and for poststructuralist psy-phi (psychoanalytic-philosophical) writing, indicating the general concern with the problematic of the death drive in culture. And, as Eliade explains, shamanism is precisely a knowledge of death:

> It is as a further result of his ability to travel in the supernatural
> worlds and to *see* superhuman beings (gods, demons, spirits of the
> dead, etc.) that the shaman has been able to contribute decisively
> to the *knowledge of death.* . . . The lands that the shaman sees and
> the personages that he meets during his ecstatic journeys in the
> beyond are minutely described by the shaman himself, during or
> after his trance. The unknown and terrifying world of death as-
> sumes form, is organized in accordance with particular patterns;
> finally it displays a structure and, in course of time, becomes familiar
> and acceptable. In turn, the supernatural inhabitants of the world
> of death become *visible.* (*Shamanism,* 509–10)

Beuys draws on both theories of death to call attention to what he feels is the "fatal character" of our era ("The process of death, in methodical terms, involves all the elements of death in our environment. . . . Yes, we are living in a death zone"), which he challenges by a special use of shamanism: "I don't use shamanism to refer to death, but vice versa—*through shamanism* I refer to the fatal character of the times we live in. But at the same time I also point out that the fatal character of the present can be overcome in the future" (*Drawings*, 94). Grammatology, too, is a way of bringing the subject into relation with death. "Spacing as writing is the becoming-absent and the becoming-unconscious of the subject. By the movement of its drift/derivation the emancipation of the sign constitutes in return the desire of presence. . . . As the subject's relationship with its own death, this becoming is the constitution of subjectivity. On all levels of life's organization, that is to say, of the *economy of death*. All graphemes are of a testamentary essence" (*Grammatology*, 69).

Beuys, then, uses shamanistic and psychoanalytic techniques to "manipulate symbols," as Lévi-Strauss described it, in order to affect others. But we should not forget, following Barthes, that the shaman and the analyst (countertransference) work in the middle voice. Beuys's use of the double inscription is as motivated by his private and unconscious interests as by this intention to address the primal levels of the public's awareness. Just as in the shaman's seance, in which healing another takes place by means of dramatizing the shaman's own illness and cure, so too in Beuys's Actions is the exploration of his own signature the means for addressing the concerns of the group. "My personal history is of interest only in so far as I have attempted to use my life and person as a tool, and I think this was so from a very early age" (*Beuys*, 10). "The life course and the work course run together, but not as autobiography. The prolonged experience of the proximity of death—initiation through resurrection" (*Secret*, 6). The "contamination" that interests Derrida in the problematic of the signature is systematically exploited by Beuys ("Fluxus, 'the flowing,' combats traditional art images and their material expectations, recalling the words of Heraclitus: 'All existence flows in the stream of creation and passing away' [the *apeiron*]. Existence in a total logical consistency is contrasted to a barely realized demand for totality, making penetrable the borders between art and life, as well as between the separate arts"—Adriani, Konnertz, and Thomas, 78).

Thus, Beuys includes in his vita his own birth date and place, as if listing an exhibition. The bathtub in which he was bathed as an infant is offered as a sculpture, but in a spirit quite different from that of the readymade, since, as Beuys explains, his stress is on the meaning of the object—not in the sense of self-reflection, but, by certain additions or modifications (adding pieces of gauze soaked in plaster and fat), in a more general sense: "the wound or trauma experienced by every person as they come into contact with the hard material conditions of the world through birth" (*Beuys*, 10). Not that the spirit of parody which informed Duchamp's mode (as well as that of Fluxus) is absent, for the tub is also meant to call to mind an old adage: "Some people say 'Beuys is crazy, his bath water must have been too hot.' Such old sayings have deep roots and some unconscious truth" (10).

Like Derrida, Beuys mixes collage principles with fetishism, integrating the anthropological and the psychoanalytic applications of the term ("decisive is an assumed content of meaning which is based in part on the fetishes of certain primitive races, which would impose its own individuality on the psychic area of the transmitted material"—Adriani, Konnertz, and Thomas, 98). Like the collageists, he uses in his works whatever he finds around him in his environment, the difference being that even the detritus, items accumulated on his studio shelves over the course of years, then introduced into works like *Stag Hunt,* not to mention more substantial items (the VW bus—the family car—which ended up as the rescue vehicle in "The pack," loaded with children's sleds each carrying a roll of felt, a flashlight, and a glob of fat), becomes charged or invested with the status of relics. The inside-outside opposition is meaningless for an organization of the human life-world, in Beuys's view, in which "the outward appearance of every object I make is the equivalent of some aspect of inner human life" (*Beuys,* 70). An important feature of these "representations" is the simplicity of the items involved: "Another decisive Fluxus element was 'the lightness and mobility of the material.' The Fluxus artists were fascinated by the opening up of the simplest materials to the total contents of the world. *Beuys:* 'Everything from the simplest tearing of a piece of paper to the total changeover of human society could be illustrated'" (Adriani, Konnertz, and Thomas, 79).

There is a continual interaction and overlapping in his works between the two domains of images (biographical and archetypal), each one used in turn to guide the research of the other. Beuys has remarked how vividly he remembers certain parts of his childhood. But he explores these memories not to recover the past but (as in the case of shamanism) in order to think with them into the future. *Tram Stop,* for example, a work reconstructing parts of the place at which the five-year-old Beuys would get on and off the tram, is described as "not so much a recollection of childhood as the carrying out of a childhood intuition" (*Beuys,* 242). Here is a description of the work (originally installed at the Venice Biennale, 1976—hence the references to the lagoon):

> The monument itself rises vertically from the ground. Round the
> upright barrel of a field cannon are clustered four primitive seven-
> teenth-century mortar bombs, their tops, like the cannon barrel, cast
> and transformed in proportion and surface from the original mon-
> ument in Cleves [Beuys's hometown]. Above the cannon, emerging
> from it, is the head of a man, modelled by Beuys in 1961 with
> *Tram stop* in mind. . . . Past the monument runs a tramline, a hori-

zontal element along the earth's surface that bends slightly and curves gently, coming up from below the surface and running down into it again. If it were extended, this curve would reach far into the Venetian lagoon. . . . On another radial axis is a bored hole, sunk down to the water of the lagoon below, and then on, 25 metres deep in all, so that it becomes an iron tube full of cold water. (*Beuys*, 242)

"Why should a head emerge from a cannon?" Tisdall asks. Beuys's intention, she says, has to do with "the war of ideas" going on in his head. But we can also see it as a version of a shamanistic motif—the suffering associated with the initiation: "First they put the shaman's head on a pole," according to one version of the myth, "Then they scatter the hacked-up flesh in all directions like an offering" (Lommel, 55). To anticipate the later reading, we can note as well the grammatological echoes in such a work. The Venetian lagoon parallels Derrida's example of the homophonic shuttle (in *Glas*) passing between *lagune* and *langue* (tongue, language), and the tram line connotes the transportation devices signified by "metaphor" as a term meaning "bus" or "vehicle." That this rhetorical dimension is systematically available in Beuys's objects and actions will be demonstrated in a later section.

SCULPTURE

The term *Plastik* (sculpture, plastic arts) functions in Beuys's program in the same way as *écriture* (writing) in grammatology. Just as Derrida went to the most fundamental level of writing—the *gramme,* the articulation of differance—in order to formulate a principle of general writing (an expansion of the term "writing" to include every manner of inscription, of coming into appearance as such), so too does Beuys turn to the most fundamental level of sculpture in order to produce a theory of creativity which cuts across all divisions of knowledge and addresses the question of human productivity as such. The pressure Beuys places on such terms as "sculpture," "science," and "art" parallels Derrida's deconstructive paleonymics—the science of old names in which the old term is retained while being extended almost catachrestically to cover a new semantic field: "All these actions were important to enlarge the old concept of Art making it as broad and large as possible. According to possibility, making it as large as to include every human activity. . . . On the other hand, this again demands that the concept of Science has achieved this expansion itself."[21]

Working in terms of their respective points of departure—theory of language and the art of sculpture—Derrida and Beuys each formulated the highest generalization yet produced to account for human creativity, which may be seen as the equivalents in cultural studies of Einstein's formula in the physical sciences (they function at the same level of generalization). Whereas Derrida's generalization is expressed in a set of terms, a semantic field including the series associated with differance (*trace, écart, gramme,* and so forth), Beuys's "formula" is presented as a sculpture—actually a word-thing, since the work consists of both an object and a discourse. This work, or genre of works (Beuys started producing it in a variety of forms around 1964), entitled *Fat Corner,* exemplifies the importance of Beuys for an applied grammatology. The lesson in Beuys's practice concerns the relation between ideas and objects, demonstrating the word-thing structure fundamental to a picto-ideo-phonographic Writing. Derrida's theories and texts (as I argued in part I) call for a new writing beyond the book in which models, in the form of objects and actions, supplement verbal discourse. The task of applied grammatology is to introduce this Writing into the classroom (and eventually into research communication in the form of video tapes). The relation of ideas to objects in Beuys's practice contributes at least one version of how the pedagogical process might be reorganized. In this section, then, I will discuss *Fat Corner* and Beuys's general sculpture (*Plastik*), focusing on his own account of how this work functions as well as noting its interlacing with Derrida's texts.

Fat Corner is not a unique work (indeed, anyone can make one) but describes an element (unit, situation, process) that Beuys has presented by itself or as part of other Actions or Environments and that he considers to be the fundamental embodiment of his principle of creativity. The title (*Fettecke*) is descriptive: the work consists of a quantity of fat (usually margarine, but a variety of other kinds of fat have been used) packed into the corner of a room to form a mass in the shape of an equilateral pyramid (the point is in the corner; only the base is visible)—the sculptural equivalent (for my purposes) of the A of differance. The material is left to putrefy, to spread and absorb whatever is in the air, and to be absorbed in turn by the walls and floor—the figure of decompositional disgust, the *vomi.* The elements of the piece are the fat; the action of putting the fat into the corner; the corner itself, a geometric form; time and the process of putrefaction; and the viewer's response.

Fat Corner is not an "aesthetic" object nor an "art" object, in the traditional sense. Beuys did not come to art by the usual route of craft or skill at producing "beautiful" objects, but because of "epistemological considerations": "It seemed to me very important to work within art with concepts [*Begriffen*]. . . . I saw here an opportunity to achieve something conceptual working with other people which would have as much importance for the understanding of art as of science."[22] What he has in mind, he says, is the convergence of "art and life, science and art," at the fundamental level of human creativity. As a kind of "conceptual art," then, his objects are offered as signifiers in a writing which joins together material and thought.

Derrida's homophonic principle permits me to approach Beuys's "rituals" or "rites" (as his Actions are sometimes described) as *writing* (the colossal homonym is the shift from noun to verb). Beuys (w)rites. Operating as a double inscription, an object-action such as *Fat Corner* Writes at two levels —one motivated, the other arbitrary (extending to the register of the unconscious the old distinction between *Sinn* and *Bedeutung,* sense and meaning). At the motivated level, the point of departure for Beuys's Actions is always selected from something available in the material itself, or in the location where the Action takes place (the coyote is used in America, instead of the hare; in Chicago an event is based on an identification with Dillinger).

Thus, Beuys interrogates materials the way Derrida interrogates terminology (as in the exploration, in *Glas,* of the "flowers of rhetoric"). His intention in this interrogation ("What is *Plastik?* I have attempted to crack open this concept in its first principles")[23] parallels Derrida's solicitation of the philosophemes of metaphysics. The examination of fat and felt—his two primary materials—exemplifies the motivated relationship between his theoretical discourse and his objects:

> This Theory of Sculpture describes the passage of everything in the world, physical or psychological, from a chaotic, undetermined state to a determined or ordered state. *Chaotic* is the state of raw material and unchannelled will power, characterized as WARM. *Ordered* is the state of material that has been processed or formed, symbolized by the heart sign of movement at the center. Here it acquires form and definition and appears in a crystalline state, represented in the diagram by a tetrahedron and characterized as COLD and INTELLEC-TUAL. If the process goes too far the crystal becomes a burnt-up, over-intellectualized "clinker," and falls out of the system. . . . Ideally a balance should be achieved, though the overriding tendency today is towards the intellectual pole. Balance, reintegration and flexible flow between the areas of thinking, feeling and will, all of which are essential, are the objective of the Theory. (*Beuys,* 72)

As Tisdall explains, *Fat Corner* is an excellent demonstration of the theory, since its elements manifest the qualities of the ideas. "Fat can exist as a physical example of both extremes, as a chaotic, formless and flowing liquid when warm, and as a defined and ordered solid when cold; a paradox that is compounded when it is placed in that most ordered of forms, a right-angled corner or wedge. . . . The corner symbolizes the most mechanistic tendency of the human mind, the cornerstone of our present society, as manifested in our square rooms, square buildings and square cities, all built on combinations of the right angle" (72). In one of his many expositions of this theory and its relation to his materials, Beuys states: "This is my sculptural theory, theory in quotation marks, since I believe that it is hardly a theory, but a reality [*Wirklichkeit*]. I am not a theorist, but I research a reality. Essentially I mean that what I do exceeds theory and is a search simply for the actual Gestalt of things." [24]

The reality or Gestalt of fat (and felt) which Beuys uses to make a theoretical statement has to do with its morphological properties: "Actually two elements, fat and felt, are closely related. Both have a homogeneous character in that they have no inner structure. Felt is a material pressed together, an amorphous material, with an uneven structure. The same is true of the nature of fat, and that interested me." [25] He does not simply remain at the level of biographical motivation—the association of fat and felt with his war trauma—but interrogates the materials in turn to discover their "own" properties, the natural motivation that would accompany their presence in a work:

> There is on the one hand a "chaotic, flowing" process of retaining heat which, as the source of "spiritual warmth," is provided with an inexhaustible source of energy. It is found in heat sensitive materials such as wax and fat, whose unformed state can be described as absolutely amorphous. On the other hand are the crystallized final forms existing in a geometrical context which are taken from the many materials during the conversion of the fluid or warm steam state into the cold, hardened state. . . . With the aid of such materials [wax and fat] it is possible to analyze this process of movement under the simplest conditions, from the organic-embryonic prototype to the orderly, crystallized systems and from the shapeless mass of fat to corners of fat, which provide a base model. (Adriani, Konnertz, and Thomas, 39–41)

The process of hardening or shaping these amorphous materials into forms (fat into corners, a suit made of felt) manifests the forming, creative activity as such. Describing this process in *Fat Corner,* Beuys declares: "The fat goes through exactly this process in my Actions. Here is warmth (left), and here is cold (right). I could say, that is a general score [*Partitur*] for almost all the Actions I have done" (Rappmann, Schata, and Harlan, 22). It is the score not only for his own works but for human creativity in general.

The first element of sculpture as writing, then, is the motivated quality of the materials as signifiers, similar to Derrida's deconstruction of the figurative-proper opposition by elaborating the literal sense of metaphor: "The art objects do not demonstrate ideas, they are embodied ideas— (there lies the metaphor)." [26] And Beuys is not at all reluctant to state specifically what he intends the objects to mean, what concepts he wants attached to the Actions. At the same time, and this point brings us to the second element of sculpture as Writing, the objects function mnemonically, with a certain arbitrariness and a certain independence from the concepts. The word-thing, that is, writes a double inscription. "Had I expressed all this in recognizably logical statements, in a book, for example, it would not have been successful, because modern man is inclined only to satisfy his intellect and to understand everything according to the laws of logic" (Adriani, Konnertz, and Thomas, 72). The first step, then, is to get the interest or attention of the audience with a memorable image—something that provokes and that persists in the memory. "If you want to explain yourself you must present something tangible," Beuys says, discussing the didactic character of his work. One of the difficulties of his work is that it "is permeated with thoughts that do not originate in the official development of art but in scientific concepts" (Sharp, 47). And his Actions and objects are models of his working through these concepts: "One is forced to translate thought into action and action into object. The physicist can think about the theory of atoms or about physical theory in general. But to advance his theories he has to build models, tangible systems. He too has to transfer his thought into action, and the action into an object. I am not a teacher who tells his students only to think. I say act; do something; I ask for a result" (47).

For Beuys, then, "the formation of the thought is already sculpture" (Sharp, 47). And the models he builds and performs exemplify the picto-ideo-phonographic Writing sought by an applied grammatology. His comparison of his models (a term he frequently uses to describe his Action-objects) with those used in scientific instruction suggests that there is as useful a role for "apparatus" and "laboratory demonstrations" in the humanities as in the sciences. The difference is that Beuys is deconstructing the scientific (positivist) attitude toward knowing and learning. That Beuys is engaged in a mode of Writing may be seen in his description of himself and his works as "transmitters": "I want the work to become an energy center, like an atomic station. It's the same principle again: transmitter and receiver. The receiver is the same as the transmitter. . . . The spectator becomes the program" (44). Indeed, the best way to appreciate the specific nature of this Writing (rite-ing) is not as art, science, or philosophy, but as pedagogy: "To be a teacher is my greatest work of art. The rest is the waste product, a demonstration. If you want to explain yourself you must present something tangible. But after a while this has only the function of a historic document. Objects aren't very important for me anymore. I want to get to the origin of matter, to the thought behind it. Thought, speech, communication—and not only in the socialist sense of the word—are all expressions of the free human being" (44).

The statement "To be a teacher is my greatest work of art" is the "holo-phrase" of this chapter. The task, however, is to determine *how* Beuys teaches. The first thing to be stressed is that all the elements of the new pedagogy are present in his work, including speech, or discourse, which is put in its place in relation to models and mimes, objects and actions. One of Beuys's principal concerns is the coordination of these elements (exemplifying the readjustment needed in our thinking in general, similar to Derrida's reversal of the logocentric trajectory of phoneticization). "It is a question of selection. In which sphere and in which sector can I reach something with these media, in which domain can I bring about something with each medium. Sometimes, I can do something with a complete, determinate combination, for example object and action or action and discourse, or only with speech or only thought or only writing or only drawing and so forth" (Herzogenrath, 33).

It may be worth emphasizing that discourse is an important part of Beuys's performances, just as it was necessary to stress the importance of images and models in Derrida's Writing—their productions are converging on the same hybrid mode. The art historians will never record the many questions posed after his Actions, Beuys complains, even though these are an important part of the total work (Vadel, 16). "Beuys's 'actions' have always been followed by exhaustive discussions to help his audience conceptualize what they had just seen. . . . The difference between open signs and normative language reflects the difference between art and science. Beuys attempts to move forward on both levels at once" (Simmen, 89). The discussion following the performances, whether led by Beuys himself or whether taking place among the spectators, is a direct part of the production (at times it even becomes nearly the whole production, as in "Honey pump," *Documenta 6* in Kassel, in which Beuys managed an information booth and organized discussion workshops throughout the one hundred days of the exhibit), manifesting the status of his Actions as "learning pieces."

In addition, as noted earlier, Beuys considers speech to be a kind of material in which to sculpt: "The speech especially is totally plastic because it already has movement. What the mouth does with speech, the blubber it releases, these are also real sculptures, although they can't physically be seen, the air is worked on, the larynx is worked on, the inside of the mouth articulates, the bite, the teeth, etc."[27] Beuys shares Derrida's interest (elaborated in *Glas*) in the "articulators," the physiology of speech, the mouth-ear circuit as the vehicle of a certain metaphorics. The interaction of discourse and objects (the speech-writing relation, unified within a larger frame in both *écriture* and *Plastik*) in Beuys's Actions makes his rite-ings an exploration of the origins of writing.

My point for now is that there is no need to translate what Beuys is doing from art into pedagogy, since he is already engaging in pedagogy. He is already performing the pedagogical implications of his art, just as Lacan, in his seminars, displayed the conversion of psychoanalysis into pedagogy. The lesson for an applied grammatology in these two presentations lies not in the art or the psychoanalysis but precisely in the pedagogy made available in each case—by the encounter of art and psychoanalysis with an educative purpose. In mentioning these two pedagogies together, we have touched on the nexus of grammatological teaching, having to do with the "psychoanalytic graphology" Derrida described as being part of a future grammatology: "Here, Melanie Klein perhaps opens the way. As concerns the forms of signs, even within phonetic writing, the cathexes of gestures, and of movements, of letters, lines, points, the elements of the writing apparatus (instrument, surface, substance, etc.), a text like *The Role of the School in the Libidinal Development of the Child* (1923) indicates the direction to be taken" (*Writing,* 231).

Beuys's inclusion and cathecting of the fundamental apparatuses of the school in his Actions—blackboards, chalk, erasers, desks, pointers, lectures—provide the best example available of how such a "graphology" (concerned directly with the unconscious investment in, the symbolic significance of, common schoolroom objects and actions) might become part of a pedagogy. Erasers, for example, being made of felt, carry all the associations related to this primary material in Beuys's system: "Felt as an *insulator,* as a *protective covering* against other influences, or conversely as a material that permits *infiltration* from outside influences. Then there is the *warmth* character, the greyness which serves to emphasize the colours that exist in the world by a psychological after-image effect, and the *silence* as every sound is absorbed and muffled" (*Beuys,* 120). In relation to fat, felt (as insulator) has the "analytical" function of separating each stage of the creative process (as embodied in *Fat Corner*) from the others—the principles of chaos, movement, and form.[28]

Blackboards, as Tisdall notes, have been part of Beuys's Actions from the beginning and have played an ever-increasing role (the Environment *Directional Forces* consisted of one hundred blackboards covered with drawings and notes produced during a month of lectures). In "Celtic" (an interpretation of the Celtic oral tradition), "Beuys made and erased a series of drawings on a single board, manoeuvring it with a shepherd's crook and holding it aloft as if it were a highly charged piece of equipment" (*Beuys,* 204). It is not just that the familiar or banal objects (whether from the classroom or other areas of life) are charged with significance by becoming part of an art Action but that they *already* carry charges of energy—a feature he expresses sometimes by including actual batteries and other electrical apparatuses in his works. The energy that interests him, of course, is psychological, spiritual, libidinal. Thus, when we are told that Beuys seeks to change the very concept of "object" (Romain and Wedewer, 76), we may assume that what is involved is this notion of the object as "energy field" or "transmitter": "The object is intended as a transmitter radiating ideas from a deep background in time through an accretion of layers of meaning and biography, functioning like a Faraday cage in which the power is retained through a kind of grid. The object transmits while the text demonstrates" (*Beuys*, 26). A part of this economy of the object as a "battery of ideas" essential to an understanding of Beuys's pedagogy has to do with the effect of such objects. How do they transmit? Although commentators have noticed a progression in Beuys's *oeuvre* from drawings to objects through Actions to speech, Beuys himself denies that his work has become too verbal: "Verbalisation has certainly acquired another character in it, and so too have other more physically realised environments, objects, sculptures, drawings, etc. But the object *Directional Forces* for example, grew in fact out of thinking and speaking. But then it led in my opinion to a more vital image."[29] The generation of the image as model is the same effect sought by Derrida.

MNEMONICS

Grammatology accounts for the functioning of Beuys's objects in terms of the scene of Writing. Beuys and Derrida, that is, are in agreement about the communication process, working with the principle that a letter does *not* always reach its destination, or that the letter's destination is not determined by the old notions of identity. Their methods of W-rite-ing are based on assumptions not only about how "ideas" are generated but (and here is a crucial lesson for the new pedagogy) on how ideas are communicated, or rather, disseminated. *Fat Corner*—the gradual staining and spreading of the fat as it is absorbed by the walls and floor (the fat in the corner being the equivalent of the *gl* in *Glas,* the hard and the soft, the fat as the flux of agglutinative processes)—is an image for Beuys of the spread of ideas, a version of dissemination. "The process of infiltration takes place as the filtered stain spreads slowly outwards with time. . . . the spreading of ideas to the different forcefields of human ability, a kind of inspiration that takes effect through a physical process of capillary absorption: psychological infiltration, or even the infiltration of institutions. . . . The smell of course permeates everything" (*Beuys,* 148). *Fat Corner,* in short, is the perfect embodiment of Derrida's new philosopheme based on the contact or subjective sense of smell and taste which is the justification for writing as decomposition. In this context it also becomes clear that felt— amorphous, made of compressed hair, shaped by stretching and pulling—is a better model for the contact philosopheme than is the textile (weaving) of textuality used throughout *Glas,* suggesting the hand-eye relation of touch and *Begriff.* Infiltration de-monstrates the principle of communication by *contamination,* the permeability of boundaries as membranes, which is one of Derrida's principal concerns.

The question for pedagogy is not Who speaks? but Who receives?—the reading or listening or spectating effect, in response to the *double inscription* of Writing. "I am aware," Beuys says, "that my art cannot be understood primarily by thinking. My art touches people who are in tune with my mode of thinking. But it is clear that people cannot understand my art by intellectual processes alone, because no art can be experienced in this way. I say to experience, because this is not equivalent to thinking: it's a great deal more complex; it involves being moved subconsciously. Either they say, 'yes, I'm interested,' or they react angrily and destroy my work and curse it. In any event I feel I am successful, because people have been affected by my art" (Sharp, 45).

Derrida speaks of the receivability of his work—specifically as thematized in *Glas*—in similar terms. Like Beuys, Derrida believes that the unreceivability of a provoking work is itself an effective mode of reception. The provoking, unreceivable work forces the various "Anonymous Societies of Limited Responsibility" (*SARL*) to reveal themselves, to expose their systems of exclusion: "For the unanimity [of a faction] already *feels* what it vomits, that from which it guards itself, it likes it in its own way, and the unreceivable is received." What he was seeking in *Glas,* Derrida explains, is the totally *unanticipated* reading—to write precisely at the point where all calculation of effects is lost: "What happens '*all unknowingly*' is always the most, let us say, marking, the most effective. And then that does not return to the presumed 'father' of the text, which is the real effect, the only effective one, of a dissemination."[30] Perceptible and acknowledged debts and connections, those that are recognized as such, Derrida argues, are the most superficial, the least transformative. "If the history of the analysis of 'reading effects' remains always so difficult, it is because the most effective pass through assimilations or rejections which I call by analogy 'primary,' the most 'unconscious.' And by rejection (for example the internal vomiting, incorporative) still more than by assimilation" ("Faux-bond," 95). The project of the double inscription, acting on this reception theory common to Derrida, Lacan, and Beuys, is to work directly at the primary, affective level of effect.

How the scene of Writing is received is, of course, a major topic in *The Post Card,* with perhaps its best definition being given in the "appended" article "Telepathy," in which Derrida compares the way the unconscious filters and selects what it receives with the way some member of the public will decide to respond personally (by return mail) to an open letter written by a newspaper columnist (this quotidian journalistic event serves as a model for the functioning of "unconscious" communication). Such a communication does not take place between two identifiable subjects:

No, of a letter which after the fact seems to have been sent towards
some unknown recipient at the moment of its writing, recipient
unknown to him or her self if one might say so, and who determines
himself upon the reception of the letter; this is then completely
different from the transfer of a message. Here, you identify yourself
and engage your life on the letter as program, or rather to a post
card, an open letter, divisible, at once transparent and ciphered. The
program says nothing, it announces or utters nothing, not the least
content. . . . In short, you say "that's me" by a sweet and terrible decision, quite different: nothing to do with the identification with
the hero of a novel. ("Télépathie," 8)

The nature of the relation between Derrida and Beuys—between theoretical and applied grammatology—is clearly evident in their respective uses
of the post card, which Derrida evokes as a theoretical model in a text, but
which Beuys literally produces as object. Indeed, one of Beuys's more
common "multiples" (simple, inexpensive, usually quotidian objects—
often ready-mades or modified ready-mades—produced in bulk for large
distribution) is the post card, signifying, in addition to its scene or message
(printed recto and verso), the phenomenon of "transmitting" as such.
Some of the cards include, for example, simple phrases such as "give me
honey," "honey is flowing," "let the flowers speak," or "name equals
address"; some simply bear his signature or one of his signet stamps. There
are cards with scenes from various Actions, pictures of Beuys himself,
scenes from cities he has visited. He has made cards from wood and from
magnetized metal; all the cards are reproduced in large editions.

The effect of the multiples, as Beuys understands it, characterizes the
reception of the scene of W-rite-ing as mnemonics. The object or image
has at one level a vehicular function—attached, even if arbitrarily, to an
idea (like the "active agents" in the old mnemonic systems), it is meant to
serve as a reminder: "The whole thing is a game, one which, with the help
of this kind of information, counts on casting the anchor of a vehicle somewhere close by, so that people can later think back on it. It's a sort of prop
for the memory, yes, a sort of prop in case something different happens in
the future. For me, each edition has the character of a kernel of condensation upon which many things may accumulate. . . . It's like an antenna
which is standing somewhere and with which one stays in touch" (Schellmann and Klüser, 1).

Beuys considers his editions to be a more effective means of spreading
ideas than writing (in the traditional sense) would be, because, in addition
to the superficial or even arbitrary connection between the vehicle and the
idea, the object works at the primary register as well, in a way that is discontinuous with any intention, beyond the reach of any possible calculation of effect. At this level the effect that Derrida tries to achieve by means

of "anasemia" comes into play, described by the third meaning of "sense" —neither "the sense" nor "meaning," but "direction" (sens): "if one has a relationship to this, one can really only have it, not based on a rational, analytical understanding, but because one has experienced something of the right direction, the direction in which the vehicles are standing, simply standing somewhere" (Schellmann and Klüser, 5).

At this primary level, the object functions according to the principle Derrida described as being at work in Mallarmé's Mime, which retained the structure of mimesis but without representing anything. In Beuys's case, the objects produce the effect of reference, but without referring to anything. Or rather, the reference is now supplied by the recipient, who in response to the stimulus produces it out of himself, like the recipient of the open letter in the newspaper who decides "that's me" and writes a reply to the journalist. "Where objects are concerned it's more the sense of an indication or suggestion. . . . But the multiples are often quite minimal allusions, just suggestions. I actually find interpretations of them harmful. You can describe a thing, say something about the intentions, and that's how to get close to the power that leaves something in the things so that they can have some effect. There is a 'more' in them that means they appeal to more than understanding" (Schellmann and Klüser, 14-15). The more is the plus of surplus value which Derrida explores in metaphor. The description of his works as referring without reference has been applied not only to Beuys's multiples but to his Action-Environments as well, such as Tram Stop, about which one commentator said: "That all leaves very distinct traces [Spüren] which are only the perceptible edges of something other: the whole work and the whole action have only the character of a hint" (Krupka, 49).

In terms of the double inscription, then, Beuys's objects are both what they are (their qualities motivate the concept attached to them) and stimulation for the general processes of memory and imagination. At the primary level, the object does not "transfer a message" but moves the spectator— remaining open in its reference, the object evokes associated memories that are motivated less by the qualities of the object than by the subject of reception: the theme of a work like Fat Corner, Romain and Wedewer argue, is not immanent in the material and is not accessible by means of interpretation but only through its appeal to the observer's associative memory. "If one wants to characterize the Beuysian object, the fat works being representative of the whole, with a term, one can best designate them by the attribute appellativ. That means, these works do not stand for something, they rather produce representations of things, feelings, relationships—or release, arouse, trigger them—and their admissibility depends not on a precise designation, but if they actually make possible the arousal in one of the general adequate idea of representation" (27-28).

It is worth reviewing several other accounts of the evocative function of the Beuysian object, *since it is precisely this primary effect that applied grammatology intends to add to pedagogical communication.* This primary effect, moreover, is what Derrida models in all his undecidable object-images of things which are at once open and closed—umbrellas, matchboxes, shoelaces (tied and untied), post cards. The apotropaic dimension of the object-image is a principal aspect of Beuys's works. Peter Handke's assessment of the effect on himself of seeing one of Beuys's performances reveals an important feature of their mnemonic character: "It must be made clear: the more distant and hermetic the results performed on the stage, the clearer and more reasonable [*sic*] can the spectator concretize this abstract in his own outside situation. . . . In memory it appears as one burned in their own life, an image, which in its nostalgic effects and the will to work on such images in oneself [*sic*]: then only as after image does it begin to work on oneself. And an excited peace overcomes one, when one thinks: it activates one, it is so painfully pretty, that it is utopic and that means: becomes political" (Adriani, Konnertz, and Thomas, 194–95).

Beuys's object-actions, that is, are expressly intended to function by means of an aftereffect, working thus directly with the "time of understanding," the way the Impressionists, for example, worked with the effects of space and light—one has to experience Beuys's works from the proper distance in time, as integrated by the operation of memory, just as one has to be at the right spatial distance from an Impressionist painting to allow the eye to integrate the colors properly. Indeed, Romain and Wedewer declare that Beuys does for the intuitive memory what the Op Artists did for optical perception—each working with the object in relation to its reception (69–70)—a comparison similar to my own discussion of Derrida's Op Writing.

Handke, it is important to add, was not particularly impressed at the time of the performance (he is discussing the Action *Iphegenie/Titus Andronicus*) which did not seem to him to be at all adequate to what its title promised (an abject performance, without pretending anything more than the simulacrum of reference). The powerful impact of the aftereffect, then, was all the more evocative, a response that others have recorded with respect to other works:

As always in Beuys's work, the logic of a distillation process interacts with the associations of the few objects and materials that
are used: the particular situation is directed at a generalized effect.
The tangibly itemized cycle as a symbolic parallel with life does
not strike the viewer through his recognition of each single item and
the subsequent perception of the whole as a shocking process. . . .
What hits home is the after-effect of the transformed objects which
completes the field of association. This potential psychic intensity

is thus achieved through the multiplication of several connections which create tensions between the individual effects of each object and their various different extended meanings. This intensity, which can register as a long-lasting shock in the mind of the confronted viewer, is certainly the most essential characteristic of Beuys's sculpture. (*Beuys*, 215–16)

Fat Corner, the score for all Beuys's Action-objects, is not only memorable *but also a model of memory*—of the psyche itself—and as such it is the equivalent of Freud's "Mystic Writing-Pad." It manifests the point that Beuys's works, in addition to being stimuli for thoughts, are the very image of thinking. Thinking for Beuys, in any case, is a kind of sculpture, to the extent that the ultimate signified, the connotation, of all his work is thinking, or human creativity, as such. "Thus the fat displaces itself from a very chaotic condition in a movement terminating in a geometric context. . . . It was power in a chaotic condition, in a condition of movement and in a condition of form. And these three elements—form, movement, and chaos —were the undetermined energy from which I drew my complete theory of sculpture, of human psychology as power of will, power of thought and power of feeling; and I found that it was a schema for understanding all the problems of society" (Vandel, 17).

As we saw in Freud's discussion of the ancient analogy comparing memory to wax, Beuys's use of fat, tallow, and wax (including beeswax) enables him to treat at the concrete level, symbolically, the same matters Freud and Derrida address textually. And before too hastily concluding that the formal structure of *Fat Corner* is not sufficiently complex to deal with the conceptual range Beuys claims for it, we should note that Michel Serres, discussing the philosophy of science, adopts exactly the same image—wax and its modification by heat into three possible conditions (liquid, solid, and the movement between)—as model for organizing the three dominant phases of modern Western epistemology: Cartesian, Bachelardian, and the present (Serresian?). "Communications carry information and engrave it in solids which conserve it. Three states: movement, propagation, communication; three states: figures, fluids, solids. The third state, solid, communication or information, could be called equally structure-application" (*L'interférence*, 91).

The sciences providing the analogies guiding each of these paradigms are, respectively, geometry (Cartesian), physics (Bachelardian), and biology. The current episteme, according to Serres, is characterized by the wax in its hardened (crystalline) state (Beuys's image of the potentially overintellectualized condition of modern thought) because of the capacity of hardened wax to record and preserve traces of information (like the Mystic Pad). Discussing the need to write a new, contemporary epistemology that brings together history and science, Serres states:

In effect, history, as such, implies an epistemological recurrence perfectly analogous to scientific recurrences: it furnishes the energy necessary to reanimate the dead information residing among the solid mnemonic stocks. At the same time, it [the non-Bachelardian epistemology] discovers, first, the fundamental mode of existence of objects: the demy of paper, the metamorphic rock, the piece of wax, some embryonic tissues, some cut stone, all supports of forms to read, all historical objects. . . . The god of the new Pantheon is universal scribe and reader: there is a code of all communication, it ciphers and deciphers all cryptograms. (*L'interférence*, 125)

My point, however, is not to give an exposition of Serres's model, whose correspondence with grammatology I noted previously in any case, but only to note that Serres's use of the image of wax in this comprehensive context supports the generalizing power of Beuys's *Plastik*. As for the direct relation with grammatology, it may be apparent that *Fat Corner* embodies the dynamics of force and form that Derrida discusses in "Force and Signification." The fat in the corner presents the opposition Derrida lists as "duration to space, quality to quantity, force to form, the depth of meaning or value to the surface of figures" (*Writing*, 19). Derrida's purpose is to deconstruct this opposition, his problem being that, working within language even while trying to expose what lies outside language, giving it its shape, he is restricted to the metaphorics of structure. What criticism should be able to treat—"that which engenders in general is precisely that which resists geometrical metaphorization"—is reduced to the "inessential," only a "sketch or debris." "*Form* fascinates when one no longer has the force to understand force from within itself. That is, to create" (4). In this early essay Derrida can but state the *other* of structure, which we have noted elsewhere with the terms *apeiron* and *Moira:* "To grasp the operation of creative imagination at the greatest possible proximity to it, one must turn oneself toward the invisible interior of poetic freedom. . . . They can only indicate it through a metaphor [of "separation" and "exile"] whose genealogy itself would deserve all of our efforts. . . . This universe articulates only that which is in excess of everything, the essential nothing on whose basis everything can appear and be produced within language" (8). Deconstruction is an attempt to harness this creative force: "a certain *strategic* arrangement which, within the field of metaphysical opposition, uses the strengths of the field to turn its own stratagems against it, producing a force of dislocation"—a force "which is pure qualitative heterogeneity within movement" (20, 21).

Beuys, however, not restricted to texts and language, *is* able to provide an image of force, which, along with "energetics," is one of the chief descriptors of the fat in his Actions. Speaking of the revolution he wishes to carry out in the arts, Beuys says, of his Actions, "that all becomes included

in a fully new statement of movement. The Action is in and for itself
another word for the nature of movement. . . . So I ground the Action
character in my work: to find the beginning of movement in the world"
(Krupka, 41). In order to transform thought, and society with it, everything must be expressed, "even those things which still lie beyond language
as we know it—a new substance that is both evolutionary and revolutionary" (*Beuys,* 179). *Fat Corner* makes directly accessible in applied grammatology the processes of movement and energy—force—which could only
be articulated negatively in theoretical grammatology.

GRAMMATOLOGY

Having remarked in the previous sections Beuys's own account of his
work, as well as some of the ways he performs the scene of Writing, I
would like now to examine more systematically the grammatological character of the Actions—to review the Actions within the context provided in
part I of this book. I will take as my point of departure one Action—"How
to explain pictures to a dead hare"—which is often designated as typifying
Beuys's work. I will first describe the work, including Beuys's statements
about it, and then discuss it as a version of grammatology.

In the performance, on 26 November 1965—Beuys's first exhibition in
the art world context, Tisdall notes—"Beuys spent three hours explaining
his art to a dead hare. The gallery was closed to the public, and the performance (though recorded on television) was visible only from the door-
way and the street window" (*Beuys,* 101). "Beuys, whose head was covered
with honey and gold leaf, held a dead hare in his arms and carried it,
walking through the exhibition and talking to it, from picture to picture,
letting it touch the pictures with its paw. After the tour was finished he sat
down on a chair and began to thoroughly explain the pictures to the hare
'because I do not like to explain them to people'" (Adriani, Konnertz,
and Thomas, 130).

> In putting honey on my head I am clearly doing something that has
> to do with thinking. Human ability is not to produce honey, but to
> think, to produce ideas. In this way the deathlike character of thinking
> becomes lifelike again. For honey is undoubtedly a living substance.
> Human thinking can be lively too. But it can also be intellectualized to
> a deadly degree, and remain dead, and express its deadliness in, say,
> the political or pedagogic fields. Gold and honey indicate a transforma-
> tion of the head, and therefore, naturally and logically, the brain
> and our understanding of thought, consciousness and all the other
> levels necessary to explain pictures to a hare: the warm stool insulated
> with felt, the "radio" made of bone and electrical components

under the stool and the iron sole with the magnet. I had to walk on
this sole when I carried the hare round from picture to picture,
so along with a strange limp came the clank of iron on the hard stone
floor. (*Beuys*, 105)

The honey on the head is another manifestation of the idea of thinking
as a sculptural activity. The process of bees making honey (honey in the
geometric beehive) is a version of the same principle de-monstrated in *Fat
Corner* (Rappmann, Schata, and Harlan, 61). Not only the honey on the
head but the hare itself is a model of thinking: "The hare has a direct relation to birth. . . . For me the hare is a symbol of incarnation. The hare
does in reality what man can only do mentally: he digs himself in, he digs
a construction. He incarnates himself in the earth and that itself is important" (Adriani, Konnertz, and Thomas, 132). The hare burrowing into the
earth is an image of thinking—of man embodying his ideas in forms. The
Action as a whole is especially useful in our pedagogical context because,
as Beuys explains, it deals with "the difficulty of explaining things"

> particularly where art and creative work are concerned, or anything
> that involves a certain mystery or questioning. The idea of explaining
> to an animal conveys a sense of the secrecy of the world and of
> existence that appeals to the imagination. . . . The problem lies in
> the word "understanding" and its many levels which cannot be
> restricted to rational analysis. Imagination, inspiration, intuition and
> longing all lead people to sense that these other levels also play a
> part in understanding. This must be the root of reactions to this ac-
> tion, and is why my technique has been to try to seek out the
> energy points in the human power field, rather than demanding
> specific knowledge or reactions on the part of the public. I try
> to bring to light the complexity of creative areas. (*Beuys*, 105)

Beuys's own accounts of his intentions do in fact articulate the program
desired for applied grammatology. My purpose, then, is to show that one
reason why Beuys's practice is so relevant to this program is that the specific elements of grammatology as Derrida defines them are also available
in Beuys's work, although Beuys himself never makes them explicit. There
is no need, in other words, to impose the categories of grammatology on
Beuys but only to call attention to the manner in which Beuys employs
them.

My procedure here will be to treat Beuys's objects or "ciphers" the
same way Derrida treats vocabulary, that is, in terms of the entire semantic
field or symbolic topos that is evoked. The hare, for example, as Romain
and Wedewer remind us, means many different things in various world
mythologies and legends besides "incarnation" or "birth," any of which
may be brought into play in the reception effect when this animal is used
in an Action (31). The hare is perhaps Beuys's chief totem animal, em-

ployed in a variety of ways, including its literal presence, as in "How to explain pictures to a dead hare," or "Siberian Symphony" (which included a dead hare hanging on a blackboard), "The chief" (with two dead hares, one at either end of a large roll of felt in which Beuys was wrapped), "Eurasia" (in which Beuys maneuvered along a line a dead hare with its legs and ears extended by long, thin, black wooden sticks), and so forth; the hare is also included as an image sculpted in chocolate, gelatin, and other materials, or as a toy; it may be evoked as an image in titles, such as "Hare's grave" (actually a "genre" of works—boxes or reliquaries of detritus).

Of the several meanings of the hare available in mythology, the most significant one in our context, the one that reveals the convergence in grammatology of Derrida and Beuys, *is the hare as an embodiment of Thoth, the god of Writing:* "The divine hare was closely connected with the Egyptian god Thoth, the Greek god Hermes, and the Roman Mercury, all of whom were supposed to have similarly invented writing."[31]

It is of no less interest, perhaps, considering Derrida's concern with the function of the copula "to be" and its confusion with the ontological "being" (in "The Supplement of Copula," or "*Ousia* and *Grammē*," for example), that the hare was in ancient Egypt the hieroglyph for the auxiliary verb "to be." The scholars noted, of course, that the hare was used to represent the copula verb for phonetic reasons—the hare hieroglyph was used whenever the phonetic value *"un"* was needed, with "to be" being the only word in which this sound occurred alone. Since we are now taking up the *Moira,* or destiny, of this term in the context of Derrida's homophonic and macaronic methods, I might add that Derrida's deconstruction of the problem of the "first" (origins) or the "one"—*Un* in French —may be transducted into Beuys's manipulation of the hare, whose name as a deity is *Un* (Layard, 156). The legendary fertility of the rabbit also motivates the hieroglyph, as shown by research into the symbolic connection of the hare to the copula, which demonstrated that the hare sign signified "leaping" and "rising" and hence, according to the argument, "being." The Greek word for "I leap," moreover, means also "emit semen" and hence "beget" (Layard, 142–43, 151). Derrida, of course, does not take such etymologies at face value, but he does play with them in order to generate texts.[32]

The hare as Thoth indicates that the special importance of Beuys for applied grammatology is not only that his Actions demonstrate a picto-ideo-phonographic Writing but that they teach the theory of grammatology in a dramatic form ("theorter" or philosophical theater). More than just a translation of the theory of writing into a performance mode, the Actions show a way to work with the question of Writing nonconceptually (non-theoretically), in a "creative" rather than in an "analytic" mode. From this perspective, agreeing with Beuys's denial that his use of animals is "ata-vistic," we can see that his principal animal imagery connotes the meta-phorics of *inventio*. His performances, following the score of *Fat Corner* (itself an embodiment of the principle of creativity), are a manner of *doing* what he is saying—they literalize and enact the philosophemes of "invention" used in the rhetorical tradition (he generates "original" works of art by performing the rhetorical description of creativity, in works whose lesson is meant to be "everyone an artist").

The structuring principle of Beuys's Actions (the metaphors of *inventio*) relates to the chapter on Mnemonics (chapter 3), in that Beuys's imagery resonates with the images used in Medieval and Renaissance commonplace books to describe the operations of "invention." As the Book achieved dominance in education, replacing the oral tradition, the location of hypo-mnemics shifted from the mind (memory) to the pages of commonplace books, those encyclopedic compendia, organized by topic, collecting and classifying a great range of materials from every imaginable source and subject area (including, of course, the "flowers of rhetoric"—the jewels, stars, or ornaments constituting the best of "everything" that had been spoken or written). As Lechner explains, the commonplace books "were often called the artificial memory. The desire for possessing a kind of uni-versal knowledge led to the distrust of the 'natural' memory and the sup-plying of an auxiliary one" (147).

Derrida's interest in hypomnemics can be seen to include this rhetorical phase in the history of knowledge (leading up to Hegel's "Absolute Knowl-edge"), as discussed in terms of the "scene of teaching" in which, in gram-matology, "nothing takes place but the place itself" (understood now as the topics or places of invention). The crucial point of Lechner's study of the commonplaces for my purpose is her account of the metaphors tradi-tionally employed to describe the use of the commonplace book as arti-ficial memory (for the generation of a composition), that is, the metaphorics of the invention process, involving the gathering together of the material to be used in a presentation. Invention in the commonplace tradition was associated with movement about a field, locating ideas stored in "seats." Two metaphors were used pedagogically to teach this process (and were repeatedly alluded to wherever the tradition was influential): "The two images which recur most frequently in the rhetorical works for describing the invention and storing of material are the bee gathering nectar and the hunter pursuing game. Both images relate to wild life in nature, which sug-gests some kind of 'searching for' or hunt, and to human life, which implies industry of some sort. Here 'invention' is seen as a search which somehow 'covers ground' " (Lechner, 137).

It is no accident, considering Beuys as an applied grammatologist, that the two most predominant, consistent images in his Actions involve some aspect of bees making honey and the hunting of the hare (the example Lechner cites does, in fact, refer to the hare: "Those that bee good hare-finders will soone finde the hare by her fourme, for when thei see the ground beaten flatte around about, and faire to the sighte: thei have a nar-rowe gesse by al liklihode that the hare was there a litle before" [144]—the example serving to show the "relation between the mark or 'identity' of the locality and the game sought in the place"). Similarly, Seneca's image of the bee, Lechner says, was echoed by many Renaissance rhetoricians: "We should follow, men say, the example of the bees, who flit about and cull the flowers that are suitable for producing honey, and then arrange and assort in their cells all that they have brought in" (138).

In this context we are reminded that Derrida's entire discussion of the flowers of rhetoric in the Genet (*genêt*) column of *Glas,* including his exposition of creating by means of dissemination (dehiscence), is a rhetoric of invention. One of Lechner's examples, taken from *Novum Organum* to show Bacon's application of the *inventio* metaphor, is especially rele-vant to Derrida (and Beuys): "Those who have handled science have been either men of experiment or men of dogmas. The men of experiment are like the ant; they only collect and use: the reasoners resemble spiders who make cobwebs out of their own substance. But the bee takes a middle course; it gathers its materials from the flowers of the garden and of the field, but transforms and digests it by a power of its own" (Lechner, 140).

Derrida, similarly, discussing the inside-outside problem in "Outwork," uses the spider metaphor, evoking specifically the one described in the *Songs of Maldoror:* " 'Every night, at the hour when sleep has reached its highest degree of intensity, an old spider of the large species slowly protrudes its head from a hole in the ground at one of the intersections of the angles of the room' " (*Dissemination,* 42)—the spider *is* the corner (rationality and form in Beuys). Derrida elaborates: "A spider emerging 'from the depths of its nest,' a headstrong dot that transcribes no dictated exclamation but rather intransitively performs its own writing." Lautré-amont's textuality as spider is beneficial transitionally in its break with the dogmas of naive realism. But Hegel's equally intransitive textuality reveals the negative limitations of this model, with the description of his method (in speculation "the conception of the concept is an autoinsemination") calling to mind the spider invoked a few pages earlier, spinning its web out of itself: "It [philosophy] must therefore produce, out of its own interior-ity, both its object and its method" (47). That Derrida is concerned with the problematic defined in Bacon's metaphor may be inferred from the etymological associations he provides for "hymen." Within the various *hymenologies,* or treatises on membranes, one finds all three of Bacon's *inventio* models—*hymenoptera* include winged insects, ants as well as bees and wasps; *huphos* includes spider webs, and so forth (213). Where Derrida's sympathies lie, however, must be surmised by the process of elimination.

From his earliest drawings and sculptures, such as *Queen Bee* (1947— but there are many works with this title), through "How to explain pictures to a dead hare," to "Honey pump" (the huge pump, made with ships' engines to circulate two tons of honey, which accompanied the information room at *Documenta 6*), Beuys has drawn upon the bee and its activities as one of his central images:

> The heat organism of the bee colony is without a doubt the essential element of connection between the wax and fat and the bees. What had interested me about bees, or rather about their life systems, is the total heat organization of such an organism and the sculpturally finished forms within this organization. On one hand bees have this element of heat, which is a very strong fluid element, and on the other hand they produce crystalline sculptures; they make regular geometric forms. Here we already find something of sculptural theory, as we do in the corners of fat. (Adriani, Konnertz, and Thomas, 41)

His explicit interest extends to the symbolic significance of bees and honey, beyond his own theory of creativity: "This warmth character is to be found in honey, in wax, and even in the pollen and nectar gathered from plants. In mythology honey was regarded as a spiritual substance, and bees were godly. The bee cult is basically a Venus cult" (*Beuys*, 44).

The point, however, is that, whatever Beuys says about his frequent use of the bee or hare images, they may also be understood as references to the rhetorical theories of creativity and composition. Thus, his Actions fulfill the grammatological goal of a *Writing which does what it says*, showing how the root metaphors or philosophemes of Western thought might be interrogated and deconstructed at the applied level.

A further insight into Beuys's principal images of creative thought (keeping in mind that the beehive filled with honey is a version of fat in the corner) is made available in Derrida's notion of the signature (the contamination between life and art, the motivated relationship between the proper name and the work). The name "Beuys" ("speculation—on 'Beuys'"), that is, *signs* the metaphorics of *inventio* mounted in the Actions (both the hunting of the hare and the bee in its hive). Although antonomasia in Beuys's case only produces a near rhyme, the relevant term does designate the elements of *inventio*, revealing that Beuys's Actions are an enactment of his name. There are in fact two feminine nouns involved— homonyms (so that Beuys's signature itself includes Derrida's homophonic principle)—with the root being *Beut* (*die Beute*). One is a hunting term, meaning "quarry" or "game," illustrated by the phrase "the hunter pursues his quarry" or "to return with a good bag." The other *Beut* means "a wooden beehive," with the verb *beuten* meaning "to stock a hive with wild bees." In short, hunting (the hare, or the stag—another one of Beuys's totems) and bees, as terms and images, line up at three levels—in the *Beut* homonyms; in the *inventio* metaphors of the hypomnemic commonplace books; and as the organizing images in many of Beuys's Actions. The *Beut* is also in "Beuys." *Beute* is to "Beuys" what *genêt* is to Genet, *die Kante* to Kant, or *éponge* to Ponge—all are rebus signatures.

To appreciate the destiny of this signature effect, it is important to note that the *t* of *Beut is* present in the signature, in that Beuys sometimes signs his name with the tail of the *u* extended (to look like an upside-down *h*— the *h* being the letter signifying *Mensch* or *Human* in the formulas presented in the Action *"24 hours . . . and in us . . . under us . . . landunder"*), the tail of the *u* not only extended but crossed, thus adding a buried *t* to his name (recalling the transduction techniques of writing-drawing Derrida recommended in his discussion of Adami).

The cross, which appears in a variety of forms in his work, is itself one of Beuys's trademarks (he uses it in his rubber signature stamp "Fluxus Zone West"), suggesting an important convergence of his program with Derrida's use of the chiasmus (which Derrida himself associated with the red cross mark in Adami). Beuys's cross is meant to suggest many other crosses, the history of this sign in religion and politics, art and science (related as much to Mondrian's abstractions as to the cross hairs on a machine-gun). "Sometimes it [the cross] is a global symbol of the earth. Often it is the schematic representation of natural structure, as in the *Queen Bee.* When used as a Christian symbol it represents those aspects of noninstitutionalized Christianity which Beuys believes to have had a powerful effect on Western thinking" (*Beuys,* 108). But whatever its embodied form, the cross, as with Derrida's chiasmus, is finally the mark of a structuring or stricturing dynamics of creativity ("X: not an unknown but a chiasmus. A text that is unreadable because it is *only* readable"—*Dissemination,* 362). In a session recorded at *Documenta 5,* Beuys, drawing the cross, stated that it symbolized "a square into which one can introduce value"[33] (recalling the "square mouth" of enframing in *Dissemination*). Again, the cross marks human creative potential—"That means, as a plus. + that is a plus," signifying individual human freedom (Ritter, 72)—the cross as "plus" being associated with Derrida's compositional "+ L." By the sixties, then, the cross in Beuys's work had become "the general medium of marking: cross as crossing two lines, defining a point. It serves as the distinguishing mark of a place . . . for example the 'shooting post in the woods' (perhaps a stag memorial) . . . as shorthand for a compilation, cross-like, covering storehouses ('information theory')" (Krupka, 55). Whether chiasmus or cross, *x* or +, the dynamics of creativity in theoretical and applied grammatology alike involves the taking place of the place itself, teaching invention by displaying and deconstructing the metaphorics of creativity.

The grammatological import of the methodology explored in "How to explain pictures to a dead hare" is also apparent in the emphasis it gives to the *step* (the "strange limp and clank of iron on the stone floor"). Derrida has applied his special techniques to an interrogation of the steps or step (*pas*) as a methodological term ("step by step"), which is the "theoretical" version of Beuys's performance movements. "It is the unimaginable logic, unthinkable even, of the *pas au-delà* ["step beyond" or "no beyond"] which interests me" ("Faux-bond," 101). Derrida experiments with the step at two levels—as homonym and as "story." (1) The term *pas* exemplifies a colossal homonym, moving undecidably between noun and adverb, between *pas* as step and *pas* as negation (*ne pas*), summarized in the phrase *pas au-delà*. The phrase refers to his revised notion of speculation—his homophonic operation—which displaces all logic of denial and disavowal, all dialectical opposition, thus enabling him (in the service of *copia*) to proceed without taking a step: "The entire system of limits (faux pas) which prohibits putting one *pas* in the other finds itself surmounted in one single step (*pas*), without the step, the activity of walking, what one does with the legs, taking place. . . . The *pas de plus* ["no more" or "one more step"] works its homonym silently, surmounting the two senses, at one stroke, the two limits. Its transgression is not therefore a work or an activity, it is passive and transgresses nothing." Such is the step with which Blanchot proceeds ("Pas," 147, 152).

(2) The other level at which Derrida experiments with the step of method, in a way that more directly resembles Beuys's performance, involves a narrative dramatization of walking with a limp (the metaphorics of method). In "Envois," that is, "Derrida" falls and fractures his ankle, forcing him to walk with a limp and lean on a crutch or cane, so that the "story" repeats the methodological metaphors. The pun is still at work here as well, since "Envois" is preface to a study of the *"legs"*—legacy— of Freud. The scene of "Derrida" hobbling around with a cast and cane prepares the way for—or performs, mimes—the method to be followed in "Speculer—sur 'Freud,'" a piece that itself mimes Freud's own speculative method. Freud, both in his letters to Fliess and in *Beyond the Pleasure Principle,* refers to his speculative procedure as an impeded walk, using a phrase cited from another author: "What we cannot reach flying we must reach limping" (*Origins,* 130). We are reminded, of course, that Oedipus limped, as did all the males of his line (as Lévi-Strauss pointed out).

Derrida mimes this limp in his own essay, trying to capture just the right gait, since its effect, as exercised in *Beyond the Pleasure Principle,* is similar to that of the *pas sans pas* (step without a step) achieved by Blanchot—an interminable detour that transgresses passively (*Carte,* 287).

Reading *Beyond the Pleasure Principle* as a "discourse on method," Derrida finds that the pleasure of method is the repetitive return of the question—rhythm. "*Fort: da.* It is necessary that the most normal step allow disequilibrium, in itself, in order to carry on ahead, to be followed by another, the same again, but as another. It is necessary that the limp be above all the rhythm of walking, *unterwegs.* . . . If speculation remains necessarily unresolved because it plays on two *tableaux,* band against band, losing to win, winning to lose, how be surprised that it [*ça*] proceeds badly? But it has to advance badly in order for it to work. It rightly limps, isn't that so?" (433).

Noting that *Beyond the Pleasure Principle* ends with the citation about limping mentioned earlier, Derrida remarks that its last chapter, in view of its uselessness to the argument, is a kind of "club foot." Yet it is effective in its own way, because it manifests the methodological value of the prosthesis. Beuys also dramatizes this methodological step, with his canes and shepherd crooks (present in many drawings and Actions) standing for the prosthesis—for the simulacrum replacing the thesis in the deconstruction of dialectics (*Carte*, 414). Beuys refers explicitly to his legs in several Actions, partly with respect to the shuttle sewing them into his signature: in terms of the anagram with "bee" (*die Beine* = legs; *die Biene* = bee) and in terms of *die Beuge* (bend—*Kniebeuge* = kneebend). The following event from the Action "Eurasian staff" is relevant: "Beuys again went to the felt sole [on the floor] and this time placed his iron-soled foot over it at right angles. Then he put a lump of fat in the right angle behind his bent knee and crouched down sharpening this angle until the fat was squeezed out on to the felt sole" (*Beuys,* 130).[34] And in a version of the Action "Celtic" performed in Basel, home of Paracelsus, Beuys highlighted "with flashlights the back of the leg above the knee, located in alchemy as a potentially powerful zone" (*Beuys,* 199). Such works embody his slogan, "I think with my knees." Discussing "The pack" (the VW bus loaded with sleds)—which reminds us that the methodological analogy actually includes the metaphors of transport as such (method's root metaphors being derived from the history of travel, messengers, the to and fro, or *fort: da,* rhythm) —Beuys states: "I compared it [the Volkswagen motor with the sled's runners] to a person who, finding himself in an emergency, says, if I cannot run any longer, I can at least still crawl" (Herzogenrath, 31). The methodological message of "The pack," in other words, is conveyed by the same slogan of speculation Freud cites at the end of *Beyond the Pleasure Principle.*

Keeping in mind the importance for Derrida of the shoes and their laces as methodological models in "Restitutions" ("the shoes or stocking with which thought advances, walks, thinks, speaks, writes, with its language provided with shoes (or as road)"—trans. Leavey, 21), we may include as an experiment with the step of deconstruction Beuys's concert in Wuppertal (1963): "Dressed like a regular pianist in dark grey flannel, black tie and no hat, I played the piano all over—not just the keys—with many pairs of old shoes until it disintegrated" (*Beuys*, 87). His intention was "homeopathic," indicating a "new beginning, an enlarged understanding of every traditional form of art."

The steps of grammatology itself are the issue here, finally. The difference between Beuys and Derrida is the difference between applied and theoretical grammatology. The interrogation of metaphors and models which Derrida addresses in his texts (using the performance capacities of literature), Beuys carries beyond the Book into literal action. Although the difference in their content or subject matter seems at times to be extreme, much of the difference may be attributed not only to the differences between their respective points of departure (philosophy and sculpture) but to the division between text and Action. *Putrefaction* is just as important to Derrida's Writing (the epithymics of decomposition) as it is to Beuys's *Plastik* (*Fat Corner*), but the *word* and the *thing* affect people differently. Beuys's perfomance mode similarly leads him to adopt certain formats that may seem alien to Derrida's position—alchemy, Kabala, or the prophet motive in general (about which more later). But scrutiny of the Actions reveals within them, operating as their organizing principles, the pedagogy of invention and the metaphorics of Writing—grammatology, in short.

The method of grammatology, then, shared by Derrida and Beuys, is the display and displacement of the literal sense of the root metaphors of Western thought—dialectic and rhetoric, science and art. At the same time that this analytical function is at work, a further pedagogy of creativity is also set in motion, intended not only to show people the principles of creativity and how to put them into practice but also—and here is the particular power of the new pedagogy, beyond deconstruction—to stimulate the *desire* to create (not necessarily in "art," but in the lived, sociopolitical world).

The image of the nomad summarizes the steps of grammatology (the nomad wanderer who crosses all boundaries), with Derrida using the image analogically, while Beuys literally enacts the shamanistic practices of the nomadic civilizations (associated with the Russian Steppes). "Ever since the very first texts I published," Derrida remarks, "the motifs of the 'margin' and of 'nomadism' are very insistent," although, he adds, their operation in his thought should be distinguished from the ideology of nomadic margins which was fashionable in Paris intellectual circles ("Crochets," 108). Perhaps, too, it is justifiable to include "margarine" in that series of terms Derrida generates around *marges*, including *marche* and *marque*. [35]

9

Film:

Sergei Eisenstein

The organizing principle of applied grammatology (hereafter AG) may be simply stated (its complexity as an operation having been discussed at length)—hieroglyphics. The hieroglyph emblematizes Derrida's lesson for didactic discourse, including its association with dephoneticization (the realignment of writing with the visual arts); with the history of writing (Champollion's decipherment of the Rosetta stone); with psychoanalysis as a science that approaches language and mind in terms of hieroglyphics (the dream as rebus); with the history of mnemonics, from the *Ad Herennium* to computer terminals, involving the technics of information storage and retrieval. The import of the hieroglyph as an emblem of the new pedagogy is that teaching must now include in its considerations the non-discursive and imagistic dimensions of thought and communication. The lesson of the Rosetta stone for AG is that academic, specialized discourse is open to translation into the popular, mass media. AG is, among other things, a strategy for popularization.

The hieroglyph, then, remarks another important dimension in which AG finds support—film. Film and video (audio-visual writing) are in fact the media in which the word-things of AG—seemingly so bizarre in Derrida's books, Lacan's seminars, or Beuys's performances—find a natural context. The pedagogy of grammatology is, finally, an educational discourse for an age of video. Its instructional procedures are the ones appropriate for students (for a culture), whose experience of language is largely shaped by continuous exposure to cinema and television. AG is a response to the increasing pressure the electronic media are placing on schools organized "by the book." A full account of the implications of AG for educational television must await another study. I must confine myself here to an articulation of the two domains (AG and film studies), taking one example—Sergei Eisenstein—as a focus for the practicality of Derrida's Writing. That Eisenstein first worked out his theory of montage using analogies drawn from hieroglyphics in general, and Japanese ideograms in particular, makes his work a good point of departure for this articulation.

THE LANGUAGE OF CINEMA

For poste-pedagogy, as was outlined in chapter 6, a good scene is preferable to a long discourse. The *mise en scène,* the form or framing, of teaching is as much a part of any course as is the content or knowledge of the discipline concerned. I have focused in part II on the import of AG for the classroom, understood as itself a medium, a multimedia performance situation. Derrida's texts offer a procedure for mounting a discourse capable of bringing into play the full possibilities of this medium. My purpose has been not only to analyze these procedures but to argue that we ourselves might consider composing texts in the manner of Derrida, lecturing in the manner of Lacan, giving de-monstrations in the manner of Beuys. In short, I have proposed mounting a pedagogical discourse that takes into account the functioning of the double inscription.

AG assumes that teacher-scholars will not only perform the double inscription in the classroom but that they will turn to film/video as the means most adequate for a postmodernized academic essay (in any case, video makes the teaching performance publishable). If Lacan provided a model for an AG lecture, and Beuys a model for an AG de-monstration, then Eisenstein offers a similar lesson for an AG essay beyond the book. Film, of course, with its several channels or tracks, is the ultimate realization of the word-thing chimera. And the film essay is part of what one commentator has called the "second film revolution."[1] In its first phase, film developed from a technological curiosity to a comprehensive mode of narrative, which has become the predominant means of story telling in our culture. Indeed, according to Christian Metz, film developed into a language precisely in learning how to tell a story. The second phase marks the maturing of film into an intellectual medium capable of carrying out the work of the disciplines of knowledge (rehearsing thus something similar to the emergence of philosophy out of myth).

The interest of film studies for AG has to do with the debate about whether or not film is a language. The argument hinges on the question of how film means—whether it is a mode of *representation,* based on the imitation of, or analogy with, reality; or whether it is a system of *writing*, based on the relational articulation of signs. Peter Wollen poses the principal question: "To what extent does film communicate by reproducing an imprint, in Bazin's terms, of reality and of the natural expressivity of the world, like a Veronica or a death-mask? Or, to what extent does it mediate and deform (or transform) reality and natural expressivity by displacing it into a more or less arbitrary and non-analogous system and thence reconstituting it, not only imaginatively, but in some sense symbolically?"[2]

In its original form, this debate included an argument about editing styles: Bazin's promotion of the long or continuous take ("deepfocus [which allowed several motifs or centers of interest to be spaced out along a depth-axis], laterally composed shots, camera movement [which brought the possibility of adding new motifs without having to "cut"]"); and Eisenstein's "fragmentation of the pro-filmic [before the camera] reality with a view to its later recombination through montage."[3] It is now recognized that these two techniques are simply "two different modalities of the montage-effect"—"the primary material of the cinema is a body of fragments of the real world, mediated through the mechanical duplication allowed by photography." By means of a vast "work of assemblage," cinema splits itself off from the real world "and becomes a discourse on the world" (*Reader*, 41). I have argued elsewhere that the gram or trace provides the "linguistics" for collage/montage—that Derrida is the "Aristotle of montage"—so I will simply allude to montage as the principle of Writing with one citation: "I insist on the word 'assemblage' here for two reasons," Derrida notes in "Differance":

> On the one hand, it is not a matter of describing a history, of recounting the steps, text by text, context by context, each time showing which scheme has been able to impose this graphic disorder, although this could have been done as well; rather, we are concerned with the *general system of all these schemata*. On the other hand, the word "assemblage" seems more apt for suggesting that the kind of bringing-together proposed here has the structure of an interlacing, a weaving, or a web, which would allow the different threads and different lines of sense or force to separate again, as well as being ready to bind others together. (*Speech*, 131–32)

The real interest of the Eisenstein-Bazin debate, according to Metz, is the sheer fact that it has recently been revived and that the montage editing style has returned to favor: "What is really at issue through montage is a concern that the writing process should be marked, a rejection of a deceptive 'transparency.' The montage in question is not therefore necessarily montage in the narrow sense (splicing), and does not necessarily exclude long takes" (*Reader*, 40). Metz himself proposes a "revisionist" theory of film as language, suggesting that cinema is a language without a system (or, at best, with only an "open" system), a *parole* without a *langue,* without a code.[4]

But Stephen Heath complains, in response, that Metz defines cinema in terms of expression as opposed to communication, resulting in a conception of cinema as "direct parole," or speech. Moreover, the image, according to Metz, is an analogon of what it represents. However much Metz qualifies this point, what remains, in Heath's view, is the notion of meaning motivated by the "impression of reality," which amounts to a forgetting of the process of the production of this impression, and thus constitutes "the denial of cinema as semiotic system" (*Reader,* 104, 106). Metz falls into the "natural attitude to cinema": "cinema becomes not process of the articulation of meaning, but direct duplication of some Reality; it represents 'reality' with 'reality.'" Against Metz's view of a cinema of speech, which is finally phenomenological, Heath proposes a cinema of *writing.* This opposition, recalling Roland Barthes's distinction between *works* and *texts,* is between film and cinetext: between film as reproduction, reflection, representation, and cinetext as production, dramatization, writing. The cinema of speech works in the mode of "natural expression, versus in the cinema of writing an activity of scription, production, transformation, analysis."

Sylvia Harvey, discussing "materialist cinema," reveals what lies behind Heath's choice of terms to describe the cinetext—the aim to change the relation of the spectator to the film, rejecting a mimetic theory of art for a theory of art as production, that is, as a transformation of reality. The cinetext, then, involves "the modernism of an experimental cinema which self-consciously sought to explore and to make apparent to its audience the devices of its own construction, attempting to call attention to the illusory nature of the film image and thus holding the audience back from an unproblematic identification with the events and characters portrayed on the screen."[5] Harvey discusses the programs of two film journals— *Cinéthique* and *Cahiers du Cinéma*—which have two different approaches to materialist cinema, representing the disagreement over whether a new practice should operate by means of avant-garde or by popular forms of mediation. AG does not regard these two possibilities as antithetical, but as supplementary. Indeed, one way to characterize AG would be as a translation into the domain of education of this debate, applying to academic discourse the problematics of the production of meaning. And it is as true to say of AG what Harvey says of the *Cinéthique* program: "This emphasis on a cinema which is able to produce knowledge about itself, and which can thus be promoted up the league table from 'ideological practice' to 'theoretical practice,' is closely bound in with the political defence of modernist aesthetics."

The *Cinéthique* theorists referred to their "self-reflexive cinema" as a cinema of "deconstruction." Heath, similarly, invokes Derrida as the theorist of writing. "Jacques Derrida has fully demonstrated to what extent the concept of the natural authentic expressivity of speech (as opposed to the artificial parasitic travesty of writing) has been fundamental in Western thinking in its constant attempt to locate some full original presence before the difference of articulation" (*Reader,* 119). Defining "filmic writing" as "an operation or process," "the activity by which the film working with and against the various codes constitutes itself as *text,*" Heath indicates that his approach is an application of Derrida to cinema: "The concept of filmic writing as displacement provides a way of formulating a radical practice of cinema in terms of *deconstruction* and *writing* in the strong, theoretically reflexive, sense that the term finds in contemporary French theory" (133). There are, he adds, still only a few extant film texts, among which the films and theories of Eisenstein figure prominently: *October,* 1927, and *Old and New,* 1929, "may now be recognised not as films, but exactly as texts" (120). Equally important to filmic writing are Eisenstein's "crucial essays" in which he "uses notions of ideogrammatic production of meaning against notions of phonetic expressivity and representation." Against Metz, who opposes the "temptation," recurrent in film theory, to compare film to ideogrammatic writing, Heath valorizes the hieroglyph analogy as part of his refutation of the mimetic and phenomenological positions.

Julia Kristeva helps explain the importance of Eisenstein's theories of montage as ideogrammatic and hieroglyphic writing as an example of grammatology (a theory itself formulated as a repetition of the history of writing) when she defines the fundamental task for "semanalysis" as the investigation of the constitutional kernel element of semiotics—the sign—in a way that would "dissolve" it, thus breaking with the Stoic notion of the sign which has dominated Western thinking. Semanalysis imposes itself now, she explains, because "a semiotic activity orientated directly towards the matrix of the sign, foundation of our culture, is the only means of thinking the constants of that culture and of posing once more, in order perhaps to formulate them in a new way, the problems of the signifying act, its relation to the material infinity, rationality, scientificity, and so on" (*Reader,* 33). AG, of course, proposes to extend the semanalytic intervention in the history of the sign to the discourse of the school.

The three factors most responsible for bringing about the current "calling into question of the sign" (and with it "the whole gnosiology—theory of knowledge—as it has been thought in the West since Zeno") are, according to Kristeva, the Marxist concept of work, the Freudian concept of the unconscious (the two concepts which she discusses), and one final factor that she lists but leaves aside, but what is especially relevant to AG: "the dramatic eruption into the world theater of long oppressed nations such as China and India with their linguistic and scriptural systems, their complex signifying practices which depart from the principles of sign and semeiosis established by the Greeks (I am thinking for example of the hieroglyphic writing of the Chinese and of the hypersemiotic practices of the Indians, their sacred texts, their rites, their mastery of the body"—*Reader, 33*).

Kristeva also credits Derrida with providing leadership in this redirection of Western gnosiology: "This reformulation is only just beginning (as, for instance, in Derrida's texts devoted to *écriture*)." The initial step is to postulate "that every process of signification is a *formal play of differences, that is, of traces.*" Writing at this theoretical level is the "neutralisation" of logocentrism, which is the support, in Kristeva's semanalysis, for a certain critical investigation of signification, to be extended "over the vast field of signifying practices (myth, religion, art, etc.)," and which takes as its specific object poetic texts, in order to consider the manner in which literary practice tends to be irreducible to and subversive of the categories of science (*Reader*, 35–36).

Derrida's theorization of grammatology as a repetition of the hieroglyphic moment in the history of writing is the same move made by theorists to account for cinematic language, from Eisenstein's formulations to Kristeva herself, who reiterates the typical analogy—"The screen offers to the camera the possibility of a spatial and dynamic inscription, in the manner of the formation of a moving hieroglyph."[6]

The general lesson to be drawn from the discussion surrounding cinetexts is that Derrida and Eisenstein together offer a way to achieve filmic writing. Indeed, one critic—Marie-Claire Ropars-Wuilleumier—has developed this comparison at length. Ropars draws on four figures, in fact, for her study of the cinetext—Derrida, Freud, Emile Benveniste, and Eisenstein. She, too, wants to inscribe the analysis of film within the general problematic of *écriture* (understood in its theoretical sense, she notes, as the substitution of trace for sign): "and which refers all processes of signification to a differential movement whose terms are neither assignable nor fixable. . . . One encounters [this perspective] at work, blindly, differently, in the last writings of Benveniste on the two orders of signification internal to language [semiotics and semantics], and, in a more diffuse way, in Freud's texts when he describes the text of the dream; it is this finally which clarifies the active contradictions which mobilise Eisenstein's discourse on montage."[7]

Ropars is interested in the way each one of these perspectives "opens a fault in the linguistics of the sign," with Freud, Eisenstein, and Benveniste each exposing a different aspect of the implications of Derrida's spatialization for text production.

This constant movement of drift [dérive]–constituting the notion of writing–designates that which in writing situates contradictorily the specificity of a language: propriety of materials, but disappropriation of their functioning, in the extent to which it is not the material itself which becomes significant, but its enchainment, comparable to other types of concatenation. In this operation of transfer, the readability of the material diminishes in the same degree that the force of writing increases. (53)

The implication is that, against Metz, filmic writing does possess its own version of double-articulation (referring to the production of meaning by means of the combination of differential units that are themselves without meaning–or, in the case of the film, of units stripped of their original sense). Writing in film resembles the rebus writing of dreams, in which the dream scene figures an abstract thought. The concept thus figured arises not in reference to any one image but as the product of the juxtaposition of images. This operation is the opposite of Cratylism, Ropars explains, in that it *demotivates* the analogon, separates the image from the object it represents, dissociates figuration and signification: it is a Writing that breaks up the sign (Ropars, 71).

Ropars finds that the unifying element articulating the ideas of Freud, Eisenstein, Benveniste, and Derrida is their appeal to the hieroglyph–specifically, to the heterogeneity of the hieroglyphic system of writing. The hieroglyph refers, she says, discussing Derrida's use of Leroi-Gourhan, to "any writing which makes coexist, at the heart of a single visualized form, nonunifiable systems of signification" (67). Studies of Aztec glyphs support Derrida's interest in the possibility of a writing that is at once plastic art and language, spatialized and nonlinear, functioning by agglutinations, joining together in one graphic code figurative, symbolic, abstract, and phonetic elements. By stressing Eisenstein's "insistence, completely 'derridean,' on seeking in non-alphabetic forms, for a linguistic model which is not subordinated to spoken language" (35), Ropars makes it obvious that the best model for what is at stake in AG's adoption of filmic writing may be found in the cinetexts of Sergei Eisenstein.

DAS KAPITAL: THE MOVIE

One of the most interesting ideas of the twentieth century, from the perspective of AG, is Eisenstein's project to make a film of Marx's *Capital.* This project is at least as fecund as Saussure's hints about the possibility of a science of signs, although it is only now beginning to find its practice.

This film was intended to be a popularization of the central theoretical work of the Russian revolution, and as such it suggests what might be the first task for a pedagogy of the video age—the translation (transduction) of the principal intellectual works of Western civilization into the language of cinema/television (similar to the task undertaken by the humanists at the time of the Renaissance, when the important works of the classical world were translated into the vulgate, for distribution by means of the new technology of print).

Although he never filmed *Capital*, Eisenstein did make a set of notes about his plans. Marx's text was to serve as the "libretto" or scenario for the film, which was not intended to be a reproduction or representation of the book, but its performance. "There are endlessly possible themes for filming in CAPITAL ('price,' 'income,' 'rent')," Eisenstein wrote, clarifying his intention. "For us, the theme is *Marx's method.*"[8] "The setting of CAPITAL develops as visual instruction in the dialectical method" ("Notes," 16).

While believing that "the most important tasks in a cultural revolution are not only dialectical demonstrations but instruction in the dialectical method," Eisenstein was also aware that "such tasks are not yet permissible. Cinema does not possess these means of expression, since there has been, until now, no demand for tasks of that sort" ("Notes," 26). Eisenstein, to invent this means of expression, developed a discursive style, organized no longer as a unified story but "de-anecdotalized," consisting of a "collection of essays" which replace the narrative organized around "the eternal themes" ("love and duty, fathers and sons, triumph of virtues, etc."—"Notes," 10), with *instruction* that will "teach the worker to think dialectically." He approaches film, in short, as a pedagogy.

Part of Eisenstein's value for AG is precisely his status as a teacher (Derrida, Lacan, and Beuys are or have been teachers), as a professor at the State Institute of Cinema where he headed the Department of Direction. Jay Leyda, who studied with Eisenstein, notes that when Eisenstein was prevented from resuming film production by the State Ministry, "the classroom of the Direction Course became his studio, his workshop, his laboratory, his stage and his screen."[9] Eisenstein himself stated, in an essay on the history of the Institute, " 'to teach' in the present stage still means really 'to create,' for this is almost a bare place where one must form one's system and method for creatively apprehending the art of film direction. And work in this constructive sense is no less and no more than one's own creative tasks" (*Essays,* 69). We may examine, then, the notes for *Capital,* along with *October,* the film in which Eisenstein developed the techniques for filming concepts, in the same way that we looked previously at *Encore* and "How to explain pictures to a dead hare," as texts modeling procedures relevant to AG as a pedagogy. The strategies available in these productions do not need to be translated into pedagogical terms, since they were explicitly elaborated in the first place as educational discourse.

In terms of its content, *Capital* would have been something like a filmed version of Roland Barthes's *Mythologies;* that is, a "collection of essays" exposing the myths (ideology) of bourgeois society. This intention is expressed partly in Eisenstein's allusion to the role of "The Glass House"—another one of his unrealized projects—in *Capital.* The relevance was in part formal: "Experimental work is needed. For that, it's 'madly' necessary first to make THE GLASS HOUSE, in which the (usual) idea of the frame is what happens to the structure of things in the fragments of OCTOBER and in CAPITAL's entire structure" ("Notes," 24). Eisenstein alludes here to the strain placed on film conventions by the demands of "intellectual montage," whose central device is "filmic metaphor" (the most controversial and most important element in filmic writing). To articulate the dialectical structuration of metaphor in film (to overcome the strictures of film form which lead some commentators to suggest that there can be no filmic metaphors), Eisenstein intended in *Capital* to challenge the "ideology of the unequivocal frame." *The Glass House,* "a satire on bourgeois society which was to have taken place in a building whose walls, ceilings and floors were made of glass," thus allowing "the inclusion within one frame of several actions," offered a situation in which to explore new dimensions of the montage principle of juxtaposition.

The subject matter of *The Glass House*—the satire of bourgeois life—is equally relevant to *Capital.* Again, the comparison with *Mythologies* indicates the aptness of Eisenstein's glass set as a visualization of the project of semioclasm in which Barthes set out to "unveil," to "demystify" that-which-goes-without-saying in bourgeois daily life. "Indifference to each other is established by showing that the characters do not see each other through the glass doors and walls because they do not *look.*" Eisenstein notes, "—a developed 'non-seeing.' Against this background one person goes crazy, because he alone *pays attention* and looks. All live *as though there are real walls,* each for himself." [10] The one who does look, in Barthes's terms, is the mythologist, for, in "liberating" or exposing the myth, the mythologist becomes estranged from his fellows, cut off from those who live the myth. Thus, the mythologist's connection with the world "is of the order of sarcasm." [11] Since he is not living in a bourgeois society, and hence is not caught in Barthes's double-bind—the bourgeois mythologist, living the contradiction that "makes sarcasm the condition of truth"—Eisenstein raises the pitch of his tone to parody, farce, the grotesque (or such were his intentions).

Barthes's collection of observations on the daily life of the bourgeoisie shows the potential fruitfulness of Eisenstein's plan to include in *Capital* considerable material drawn from *"fait divers"* (news items) reported in French newspapers, such as the "evening ball of the First Empire" recounted in *Le Figaro,* illustrating "the way in which the French bourgeoisie yearns for a king." It was a costume ball with "antique coaches conveying famous historic personalities," including Napoleon with his entourage. Other items Eisenstein clipped and noted for his project included the Aga Khan, "playing rugby and ping-pong and accepting the prayers of the faithful (God—a graduate of Oxford University). . . . An economic invasion and construction of new cities. *Hansa-Bund* . . . setting up jewelry stores within a week, hiding the filth of the streets with carpets. . . . A great episode from Paris. A war victim. Legless man on a cart commits suicide—he throws himself into the water. . . . A factory where it is possible to pinch parts and tools. No search of workers made. Instead, the exit gate is a *magnetic* check point. No comment needed" ("Notes," 8–9). In short, France is to be ransacked "for petit-bourgeois, philistine material." The technique: "generalizations, from given cases to ideas (this will be completely primitive, especially if we move in a line from bread shortages to the grain shortage [and] the mechanics of speculation. And from a button to the theme of overproduction. . . . The form of *faits divers* or collections of short film-essays is fully appropriate for replacement of 'whole' works" ("Notes," 7, 9).

At the same time that he was preparing his "Notes," Eisenstein was also reading Joyce's *Ulysses* (of which he also hoped to make a film). The formal part of *Capital* was to be dedicated to Joyce, from whom Eisenstein gleaned several major lessons. He planned, for example, to borrow from *Ulysses* the organizational focus on one typical day in the life of a worker. Nor would this focus, as Stanley Edgar Hyman pointed out, be an imposition external to Marx's own structure: "I would suggest that we see Marx's book as a melodrama called something like *The Mortgage on Labor-Power Foreclosed.* In the first act the villain mistreats the virtuous wife and injures her poor little child; in the second act the young laboring hero himself is maimed and sits paralyzed in a wheelchair while the child dies; in the third act they are thrown out into the snow and take refuge in a miserable hovel; in the fourth act the discovery is made that the villain stole the mortgage originally and has no legal or moral rights over our heroes. It needs a fifth act in which the working-class family is rescued and restored to its happy home, but only the proletarian revolution could produce that final curtain."[12] Such is the dramatic movement that Hyman observed in *Capital,* which includes "four descents into suffering and horror," with the first act being "The Working-Day" chapter (143).

Eisenstein's strategy was to use parallel montage, in which the mythologies of bourgeois society would be intercut with the worker's day, culminating in his return in the evening to the petty comforts of his humble home, which represents, Eisenstein says, the major obstacle to the revolution. Specifically, it is the wife who consitutes "the greatest evil." "A German worker's wife will always have something warm for her husband, will never let him go *completely* hungry. And there is the root of her negative role which slows the pace of social development. In the plot, this could take the form of '*hot slop*,' and the meaning of this on 'a world scale'" ("Notes," 16). An important feature of Eisenstein's formal technique, credited to Joyce, is illustrated in this example of the "slop" enlarged to a "world scale." The technique is the pun. "The elements of the *historiette* itself are thus chiefly those which, *in the form of puns,* provide the impulse towards abstraction and generalization (mechanical spring-boards for patterns of dialectical attitudes towards events)" (16). The structuring function of the pun (a crucial link with AG) operates at two levels. First, directly, in that the "hot slop" (or soup) may allude to the "sloppiness" of the Russian worker: "In case CAPITAL is restricted (in its basic 'intrigue') to the 'world scale' and the Second International to the 'pedagogic' framework of USSR boundaries," Eisenstein states, he would "show the way in which our *slovenliness,* hooliganism, etc., is a social betrayal of the working class as a whole" (24). To implement the pun as an organizing device, Eisenstein planned to build "a demonstration of the mechanisms of associative thinking" (19). He would build into the alternating montage, paralleling the home-returning husband and the slop-cooking wife, "associative moves from the pepper with which she seasons food. Pepper. Cayenne. Devil's Island. Dreyfus. French chauvinism. *Figaro* in Krupp's hands. War. Ships sunk in the port. . . . It would be good to cover the sunken English ships with the lid of a saucepan. It could even be not pepper—but kerosene for a stove and transition into oil" (17). The initial move from "pepper" to "cayenne" is, of course, a metonymy, similar to the conventional example of Bordeaux, in which the name of the place becomes also the name of the product. In the case of "cayenne," we have the name of the capital of French Guiana, on an island at the mouth of the Cayenne River, the original source of cayenne pepper. Devil's Island, where Dreyfus was imprisoned, is off the coast of French Guiana. The technique, in which the viewer is expected to activate these puns and follow this metonymic slide, is based on the concept of "inner speech," to be discussed later.

Perhaps the most important part of the "Notes" is Eisenstein's frequent reference to *October,* the film on which he was working while planning *Capital,* which demonstrates in practice the formal devices for the filmic writing known as intellectual montage: "About the structure of the work which will derive from the methodology of film-word, film-image, film-phrase, as now discovered (after the sequence of 'the gods' [in *October*]"— "Notes," 7).

INTELLECTUAL MONTAGE

October (1927), made to celebrate the tenth anniversary of the 1917 revolution, deals with the events extending from the February Revolution to the taking of the Winter Palace and the opening of the Second Congress of Soviets. Based on the book *Ten Days that Shook the World* by John Reed, it also is informed (as Eisenstein explains) by episodes of his own biography, his own experience of the revolutionary period. With respect to the latter dimension, Eisenstein developed his style of editing to break with notions of film as "passive reproduction" of the real. Not the real, but the filmmaker's attitude to the real, was to be presented, undermining the "stagnant order of things" by recombining the images to produce a new interconnection among things.[13]

Eisenstein acknowledged D. W. Griffith as the originator of montage and of the close-up shot, which is an essential feature of this style, but he also stressed his own distinctive use of the technique as a means to convey thought rather than (or as well as) action. The American term—"close-up" —refers to the nearness of the view, Eisenstein explained, whereas the Russian translation—"large-scale"—indicates the *value* of what is seen (in the manner of Egyptian wall paintings). The function of the close-up for the Russians is "not only and not so much to *show* or to *present,* as to signify, to *give meaning,* to *designate.* . . . The first factor that attracted us in the method of the close-up was the discovery of its particularly astonishing feature: to create a *new quality of the whole from a juxtaposition of the separate parts.*"[14] Griffith and the Americans used parallel editing (cross-cutting between separate scenes of simultaneous action) for narrative purposes (girl tied to the tracks/train approaching). Eisenstein applied the device to discursive ends, to construct metaphors or "montage imagery":

> In *October* we cut shots of harps and balalaikas into a scene of Mensheviks addressing the Second Congress of Soviets. And these harps were shown not as harps, but as the imagist symbol of the mellifluent speech of Menshevik opportunism at the Congress. The balalaikas, but as an image of the tiresome strumming of these empty speeches in the face of the gathering storm of historical events. And placing side by side the Menshevik and the harp, the Menshevik and the balalaika, we were *extending the frame of parallel montage into a new quality, into a new realm:* from the sphere of action into the sphere of significance. ("Film Form," 245)

Under pressure from the proponents of socialist realism, and partly in response to the incomprehension and hostility that greeted *October* (at least in Russia), Eisenstein eventually considered montage imagery to be a mistake, or an abuse. But it is this technique that he had in mind while planning *Capital* and that is currently the center of theoretical interest.

Social realists, and realists of all stripes, oppose montage imagery precisely because it substitutes discourse for representation. Eisenstein initially pursued his experiments with montage imagery because he associated the new style with the ideology of the revolution: "The liberation of the consciousness from all that representational structure linked to the bourgeoisie; a new world revealed in the entrance of a new class upon the arena of world history; October—and the rising ideology of the victorious proletariat: these are the premises from which arose the possibilities of a new language in culture and the arts" (*Essays,* 98). His style itself, he believed, was revolutionary not only in the manner of the constructivists and futurists who had broken with the Western aesthetic tradition but, in the juxtaposition and collision of contrasting images in montage, it was *dialectical.*

The notes for *Capital* begin with a review of the development of montage imagery in Eisenstein's first three films. In *Strike* ("educational and methodological film on the methods and processes of class and of underground work"), Eisenstein intercut a scene of the Czar's soldiers firing on the workers with a scene of a bull being slaughtered in an abattoir. In *Potemkin* he intercut shots of the battleship's guns firing with shots of three stone lions (one sleeping, one awaking, one rising), ordered so as to depict the lion rising to its feet, "as if in protest against the blood-shed on the Odessa steps." Finally, in *October,* the sequence "In God's Name" "becomes a treatise on deity" ("Notes," 3–4).

Eisenstein's confidence in the capacity of montage imagery to function discursively, making possible a film treatise, was based on an analogy between film and Japanese writing. "The point is that the copulation (perhaps we had better say, the combination) of two hieroglyphs of the simplest series is to be regarded not as their sum, but as their product, i.e., as a value of another dimension, another degree; each, separately, corresponds to an *object,* to a fact, but their combination corresponds to a *concept.* From separate hieroglyphs has been fused—the ideogram. By the combination of two 'depictables' is achieved the representation of something that is graphically undepictable" ("Film Form," 29–30). The combination of depictive shots (as in the ideogram "knife + heart = sorrow") to produce intellectual series is "the starting point for the 'intellectual cinema' " (30).

Eisenstein's discussion of montage, including his belief that it affected the viewer physiologically, provides a context for the poststructuralist turn to the body and for Derrida's remarks on tone and rhythm as the terms most descriptive of Writing as a movement of differance. Eisenstein identified five formal categories of montage: (1) metric (based on the sheer length of the pieces to be spliced); (2) rhythmic (taking into account the content within the frame in determining the length of the pieces); (3) tonal (concerned with the dominant emotional quality of the pieces produced by a combination of the first two rhythms, comparable to the way melody arouses feeling); (4) overtonal ("the collective calculation of all the piece's appeals," including not only the dominant emotion but associated emotional overtones as well); and (5) intellectual (the intellectual or conceptual associations accompanying the emotional effects) ("Film Form," 72–82). The similarity with Freud's view that conscious ideation follows the traces already laid down by the drives is noteworthy. All five levels share the property of rhythm, which Eisenstein identifies with the "movement" of dialectics. The ambition of intellectual cinema, by resolving the "conflict-juxtaposition of the physiological and intellectual overtones" (presuming, following Hegel and Lenin, that there is a continuity linking the lowest with the highest orders of life), is to "build a synthesis of science, art, and class militancy" ("Film Form," 83).

The closest he came to producing this montage in practice, Eisenstein felt, was in certain sequences in *October*.

> Kornilov's march on Petrograd was under the banner of "in the Name of God and Country." Here we attempted to reveal the religious significance of this episode in a rationalistic way. A number of religious images, from a magnificent Baroque Christ to an Eskimo idol, were cut together. The conflict in this case was between the concept and the symbolisation of God. While idea and image appear to accord completely in the first statue shown, the two elements move further from each other with each successive image. Maintaining the denotation of 'god,' the images increasingly disagree with our concept of God, inevitably leading to individual conclusions about the true nature of all deities. In this case, too, a chain of images attempted to achieve a purely intellectual resolution, resulting from a conflict between a preconception and a gradual discrediting of it in purposeful steps. ("Film Form," 62)

The scene functions as a filmic reasoning, he says, formally identified with the process of logical deduction. Didactically, the montage sequence is comparable to the "break-down" method by which even the rawest recruits in the army learn to handle a rifle ("Film Form," 44). In the "gods sequence" the pieces "were assembled in accordance with a descending intellectual scale—pulling back the concept of God to its origins, forcing the spectator to perceive this 'progress' intellectually" (82).

Noel Carroll agrees with Eisenstein's analysis of the sequence, stating that it suggests the possibility that the standard patterns of argument may be used as models for editing structures.[15] The gods sequence itself, Carroll observes, has the form of a "reductio ad absurdum," which derives a contradiction from the standard conception of God, beginning with the premise (inferred by the audience) that "there is a God such that God is all-benevolent." But in the chain of images of the gods, each one moving further away from the familiar one, the idea of God as a "deceiver" (a self-contradictory condition, as Descartes argued in his *Meditations*) is evoked, calling into question the original premise. Moreover, the use of statues throughout the sequence evokes Marx's view that religion is "manmade," with its dominance over man being a symptom of alienation.

Eisenstein considered the "gods sequence" to be just an embryonic step toward a purely intellectual film, capable of directly treating ideas, systems, and concepts. His call for a filmic essay is couched in the same terms used today by textualists to characterize the new hybrid mode joining theory and practice in paraliterature, paracriticism, postcriticism—a merger of science and art. Given the nature of film as photography, and of the montage image transforming juxtaposed representations of objects, events, people, into discursive abstractions, the new intellectual cinema would "restore sensuality to science . . . give back to emasculated theoretical *formulas* the rich exuberance of life-felt *forms*" (*Essays*, 45). "The cinema is capable of, and consequently must achieve, a concrete sensual translation to the screen of the essential dialectics in our ideological debates. Without recourse to story, plot, or the living man" (46). Sound films lend themselves to this project of an "intellectual concrete film" as much as do silent ones, although Eisenstein's acknowledgment of this fact recalls the principle in AG of not excluding verbal language but of putting it in its place: "In the intellectual film sound will receive its humble necessary place among the other means of effect" (45).

The example given for the effect this cinema is intended to have, interestingly enough, is Eisenstein's recollection of his mathematics professor at the engineering academy, Sokhotzki, "one of those flaming old fanatics . . . who could by the hour and with the same fire or enthusiasm, discourse on integral calculus and analyse in infinite detail how Desmoulins, Danton, Gambetta, or Volodarsky thundered against the enemies of the people and the revolution" (*Essays*, 43). The mathematical abstraction is given "flesh and blood" in the temperament of the lecturer, which absorbs and unifies the audience, comparable to the absorption of "attractions" occurring at the theater or the sports arena. A good lecture from this professor, in Eisenstein's experience, was better than a book for scientific instruction ("Book. Printed word. Eyes. Eyes—to brain. Bad!"). And better than this perfected oratory would be the intellectual cinema, with the rhythms of montage replacing and perfecting the rhythmic breathing of the audience absorbed by the attraction.

Of course, as this example indicates, all too Hegelian in its pedagogy, Eisenstein's intellectual montage, if it is to serve as a model for AG, must be separated to some extent from its ideological tendentiousness. "Its task is the deep and slow drilling in of new conceptions or the transplanting of generally accepted notions into the consciousness of the audience. . . . The new cinema must include deep reflective processes, the result of which will find expression neither immediately nor directly" (*Essays*, 34). What is valuable here is the pedagogy of change, addressing concept formation by means of film. But in reopening the discussion of montage imagery, contemporary textualists have already shifted Eisenstein's devices from dialectical to deconstructive ends. AG intervenes at this point, to carry the device beyond deconstruction.

OCTOBER

There is general agreement among critics interested in the problematics of film language that *October* is perhaps the most representative example of a cinetext. Indeed, a group of researchers at the University of Paris, Vincennes, including Marie-Claire Ropars-Wuilleumier, devoted a year-long seminar to this film.[16] Ropars, working explicitly with Derrida's theories, has produced the most detailed analysis of Eisenstein's filmic writing, including a brilliant article on the montage image in *October*. A review of her argument will confirm the relevance of intellectual cinema to AG.

Ropars designates the gods sequence as the best example of Eisenstein's break with visual denotation, demonstrating in one sequence how *October* as a whole renounces any attempt to recount the events of the revolution, to represent it in a historical reconstruction, electing instead to perform its signification or meaning. Given the exemplary status of this sequence, it may be worthwhile to include here a slightly modified version of the shot-list from Ropars's article.

1. (Titles) "In the name of God and Country." 2. (Titles) "In the Name." 3. (Titles) "OF GOD." 4. Four cupolas of a church, topped by crosses (Long Shot [LS]). 5. Bust of a Baroque Christ "in glory" —rays behind it (Medium Shot [MS]). 6. The four cupolas, left angle (LS). 7. Two of the cupolas, right angle (MS). 8. Christ standing (LS). 9. One cupola, left angle (Close-up [CU]). 10. One cupola, right angle (Extreme Close-Up [ECU]). 11. Bust of a Hindu god, radiating arms (MS). 12. The Hindu god standing (LS). 13. The cupola of a mosque (CU). 14. The mosque cupola, right angle (CU). 15. Mosque cupola, front (CU). 16. Face of a Buddha, incense smoke (CU). 17. The Buddha's hands resting on its knees (CU). 18. Seated Buddha (LS). 19. A Lion's head, jaws open, turned to the right (CU). 20. Fat Buddhist divinity, shining marble, turned to left (MS). 21. Anthropomorphic head with eagle's beak, turned to right (CU). 22. Another such head with animal's snout, whiskers, turned left (CU). 23. Japanese mask (CU). 24. Painted wooden mask, African, front (CU). 25. The Japanese mask (CU). 26. Wooden mask, elon-

gated cranium, turned left, high angle (CU). 27. Same mask, turned right (CU). 28. Same mask, front (CU). 29. Crude object, oval shape, a fetish head? (CU) 30. Feet and hands of a wooden fetish (MS). 31. Two wooden fetishes, standing (LS). 32. Trunk and head of an idol (MS).

Ropars, following Eisenstein's suggestion, explains that the sequence involves a double process—the simultaneous construction and deconstruction of the concept of "god." The concept is constructed or established through the juxtaposition and accumulation of the figures, which by association compose a set, including representative examples of the principal incarnations of "god" from the principal cultural areas—Europe, Asia, Africa, and the North Pole. The set is deconstructed in that the representations are ordered in a way displaying a transformation of the concept, perhaps even its reduction or degradation. The order in which the images are shown constitutes the deconstruction. "If every concept issues historically, according to Eisenstein, from a condensation of concrete images, it is not the work of elaboration which one finds restored here, but it is on the contrary the decomposition. It is a question not only of producing the concept, but especially of tracing it to its origins, that is to the components which permitted its production: the final block of wood is but a content of the container God." [17]

Ropars's most valuable insight comes in her analysis of how this decomposition or deconstruction (decondensation) of the concept works, for she characterizes the procedure in terms very similar to those used to define the practice of *anasemia,* which Derrida borrows from Nicolas Abraham (see chapter 3). "It is no longer the images which are metaphors of the concept, it is the concept which rejoins a metaphorical origin, under the pressure of images become objects and no longer symbols: each object is but a synecdochic fragment of a notion whose generalizing abstraction sublates the metaphor. Or, in other terms, it is the concept which resembles the images, not the images which resemble the concept: God is but a metaphor, says in reality this accumulation of the metaphors of God" (Ropars, "Fonction," 124). The process is in fact a kind of interaction: "This unveiling may work in inverse directions, whether it is a question of referring the idea to its real origin, or on the contrary whether the reality is to be referred to the signification which situates it and allows it to be grasped" (125).

This reduction of the concept to its metaphor, as in the case of Derrida's deconstruction of the philosophemes of metaphysics, is only part of the procedure, which ultimately involves not resemblances, not representation, but the articulation (by montage) that demotivates and remotivates the links between concepts and images, signifieds and signifiers. The exemplary value of the gods sequence, Ropars says, is that the concrete reduction does not imply a realistic representation. Rather, the objects shown are "non-diegetic inserts" whose appearance in the film is not motivated by the referential space of the depicted event (General Kornilov's march). "It is from the montage hence of their place, that they receive their function. Circulating in the film [the figures] constitute the textual material, supported no doubt by the decor of Saint Petersburg, but assuring complete autonomy, outside of any referential perspective the basis for a discourse in which the figures take effect only with respect to the text and not to the context" ("Fonction," 125).

The procedure, in other words, does not confine itself to the Nietzschean move, described in Derrida's "White Mythologies" (as Ropars notes), of desublimating the concept. Rather, the figures of the gods, joined by the statuary of all types, are mounted as a commentary that recurs periodically throughout the film: the film opens with a sequence showing the crowd tearing down a statue of the czar; Kornilov and Kerenski are both mocked as "little Napoleons" by inserting shots of figurines and statues of Napoleon into scenes depicting their historical actions, and so forth. Separated from their specific referential context, the figures become available for a "metonymic articulation." Derrida, Ropars adds, treats in "White Mythologies" the "invariant feature of the concept of metaphor, the subordination of the syntactic to the semantic, and seeks in the syntactic resistance one of the means of the auto-destruction of the metaphor, 'which always carries its death within itself.' It is precisely in this direction that eisensteinian montage works" ("Fonction," 127).

Ropars sees in this montage articulation of the figures and their arrangement a prefiguration of the Lacanian reading of Freud, and the double-system of signification which Benveniste discerned in language (the coexistence in language of the semantic and semiotic systems). Eisenstein's proposal, the basis for a nonverbal writing, is that "no representation signifies the reality whose appearance it imitates. Constituted in the effacement of the denotation as of the symbolization, signification emerges then as a semantic of writing, in which the negation of the sign and of the symbol give the sense to construct in the sole process of its production" ("Fonction," 128). "The repetitive syntax lends a metonymic base to the metaphoric effect: the similarity of the elements [in the gods sequence] is created by their contiguity; the resemblance is but an illusion, with only the syntactic liaison being real" (123).

The point, at both the formal and ideological levels, in cinema and politics alike, is that the real is constructed, not received as a given. "It is in the production of meaning that one grasps the world, not in the reproduction of its appearance; to *representation* as figurative imitation of reality, Eisenstein opposes the image as abstracted element produced by montage in perfect independence with respect to the represented element"

("Fonction," 128). The decomposition noted in the gods sequence is the principle by which the entire film is constructed. "To return the cinematographic material—and its illusory reality—to the state of raw material; to repossess these liberated fragments in a whole which recomposes the contradictory image of reality and its significative orientation. The movement of writing, then, retraces with its dynamic constitution of the text that of the dialectic which constitutes history" (126). This homology between the dialectics of montage and of history is what led Eisenstein to believe that he could use cinema to teach Marx's method to the Russian people.

The writing process, moreover, frequently involves a certain "literalization," the literal depiction of a linguistic cliché or commonplace phrase. The technique is to substitute a material image for an abstract notion, as in the ironic depiction of Kerensky's rise to power, his political version of social climbing and *arrivisme,* in terms of his arrival at the Winter Palace and his interminable climbing of the stairs, intercut with titles identifying each new title of office bestowed upon him. This procedure of literalization extends further than Ropars herself indicates, including, as in the cases of Derrida, Lacan, and Beuys, reflexive reference to the very function of the examples themselves. Thus, we may discern in Ropars's description of the function of the cupola in the sequence ("With the changing of the cupolas begins the plastic modification which leads from a radiating morphology to a rounded morphology; but the syntactic woof at the heart of which the change intervenes constitutes the unity of the old and the new cupolas: it relates thus, under the theme 'cupolas,' the morphological and cultural differences"—"Fonction," 121) Derrida's "shuttle" at work (not to mention Eisenstein's own technique of the pun), for the cupola literalizes the *copula,* the syntactic *copulation* remarked in Eisenstein's account of this sequence cited earlier.

In the same vein, it is not insignificant, given the *Moira* of *idea* pursued in AG, that the exemplary example of Eisenstein's montage image (the basic device of intellectual montage) concerns fetish images. All examples, from the point of view of AG, have the structure of fetishism. More importantly, the fact that Eisenstein elects to produce the intellectual commentary in *October* by means of the repeated insertion of shots of statues into the documentary portion of the film (thus confusing and collapsing the distinction between referential and discursive space) is itself a literalization of the principle of *poiesis,* which etymologically is linked with the setting up or erecting of statues in a temple (as was noted with respect to Heidegger and Derrida in chapter 1). Although Ropars mentions this aspect of montage imagery only in passing, the verbal dimension of the images as literalisms of key words is one of the features of Eisenstein's practice most relevant to AG. The imagistic comment about the Menshevik speeches, for example, which required two instruments in Russian in order to convey the sweet but tiresome quality of the oratory, could be combined into one image in English, in which the term "harping" states concisely the point Eisenstein wanted to make. This strategy of "verbal images" will be treated in the next section.

For now it may be worth noting a possible intertextual frame, if not an inspiration, for the poetics of statuary mounted in *October,* observable in the hint provided by the sarcastic juxtaposition of Kerensky and the statuettes of Napoleon (the montage image that organizes the "Country" part of the "For God and Country" sequence). On the one hand, the historical authenticity or relevance of the metaphor is substantiated by John Reed's account, in which it is mentioned, as an indication that the forces of reaction were gaining confidence after the February revolution, that "certain newspapers began to sigh for a 'Russian Napoleon.'"[18] On the other hand, there is the similarity between the way Eisenstein ridicules Kerensky and the way Marx treats Louis Bonaparte in *The 18th Brumaire of Louis Bonaparte.* Reed's book, which deals almost exclusively with the debates in the Congress, seems an unlikely or unpromising basis for a film, unless Eisenstein's intellectual aims are taken into account. In any case, the parliamentary theme of *Ten Days that Shook the World* recalls Marx's own focus on the parliamentary history of the 1848 revolution in France. Perhaps one reason why Eisenstein became inspired by the possibility of filming *Capital* during the shooting of *October* was his realization that he was in a sense already making a version of Marx's *Brumaire.*

October, of course, reverses the direction of events which Marx recorded in his study of the February revolution in France: "Hegel remarks somewhere that all facts and personages of great importance in world history occur, as it were, twice," Marx wrote in his famous opening to *Brumaire.* "He forgot to add: the first time as tragedy, the second as farce."[19] In Russia, the February revolution (this coincidence of months might have appealed to Eisenstein, who was well read in Marx's texts), in which Kerensky came to power, was the farce, preceding the authentic revolution in October. Eisenstein treats Kerensky with the same sarcasm and savage irony Marx applied to Louis, whose coup d'état and restoration of the Empire is characterized as a parody of the Napoleonic era. Eisenstein's satiric intentions (his sensibility in this respect is very much like Marx's own) are typified in this account of the stair-climbing sequence:

> A comic effect was gained by sub-titles indicating regular ascending
> ranks ("Dictator"—"Generalissimo"—Minister of Navy—and of
> Army—etc.) climbing higher and higher—cut into five or six shots
> of Kerensky, climbing the stairs of the Winter Palace, all with
> exactly the *same* pace. Here a conflict between the flummery of the
> ascending ranks and the "hero's" trotting up same unchanging
> flight of stairs yields an intellectual result: Kerensky's essential non-

entity is shown satirically. We have the counterpoint of a literally expressed conventional idea with the *pictured* action of a particular person who is unequal to his swiftly increasing duties. The incongruence of these two factors results in the spectator's purely *intellectual* decision at the expense of this particular person. ("Film Form," 61–62)

Such ironic counterpoints also structure Marx's style: "Finally, the scum of bourgeois society forms the *holy phalanx of order* and the hero Crapulinski [Louis] installs himself in the Tuileries as the *'saviour of society'* " (26). The famous conclusion of the *18th Brumaire,* although it is Marx's only allusion to a statue, is perhaps rhetorically effective enough to stimulate Eisenstein's thinking along the lines realized in *October:* "but when the imperial mantle finally falls on the shoulders of Louis Bonaparte, the bronze statue of Napoleon will crash from the top of the Vendôme Column" (135).

INNER SPEECH

In the context of intellectual cinema, we may see both what AG has to learn from Eisenstein and what AG in turn has to offer to the contemporary renewal of interest in Eisenstein's project. The point to be emphasized is that the aspect of Eisenstein's experiments which has been renewed—his use of filmic metaphors, the montage imagery of the gods sequence—is precisely the dimension of his work most relevant to AG. The most innovative or experimental feature of grammatology—the foregrounding of the homonym, homophone, or pun—may be recognized in this context as the enabling device for the rhetoric of filmic writing. The experiments with montage imagery were halted in Russia by the turn to socialist realism and were similarly resisted in other cinemas because of their violation of the assumptions of realism. Thus, my earlier claim—that the practice of AG, however bizarre it may appear to be in book form, is natural to cinema—should be modified to read "discursive" cinema, cinetext.

AG intervenes in the discussion of filmic writing with respect to the question of the relation of words to images, of word-presentations to thing-presentations. Film theorists have returned to Eisenstein's silent films in order to note an aspect of the word-image relation which has been neglected since the advent of sound films. There have been important experiments with the possible combinations of sounds and images in film, whether they should be synchronized, as in most commercial films, or separated and allowed to function with more or less autonomy. The Russian theorists had observed, however, that silent films were themselves organized verbally, not only with respect to the intertitles, or to the mimed speech visible in the images, but, more importantly, with respect to the image track itself.

The formalist critic Boris Eikhenbaum first stated the verbal dimension of the image track in his important essay "Problems of Film Stylistics," written in 1927, the same period in which Eisenstein was working out the devices of *October* and *Capital.* Although film represented for Eikhenbaum the attempt by modern culture to escape from domination by the word, he recognized that what was involved was not an abandonment of the verbal but its displacement into what he took to be a new mental operation called "inner speech." He elaborated this concept as an answer to the question of how a viewer comprehends a film, which he identified as the most important question facing film theory. Film textualists today agree with Eikenbaum's judgment, while noting that research on this question is only now beginning. According to Eikhenbaum,

> the film viewer finds himself in completely new conditions of perception which are opposite to those of the reading process: from the subject—visible movement—he progresses to comprehension of it, the construction of internal speech. . . . For the study of the laws of film (especially of montage) it is most important to admit that perception and understanding of a motion-picture is inextricably bound up with the development of internal speech, which makes the connection between separate shots. . . . He [the viewer] must continually form a chain of film-phrases, or else he will not understand anything. . . . One of the chief concerns of the director is to make sure that the shot is "accessible" to the viewer; in other words, that the viewer is able to divine the episode's meaning, that he is able to translate it into the language of his own internal speech. Thus, internal speech must be taken into consideration in the very construction of a film. [20]

Eikhenbaum's essential point has to do with the difference between the way a reader comprehends a book and the way a viewer comprehends a film. Whereas the reader progresses from the printed word to a visualization of the subject, the viewer processes the images in the opposite direction, from the comparison of the moving frames to the naming of the images—to internal speech, which amounts to "a new and heretofore undeveloped intellectual exercise." [21] In this linking together of the fragments juxtaposed in the editing, the viewer extends this naming activity to fill in the intervals between segments, in order to make sense of the sequence. Most importantly for my purposes, Eikhenbaum specified that this naming process operated chiefly by means of metaphor.

> One more general question remains, concerning cases when the director must give a semantic commentary to the film in whole or in part, when "something from the author" must appear in a film over and above the plot itself. The easiest method is to give commentary in intertitles, but contemporary cinema is already making attempts to function by different means. I have in mind the appearance in cinema

of metaphor, which sometimes even bears the characteristics of symbol. From the semantic point of view, the introduction of metaphor into film is of particular interest because it confirms again the real significance of internal speech, not as an accidental psychological element of film perception, but as an integral structural element of a film. Film metaphor is entirely dependent on verbal metaphor. The viewer can understand it only when he possesses a corresponding metaphoric expression in his own verbal baggage. . . . A film metaphor is a kind of visual realization of a verbal metaphor. ("Problems," 30)

Eikhenbaum argues that directors deliberately construct scenes "the meaning of which depends directly on current verbal metaphors." He offers this example: "In [*Devil's Wheel*] the sailor Shorin chances into a tavern and joins a billiard game. His ball *falls* into the pocket. The absolutely episodic quality of this scene gives the viewer to understand that it is significant, not for story-line development, but as commentary: the hero's 'fall' begins" ("Problems," 30).

In noting now the operation of inner speech in montage imagery I am touching on the central significance of intellectual montage for AG. For the question posed by Eikhenbaum with respect to film is the same one to be posed for Writing—how does a student understand a pedagogical discourse? Everything discussed here concerning the comprehension of films, especially the role of verbal images and filmic metaphors, is especially relevant to the way AG functions, both in terms of the way it is composed and the way it is comprehended. An AG lecture (seminar-performance) will include the equivalent of "non-diegetic inserts," that is, it will mount scientific information in its discourse which will have the status not of disciplinary content but of metaphor, just as in Eisenstein's intellectual cinema images were mounted to function not as representations of reality but as metaphorical comments.

Eisenstein explicitly formulated his account of montage imagery in terms of inner speech. Indeed, Eikhenbaum's appeal for a theory of montage which would take into account inner speech (criticizing Timoshenko's study, which ignored that dimension) could be read as a direct charge to Eisenstein, who, in any case, was already at work on just such a theory. Paul Willemen, one of the leading proponents of inner speech among textualists, has noted the presence of verbal images (filmic metaphors constructed to evoke inner speech) in *October,* although the example he provides is perhaps too modest: "Other major examples can be found in Eisenstein's *October,* such as the Czar's 'fall' being suggested by the crashing down of the Czar's statue."[22]

In this same vein, I suggested earlier that the gods sequence is doubly exemplary—as the primary example of filmic writing, de-monstrating the discursive capacities of film, and as a manifestation of the exemplarity of the film example as such (poiesis). That this sequence is also a verbal image, indeed, that it is a comment on verbal imagery, may be seen when it is read as a literalization of the term Eikhenbaum used to characterize the viewer's activity. "Cinema demands of the viewer a certain special technique for *divination*," Eikhenbaum argued. "The film viewer must *divine* a great deal" ("Problems," 14, 28). Thus, in giving a name to the theme of the gods sequence, the viewer is also naming the very mental activity he must use to understand the sequence. The deities or divinities imaged in the gods sequence name in a pun the "divination" process Eikhenbaum identified with the formation of internal speech. At this formal level, then, the gods refer not only to religious concepts but to film concepts as well.

The literalisms (as the verbal images are often called) at work in *October* indicate that there is a continuity relating Eisenstein's later development of the notion of inner speech (which David Bordwell suggests dominates Eisenstein's technique after 1930) to the formulation of intellectual montage (dominant from 1923 to 1930).[23] There is some disagreement, that is, about whether inner speech extends, or breaks with, intellectual montage. Bordwell argues that, in taking up inner speech, Eisenstein alters his epistemology, switching from a materialist constructivism based on the theories of Marx, Lenin, and Pavlov to an associationist organicism that is finally a kind of romanticism, concerned not with logic but emotion, not with abstract, ideological reason but with pathos and ecstacy. As Bordwell explains, accounting for the differences between *October* and *Ivan the Terrible,* the reason for Eisenstein's shift in approach was political: "By 1929, power in the philosophical academy had been won by Deborin and his followers, who stressed a Hegelian-idealist dialectic. And in 1931, the January 25 decree of the Central Committee of the Bolshevik Party abolished all dispute on the matter and asserted 'the impossibility of reducing phenomena of higher order to those of lower order'" (45). In short, the Central Committee banned materialist cinema.

That Eisenstein modified his style is obvious, but that this modification marks an abandonment of intellectual montage is less clear. Eisenstein himself described his later theory of montage as a less naive solution to the problems of intellectual cinema, whose difficulties were impressed on him by the poor reception accorded *October.*

> Is it then necessary to jettison all the colossal theoretical and creative material, in the turmoil of which was born the conception of the intellectual cinema? Has it proved only a curious and exciting paradox, a *fata morgana* of unrealized compositional possibilities? Or has its paradoxicality proved to lie not in its essence, but in the sphere of its application, so that now, after examining some of its principles, it may emerge that, in new guise, with new usage and new application,

the postulates then expressed have played and may still continue to
play a highly positive part in the theoretical grasping and understanding and mastering of the mysteries of the' cinema? The reader
has already guessed that this is precisely how we incline to consider the situation. ("Film Form," 125–26)

What was required in response to the emergence of socialist realism as the
official art of the Party was "the demonstration of such conceptual postulates by agency of concrete actions and living persons." Realizing that his
attempt to deanecdotalize the cinema in order to directly convey the whole
process of thought ran counter to the developing insistence on dramatizing
the virtues of socialist life by means of protagonists and plots, Eisenstein
decided to frame intellectual cinema within the point of view of a character,
thus disguising its "written" or discursive nature.

The "double science" of grammatology, placing science (the disciplinary
discourses) in the frame of the subject of knowledge (the signature effect),
may be seen at work in this compromise. In any case, Eisenstein modeled
his shift on the example of James Joyce.

Montage very quickly realized that "affective logic" is the chief
thing, but for finding all the fullness of its system and laws, montage
had to make further serious creative "cruises" through the "inner
monologue" of Joyce, through the "inner monologue" as understood
in film, and through the so-called "intellectual cinema," before
discovering that a fund of these laws can be found in a third variety
of speech—not in *written*, nor in *spoken* speech, but in *inner speech*,
where the effective structure functions in an even more full and
pure form. But the formation of this inner speech is already inalien-
able from that which is enriched by sensual thinking. ("Film Form,"
250–51)

Eisenstein was interested in a kind of "arche-writing," then (to use Derrida's
term). Joyce, in *Ulysses* and *Finnegans Wake*, had developed the double
method, combining subjective and objective presentation as far as it could
go in literature. "Joyce's originality is expressed in his attempt to solve this
task, embracing in one work the inner and outer worlds, with a special
dual-level method of writing: unfolding the display of events simultaneously
with the particular manner in which these events pass through the consciousness and feelings, the associations and emotions of one of his chief
characters" ("Film Form," 184–85). Cinema, Eisenstein believed, could go
beyond Joyce, being able to accomplish the double perspective without
the extreme distortions forced upon Joyce: "How easily the cinema is
able to spread out in an equal graphic of sound and sight the richness of
actuality and the richness of its controlling forces" (186).

Eisenstein's immediate inspiration for the shift to a narrative enframing
of montage imagery, in other words, came before 1930 with the reading of

Ulysses, mentioned as a model for the formal aspect of *Capital.* Specifically, Eisenstein was interested in adapting Bloom's interior monologue to film, and inner speech offered a mode of presentation peculiar to cinema. "When Joyce and I met in Paris, he was intensely interested in my plans for the inner film-monologue, with a far broader scope than is afforded by literature. Despite his almost total blindness, Joyce wished to see those parts of *Potemkin* and *October* that, with the expressive means of film culture, move along kindred lines" ("Film Form," 104).

Montage composed in accord with the principles of inner speech, then, may seem to convey a kind of monologue. "How fascinating it is to listen to one's own train of thought, particularly in an excited state, in order to catch yourself, looking at and listening to your mind. How you talk 'to yourself,' as distinct from 'out of yourself.' The syntax of inner speech as distinct from outer speech. The quivering inner words that correspond with the visual images. Contrasts with outer circumstances. How they work reciprocally" ("Film Form," 105). Inner speech, of course, raises the question of "voice" in film. The first thing to be stressed in this context is that inner speech is the opposite of that autotelic activity of logocentrism which Derrida deconstructed in *Speech and Phenomena.* Derrida's experiment with "apostrophe" in *La carte postale,* addressing oneself as if to another, is a version of inner speech, which is materialist rather than idealist in its acknowledgment of the externalized, mediated quality of introspection.

Inner speech, that is, involves a process of incorporation, being an internalization of social discourse. But the peculiar nature of this mode is due precisely to the fact that the addressee is oneself. Summarizing Vygotsky's discussion of inner speech (outlined in a book published in Russia in 1934), Willemen notes that

> in thought, addresser and addressee are identical, and this means that the context within which the communication takes place does not have to be rendered more explicit nor do the problems raised by the mode of contact have to be taken into account. . . . In short, internal speech (thought) can operate with extreme forms of abbreviation, condensations, image equivalents or fragments of image equivalents, extraordinary syntagmatic distortions, and so on. In fact, all the mechanisms which Freud detected to be at play in dream work, can be seen to be at work in internal speech as well. [24]

Willemen's point is not that inner speech is a psychoanalytic theory but that Lacanian psychoanalysis, with its notion of the unconscious as "the discourse of the Other," which is "structured like a language," produces an account very similar to that provided by the Russian psychologists and linguists, for whom "the problem of individual consciousness as the *inner word* (as an *inner sign* in general)," as V. N. Volosinov put it in a book published in 1929, "becomes one of the most vital problems in philosophy of language."[25] At the level of the description of this third mode of discourse, neither speech nor writing, there is little to distinguish Lacan's *lalangue* (described in chapter 7) from inner speech. AG assumes that this convergence (to which may be added descriptions of right-brain processing from cognitive psychology), and not the diverging rationales that differing theoretical positions offer to explain "inner speech," is the crucial fact that a pedagogical discourse must take into account.

As indicated in this summary of the notion, the Russian theorists stressed the social, and hence the ideological, origin and quality of inner speech:

> The first investigations of inner speech carried out in the Soviet Union
> . . . made it clear that despite its specificity (soundlessness and
> fragmentariness), inner speech, far from being an independent entity,
> is a secondary phenomenon derived from external speech—auditory
> perception of the speech of other persons and active mastery of all the
> forms of the spoken and written word. Seen from this viewpoint,
> inner speech represents a psychological transformation of external
> speech, its "internal projection," arising at first as a repetition (echo)
> of the speech being uttered and heard, but becoming later its in-
> creasingly abbreviated reproduction in the form of verbal designs,
> schemes, and semantic complexes operating not unlike "quanta"
> of thought.[26]

The main feature of this mode is its peculiar syntax, disconnected, incomplete, nearly a "pure predication," radically simplified, producing "agglutinated" words. But however much like a monologue the speech seems to be, it most resembles, finally, according to Volosinov, "the alternating lines of a dialogue," which are connected (being "total impressions of utterances" rather than explicitly formulated sentences) "not according to the laws of grammar or logic but according to the laws of evaluative (emotive) correspondence, dialogical deployment, etc., in close dependence on the historical conditions of the social situation and the whole pragmatic run of life" (Volosinov, 38). Derrida's concern with the collapse of inner and outer oppositions and his inclination to compose his texts (in a number of important instances) as dialogues links him with the problematic of inner speech.

Once internalized, inner speech resembles in its operations the sensual logic of primitive language, relevant to the shamanism of psychoanalysis and of Joseph Beuys, not to mention Eisenstein's own tendency to use analogies derived from anthropologists to characterize the "concrete" logic of montage. In fact, the theorists sought analogies for inner speech in the operation of every "alternative" mode of language—in the language of schizophrenics, primitives, children, and in ancient languages—especially with respect to the phenomenon of "undecidable" terms. Vygotsky treats this "concrete" quality as a form of developmental psychology, arguing that inner speech duplicates a stage of concept formation typical of children's thinking, in which terms are treated not as concept names but as family names, as proper nouns (comparable to Derrida's signature principle). The pedagogical implication of his developmental reasoning for Vygotsky is that instruction in systematic knowledge must be approached through this pre- or pseudo-conceptual thinking. The lesson for AG is that all these alternative discourses work by means of the literalisms of verbal imagery.

THE VERBAL IMAGE

Before elaborating on the literalisms operating in filmic inner speech, I should review the revival of inner speech in contemporary textualist theory. Paul Willemen has produced the most complete discussion of the continuity between the investigations undertaken during Eisenstein's period (showing that inner speech figured not only in the discussions of Vygotsky, Volosinov, and Luria but also in those of the Prague Linguistic Circle, Jakobson, Pierce, and others outside Russia) and the current critical scene. Willemen observes, based on this investigation, that "the non-verbal is never totally separate from the verbal, but always to be grasped in its relation to it." His conclusion is that "language is the symbolic expression *par excellence* and all other systems of communication are derived from it and presume its existence." The point is not that all signification is verbal but that there is no signification without a verbal dimension ("Discourse," 64).

I should stress that AG views this proposition not as a necessity but as the current logocentric condition of semiotics. Inner speech helps clarify the link between the domination of voice in metaphysical thinking and the dominance of verbal language in all manner of discursive formations. Hence it does not suffice, in order to undo logocentrism, simply to switch media (from book to film), not only because film operates with the "intellectual" sense of sight and hearing, but because images and sounds are "lined with verbal discourse." But just as in the case of the deconstruction of the sign, whose point of departure was Saussure's own notion of "difference," AG finds that the peculiar nature of the verbalization (the verbal image) involved in inner speech offers a point of departure for releasing filmic practice from its logocentric captivity.

The main point of contact between the Russian theories of inner speech and the cinetextualists, working with Lacan, is the notion that the unconscious is structured like a language. "The psychoanalysis of Freud and Lacan engages the unconscious *as a kind of inner speech,* where this latter is neither 'social' nor 'individual,' still less the site of some universal symbolism, but, exactly, linguistic in a new assumption of the—complex, heterogeneous—reality of language as a site of history."[27] Stephen Heath provides a current version of inner speech:

> What is needed, still, and it is here that the status of inner speech could be thought through, the question of cinema and language taken up again today, is a theory of cinematic enunciation. . . . Yet in that fixity, that givenness of the film, there is always a present enunciation, the making of the film by the spectator ('making' here the join of the one and the other, the spectator making it as one makes a train, catching it, taken up in its movement, and as one makes, fashions something, articulating it, creating that movement). . . . There is another enounced in this performance-enunciation of the film: all the meaning I am, that is me, all my identity, the history I have for-and-against the film and in-and-across the very institution of the view of the film, the institution of the regulation of the exchange, the exchange at stake in the process of cinematic enunciation. What we know predominantly are institutions of which the force and the reason is facilitation of that exchange, the ease, the flow, the assurance the pacification of the passage across from film to spectator, spectator to film in orders of identity. (*Questions,* 216–17)

Heath is concerned here with the ideological "production of the subject" in the process of "thought work" associated with the comprehension of any discourse, a process he calls "passage." "Passage is the performance of the film, the movement of the spectator making the film, taken up as subject in its process" (*Questions,* 173).

The institutional facilitation of the passage between the film and the viewer involves, of course, the question of the "suture," the identification of the subject with the film. Kaja Silverman reveals what is at stake for AG in this suturing passage when she reminds us of Althusser's insight that a discourse can take place between a person and a cultural agent (a person or a textual construct that relays ideological information). The primary cultural agents in the modern world, Althusser observes, are educators. "The agent addresses the person, and in the process defines not so much its own as the other's identity," Silverman explains, citing "Ideology and the Ideological State Apparatuses" in which Althusser refers to the agent's address as "hailing": "Ideology 'acts' or 'functions' in such a way that it 'recruits' subjects among the individuals (it recruits them all) or 'transforms' the individuals into subjects (it transforms them all) by that very precise operation which I have called *interpellation* or hailing, and which can be imagined along the lines of the most commonplace police (or other) hailing: 'Hey, you there!' "[28] Supposing that the scene takes place in the street, when the person turns around, in response to the hailing, he becomes a subject having recognized himself as the addressee. Derrida suggests that the "scene of writing" is constituted in exactly this way, although the imaginary scene he describes is that of a reader writing a letter in response to a newspaper columnist. "The receiver is determined at the moment of reception of the letter."[29] Such is the functioning of the unconscious.

AG attempts to develop a pedagogy capable of exposing, if not of escaping, the ideological nature of the educational apparatus. And the articulation of inner speech with psychoanalysis, as Willemen notes, "opens up the question of verbal discourse in relation to imaged discourse in terms of ideology and politics" because inner speech is a process that "lines every signifying practice, operates to articulate the laws of unconscious signification into the social" ("Discourse," 90–91). Inner speech, that is, is a "frontier" discourse, the place of overlap and contamination between the inner and outer dimensions, between the imaginary and the symbolic. "In so far as the unconscious impinges upon the formation of inner speech, the latter is trans-individual, that is to say, profoundly social. The unconscious, if it is to be defined topographically, is a *locus communus* where locutions are indeed 'in common'" (92). Concerning at once that which is most private and most social, transgressing the inside/outside dichotomy, "the traces of inner speech in the visual, in the figuration of a narrative or a tableau, take the form of, precisely, *loci communi* of the socially and linguistically commonplace. This would be one more argument why 'images' should be considered products of secondary elaboration, that is, displaced enunciations invested by/with unconscious discursive processes" (92). Inner speech, then, far from constituting a "private language," is related rather to dream images in that "both can be regarded as 'grounded in folklore, popular myths, legends, linguistic idioms, proverbial wisdom and current jokes'" (93).

The first point to stress here is the link between inner speech as consisting of "commonplaces" and "the taking place of the place" in Derrida's foregrounding of hypomnesis. Inner speech is the concept that makes possible (and that reveals the political dimension of) Derrida's project to study all manner of inscription, since all are "lined with inner speech," which is to say that all signifying processes are permeated by logocentrism. The point is not to eliminate verbalization but to identify its place in the process of comprehension. The goal is not to replace the verbal with the nonverbal but to develop a heterogeneous discourse, mixing word and thing presentations. As Willemen argues, "What is at stake here is precisely the possibility of a discourse which, although structured 'like' a language nevertheless works with the widest variety of signifiers, and thus can be sited at the join of the unconscious and preconscious/conscious systems, the site of the processes of resistance" ("Discourse," 74). Derrida's attempt to Write from the position of the censor (discussed in chapter 5), and all his explorations of word/image interaction, may be understood as a strategy to attain access to the ideological component of knowledge.

> It is in this space that the repressed signifier that gave itself up under the guise of an image, re-finds a verbal signifier. . . . Just as the unconscious persists in all discursive practices, so does verbal language, even when repressed. The discourse of attention, thought, has been conceptualized as inner speech (intrapsychic speech, in Jakobson's terminology). Inner speech, like the ego, is a frontier creature. . . . The secondarising work of inner speech, providing the initial stabilisation of the signifying process according to the contradictory demands the ego is there to bind, constitutes thought. ("Discourse," 78)

The practical value of inner speech may be better appreciated when it is realized that Roland Barthes's *S/Z* expounds a version of this theory. In this context, *S/Z* may be recognized as a useful text for AG in that its theory of codes is as applicable to pedagogical narratives as it is to literary and cinematic ones. It suggests how the psychoanalytic dimension (the symbolic code) interacts with the Cultural or referential code (the domain of inner speech). The cultural code, revelant to the body of knowledge transmitted in a discipline, is the code of received knowledge: "The locus of an epoch's codes forms a kind of scientific vulgate which it will eventually be valuable to describe. . . . If we collect all such knowledge, all such vulgarisms, we create a monster, and this monster is ideology. As a fragment of ideology, the cultural code *inverts* its class origin (scholastic and social) into a natural reference, into a *proverbial statement. Like didactic language* and political language, which also never question the repetition of their utterances (their stereotypic essence), the cultural proverb vexes, provokes an intolerant reading."[30] AG wants to identify these proverbs, the commonplaces of knowledge.

The difference between reading a narrative fiction and an academic discourse using Barthes's terms will involve a shift of emphasis away from the symbolic code, which dominates "Sarrasine," to the cultural code. But the reading of "Sarrasine" shows that the latter code

> forms an anonymous Book whose best model is doubtless the School Manual. For, on the one hand, this anterior Book is both a book of science (of empirical observation) and a book of wisdom, and on the other hand, the didactic material mobilized in the text . . . generally corresponds to the set of seven or eight handbooks accessible to a diligent student in the classical bourgeois educational system. . . . Although entirely derived from books, these codes, by a swivel characteristic of bourgeois ideology, which turns culture into nature, appear to establish reality, "Life." (*S/Z*, 205–6)

It is precisely this cultural material that dates Balzac, Barthes adds, representing in the classic text "a nauseating mixture of common opinions, a smothering layer of received ideas. . . . In fact, the cultural code occupies the same position as stupidity" (*S/Z*, 206). Lacan also tried to work with this stupidity, the "bêtise" mentioned in chapter 7.

Inner speech, which takes the form of "commonplaces," draws its materials from the cultural code. The reading process, as Barthes describes it, is just this activity of inner speech: "Thus begins a process of nomination which is the essence of the reader's activity: to read is to struggle to name, to subject the sentences of the text to a semantic transformation. This transformation is erratic; it consists in hesitating among several names" (*S/Z*, 92). "What we hear, therefore, is the *displaced* voice which the reader lends, by proxy, to the discourse: the discourse is speaking according to the reader's interests. Whereby we see that writing is not the communication of a message which starts from the author and proceeds to the reader; it is specifically the voice of reading itself: *in the text only the reader speaks*" (151). In classical reading, the work of nomination produces a "thematics" coded by the "implicit proverbs" of the cultural code.

This nomination process informed by the cultural code functions in films as well as in literature and is the basis for the production of verbal images—the essential device of intellectual montage. As mentioned earlier, verbal images may be described as "literalisms"—"the use of non-verbal stand-ins for verbal signifiers, a result of repression" ("Discourse," 83). The reader or viewer, as Noel Carroll explains in his "rhetoric" of the verbal image, names the images with terms drawn from the commonplaces of the cultural code. Carroll, however, prefers to use speech act theory, rather than the theory of inner speech, to account for the functioning of the verbal image. The verbal image, he argues, is an illocutionary act, which performs precisely the evocation of words in the spectator's mind (even if these words are not fully conscious). He wants to confine the device (artificially, from the point of view of AG) to deliberate acts by the filmmaker.[31]

In his excellent explication of the device, Carroll lists these conditions for the verbal image:

1. The image, or image part, or succession of images under consideration is literally describable by a certain word or string of words.
2. The word or string of words evoked as a description of the image must have some extended meanings beyond its literal meaning and at least one of those extended meanings applies as a comment on the subject of the image.
3. Both the literal and extended meanings of the words or strings of words putatively evoked by the image must exist in the language (or languages) of the filmmaker (or filmmakers).

He supplements this list with a further list of constitutory conditions. An image is a verbal image if

    a. the elements that give rise to the putative verbal image are salient
    and hypothesizing the verbal image gives us our best explanation
    of the otherwise unmotivated prominence of the elements;

    b. its postulation fits as a coherent (i.e. consistent) remark upon the
    developing narrative

and/or

    c. a developing character

and/or

    d. a developing theme;

    e. its postulation fits the discursive context of the film's production
    and it does not contradict the overt meanings internal to the struc-
    ture of the film.

Rather than cite Carroll's examples, I will provide several of my own which were evoked in me by certain narrative films and which confirmed for me the practicality of the principle involved. In *The Birds,* Alfred Hitchcock's notorious fondness for playing with Freudian themes and symbols is couched as a verbal image in the scene in which Melanie, having (unnecessarily) gone to the attic by herself, is attacked by the birds. The birds, of course, nearly "peck her" (pecker) to death. This "pecker" at the thematic level is the phallus whose power Melanie challenged: "This is the birds' final attack on Melanie," Bill Nichols notes. "It drives her from the Brenner house (indirectly) and pushes the theme of aggression against the (erotic) image of the other to its extreme."[32] The "pecker" is also the signature, signing the "cock" in Hitchcock's proper name (Derrida might read all of Hitchcock's self-conscious manipulation of phallic imagery in terms of the signature).

Another example that meets Carroll's conditions is evoked by the last scene of *McCabe and Mrs. Miller,* which shows Mrs. Miller (the heroine, Julie Christie) smoking her opium pipe (a "free motif") while McCabe (Warren Beatty), having managed to kill all three of the hired guns sent after him, dies, wounded, in a snowbank. The opium evokes rather its derivative, heroin, a literalism for "heroine," which serves to comment on the effect the woman had on McCabe, who never would have "played the hero" (as established in the early part of the film) had he not been trying to impress Mrs. Miller. To live by the clichés of the cultural code can be deadly, as Barthes pointed out with respect to the fate of the hero in "Sarrasine."

For that matter, it may be seen in this context that the castrato functions as a kind of "literalism" (Barthes selected the story for analysis because of this happy convergence of the narrative with the symbolic code). Sarrasine, that is, is literally castrated, while access to the Symbolic requires symbolic castration. Brecht similarly takes advantage of the convergence of the political and narrative lines in *Galileo.* Galileo's discovery that the earth revolves is "revolutionary." Brecht is able to evoke his Marxist message of political revolution by means of the literal revolutions manifested in Galileo's position.

The crucial point to keep in mind in discussing the nomination process of inner speech, however, is that Eisenstein, for example, used verbal images as a means of adding a commentary to a nonverbal channel, thus creating a heterogeneous system. As Stephen Heath emphasizes, verbalization may function in filmic writing the way spatialization functions in grammatological discourse. AG, that is, operates at the meeting point of nonverbal and verbal systems, balancing the spatialization of the verbal and the verbalizing of the spatial. Thus, Heath promotes inner speech precisely as a means of countering the attempt to pacify images by banishing from them the nomination process productive of concepts (*Questions,* 216–17).

Heath's observation that "independent, avant-garde, and political filmmakers" have turned to inner speech and its verbal images "to produce alternative institutions, different 'viewings,' new hearings" is confirmed by Carroll, who is interested in the way that avant-garde "film-essays" construct verbal images that are literalizations, not of the commonplaces of the cultural code, but of slogans or terms specific to the polemics of specialized artistic or theoretical fields. What all these commentators suggest is that, once this process has been identified, it may be used to mount a counterideological discourse. Arguing against those who might interpret inner speech as an attempt to reintroduce the old supremacy of literature over cinema, Willemen insists that verbal images may be used in filmic writing to break with the ideology of realism and representation in cinema. Nor is the film text totally translatable into verbal language, he adds ("Reflections," 62–63). Rather, without concerning oneself about the intentionality of the verbal image, the fact is that the interaction of verbal language and images can produce "metaphoric effects," "literalisms," which involve "the type of play on words Freud analyses in his books on jokes, rather than metaphors properly speaking. These verbo-visual puns often involve a play on the polysemic aspects of the image as well as the polysemic qualities of the verbal terms involved." Willemen likes to think of the device as offering "a radically new perspective which, unfortunately, has never been followed up" and which provides a new strategy both for the writing and the reading of films. Indeed, the viewer's inner speech is as important as the filmmaker's in the generation of verbal images.

With such literalisms in mind, we may return for a moment to Eisenstein's project, in order to note that *Ivan the Terrible* might be read as a remake of *October,* at least to the extent of retaining the basic principle of montage imagery activated by inner speech. This final example should help clarify the laconic quality of the film-essay, operating with verbal images to organize the translation into film of a verbose theoretical discourse such as Marx's *Capital.* As Eisenstein states in his "Notes" for *Capital,* his general rule is "that picture is cinematic whose story can be told in two words." Organized around a single concept, *Capital* or *October,* Eisenstein believed, could accommodate any number of shifts at the level of anecdote. "Furthermore, one realizes that without even chasing around after the flavor of Egypt, the whole of CAPITAL could be 'constructed' on a set. *Schuftan* ["an illusionistic process designed to perfect, through the use of reduced models drawn on glass, the integration of *décor* into film"] Glass. [*Glas?*] Model. . . . Film language is not *terrifying as far as footage is concerned.* On the contrary, it is the maximally succinct expressive mode; within fifteen meters the idea of Deity disqualifies itself" ("Notes," 13–14). Willemen's experience with verbal images reveals what this succinctness implies for practice: "After the elaborate analysis of some sequences of Raoul Walsh's *Pursued* (1947) it appeared that the circulation of a few privileged but repressed verbal signifiers (e.g. 'phallus' and 'to shoot' in the sense of 'consummating the sex act') put into place not only visual signifying configurations (flashes of light) but also produced distortions on the sound track (noise level of gunshots), determined camera set ups and even physical attributes of characters (e.g. the one-armed Grant Callum"–"Reflections," 66).

The key signifiers organizing a film-essay, as opposed to a narrative film, will, of course, be theoretical terms, philosophemes, concepts or proper names treated as literalisms. To see how this literalization works in *Ivan,* I should first note that *October* is famous for being the first film to depict Lenin as a character, which contributed eventually, it is said, to Lenin's "cult of personality." [33] *October* has even been described as marking the turn toward socialist realism because of its "heroicisation" of reality, resulting from its refusal to reproduce historical fact, which it replaced with an invented revolutionary reality while retaining a documentary style. In short, it rewrote Russian history. The tendency of subsequent presentations of the October days to use footage from *October* rather than (or even because of the absence of) documentary evidence marks its effectiveness as a propaganda film (Taylor, 93).

But if *October* can be read as a precursor of Eisenstein's films of the Stalinist period, so may *Ivan* be understood as an exercise, on a massive scale (many scenes, one idea–the principle of intellectual montage), of montage imagery. Consider, for example, this remark Eisenstein made about the status of Ivan as a character:

The "great" and "illustrious" personages of the past ruled the fate of millions according to their limited views. They were "gods"

invented out of whole cloth. It is time to reveal the truth about
these paid romantic heroes. The concealed traps of official history
must be exposed. We want to know the social basis of these fab-
ulous figures, glorified by hired scholars in the interests of their class
and their descendants. Ivan the Terrible as a personality in the manner of Edgar Allan Poe will hardly interest the young Soviet worker;
but as *the creator of the linen trade,* the Czar who enriched and
strengthened Russia's economic position, he becomes a more interesting figure. (*Essays,* 26–27, my emphasis)

Ivan, that is, may be read as another gods sequence, demystifying a legend
if not a religion. More importantly, the "god" being demystified, at the
level of inner speech, at least, may not be Ivan but Lenin himself (his cult
of personality fostered by Stalin), for the verbal image working here is the
pun associating Lenin with linen (by antonomasia). The pun is English, of
course, but then Eisenstein was fluent in English. In any case, as Willemen
notes, the verbal image must work twice—once in the language of the filmmaker, once in the language of the viewer. The allusion links Lenin's signature with Marx in that one of the principal examples of the theory of the
commodity in *Capital* is the linen trade in England. The comment articulated in *Ivan* might be that Stalin is capitalizing on Lenin's sacred status to
create a power as fetishistic and alienated as that originally deconstructed
in the gods sequence.

Or, to put it another way, the Signature effect of Lenin/linen in *Capital*
might provide a verbal image capable of organizing a film of *Capital,* should
anyone ever decide to make it. But then, Jean-Luc Godard, the leading
cinetextualist of our time, has already made his own version of *Capital* in
Two or Three Things I Know about Her. In this film (and in a number of
others) Godard uses "prostitution" as a metaphor of capitalism, a metaphor
which, as Hyman's reading of Marx indicates, is Marx's own: "As intangi-
bles become commodities, man becomes 'a thing, although a living conscious thing.' Women, of course, become prostitutes—what better symbol
for turning flesh into commodity, people into things? Prostitution is everywhere in the book [*Capital*]" (Hyman, 132). The verbal image in *Two or
Three Things* which evokes the name "prostitute" (and which functions as
the mnemonic device organizing the concept) involves, as Alfred Guzzetti
explains, the construction cranes used in the building projects that constitute the setting of the film. "This cut [from Juliette to the construction
site, showing the crane] also serves to evoke the woman/region equivocation in a pun of which Godard can scarcely be presumed innocent: *grue,*
the word for crane, is also slang for 'prostitute.' "[34] That Godard whispers
his voice-over commentary may be a reference to inner speech, in that
according to one theory, the passage from external to internal speech involves a middle phase during which the child whispers to itself.

THE ELECTRONIC PARADIGM

"Now I know how to go on." Can anyone say this with respect to AG? Is anyone prepared to apply grammatology? Is grammatology an emergent discipline, field of study, a new discursive formation? All that has been established to this point is that there is available in Derrida's texts both a theory and a demonstration of a heterogeneous scripting, articulating word and thing presentations; that there are also available in the arts—especially in performance art and video/film cinetexts—models exploring the possibilities of this practice, already directed to didactic ends. What remains, of course, is to bring these examples to bear on our own discourse.

In principle, this application could begin in the educational institution as it exists today, leaving everything to do with curriculum and evaluation in place while transforming first of all the language used, the medium in which professors and students communicate. The assumption is, however, that in tampering with this language something "happens" (takes place) that alters the entire ecology of learning. I must avoid the temptation to speculate on the specifics of this change, as well as the temptation to outline a kind of teacher's manual for the new pedagogy. But as long as this chapter is already, I feel obligated nonetheless to continue on a bit further in order to reiterate the principal value of AG—that it shows us how to adapt the dominant medium of mass communication (television) to the critical, theoretical, and creative interests of academic discourse. The necessity justifying AG is the existence of a new technology of writing. Every teacher today, at every grade level from kindergarten to graduate school, is in a position similar to the one Socrates confronted when he caught Phaedrus with the written speech concealed in his robe. The television set, the poste, is the concealed (unacknowledged) device that, with or without Derrida, is transforming our situation.

Emilio Garroni, in an essay dealing with the importance of inner speech for the theory of filmic writing, has stated the central question facing AG. Garroni first formulates his question with respect to the problem addressed by Russian montage: "Is it possible to develop the pertinent procedures, in the realization of filmic and televisual messages, in a way that such messages approximate as closely as possible the very processes of thought?"[35] Then, reflecting on the way these messages lend themselves to "mystifying acritical, rhetorical, emotional, fallacious, etc. operations," Garroni restates his question: "Is the filmic or televisual message made in a way such that it renders insurmountable this acritical situation, even if the sender is motivated by the best intentions of communication?" (120). Garroni himself does not accept as inevitable or necessary the current acritical use of film and television, although he admits that many observers would not agree with him.

Derrida (as I mentioned in chapter 1) called upon the educators assembled for the Estates General of Philosophy (June 1979) to include the study and use of the media in their educational work. He added that this project must be carried out *within* the media themselves. Régis Debray, spokesman for the workshop on teaching and media at this meeting, made the classic argument against television as a means of philosophic teaching. No real thinking, Debray insists, can occur by means of television for reasons inherent in the medium: "The mass media are not neutral forms susceptible to carry no matter what cultural material. They entail necessarily a regression of discursive forms, a decomposition of analytical procedures inherent in critical thought, the progressive abandonment of a certain number of constraints proper to the philosophical effort such as demonstration, definition, or interpretation" (*Etats,* 160–61). Television is incapable of doing philosophy (certainly of doing it "philosophically"), not only because of its discursive regressiveness, but also because of the nature of the mass audience, for whom "existential thrills and emotive amalgations have always been more gratifying than an apprenticeship in the technique of discernment." Debray goes on to specify his criticisms, objecting that television (1) is a communication without reciprocity; (2) replaces the value of truth with the pursuit of seductive effects; and (3) is ephemeral, prohibiting verification by the inhibition of memory. He summarizes his attack, aimed at the tendency of television to pacify rather than stimulate its audience, by noting that certain institutions are putting philsopohy on cassettes, thus "replacing the living pedagogical word with audio-visual programs (all of metaphysics in three hours, at home, on videodiscs)" (163).

At the same time, Debray expresses his anxiety over his own Platonic critique, because he joins Derrida in recognizing the political necessity (again like Plato) for academics to work with the contemporary media. Debray's mistake, from the point of view of AG, is to imagine that the traditional mode of philosophizing, which developed out of alphabetic writing, is the only kind of philosophy possible, instead of considering that the philosophical project, in order to operate within film/video, should be rethought, redefined, redesigned to exploit the virtues specific to these media (the same point applies to deconstructionists who can think only in terms of *literary* criticism). Moreover, Eric Havelock, anticipating Derrida's own assessment of the contradiction in Plato's relationship to writing, has shown that, despite Plato's explicit statements condemning writing, Platonic philosophy fully manifests a mode of thought made possible only by alphabetic writing. Walter Ong says, referring to Havelock, "The Greek philosopher's thought is essentially the thought released by a rather thoroughly alphabetized culture taking issue with the thought of the old oral-aural world, newly superseded in Plato's day."[36] The passage from mythology to philosophy is a product, in part at least, of the shift from an oral to a written culture.

My argument is that Derrida's texts similarly already reflect an internalization of the electronic media, thus marking what is really at stake in the debate surrounding the closure of Western metaphysics. A fuller appreciation of the import of Derrida's style for philosophy is possible in the context of this technological transformation, indicating the position that enables him to compose scripts "beyond the book." Nor is Derrida's program another version of a technological determinism, à la Marshall McLuhan. Rather, it represents a deliberate choice to accept the new paradigm. Walter Ong reminds us, in a way that accounts for Derrida's willingness to take issue with the entire (preelectronic) era from Plato to Freud, of the major role played in cultural shifts by the changes in the dominant technology of communication. Following Ong, if Plato marks the turn from a civilization based on orality (speech) to one based on alphabetic writing, Derrida marks a similar shift from alphabetic writing in its print stage to filmic writing.

Derrida's own negotiation of the transition between the print and electronic eras has principally concerned a critique of the alliance of Book and Voice. His analysis of the interdependence of logocentrism (centered in philosophy) and alphabetic writing (chirography subordinated to orality) has been misunderstood as a simple attempt to invert the opposition voice/writing. In fact, he has sorted out the vestiges of orality which persist in our concepts, while revealing that the actual character of Western thinking is governed by chirography and print. The point is that these governing structures are in the process of being subverted in turn. Thus, two of Derrida's major topics—the "margin" and the "signature"—may be recognized as features peculiar to alphabetic writing, whose effects are to be identified and displaced in the electronic paradigm.

With respect to these effects, Jack Goody points out that the presentation of information in the form of lists is one of the special capacities of alphabetic writing: "The list relies on discontinuity rather than continuity; it depends on physical placement, on location; it can be read in different directions, both sideways and downwards, up and down, as well as left and right; it has a clear-cut beginning and a precise end, that is, a boundary, and edge, like a piece of cloth. Most importantly it encourages the ordering of the items, by number, by initial sound, by category, etc. And the existence of boundaries, external and internal, brings greater visibility to categories, at the same time as making them more abstract."[37] Derrida's critique of margins may be associated with the meaning of the word "list," which, as Goody remarks, has to do with " 'the border, edging, strip, selvage of a cloth,' " with which is associated "the notion of a boundary" (80).

Along with the list and its relatives, the formula and the table—the principal devices by which writing tames the "savage mind"—Goody observes that the growth of individuality is directly linked to the fact that a written work may be signed. "If a mutation [in an oral culture] is adopted, the individual signature (it is difficult to avoid the literate image) tends to get rubbed out, whereas in written cultures the very knowledge that a work will endure in time, in spite of commercial or political pressures, often helps to stimulate the creative process and encourage the recognition of individuality" (14). Part of the relevance of the psychoanalytic model to this investigation of the effects of the technology of communication in thought has to do with Freud's self-analysis, which represents a limit-case exemplifying the kind of introspection which alphabetic writing made possible. In the context of the transformation brought about in cognition by the Book, Goody stresses "the relevance of this internal aspect since the role of the inner ear and the contribution of writing in clarifying one's own thoughts are rarely given much recognition by those who see the elements in communication as a matter of the external relations between human beings; the outstanding case, not always the limiting one, is the audience of one, myself, for even at this level the 'social setting' is all-important, an essential prerequisite of the kind of cognitive process we are familiar with" (160). He argues, that is, that communication with oneself is as susceptible to cultural transformation as every other aspect of civilization, hence that the dominant medium of communication in a culture—voice, book, or electronics—directs thought. The theory of inner speech outlined in this chapter seems to offer a clue to the transformation now under way in communication with oneself and to the new cognitive style in general emerging in an electronic culture. In short, the signature itself, the relation of the speaker-writer to his discourse, is changing.

Walter Ong's observation that our culture is now drawn to open-system models for conceptual representation, which he links to our "new orality," identifies what is at stake in AG. For Ong, if Kant is the exemplar of a thinking that maximizes a closed system (in which borders, distinctions—such as those separating noumena and phenomena, or practical and pure reason—are stressed), then television may be seen as the fullest embodiment of an open system because of the large-scale blur it permits between fiction and life.[38] Ong uses the analogy of the Klein bottle to illustrate the merger that videotape creates between live or direct broadcast and pre-recorded images. Quiz shows further reflect the controlled spontaneity characteristic of open systems (*Interfaces,* 319, 324). Ong adds that open-system thinking, defined as being interactional, transactional, developmental, process-oriented, has already deeply affected the university curriculum in the form of interdisciplinary courses of study and "open" classroom procedures. He states that in these new circumstances the "participatory study of humanistic subjects encouraging creative or imaginative work" is going to play a part in the education of the future (*Interfaces*, 329).[39]

Ong's assumptions are shared by those theorists who have begun to argue for the promotion of the audio-visual media from an auxiliary to a primary role in education. The most succinct statement of the assumptions motivating this argument has been formulated by Gavriel Salomon. Salomon offers, to begin with, an important corrective to the way theorists of inner speech, from Eikhenbaum to Garroni, have posed the question of the relationship between film and thought. It is not so much that film can or should correspond to our processes of thinking (which is finally to pose the question within the model of representation, repeating the gesture of logocentrism). Rather, Salomon suggests that our modes of thought themselves change, that we are internalizing the symbolic system of film and beginning to think by means of filmic structuration (editing, camera movements, and the like). Part of the strangeness of Derrida's texts, in this view, would be that he is already thinking filmicly, already exploiting the philosophical potential of bookish equivalents of montage imagery.[40]

Salomon further suggests that television (and film) develops skills that in turn become tools of thought applicable to matters outside the demands of a particular medium (83). With respect to inner speech, Salomon notes that the "extraction of knowledge" from any system of representation proceeds by the translation from an external code of meaning to an internal code. Salomon is not convinced, however, that verbal language is the only possible code by means of which this extraction may take place. To learn from a model it is necessary to recode it, but this recoding may occur directly in visual codes as well as in verbalization (115, 152).

Another point in Salomon relevant to AG is that the new media should not be used (or are ineffective when used) for purposes originally devised for other media. Rather, new ends that exploit the strengths of the new media should be developed. The ambiguity inherent in images, for example, should not be considered as a fault, but, along with all the other features of filmic writing, should be explored to discover what contribution it might make to a new discourse. Thus, to the extent that educational films attempt to limit the ambiguity of the images by adding spoken explanations, they lose much of their specific and unique contribution to learning (56). He concludes that while television *allows* "shallow processing" (the acritical condition), it does not *require* it. On the contrary, television has the potential for deep processing of thought, but for this potential to be realized new compositions must be devised that make use of the specific capacities of the medium for cognitive ends.

Following Salomon's lead, Geneviève Jacquinot (who edited a special issue of *Communications* [33 (1981), "Apprendre des medias"]) has called for the development of an intellectual, educational use of film/video. She applies Barthes's readerly-writerly opposition to film, reminding us that, if academic discourse is at present understood in a readerly way, it may also be treated in a writerly way (which is what AG attempts to do). Inner speech as that process of nomination which Barthes describes as reading need not confine itself to a passive consumption of ideology but may become an active construction of the "plurality" of a text: "Yet reading does not consist in stopping the chain of systems," Barthes declares, "in establishing a truth, a legality of the text, and consequently in leading its reader into 'errors'; it consists in coupling these systems, not according to their finite quantity, but according to their plurality (which is a being, not a discounting): I pass, I intersect, I articulate, I release, I do not count. Forgetting meanings is not a matter for excuses, an unfortunate defect in performance; it is an affirmative value, a way of asserting the irresponsibility of the text, the pluralism of systems" (S/Z, 11). Thus, "reading is not a parasitical act, the reactive complement of a writing which we endow with all the glamour of creation and anteriority. It is a form of work (which is why it would be better to speak of a lexeological act—even a lexeographical act, since I write my reading"—10).

Jacquinot notes that the film image does not lend itself to the traditional model of pedagogy, and her remarks imply that the reason the readerly-writerly distinction translates so readily into a film context is that the writerly approach to literature is in fact precisely a filmic mode of comprehension. Indeed, we might understand Barthes's interest in photography in his later career as the consequence of pursuing this writerly mode. Paul Willemen, in any case, considers Barthes's notion of "third meanings," developed in a reading of some stills from Eisenstein's films, to be an attempt to exploit the cognitive work of inner speech. That an image can never be completely rendered in words, that the heterogeneous systems in filmic writing are irreducible to any unity, is the condition within which inner speech functions—"the mode of presence of the verbal geno-text within the film is primarily that of the traces of its absence, the marks of the fact that the material was modelled by words which themselves have disappeared" ("Reflections," 6). Or, from the viewer's perspective, there is the possibility and necessity to name the excess of signifiers available in the image. "This thing which always escapes and yet is present, this vital something which one can't quite get hold of but nevertheless constitutes the essential distinguishing mark between the order of language and the image, is this perhaps the 'ineffable' third sense Roland Barthes speaks of?" (68).

Barthes's work with the third sense, because it addresses precisely the problem of the cognition of images, the excess of meaning available in images beyond the obvious meanings of the cultural code (in Eisenstein's case, the obvious meaning is "revolution"), is of major importance for AG, further justifying its concern with the puns in montage imagery: "The obtuse meaning appears to extend outside culture, knowledge, information; analytically, it has something derisory about it; opening out into the infinity of language, it can come through as limited in the eyes of analytic reason; it belongs to the family of pun, buffoonery, useless expenditure. Indifferent to moral or aesthetic categories (the trivial, the futile, the false, the pastiche), it is on the side of the carnival."[41]

The question Jacquinot raises in the context of Barthes's writerly reading reflects her belief that a new medium requires a new pedagogy: "But to the question of whether the proposal to obtain a pedagogical televisual image does not reduce to the impossible project of transforming a cool medium into a hot medium, couldn't one substitute the question: isn't it possible to transform a closed pedagogy into an open pedagogy?"[42] Traditional pedagogy, Jacquinot argues, based on the myth of unique interpretation and the ideology of good (well-made) communication, considered learning to involve the transmission of a constituted knowledge by someone who knows to someone who does not know. She opposes to the traditional model a modernist, constructivist epistemology. In place of a prestructured, predigested product designed for consumption by a homogeneous group, the open pedagogy will expose the work of production, will "make of the didactic act a process of production of sense" (17).

The ambiguity of the film image lends itself to a "pedagogy of difference or of the singularity as soon as one liberates it from its referential function" (Jacquinot, 117). Instead of the ideology of communication, open pedagogy adheres to the ideology of signification, "which takes into account all the systems of codes, seeks to make them explicit in order better to analyze their origin and their mode of functioning." The filmic message is didactic, "no longer because it transmits a knowledge, but because it permits the elaboration of a knowledge." This elaboration is undertaken not by the one who teaches but by the one who learns, based on a presentation that provides the raw materials for an *inventio*. Pedagogy becomes process, not product. Against the model of natural science, which values "information over evasion, and perception over imagination," the open pedagogy promotes a heuristic, inventive mode, in which the aesthetic dimension replaces the referential as the guide for the productive participation of the addressee. What must be emphasized with respect to this argument, of course, is that it assumes that the open pedagogy, fostering the writerly student, is not simply one style among others but is the one necessary for the cognitive use of film/video in education.

Although Jacquinot points out that there are almost no available examples of "modernist" educational films, she mentions Eisenstein's intellectual montage and Brecht's "learning plays" as possible models for a practice, with the theories of Lévi-Strauss and Umberto Eco offering a rationale for the project. It may be useful to conclude my study with a discussion of Eco, since he has explored most fully the "openness" that must inform the new pedagogy. Moreover, if deconstruction (as in Culler's discussion mentioned at the beginning of this book) tends to emphasize the negative or critical relationship of Derrida to semiotics, grammatology explores the positive dimension of this relationship (in which the gram subsumes the sign).

The chief link between Derrida and Eco is that both see *Finnegans Wake* as the touchstone for thinking about language in our time. David Hayman has identified the principal lesson of the *Wake* as having to do with its being "open" or "writeable": "The *Wake* belongs to a class (not a genre) of works which invite the reader to perpetuate creation."[43] Eco agrees: "The search for 'open' models capable of guaranteeing and founding the mutation and the growth and, finally, the vision of a universe founded on possibility, as contemporary philosophy and science suggest to the imagination, encounters perhaps its most provoking and violent representation—perhaps its anticipation—in *Finnegans Wake*."[44] Eco believes that works constructed in accord with an open aesthetic are inherently didactic, are "epistemological metaphors": "It has to do with elaborating models of relations in which ambiguity finds a justification and acquires a positive value. . . . Contemporary art attempts to find—anticipating science and social structures—a solution to our crisis, and encounters it in the only mode possible, with an imaginative guise, offering images of the world which amount to epistemological metaphors" (*Obra*, 11).

Contemporary art, with its "continuous exercise of free selection and of conscious and continuous breaks with established methods," may well represent, Eco suggests, an "instrument of liberation," providing us with an education in "self-direction" (*Obra*, 127). Eco's discussion of avant-garde art in terms of "information theory" provides a clue to the nature of an "open" pedagogy. The clue is based on the homonym in "information." If traditional pedagogy attempted a transparent, univocal transmission of a body of information, understood as the content or signifieds of a discipline, an open pedagogy concerns itself with information as it is understood in General Systems Theory, cybernetics, and the like, defined in terms of the probability or improbability of a message within a rule-governed system. The more probable (banal) the message, the less information it conveys. "Information" here is statistical, referring not to what one says but to what one *could* say, the extent of liberty of selection (103). Ordinary languages, such as English, Eco notes, tend to be balanced at a statistical rate of fifty percent redundancy.

AG, then, deals with information in this statistical sense, adopting a style from the experimental arts, which favor a high improbability, as opposed to the clarity (low information) favored in traditional pedagogy. "While classic art introduced original movements within a linguistic system which substantially respected the basic rules, contemporary art realizes its originality in proposing a new linguistic system which carries within itself new laws" (*Obra,* 106). In the tension between form and possibility, the artists strive to augment the possibilities of information by means of an "organized disorder." "In consequence, information associates itself not with order, but disorder, or at least with a certain type of order-not-habitual-forseeable. Could we say that the positive measure of such information (distinct from signification) be entropy?" (101).

The pun or homophone acquires a new status with respect to the new sensibility, attuned no longer to the expectations of cause and effect, the logic of the excluded middle, but to the pleasure of surprise, in that homophones represent "the bridge of least motivation," thus generating the greatest "information." Eco establishes the epistemological importance of the pun by identifying it as the principal figure of *Finnegans Wake,* understood itself to be an "epistemological metaphor" of "unlimited semiosis" (the *apeiron,* in Derrida's terms). "In proposing itself as a model of language in general, *Finnegans Wake* [FW] focuses our attention specifically on semantic values. In other words, since FW is itself a metaphor for the process of unlimited semiosis, I have chosen it for metaphoric reasons as a field of inquiry in order to cover certain itineraries of knowledge more quickly."[45] The crucial point of Eco's analysis for AG is his observations on how the *Wake* functions: "We should be able to show that each metaphor produced in FW is, in the last analysis, comprehensible because the entire book, read in different directions, actually furnishes the metonymic chains that justify it. We can test this hypothesis on the atomic element of FW, *the pun,* which constitutes a particular form of metaphor founded on subjacent chains of metonymies" (*Role,* 72).

For specific examples of how the pun operates in the *Wake* ("meander-tale" is a key illustration of this "nomadic" writing) I refer the reader to Eco's study. What interests me here, and what may serve as a model for the intelligibility of AG, is Eco's description of the homophonic system.

The pun constitutes a forced contiguity between two or more words: *sang* plus *sans* plus *glorians* plus *riant* makes "Sanglorians." It is a contiguity made of reciprocal elisions, whose result is an ambiguous deformation; but even in the form of fragments, there are words that nonetheless are related to one another. This *forced contiguity* frees a series of possible readings—hence interpretations—which lead to an acceptance of the terms as a metaphoric *vehicle* of different *tenors.* . . . We can in theory distinguish between two types of puns, in accordance with the reasons that established the contiguity of terms: contiguity of resemblance of signifiers. . . . contiguity of resemblance

of signifieds. . . . As one can see, the two types refer to each other,
even as contiguity seems to refer to the instituting resemblance, and
vice versa. In truth, though, the force of the pun (and of every successful and inventive metaphor) consists in the fact that prior to it no
one had grasped the resemblance. . . . The resemblance becomes
necessary only after the contiguity is realized. Actually (FW is itself
the proof), *it is enough to find the means of rendering two terms
phonetically contiguous for the resemblance to impose itself;* at best,
the similitude of signifiers is that which precedes, and the similitude of signifieds is a consequence of it. The exploration of the field
of FW as a contracted model of the global semantic field is at once
useful and derisive. It is useful because nothing can show us better
than a reading of FW that, even when semantic kinship seems to pre-
cede the coercion to coexist in the pun, in point of fact a network
of subjacent contiguities makes necessary the resemblance which was
presumed to be spontaneous. It is derisive because, everything being
given in the text already, it is difficult to discover the "before"
and the "after." (*Role,* 73–74)

Eco's account clarifies the epistemic foundations of Derrida's decision to
experiment with a mimesis of signifiers.

The *Wake* is an epistemological metaphor showing the consequences
for cognition of field theory. The reader's relationship to the *Wake* models
the relationship of the poststructuralist student to the fields of knowledge,
whose "content" may be identified with the encyclopedia. "Some scholars
have proposed a semantic representation with the format of an encyclopedia, and this solution seems to be the only one capable of conveying the
whole information entailed by a given term" (*Role,* 176). Grammatology
intervenes here in terms of mnemonics—the evolution of writing as artificial
memory (hypomnesis), as a technology for the storage and retrieval of
information. (Compare Sperber's use of the encyclopaedia in chapter 3.)
As noted in the discussion of Beuys, mnemonics shifted, with the development of writing, from the orator's memory technique to the humanist's
commonplace book, from mind to page. The final stage of the alliance
between memory and the book is the encyclopedia, which itself constitutes
the hypertrophy of the commonplace book. The encyclopedia is the final
stage of the book as hypomnemic device, which is giving way, in the electronic paradigm, to the computer. Indeed, the homophonic structure of
the *Wake* anticipates a computerized version of reading.

This means that all connections were already codified before the
artist could recognize them by pretending to institute or discover
them. This allows us to affirm that it is in theory possible to construct
an automaton whose memory would conserve all the semantic fields
and axes which we have just mentioned; it is thus within its capacity
to establish the connections which we have indicated (or, as it were,

to attempt to make others; this could mean writing a new FW or reading FW in a way different from our own). What makes the pun creative is not the series of connections (which precedes it as already codified); it is the decision of the short circuit, the so-called metaphoric one. (*Role,* 77-78)

Ropar's argument that Eisenstein's filmic metaphors are in fact based on metonymic contiguities, established within the syntax of the film, not by semantic resemblance or referentiality, finds support in Eco's account, according to which "a metaphor can be invented because language, in its process of unlimited semiosis, constitutes a multidimensional network of metonymies, each of which is explained by a cultural convention rather than by an original resemblance" (*Role,* 78). The advantage of working with contiguity rather than similarity, Eco explains, is that it avoids the procedure of analogy and the metaphysical or "idealist doctrine of linguistic creativity" which goes with it. The "Kuleshov" effect of montage juxtaposition, inducing the "post hoc ergo propter hoc" "fallacy" of filmic writing, is the film equivalent of the logic of the pun, the point being in both cases to set aside the limitations of the referent and create connections which as of yet do not exist, thus enriching the code's possibilities (79).

The question for AG concerns how the student might operate in accord with the hypomnemics of the electronic paradigm. At this stage of transition, the fields of knowledge, as represented in encyclopedias, textbooks, and the like, may be manipulated by the learner as if reading were computing. Derrida, in effect, shows that it is possible to treat the realm of discourse as if it were composed in the manner of *Finnegans Wake,* with the pun as the atomic unit organizing and bringing into relation the intertextuality of all the systems of knowledge. In this context, Derrida's extensive use (especially in *Glas*) of encylopedic dictionaries finds its justification as an *inventio*. AG distinguishes itself from the psychologisms of current reader-response subjectivism by concerning itself not only with the "field of oriented possibilities" (that which actually or phenomenologically occurs in the inner speech of a student) but with *constructing* connections among the systems in relation to the field of *all* possibilities.

One consequence of the open aesthetic on which the open pedagogy is based is a new definition of "form"—"form as a field of possibilities" (*Obra,* 156). Thus, "the uncertainty which gives information is the fruit of an organization of possibilities instead of a univocal determination: it is uncertainty in an 'open' situation because it is organized as open, not from being casually disorganized" (104). Derrida's use of "undecidability" is designed to promote just this enhancement of information. Eco uses Pierce's notion of the "interpretant" in order to explain how an open form is comprehended. In Pierce's pragmatism, Eco notes, reality is a *result,* not a datum. To understand a sign amounts to learning what to do in order to gain acquaintance with the object of the term. This object is not the item itself in reality, however, but is the "dynamic object," constituted by "all the information available about the object," the semantic spectrum through which many possible paths may be taken. "A term entails the globality of information about it" (*Role,* 188). The interpretant is that part of the global possibilities activated or selected by the knower. In an epistemology of unlimited semiosis, the meaning of a representation can only be another representation. Understanding, in this situation, may be redefined in terms of action:

> An energetic response does not need to be interpreted; rather, it produces a change of habit. This means that, after having received a series of signs and having variously interpreted them, our way of acting within the world is either transitorily or permanently changed. This new attitude, this pragmatic issue, is the final interpretant. At this point the unlimited semiosis stops. . . . The missing link between semiosis and physical reality as practical action has been found. The theory of interpretants is not an idealistic one. (*Role,* 194)

The notion of the interpretant, as Eco explains, solves all the problems of meaning raised by the spectrum of positions from subjectivist psychologism to behaviorism. Eco uses the example of the Rosetta stone to make his point, which links his program to the hieroglyphic principle of AG. The interpretant

> saves the category of content (and of meaning) from being an ungraspable platonic abstraction or an undetectable mental event. Once the interpretant is equated with any coded intentional property of the content, since these properties cannot be isolated but under the form of the other signs, the elements of the content become something physically testable. A given culture displays, in any of its activities, accepted correlations between representamens (or expressions), each becoming in turn the interpretant of the other. In order to understand how an explicit correlation of expressions makes the content analyzable, think of the Rosetta stone, carrying the simultaneous translations of a hieroglyphic text in Demotic and Greek. The content of the first Egyptian text has become testable because of the mediation of the Greek one, this latter being in its turn interpretable, not only because there existed public lexicons equating given words with given contents, but also because these contents were already largely analyzed by the Western culture. (*Role,* 197)

This accessibility of the interpretants in the open field is what makes it possible for the learner to construct another text, to mark a new path through the encyclopedia. "Interpretants are the testable and describable correspondents, associated by public agreement to another sign. In this way the analysis of content becomes a cultural operation which works only on physically testable cultural products. . . . Semiosis explains itself by itself" (*Role,* 198). Moreover, these interpretants require a combination of word and thing presentations. "The compositional analysis of a verbal term should not consider as its interpretants only linguistic terms. Among the interpretants of the word 'dog' are all the images of dog displayed by encyclopedias, zoological treatises, and all the comic strips in which that word has been associated to these images, and vice versa. . . . But no semantic analysis can be complete without analyzing verbal expressions by means of visual, objectal, and behavioral interpretants, and vice versa" (*Role,* 197). In short, Eco's account of the interpretant indicates how the principle of inner speech connected with montage imagery might be extended into a new, heterogeneous construction. These constructions, built in terms of the open aesthetic, offer a clue to the pedagogy of grammatology.

In this context, in which "a sign is a textual matrix," in which "the content of a single term becomes something similar to an encyclopedia," the "unconscious" associated with the cultural code may be understood as that vast body of knowledge, produced by the information explosion, which exists outside the "living memory" of any individual and to which access may be attained only by artificial memory techniques. AG proposes to supplement the conventional means by which scholarship works this knowledge with strategies derived precisely from the history of hypomnesis (from the *Ad Herennium* to the computer). The basic principle is similar to the one suggested in Wittgenstein's *Blue Book:* "There is one way of avoiding at least partly the occult appearance of the processes of thinking, and it is, to replace in these processes any working of the imagination by acts of looking at real objects . . . or by painting, drawing or modelling; and every process of speaking to oneself by speaking aloud or by writing."[46] AG extends this procedure to include not only what one might imagine but what one might find in the "encyclopedia."

Eco's description of creativity as knowledge provides one context for AG as *inventio.* "The majority of our messages, in everyday life or in academic philosophy, are lined with metaphors. The problem of the creativity of language emerges, not only in the privileged domain of poetic discourse, but each time that language—in order to designate something that culture has not yet assimilated . . . must *invent* combinatory possibilities or semantic couplings not anticipated by the code. . . . In this sense, [metaphor] assumes a value in regard to communication and, indirectly, to knowledge" (*Role,* 183). One of the most fascinating or disturbing features of Derrida's practice is his ability to demonstrate the "necessity" of meanings or associations produced by punning. Eco explains the basis for such demonstrations of the interdependence of chance and necessity, noting how metaphor simulates the productivity of factual judgments based on empirical discoveries. The manner in which a new factual judgment, derived from a discovery

(for example, the findings of a Galileo or a Darwin), reorganizes the
semantic system may be *simulated* (AG mimes knowledge) in the absence
of facts from within language by tracing the paths of unlimited semiosis.

> The factual judgment is born from a physical mutation of the world
> and only afterwards is transformed into semiotic knowledge. The
> metaphor is born from an internal disturbance of semiosis. If it suc-
> ceeds in its game, it produces knowledge because it produces new
> semiotic judgments and, in the final outcome, obtains results which
> do not differ from factual judgments. . . . If they are inventive (and
> thus original), they cannot be easily accepted; the system tends
> not to absorb them. They then produce, prior to knowledge, some-
> thing which, psychologically speaking, we could call "excitation,"
> and which, from a semiotic point of view, is none other than "infor-
> mation" in the most proper sense of the term: an excess of disorder
> in respect to existing codes. (*Role,* 86–87)

AG as a methodology works in accordance with the situation Eco describes, operating on every manner of inscription, circulating in the universe
of discourse as an interruption, a disturbance that excites (incites, not insights), generating "information." The initial move is to examine the metaphors (verbal images) lining every discourse, in order to decompose or
unfold and redirect the possibilities of meaning inherent in the material.
Consider, for example, the question of the electronic paradigm itself. AG
might investigate the possible character of this episteme in a way similar
to Ong's approach to the printing press. Ong proposed his own version of
the "ages of man," noting an analogy between the oral, written (printed),
and electronic evolution of communications technology and the oral, anal,
and genital stages of maturation. Ong observed that the parallel between
anality and typography is "spectacular":

> For, if constriction is closely associated with writing, it is of the
> absolute essence of print. The concept of "print" itself necessarily
> involves pressure. The key instrument of printing is the press. . . .
> Type is "set," placed in rigid lines, by hand or by a machine. The
> lines, of uneven lengths, are "justified"–spaced out to the same
> length–which is to say forced to comply to a set measure. . . . How
> strange is this typographical world of compression and visually in-
> spected, locked-up chunks of metal and wood when compared with
> the world of speech in its original, oral-aural habitat, where words
> "flow" and indeed must flow without constraint. (*Presence,* 97)

Ong admits that he has little to say about the electronic paradigm, other
than that its effects will be as drastically different from the print paradigm
as print was from the oral paradigm. AG's approach to this metaphorical
speculation, following Derrida's lead in a piece such as "Tympan" (which
exercises the terminology of the printing press), would be to explore video

and computer technology, both as things and as vocabularies (word-thing presentations of hypomnemic devices), and then to cross-reference this "information" with the semantic fields of cultural studies. Let that be our first assignment, to let language do some thinking for us. If the resultant metaphors (based on puns) become knowledge, they will have completed their cycle, according to Eco (*Role,* 86–87). "They become catachreses. The field has been restructured, semiosis rearranged, and metaphor (from the invention which it was) turned into culture."

Notes

CHAPTER ONE: GRAMMATOLOGY

1. Rodolphe Gasché, "Deconstruction as Criticism," in *Glyph 6: Textual Studies* (Baltimore, 1979), 180.

2. Michael Ryan, "New French Theory in New German Critique," *New German Critique* 22 (1981): 145.

3. Edward Said, "Reflections on Recent American 'Left' Literary Criticism," *Boundary2* 8 (1979): 12–15. This whole issue is relevant to the debate concerning the status of deconstruction.

4. Gerald Graff, *Literature against Itself* (Chicago, 1979), 12–13, 239.

5. Jonathan Culler, *The Pursuit of Signs* (Ithaca, 1981), 42–43. My disagreement is not so much with Culler's description of deconstruction (although I read *Of Grammatology* as a subsumption rather than as a subversion of semiotics) but with his confinement of the question to literary studies.

6. See David Diringer, *Writing* (London, 1962); Ignace J. Gelb, *A Study of Writing: The Foundations of Grammatology* (London, 1952); André Leori-Gourhan, *Le Geste et la Parole* (Paris, 1964); and Jack Goody, *The Domestication of the Savage Mind* (London, 1977).

7. Jacques Derrida, *Of Grammatology*, trans. Gayatri Spivak (Baltimore, 1976). Originally published in France, 1967. Cf. Maurice Pope, *The Story of Archaeological Decipherment* (New York, 1975).

8. George Steiner, *Language and Silence* (New York, 1967), 17.

9. Jacques Derrida, *Positions*, trans. Alan Bass (Chicago, 1981), 35–36.

10. Jacques Derrida, *Writing and Difference*, trans. Alan Bass (Chicago, 1978), 15–16.

11. Jacques Derrida, *La carte postale: De Socrate à Freud et au-delà* (Paris, 1980), 325.

12. Jacques Derrida, "Philosophie des Etats Généraux," in *Etats Généraux de la Philosophie* (Paris, 1979), 39.

13. Martin Heidegger, *The Question Concerning Technology*, trans. William Lovitt (New York, 1977), 15.

14. Edward Said, "Textuality (Derrida-Foucault)," *Critical Inquiry* 4 (1978): 702.

15. Jacques Derrida, *Dissemination*, trans. Barbara Johnson (Chicago, 1981), 184-88.

16. Jacques Derrida, "Differance," in *Speech and Phenomena*, trans. David B. Allison (Evanston, 1973), 132. The term, in my opinion, should be written "DifferAnce," in order to retain the visual image of the pyramid.

17. Jacques Derrida, "Scribble (writing-power)," *Yale French Studies* 58 (1979), for a fuller discussion of Warburton than that found in *Of Grammatology*.

18. See Maureen Quilligan, *The Language of Allegory: Defining the Genre* (Ithaca, 1979). This is an excellent study, clarifying the relationship of allegory to pun in a way that illuminates Derrida's strategy, as does her stress on the distinction between "allegoresis" (what Northrop Frye had in mind when he described contemporary critical methods as "allegorical") and "allegory" (personification). Deconstruction tends to employ the former (suspicious reading) and grammatology the latter mode. Theoretical grammatology is an allegory (a narrative investigation of a threshold text) of the history of the decipherment of the Rosetta stone.

19. W. Haas, *Writing without Letters* (Manchester, 1976), 171. Defines the "grapheme" as any minimal, distinctive functional unit of writing. Cf. Massin, *Letter and Image*, trans. C. Hillier and V. Menkes (New York, 1970).

20. Jacques Derrida, "Signéponge," in *Francis Ponge* (Paris, 1977), 144. Another part of this text on Ponge is published in *Digraphe*, No. 8 (1976): 17-39. Cf. *Signéponge/Signsponge*, trans. Richard Rand (New York, 1984). The title may also read "Signed Ponge."

21. See E. A. Wallis Budge, *Egyptian Language* (London, 1970), 13-27.

22. See Jacques Derrida, "Economimesis," in Sylviane Agacinski et al., *Mimesis: Des articulations* (Paris, 1975). A translation by R. Klein is available in *Diacritics* 11 (1981).

23. Alphonse De Waelhens, *Schizophrenia: A Philosophical Reflection on Lacan's Structuralist Interpretation*, trans. W. Ver Eecke (Pittsburgh, 1978), 205.

24. Geoffrey H. Hartman, *Saving the Text* (Baltimore, 1981), p. 85. This collection of essays encouraged me to pursue the line of thinking developed in part 1 of my book. Like Hartman, I approach Derrida through his style rather than through his philosophical arguments.

25. Jacques Derrida, *Glas* (Paris, 1974), 40.

26. Michael Devitt, *Designation* (New York, 1981), 14-22. Derrida's "signature" theory should be analyzed in the context of the considerable work done in Anglo-American philosophy on the "proper name."

27. Stanley Rosen, *The Limits of Analysis* (New York, 1980), 153.

28. Plato, *The Collected Dialogues*, ed. Edith Hamilton and Huntington Cairns (Princeton, 1961), 522.

29. Jacques Derrida, "Limited Inc," *Glyph 2: Johns Hopkins Textual Studies* (Baltimore, 1977), 197.

30. See Angus Fletcher, *Allegory: The Theory of the Symbolic Mode* (Ithaca, 1964), 198–99. Derrida uses the document and the scholarly (naturalistic) detail in the manner of what Fletcher describes as "ornament" (*kosmos*), playing on the devaluation in logocentrism of writing and style as "merely" ornamental. He plays similarly on "signature," evoking, with this theory of "signing" as a contamination between inside/outside, the hermetic significance of signature. Fletcher cites Jolande Jacobi's glossary to Paracelsus's "doctrine of signatures": "*Signature:* External characteristics corresponding to inner qualities, which serve as signs, by which everything internal and invisible can be discovered" (194). Joseph Beuys (see chapter 8) makes explicit use of Paracelsus and signature.

31. Gaston Bachelard, *The Philosophy of No: A Philosophy of the New Scientific Mind*, trans. G. C. Waterson (New York, 1968), 32.

32. Jacques Derrida, "White Mythology: Metaphor in the Text of Philosophy," trans. F. C. Moore, *New Literary History* 6 (1974): 40–41.

CHAPTER TWO: THEORIA

1. Michel Foucault, *Language, Counter-Memory, Practice*, trans. Donald F. Bouchard and Sherry Simon (Ithaca, 1977), 33.

2. Jacques Derrida, *Edmund Husserl's "Origin of Geometry": An Introduction*, trans. John P. Leavey, Jr. (Stony Brook, N.Y., 1978), 52.

3. Jacques Derrida, "Tympan," in *Marges de la philosophie* (Paris, 1972), xx.

4. Walter J. Ong, *The Presence of the Word* (Minneapolis, 1981), 8. Ong's concern, in several of his books, with the three ages of communication (oral, alphabetic, electronic) identifies him as a theoretical grammatologist. The writings of George Steiner and Marshall McLuhan could be similarly classified. The bibliographies in the books of these critic-scholars are a valuable resource for the background of grammatology.

5. Alfred Korzybski, *Science and Sanity*, 4th ed. (Lakeville, Conn., 1958), 643. This eccentric book by the founder of "General Semantics," despite its positivism, anticipated certain facets of deconstruction.

6. Jacques Derrida, *Spurs: Nietzsche's Styles* (Chicago, 1979), 87–88.

7. Martin Heidegger, *"Moira,"* in *Early Greek Thinking*, trans. David Farrell Krell and Frank A. Capuzzi (New York, 1975), 97.

8. Roman Jakobson, "Poetry of Grammar, Grammar of Poetry," *Lingua* 21 (1968): 605.

9. See Wendy Steiner, *Exact Resemblance to Exact Resemblance: The Literary Portraiture of Gertrude Stein* (New Haven, 1978), 150.

10. Friedrich Nietzsche, "Twilight of the Idols," in *The Viking Portable Nietzsche*, trans. and ed. Walter Kaufmann (New York, 1968), 483.

11. Willy Rotzler, *Constructive Concepts* (New York, 1977), 148. Cf. J. O. Robinson, *The Psychology of Visual Illusion* (London, 1972), and R. L. Gregory, *The Intelligent Eye* (New York, 1970).

12. E. H. Gombrich, *The Sense of Order* (Ithaca, 1979).

13. Jacques Derrida, "Structure, Sign, and Play in the Discourse of the Human Sciences," in *The Structuralist Controversy: The Languages of Criticism and the Sciences of Man*, ed. Richard A. Macksey and Eugenio Donato (Baltimore, 1972), 248, 260. This essay, minus the discussion following the paper, is included in *Writing and Difference*.

14. James Ogilvy, *Many Dimensional Man* (New York, 1977), 46–47.

15. Jacques Derrida, "Pas I," *Gramma: Lire Blanchot I*, no. 3–4 (1976): 111–215.

16. Sigmund Freud, *The Origins of Psychoanalysis: Letters to Wilhelm Fliess, Drafts and Notes: 1887–1902*, trans. Eric Mosbacher and James Strachey (New York, 1954), 232.

17. Raymond Williams, *Keywords: A Vocabulary of Culture and Society* (New York, 1976), 265.

18. F. E. Peters, *Greek Philosophical Terms* (New York, 1967), 6.

19. Jacques Derrida, "The 'Retrait' of Metaphor," *Enclitic* 2 (1978): 23.

20. Harold M. Kaplan, *Anatomy and Physiology of Speech* (New York, 1960), 232.

21. Jacques Derrida, "Entre crochets," *Digraphe* 8 (1976): 100.

22. Jacques Derrida, "Signature Event Context," *Glyph* 1: *Johns Hopkins Textual Studies* (Baltimore, 1977), 185. Cf. *Marges*, 381.

23. For a discussion of Derrida as the "Aristotle of Collage/Montage," see Ulmer, "The Object of Post-Criticism," in *The Anti-Aesthetic*, ed. Hal Foster (Port Townsend, Wash., 1983), 83–110.

24. Jacques Derrida, "Fors," trans. Barbara Johnson, *Georgia Review* 31 (1977): 114. An introduction to Nicolas Abraham and Maria Torok, *Cryptonymie: Le verbier de l'Homme aux Loups* (Paris, 1976).

25. J. Laplanche and J.-B. Pontalis, *The Language of Psychoanalysis*, trans. Donal Nicholson-Smith (New York, 1973), 287.

26. Jacques Derrida, "Mallarmé," in *Tableau de la littérature française: De Madame Staël à Rimbaud* (Paris, 1974), 375–76.

CHAPTER THREE: MNEMONICS

1. George A. Kennedy, *Classical Rhetoric and Its Christian and Secular Tradition from Ancient to Modern Times* (Chapel Hill, 1980), 96.

2. Frances A. Yates, *The Art of Memory* (Chicago, 1966), 6–7.

3. James Bunn also makes this observation (see below, n. 9). I will cite the classic example used to illustrate memory for things, because it arouses numerous associations with the themes of grammatology. The following image is intended to remind a lawyer of the accusation against his client (the defendant poisoned a man in order to gain his inheritance): "We shall imagine the man in question lying ill in bed, if we know him personally. If we do not know him, we shall yet take some one to be our invalid, but not a man of the lowest class, so that he may come to mind at once. And we shall place the defendant at the bedside, holding in his right hand a cup, in his left, tablets, and on the fourth finger, a ram's testicles. In this way we can have in memory the man who was poisoned, the witnesses, and the inheritance" (Yates, 11)—cited from the *Ad Herennium*. After my book was in press I discovered that Michel Beaujour makes the Luria–*Ad Herennium* comparison in *Miroirs d'encre* (Paris, 1980). His notion of "autoportrait" seems relevant to the signature effect in Derrida.

4. A. R. Luria, *The Mind of a Mnemonist*, trans. Lynn Solotaroff (Chicago, 1968), 32.

5. Robert Sonkowsky, "Euphantastik Memory and Delivery in Classical Rhetorical Tradition," *Rhetoric 78: Proceedings*, ed. Robert L. Brown, Jr.,

and Martin Steinmann, Jr. (Minneapolis, 1979), 378. The point is that a scene is constructed in order to remember a verse.

6. The same problem is discussed in *Of Grammatology*, 45: "One must therefore challenge, in the very name of the arbitrariness of the sign, the Saussurian definition of writing as 'image'—hence as natural symbol—of language. Not to mention the fact that the phoneme is the *unimaginable* itself, and no visibility can *resemble* it, it suffices to take into account what Saussure says about the difference between the symbol and the sign in order to be completely baffled as to how he can at the same time say of writing that it is an 'image' or 'figuration' of language and define language and writing elsewhere as 'two distinct systems of signs.' For the property of the sign is not to be an image." This contradiction offers the entry point for Derrida's deconstruction of Saussure. It also suggests Derrida's interest in the general problematic of allegory and the "abject image" with respect to the "motivation" of the sign ("abject" images acknowledge their complete inadequacy to that which they nonetheless copy).

7. Sonkowsky makes the comparison between ancient mnemonic systems and Freud's theory of dreams. He suggests, however, that Derrida's "Freud and the Scene of Writing" would have been improved by an awareness of mnemonics. My point is that Derrida's work since the essay in question, if not including it, does reflect a familiarity with the sophists' artificial memory.

8. Jacques Derrida, "Ousia and Grammē: A Note to a Footnote in *Being and Time*," in *Phenomenology in Perspective*, ed. F. Joseph Smith (The Hague, 1970), 91–92. Cf. *Dissemination*, 8: "These questions will not be answered, at least not finally in the declarative mode. *Along the way, however*, a certain *protocol* will have—destroying this future perfect—taken up the preoccupying place of the *preface*. If one insists on fixing this protocol in a representation, let us say in advance that, with a few supplementary complications, it has the structure of a *magic slate*."

9. James H. Bunn, *The Dimensionality of Signs, Tools, and Models* (Bloomington, Ind., 1981), 6. "Daedalian wings belong to the class of artificial limbs which includes all signs, tools, and models. Semiotics is a study of that class." This excellent study, relevant especially to chapter 4, indicates that the relationship between grammatology and semiotics is something other than the oppositional antagonism relating deconstruction and semiotics (in Culler's description).

10. Jacques Derrida, "Living On: Borderlines," trans. James Hulbert, in *Deconstruction and Criticism* (New York, 1979), 145–46.

11. He deals here with the question, "What is a father?" In the traditional metaphor, "father of logos," one imagines or understands the process of the logos by means of a domain apparently foreign to it, the transmission of life through the relations of generation. But the father is only the "real" procreator by means of language, because the link between father-son and cause-effect is possible only with the assistance of the word—the father must *declare* his parenthood (ownership), since the obvious (literal) parent is the mother from whose body the child issued. Derrida makes this point, apropos of the question of representation, of the relation of copy to model, in a discussion of Titus-Carmel's *La grande bananéraie culturelle,* a display consisting of one real banana and fifty-nine copies (plastic), with the former turning black and rotting (detumescing) during the course of

the exhibit. The real banana reveals its organic nature and its status as model, and hence *is in the maternal position,* according to Derrida—*La vérité en peinture* (Paris, 1978), 249-54 (another major text for grammatology, discussed in chap. 4). At the same time, "If there were a simple metaphor in the expression 'father of logos,' the first word, which seemed the more *familiar,* would nevertheless receive more meaning *from* the second than it would transmit *to* it. The first familiarity is always involved in a relation of cohabitation with *logos.* Living-beings, father and son, are announced to us and related to each other within the household of *logos*" (*Dissemination,* 80-81). The general argument, essential to applied grammatology, is that exposition, if it is to convey knowledge, to make itself known, hence familiar, must mime the qualities of the family—the process of procreation in which the father (discourse) and mother (image) have an equal part. Translated into pedagogy, discourse must always be supplemented by the image system (against the logocentric bias favoring the verbal, the discursive, in teaching and scholarship). Another major image Derrida uses to make this same point is the escutcheon, the coat of arms bearing in its field representations of both the paternal and maternal lines.

12. "Fors," 64—translator's footnote.

13. Nicolas Abraham, *L'ecorce et le noyau* (Paris, 1978), 262.

14. In shifting his approach to philosophical questions from the conceptual and expository to the dramatic and exemplary, Derrida uses anasemia as a strategy of obliqueness in his own narrative.

15. Nicolas Abraham, "The Shell and the Kernel," trans. Nicholas Rand, *Diacritics* 9 (1979): 19.

16. Jacques Derrida, "Me—Psychoanalysis: An Introduction to the Translation of 'The Shell and the Kernel' by Nicolas Abraham," trans. Richard Klein, *Diacritics* 9 (1979): 7-8.

17. See Craig Owens, "The Allegorical Impulse: Toward a Theory of PostModernism," *October* 12 (1980): 67-86; *October* 13 (1980): 59-80.

18. Paul de Man, "Proust et l'allegorie de la lecture," in *Mouvements premiers: Etudes critique offertes à George Poulet* (Paris, 1972), 238. I use this same example in Ulmer, "Jacques Derrida and Paul de Man on/in Rousseau's Faults," *Eighteenth Century* 20 (1979): 176-77.

19. J. Hillis Miller, "Walter Pater: A Partial Portrait," *Daedalus* 105 (1976): 111.

20. Quilligan, *Language of Allegory,* 32.

21. Jacques Derrida, "Parergon," in *La vérité en peinture,* 151.

22. Daniel Sperber, *Rethinking Symbolism,* trans. Alice Morton (Cambridge, 1975).

CHAPTER FOUR: MODELS

1. John T. Irwin, *American Hieroglyphics: The Symbol of the Egyptian Hieroglyphics in the American Renaissance* (New Haven, 1980; Baltimore, 1983), 6. This book signals the renewed interest in hieroglyphics, as does *Digraphe* 4 (1974), a special issue devoted to hieroglyphics.

2. My discussion of Montaigne here is indebted to Victoria Kahn, "The Sense of Taste in Montaigne's *Essais,*" *Modern Language Notes* 95 (1980): 1269-91.

3. Jacques Derrida, "The Purveyor of Truth," trans. Willis Domingo et al., *Yale French Studies* 52 (1975): 88. The original of this piece is collected in *La carte postale*.

4. Jacques Derrida, "The Law of Genre," in *Glyph 7: Textual Studies* (Baltimore, 1980), 206.

5. See Ruben Berezdivin, "Gloves: Inside-Out," *Research in Phenomenology* 8 (1978): 112-26. Most of this number is devoted to a collection of articles on Derrida.

6. P. T. Saunders, *An Introduction to Catastrophe Theory* (Cambridge, England, 1980), 1.

7. Jacques Derrida, *The Archeology of the Frivolous: Reading Condillac,* trans. John P. Leavey, Jr. (Pittsburgh, 1980), 73, 82.

8. C. C. T. Baker, *Introduction to Mathematics* (New York, 1974), 51–52. Cf. Patrick Hughes and George Brecht, *Vicious Circles and Infinity* (New York, 1979). An excellent discussion of Gödel's theorem, relevant to these figures, is Douglas Hofstadter, *Gödel, Escher, Bach: An Eternal Golden Braid* (New York, 1979), 15–24.

9. Lucien Dällenbach, *Le récit spéculaire: Essai sur la mise en abyme* (Paris, 1977), 17, 18. Derrida discusses *Arnolfini and His Bride* in "Restitutions" (*La vérité en peinture*, 399) and the notion of *"mise en abyme"* in general, about which he has some reservations, although he borrows its effect. The "speculation" in "Spéculer—sur 'Freud' " (see chap. 5) is a version of this *récit spéculaire* (again invoked with qualifications).

10. Jacques Derrida, "The Supplement of Copula: Philosophy *before* Linguistics," trans. James Creech and Josué Harari, *Georgia Review* 30 (1976): 553.

11. See Jacques Derrida, "Restitutions of Truth to Size," trans. John P. Leavey, Jr., *Research in Phenomenology* 8 (1978): 8, a partial translation, breaking off at page 358 of *La vérité en peinture*. I cannot reiterate too often the importance for applied grammatology of Derrida's theory that the example functions in the manner of a fetish (related to the signature), that desire is active in scholarship at the level of the example.

12. See Hartman, *Saving the Text,* 60–63, for the full play on Ich and Chi.

13. "Phonex" is introduced by A. A. Roback, *Destiny and Motivation in Language: Studies in Psycholinguistics and Glossodynamics* (Cambridge, Mass., 1954). This title could serve as a subtitle for much of Derrida's work, beginning especially with *Glas*. Roback's attitude toward the "signature effect" is noncommittal, scholarly, whereas Derrida's tone is parodic, having no desire to "prove" the destiny of a name (the *Moira* effect). With respect to the *tr* itself, Derrida no doubt chooses to "transduct" the drawings in the key of tr, since tr is the abbreviation of "translator"—see Tom Conley's tr notes to Derrida's "Title (to be specified)," *Sub-Stance* 31 (1981): 22.

CHAPTER FIVE: SPECULATION

1. In addition to "The Purveyor of Truth," two pieces from "Spéculer—sur 'Freud' " have appeared in translation (their selection constituting a kind of emphasis): "Coming into One's Own," trans. James Hulbert, in

Psychoanalysis and the Question of the Text, ed. Geoffrey Hartman (Baltimore, 1978), 114-48; "Speculations—on Freud," trans. Ian McLeod, *The Oxford Literary Review* 3 (1978): 78-97.

2. For a review of the aesthetics of the essay (of which "Envois" is something of a parody), see Peter M. Schon, *Vorformen des Essays in Antike und Humanismus* (Wiesbaden, 1954); and Gerhard Haas, *Essay* (Stuttgart, 1969).

3. Jacques Derrida, "Télépathie," *Furor* 2 (1981): 5-41. "D'un ton apocalyptique" is in *Les fins de l'homme: A partir du travail de Jacques Derrida* (Paris, 1981), 445-79. A translation of this text, by John P. Leavey, Jr., is forthcoming in *Semeia.* The proceedings of a colloquium held on *La carte postale,* including Derrida's remarks made in discussions after the papers, is available: René Major, ed., *Affranchissement du transfert et de la lettre* (Paris, 1982).

4. Sigmund Freud, "Dreams and the Occult," in *New Introductory Lectures on Psycho-analysis,* trans. W. H. H. Sprott (New York, 1933), 59.

5. Freud, *Origins,* 232.

6. See Jonathan Culler, "Apostrophe," in *The Pursuit of Signs.* Derrida's comments on Nietzsche's signature apply to his own as well; for example, when he stresses that in *Ecce Homo* Nietzsche says, "I am going to tell *myself* the story of my life. I am going to recite it and recount it now *for me.*" The value of such an activity (which is the model for the explicit introduction in applied grammatology of the subject into research) has to do with the relationship of the proper name to the signature: "The relationship of a philosopher to his 'great name'—to what borders a system of his signature—pertained to a psychology, and one so new that it would no longer be legible *within* the system of philosophy as a part of it." In this new psychology the signature is a "homonym" of the proper name. See Derrida, "Nietzsche's Otobiography," a lecture first delivered at the University of Virginia in 1977, a fragment of which is available in *Yale French Studies* 63 (1982).

At stake in this discussion is the manner in which books and babies are conceived, a question shared by Freud and the sophists. Freud noted that the answer the child receives in trying to find out where he/she comes from—motivating an interest in the mother's desire—is the name of the father. This name, assigned to the child, invested with the desire to know, becomes associated with the need *to be known,* immortalized (in a sense). The sophists based their practice on this desire, on the "will to fame." Fame is to the world of letters what lust is to sexuality. Ancient rhetoric perfected the form of praise, celebrating the name. Isocrates, the father of Paideia, brought *logos* to the level of *legend* (cf. Derrida's treatment of Freud's *legs*—legacy). Man's logos, then, is the name—all that can be said about him. In this view, which Plato labeled *"doxa,"* praise is the essence of poetry, giving glory. Experimenting with the "will to knowledge," Derrida deconstructs logocentrism precisely at its root—its name. Grammatology assumes that institutions and organisms share the same dynamics, that the drives of death and survival (which Nietzsche associated respectively with the patronym and the mother) inform the functioning of the knowledge apparatus. See Samuel Ijsseling, *Rhetoric and Philosophy in Conflict: An Historical Survey* (The Hague, 1976). Cf. *L'oreille de l'autre:*

Otobiographies, transferts, traductions, ed. Claude Lévesque and Christie McDonald (Montréal, 1982).

7. An interview of Lucette Finas with Jacques Derrida: "Avoir l'oreille de la philosophie," in *Ecarts, quatre essais à propos de Jacques Derrida* (Paris, 1973), 309.

8. See Laplanche and Pontalis, 66. This experiment is particularly important for the development of a pedagogy, given that, according to the analyses discussed in chapter 6, the pedagogical effect is dependent upon the context of authority. Hence, the operations of the censoring superego must not be ignored or exploited but exposed, as part of an institutional deconstruction.

9. Mark Kanzer and Jules Glenn, eds., *Freud and His Self-Analysis* (New York, 1979), 61. Cf. John E. Gedo and George H. Pollock, eds., *Freud: The Fusion of Science and Humanism: The Intellectual History of Psychoanalysis* (New York, 1976). These books deal historically with materials Derrida treats theoretically.

10. Roland Barthes, *Pleasure of the Text* (New York, 1975), 53.

11. The phrasing is important, since it is only with the feminine ending that the *d* of "froid" is pronounced, thus completing the pun on *Freud.*

12. Peters, *Greek Philosophical Terms,* 19. It may be worth noting that *apeiron* contains *eiron*, a propos of Derrida's ironic tone.

13. Michel Serres, *Hermes I: La communication* (Paris, 1968), 29–30.

14. Michel Serres, *Hermes II: L'interférence* (Paris, 1972), 13, 16.

15. Michel Neyraut, *Les logiques de l'inconscient* (Paris, 1978), 46. Neyraut credits as the source of this anecdote G. Bodifée, in an article published in *L'astronomie* 91 (1977).

16. Gregory, *The Intelligent Eye,* 157. It is especially relevant to applied grammatology that Gregory's examples are drawn from the history of electrical apparatuses.

CHAPTER SIX: THE SCENE OF TEACHING

1. *GREPH, Qui a peur de la philosophie?* (Paris, 1977).

2. Michel Foucault, "Les jeux du pouvoir," in *Politiques de la philosophie,* 173.

3. Jacques Derrida, "Où commence et comment finit un corps enseignant," in *Politiques de la philosophie,* ed. Dominique Grisoni (Paris, 1976), 62.

4. Post(e)-pedagogy works toward a new relationship between humanities and the sciences (and is in any case a "style" intended for the era of "artificial intelligence"–hypomnemics). The interest of Derrida's circle in the early German Romantics (cf. Hartman and Bloom and the English Romantics), who desired a fusion of philosophy with literature, should be noted as indicating the current attitude favoring a science-art interaction (albeit a critical one). See Philippe Lacoue-Labarthe and Jean-Luc Nancy, *L'absolu littéraire: Théorie de la littérature du romantisme allemand* (Paris, 1978). Poststructuralism, that is, has reopened the question of the *epistemic* quality of the arts. Cf. Jochen Hörisch, *Die fröliche Wissenschaft der Poesie* (Frankfurt am Main, 1976). For an arts perspective, see Stewart Kranz, *Science and Technology in the Arts* (New York, 1974).

5. A hidden theme of my book—to be made more explicit elsewhere—is that one of the principal uses of Writing is popularization. For discussions of some of the issues involved, see Philippe Roqueplo, *Le partage du savoir: Science, culture, vulgarisation* (Paris, 1974); Stacey B. Day, ed., *Communication of Scientific Information* (Basel, 1975); Bill Nichols, *Ideology and the Image* (Bloomington, Ind., 1981).

6. William M. Bryant, *Hegel's Educational Ideas* (Chicago, 1896; reprint ed., St. Clair Shores, Mich.), 73–74. For background on Derrida's discussion of Victor Cousin (credited with translating Hegel's thinking into the French educational system), see Walter Vance Brewer, *Victor Cousin as a Comparative Educator* (New York, 1971).

7. Michel Foucault, "The Discourse on Language," in *The Archaeology of Knowledge*, trans. A. M. Sheridan Smith (New York, 1972), 232.

8. Michel Foucault, *Discipline and Punish: The Birth of the Prison* (New York, 1977), clarifies the link between "discipline" as noun and as verb.

9. See Harold Bloom, *The Anxiety of Influence* (New York, 1973). Applied grammatology is also concerned with the scene of instruction, except that it follows Derrida's notion of differance and therefore rejects Bloom's effort to distinguish between speech and writing. Differance enables one to see the hegemony of logocentrism through the reversal that has made the oral (speech-oriented) classroom a representation of the Book (printing) format. The dominance of the Book does not mean that Writing has triumphed over Voice, since the metaphysics of Voice informs the Book. On the deconstruction of the Book, see Claude Lévesque, *L'etrangeté du texte: Essais sur Nietzsche, Freud, Blanchot, et Derrida* (Montréal, 1976). Bloom's opening remarks in "The Breaking of Form," in *Deconstruction and Criticism*, provide a valuable perspective on the pedagogy of *inventio* derived from Derrida: "All that a poem can be about, or what in a poem *is* other than trope, is the skill or faculty of invention or discovery, the heuristic gift. Invention is a matter of 'places,' of themes, topics, subjects, or of what Kenneth Burke rephrased as the implicit presence of forms in subject-matter, and named as 'the Individuation of Forms' " (1).

10. Pierre Bourdieu and Jean-Claude Passeron, *Reproduction in Education, Society, and Culture* (London, 1977; French edition published 1970), 54.

11. Jacques Derrida, "Scribble," 118.

12. For the script and a commentary by Daniel Gerould (published together with Mallarmé's "Mimetic"), see *Drama Review* 23 (1979): 103–19. (Autoperformance Issue).

13. For a theoretical discussion of "rebus work in discourse," see Jean-François Lyotard, *Discours, figure* (Paris, 1978), 300–310. Lyotard is one of the first to bring together contemporary theoretical movements with avant-garde arts, a project later taken over by the journal *October*. In a similar vein, the articulation of Derrida and Joseph Beuys provides an orientation for applied grammatology.

14. Sister Joan Marie Lechner, *Renaissance Concepts of the Commonplaces* (New York, 1962).

15. Derrida, "Pas I," 136.

16. Friedrich Albert Zorn, *Grammar of the Art of Dancing* (Boston, 1905), 16, 41, 52, 105, 108–9. Dance and Mime are relevant to applied

grammatology in terms of performance art. Joseph Beuys, for example, is influenced by the "eurythmics" developed by Rudolf Steiner.

17. Walter Ong, *Ramus: Method and the Decay of Dialogue* (Cambridge, Mass., 1958).

18. Roland Barthes, *Roland Barthes,* trans. Richard Howard (New York, 1977), 90.

19. Ludwig Wittgenstein, *Philosophical Investigations,* trans. G. E. M. Anscombe (Oxford, 1968), 59. On the question of knowing one's own name, see Wittgenstein, *On Certainty* (New York, 1972).

20. Gerald Holton, *Thematic Origins of Scientific Thought: Kepler to Einstein* (Cambridge, Mass., 1973), 15. Derrida's notion of "stricture" is relevant to the kernel-shell rapport between invention and institution. Cf. Gerard Lemaine et al., eds., *Perspectives on the Emergence of Scientific Disciplines* (The Hague, 1976); Stephen Toulmin, *Human Understanding,* vol. 1 (Princeton, 1972).

CHAPTER SEVEN: SEMINAR: JACQUES LACAN

1. Sherry Turkle, *Psychoanalytic Politics: Freud's French Revolution* (New York, 1978), 165.

2. Shoshana Felman, *La folie et la chose littéraire* (Paris, 1978), 227. Cf. Felman, "Psychoanalysis and Education: Teaching Terminable and Interminable," *Yale French Studies* 63 (1982). I share Felman's analysis of Lacan's teaching, and I attempt in this chapter to demonstrate the specific strategies he uses in practice to achieve these theoretical aims.

3. Jacques Lacan, *Le séminaire, livre II: Le moi dans la théorie de Freud et dans la technique de la psychanalyse* (Paris, 1978), 171.

4. Jacques Lacan, *Ecrits* (Paris, 1966), 867-68.

5. Jacques Lacan, *Ecrits: A Selection,* trans. Alan Sheridan (New York, 1977), 76.

6. Jacques Lacan, *Speech and Language in Psychoanalysis,* trans. Anthony Wilden (Baltimore, 1981), 71.

7. Jacques Lacan, *Le séminaire, livre XX: Encore* (Paris, 1975), 70-71 (excerpted on back cover).

8. Jacques Lacan, *Le séminaire, livre I: Les écrits techniques de Freud* (Paris, 1975), 201.

9. Stephen Heath, "Difference," *Screen* 19 (1978). Jane Gallop's response to Heath confirms my own impression. See *The Daughter's Seduction: Feminism and Psychoanalysis* (Ithaca, 1982), 49-55.

10. Jacques Lacan, *The Four Fundamental Concepts of Psycho-Analysis,* trans. Alan Sheridan (New York, 1978), 160.

11. Turkle's description, *Psychoanalytic Politics,* 147.

12. Max Black, *Models and Metaphors: Studies in Language and Philosophy* (Ithaca, 1962), 229.

13. Jacques Lacan, *Télévision* (Paris, 1973), 19-21.

14. Jean-Claude Milner, *L'amour de la langue* (Paris, 1978).

15. Baudelaire, "A Journey to Cythera," in *The Penguin Book of French Verse,* ed. Anthony Hartley (Baltimore, 1957), 159.

16. Jacques Lacan, ("Temoignage"), in *Vincennes ou le désire d'apprendre* (Paris, 1979), 90-91.

17. Jean Laplanche and Serge Leclaire, "The Unconscious: A Psychoanalytic Study," *Yale French Studies* 48 (1972): 118-75.

18. Jacques Lacan, "Of Structure as an Inmixing of an Otherness Prerequisite to Any Subject Whatever," in Macksey and Donato, eds., *The Structuralist Controversy*, 192.

19. David MacDermott, *Meta Metaphor* (Boston, 1974), 58. "Electronic circuits are conductors for electricity having many of the characteristics of knots. And the same can be said of the flow of information in computers."

20. Mircea Eliade, *Images and Symbols: Studies in Religious Symbolism*, trans. Philip Mairet (New York, 1961), 115-16. My point is not to interpret Lacan but to suggest that which is available in the overdetermined field of the double inscription (other meanings are available in the cultural field, not to mention that which might be evoked in the Imaginary).

21. Mircea Eliade, *Mephistopheles and the Androgyne*, trans. J. M. Cohen (New York, 1965), 177.

22. A discussion of shamanism is developed in chapter 8 with respect to Beuys. Shamanism provides a model, much exploited in performance art, for the "objective" use of the autobiography as a research tool applied to fields of knowledge beyond itself.

23. Derrida remarks on discovering, years later, that he shared this interest in Poe's Valdemar and "I am dead" with Roland Barthes: Derrida, "Les morts de Roland Barthes," *Poétique* 47 (1981). The themes of destiny, *Moira*, and stricture are all interlaced with the problematics of "death" in writing.

CHAPTER EIGHT: PERFORMANCE: JOSEPH BEUYS

1. Allan Kaprow, "Manifesto," in *The Discontinuous Universe*, ed. Sallie Sears and Georgianna W. Lord (New York, 1972), 292. Cf. Kaprow, "The Education of the Un-Artist III," in *Esthetics Contemporary*, ed. Richard Kostelanetz (Buffalo, 1978), 398-410.

2. Foucault, *Language, Counter-Memory, Practice*, 50.

3. Bernard Lamarche-Vadel, "Qui a peur de Joseph Beuys?" *Artistes* 3 (1980): 6. See *Der Spiegel*, 5 November 1979, 250-70.

4. Johannes Stuettgen, "The Warhol-Beuys Event: Three Chapters from the forthcoming book *The Whole Ream*" (Free International University, 1979).

5. Reported in *Der Spiegel*, 251.

6. Caroline Tisdall, "Beuys–Coyote," *Studio International* 192 (1976): 37.

7. Götz Adriani, Winfried Konnertz, and Karin Thomas, *Joseph Beuys: Life and Works*, trans. Patricia Lech (Woodbury, N.Y., 1979), 274-75.

8. Caroline Tisdall, *Joseph Beuys* (New York, 1979), 7. This is the catalogue for Beuys's Guggenheim exhibit and is a major, indispensable resource for anyone interested in Beuys.

9. Anecdote told by Derrida in a letter to the author.

10. Lothar Romain and Rolf Wedewer, *Über Beuys* (Düsseldorf, 1972), 36-37.

11. Michel Benamou, "Presence and Play," in *Performance in Postmodern Culture*, Benamou and Charles Caramello (Madison, 1977). Cf. RoseLee Goldberg, *Performance: Live Art 1909 to the Present* (New York,

1979); Chantal Pontbriand, ed., *Performance, Text(e)s, and Documents* (Montréal, 1981).

12. Jack Burnham, *Great Western Salt Works: Essays on the Meaning of Post-Formalist Art* (New York, 1974), 139.

13. Roland Barthes, "To Write: An Intransitive Verb?" in *The Structuralists from Marx to Lévi-Strauss*, ed. Richard and Fernande DeGeorge (Garden City, N.Y., 1972), pp. 164–65.

14. Roland Barthes, "The Death of the Author," in *The Discontinuous Universe*, ed. Sallie Sears and Georgianna W. Lord (New York, 1972).

15. Andreas Lommel, *Shamanism, The Beginnings of Art* (New York, 1967), 10, 12.

16. Claude Lévi-Strauss, *Structural Anthropology* (Garden City, N.Y., 1967), 196.

17. Joseph Beuys, "Interview: 'If nothing says anything, I don't draw,'" in *Joseph Beuys: Drawings* (Munich, 1979), 93–94.

18. *Joseph Beuys: The Secret Block for a Secret Person in Ireland* (Oxford, 1974).

19. Jeannot Simmen, "Shadows of Reality," in *Joseph Beuys: Drawings* (Munich, 1979), 86.

20. Mircea Eliade, *Shamanism: Archaic Techniques of Ecstacy* (Princeton, 1964), 4.

21. Joseph Beuys, interview, in Robert Filliou, *Teaching and Learning as Performing Arts* (Cologne and New York, 1970), 169. Cf. Tisdall, "Coyote," 37: "The expansion of terms and definitions beyond their restricted applications is the key to the *Energy Plan for the Western Man*, and to all of Beuys's activity. To present the *Energy Plan* he used his voice, extending the definition of sculpture to the moulding of thought forms into words, words arranged into the lecture format and determining the visual structure of the diagrams that accompanied them. . . . Language is the great transformer, since all problems are basically language problems, and language gives form. But language itself must be transformed. . . . 'For me it is the *word* that produces all images. It is the key sign for all processes of moulding and organising. When I speak, using a theoretical language, I try to induce the impulses of this power, the power of the whole understanding of language which for me is the spiritual understanding of evolution.' But language is not to be understood simply in terms of speech and words. That is our current, drastically reduced understanding of politics and economics. Beyond language as verbalisation lies a world of sound and form impulses, a language of primary sound without semantic content, but laden with completely different levels of information." *Lalangue* and Derrida's use of the homophone relate to Beuys's extended theory of language.

22. Joseph Beuys, interview, in Wulf Herzogenrath, *Selbstdarstellung: Künstler über sich* (Dusseldorf, 1973), 24–25.

23. Rainer Rappmann, Peter Schata, and Volker Harlan, *Soziale Plastik: Materialien zu Joseph Beuys* (Achberg, 1976), 20.

24. Joseph Beuys, "Krawall in Aachen," interview in Franz Meyer, ed., *Joseph Beuys—Werke aus der Sammlung Karl Ströher* (Basel, 1970), 38.

25. Willoughby Sharp, "An Interview with Joseph Beuys," *Artforum*, December 1969: 40–47.

26. Ingrid Burgbacher-Krupka, *Prophete rechts, Prophete links: Joseph Beuys* (Stuttgart, 1977), 78.

27. Clara Bodenmann-Ritter, *Joseph Beuys: Jeder Mensch ein Künstler –Gespräche auf der Documenta 5, 1972* (Frankfurt-Berlin-Vienna, 1975), 94.

28. Sarenco, "Gespräch mit Joseph Beuys," *De Tafelronde/Impuls* 3 (1980), 18.

29. Jörg Schellmann and Bernd Klüser, eds., *Joseph Beuys: Multiples,* trans. Caroline Tisdall (New York, 1980).

30. Jacques Derrida, "Ja, ou le faux-bond," *Digraphe* 11 (1977): 94–95.

31. John Layard, *The Lady of the Hare* (1944; reprint ed., New York, 1977), 138.

32. There is a certain *Moira* effect—the destiny of wordplay—having to do with the "hare" as "copula." I am thinking of the shuttle joining the vulgar *foutre* ("fuck") with *feutre* ("felt"—which, as Beuys points out, is made of animal hair, often hare's hair). In any case, not only does Beuys deliberately associate the felt material with the hare symbol, he also identifies the energy or force represented by the felt and the fat as "love" (hence the series *foutre-feutre* could be expanded to include *foudre—Coup de foudre,* love at first sight).

33. Bodenmann-Ritter, 71. In addition to the association linking Derrida's chiasmus with Beuys's cross, there is also an interesting convergence of "corners" in the respective texts. See especially Derrida's discussion of the corner in *Numbers,* which suggests that the enframing fourth side could be for Derrida what the fat is in Beuys's *Fat Corner:* "Hazarding themselves out into that night, pressing into the corners that squarely relate the three surfaces of the imperfect to the single surface of the present, our superadded inscriptions will only, in the end, have succeeded in remarking the passage itself in its own insistence, repeating the square by the closing of the angle, fictively loosening the rigor of the text through the opening of another surface of writing to come, in a certain play of the cardinal points or the hinges (*cardo* = hinge) that has been triggered off. What sort of angle is this angle writing? concave? projecting? an angle of reflection? Because we cannot yet know what that will all have meant, let us put 'this' writing forth as a kind of *angle remark,* considering all lines broken" (*Dissemination,* 295). This *angle* shuttles to Lacan's *angel.* Cf. Hartman, 85, discussing the meanings of *"je m'éc. . . ."*—"(*EC: Ecke,* the German word for *carré*). *Ecke* also means corner, or (French) *coin,* which is what circulates in an economy. But *Ecke* is also the word for angle."

34. Derrida puns on *genoux* (knees) as *je-nous* (I-we, us).

35. "The mark is also the *marginal* limit, the *march,* etc." (*Positions,* 43). There is a spectacular connection between the margarine, which Beuys tends to use in his fat works, and Beuys's autography: "In Beuys' own biography his parents would have favored a good steady job for him in the local margarine factory in Cleves" (*Beuys,* 74).

CHAPTER NINE: FILM: SERGEI EISENSTEIN

1. Yvette Biró, *Profane Mythology: The Savage Mind of the Cinema* (Bloomington, Ind., 1982), 5.

2. Peter Wollen, *Readings and Writings: Semiotic Counter-Strategies* (London, 1982), 5.

3. Christian Metz, "Current Problems of Film Theory: On Jean Mitry's *L'Esthetique et psychologie du cinéma vol. II*," in *Screen Reader 2: Cinema and Semiotics* (London, 1981), 40.

4. See Christian Metz, *Film Language: A Semiotics of the Cinema*, trans. Michael Taylor (New York, 1974).

5. Sylvia Harvey, *May '68 and Film Culture* (London, 1978), 38.

6. Cited in Barthélémy Amengual, "Cinéma et écriture," in *Cinéma: Théorie, lectures*, ed. Dominique Noguez (Paris, 1973), 147.

7. Marie-Claire Ropars-Wuilleumier, *Le texte divisé: Essai sur l'écriture filmique* (Paris, 1981), 18.

8. Sergei Eisenstein, "Notes for a Film of *Capital*," *October* 2 (1976): 23.

9. Sergei Eisenstein, *Film Essays*, ed. Jay Leyda (Princeton, 1982), 66.

10. Jay Leyda and Zina Voynow, *Eisenstein at Work* (New York, 1982), 36.

11. Roland Barthes, *Mythologies*, trans. Annette Lavers (New York, 1975), 156-57.

12. Stanley Edgar Hyman, *The Tangled Bank: Darwin, Marx, Frazer, and Freud as Imaginative Writers* (New York, 1966), 146.

13. Sergei Eisenstein, *Notes of a Film Director*, trans. X. Danko (London, 1959), 125.

14. Sergei Eisenstein, *"Film Form" and "The Film Sense,"* trans. Jay Leyda (Cleveland, 1957), 238.

15. Noel Carroll, "For God and Country: Eisenstein," *Artforum* 11 (1973): 56-60.

16. Marie-Claire Ropars-Wuilleumier and Pierre Sorlin, *"October"—écriture et idéologie* (Paris, 1976).

17. Marie-Claire Ropars-Wuilleumier, "Fonction de la métaphore dans *Octobre* d'Eisenstein," *Littérature* 11 (1973): 124.

18. John Reed, *Ten Days that Shook the World* (New York, 1935), 7.

19. Karl Marx, *The 18th Brumaire of Louis Bonaparte* (New York, 1975), 15.

20. Boris Eikhenbaum, "Problems of Film Stylistics," *Screen* 15 (1974/75): 13-14.

21. Boris Eikhenbaum, "Literature and Cinema," *Russian Formalism*, ed. Stephen Bann and John E. Bowlt (Edinburgh, 1973), 123.

22. Paul Willemen, "Reflections on Eikhenbaum's Concept of Internal Speech in the Cinema," *Screen* 15 (1974/75): 64.

23. David Bordwell, "Eisenstein's Epistemological Shift," *Screen* 15 (1974/75).

24. Paul Willemen, "Cinematic Discourse—The Problem of Inner Speech," *Screen* 22 (1981): 61. See also L. S. Vygotsky, *Thought and Language*, trans. Eugenia Hanfmann and Gertrude Vakar (Cambridge, Mass., 1962), 139-40.

25. V. N. Volosinov, *Marxism and the Philosophy of Language*, trans. Ladislav Matejka and I. R. Titunik (New York, 1973), 14. Volosinov's interest in inner speech as part of his effort to define a specifically Marxist linguistics suggests that Eisenstein's turn to inner speech in his second period does not necessarily imply a break with his earlier materialist principles.

26. A. N. Sokolov, *Inner Speech and Thought* (New York, 1972), 1.

27. Stephen Heath, *Questions of Cinema* (Bloomington, Ind., 1981), 212.

28. Kaja Silverman, *The Subject of Semiotics* (New York, 1983), 48.

29. Derrida, "Télépathie," 8.

30. Roland Barthes, *S/Z*, trans. Richard Miller (New York, 1974), 97–98.

31. Noel Carroll, "Language and Cinema: Preliminary Notes for a Theory of Verbal Images," *Millennium Film Journal* 7/8/9 (1980–81): 186–215.

32. Bill Nichols, *Ideology and the Image* (Bloomington, Ind., 1981), 152.

33. Richard Taylor, *Film Propaganda: Soviet Russia and Nazi Germany* (New York, 1979), 74.

34. Alfred Guzzetti, *"Two or Three Things I Know about Her": Analysis of a Film by Godard* (Cambridge, Mass., 1981), 35. John Pieters, in an article forthcoming in *Soundings,* analyzes this verbal image at length.

35. Emilio Garroni, "Langage verbal et éléments non-verbaux dans le message filmico-télévisuel," in *Cinéma: Théorie, lectures,* 119.

36. Walter J. Ong, *The Presence of the Word* (Minneapolis, 1981), 33. See Eric A. Havelock, *Preface to Plato* (Cambridge, Mass., 1963), and Havelock, *The Literate Revolution in Greece and Its Cultural Consequences* (Princeton, 1982).

37. Jack Goody, *The Domestication of the Savage Mind* (Cambridge, 1977), 81.

38. Walter J. Ong, *Interfaces of the Word* (Ithaca, 1977), 314, 332. Umberto Eco makes a similar comparison between television and the open aesthetic of avant-garde art. See John Fiske and John Hartley, *Reading Television* (London, 1978), for a discussion of "bardic television" relevant to the theme of shamanism, and television as the "inner speech" of a culture—the means by which a culture communicates with itself.

39. See also Walter J. Ong, *Rhetoric, Romance, and Technology* (Ithaca, 1971), 333.

40. Gavriel Salomon, *Interaction of Media, Cognition, and Learning* (San Francisco, 1979).

41. Roland Barthes, *Image, Music, Text,* trans. Stephen Heath (New York, 1977), 55.

42. Geneviève Jacquinot, *Image et pédagogie: Analyse sémiologique du film à intention didactique* (Paris, 1977), 145.

43. David Hayman, "Some Writers in the Wake of the *Wake,*" in *The Avant-Garde Tradition in Literature,* ed. Richard Kostelanetz (Buffalo, 1982), 177.

44. Umberto Eco, *La obra abierta* (Barcelona, 1965), 12. Cf. Eco, *L'oeuvre ouverte* (Paris, 1965).

45. Umberto Eco, *The Role of the Reader* (Bloomington, Ind., 1979), 70.

46. Ludwig Wittgenstein, *The Blue and Brown Books* (New York, 1958), 4.

Index

The Johns Hopkins University Press

APPLIED GRAMMATOLOGY

This book was set in Helvetica Light display by BG Composi-
tion and Press Roman text type by A. W. Bennett, Inc., from
a design by Susan P. Fillion. It was printed on S. D. Warren's
50-lb. Sebago Eggshell Cream paper and bound in Holliston
Roxite A by The Maple Press Company.